Student Solutions Manual

Business Statistics:
A Decision-Making Approach
Eighth Edition

David F. Groebner
Patrick W. Shannon
Phillip C. Fry
Kent D. Smith

Prentice Hall

Boston   Columbus   Indianapolis   New York   San Francisco   Upper Saddle River

Amsterdam   Cape Town   Dubai   London   Madrid   Milan   Munich   Paris   Montreal   Toronto

Delhi   Mexico City   Sao Paulo   Sydney   Hong Kong   Seoul   Singapore   Taipei   Tokyo

Editor-in-Chief: Eric Svendsen
Senior Acquisitions Editor: Chuck Synovec
Editorial Project Manager: Mary Kate Murray
Production Project Manager: Kerri Tomasso
Operations Specialist: Arnold Vila

Prentice Hall
is an imprint of

www.pearsonhighered.com

10 9 8 7 6 5 4 3 2 1

ISBN-13: 978-0-13-612296-8
ISBN-10: 0-13-612296-5

Table of Contents

Chapter 1	The Where, Why, and How of Data Collection	1
Chapter 2	Graphs, Charts, and Tables—Describing Your Data	5
Chapter 3	Describing Data Using Numerical Measures	31
Chapters 1-3	Special Review Section	55
Chapter 4	Introduction to Probability	56
Chapter 5	Discrete Probability Distributions	70
Chapter 6	Introduction to Continuous Probability Distributions	88
Chapter 7	Introduction to Sampling Distributions	102
Chapter 8	Estimating Single Population Parameters	123
Chapter 9	Introduction to Hypothesis Testing	137
Chapter 10	Estimation and Hypothesis Testing for Two Population Parameters	154
Chapter 11	Hypothesis Tests and Estimation for Population Variances	173
Chapter 12	Analysis of Variance	183
Chapters 8-12	Special Review Section	206
Chapter 13	Goodness-of-Fit Tests and Contingency Analysis	210
Chapter 14	Introduction to Linear Regression and Correlation Analysis	225
Chapter 15	Multiple Regression Analysis and Model Building	253
Chapter 16	Analyzing and Forecasting Time-Series Data	301
Chapter 17	Introduction to Nonparametric Statistics	337
Chapter 18	Introduction to Quality and Statistical Process Control	352
Online Chapter 19	Introduction to Decision Analysis	364

Chapter 1
The Where, Why, and How of Data Collection

Section 1.1

1.1 This application is primarily descriptive in nature. The owner wishes to develop a presentation. She will most likely use charts, graphs, tables and numerical measures to describe her data.

1.3 A bar chart is used whenever you want to display data that has already been categorized while a histogram is used to display data over a range of values for the factor under consideration. Another fundamental difference is that there typically are gaps between the bars on a bar chart but there are no gaps between the bars of a histogram.

1.5 Hypothesis testing uses statistical techniques to validate a claim. With hypothesis testing, sample data is used to make an inference about the larger population from which the sample was drawn. Student provided examples will differ depending on their experiences.

1.7 Hypothesis testing is used whenever one is interested in testing claims that concern a population. Using information taken from samples, hypothesis testing evaluates the claim and makes a conclusion about the population from which the sample was taken. Estimation is used when we are interested in knowing something about all the data, but the population is too large, or the data set is too big for us to work with all the data. In estimation, no claim is being made or tested.

1.9 By its nature, a single measure is just one value and therefore is simpler than a table. It allows an easy method of comparison between two or more data sets, something that is more difficult if the data sets are represented in tabular form. In addition, although not mentioned in this chapter, additional statistical techniques, such as hypothesis testing and estimation, involve calculations based on a single measure from a subset of population data.

1.11 Student answers will vary depending on the periodical selected and the periodical's issue date, but should all address the three parts of the question.

1.13 Because it would be too costly, too time consuming, or practically impossible to contact every subscriber to ascertain the desired information, the decision makers at *Fortune* might decide to use statistical inference, particularly estimation, to answer its questions. By looking at a subset of the data and using the procedures of estimation it would be possible for the decision makers to arrive at values for average age and average income that are within tolerable limits of the actual values..

1.15. Student answers will vary. However, the examples should illustrate how statistics has been used and should clearly indicate the type of statistical analysis employed.

Section 1.2

1.17 As discussed in this section, the pet store would most likely use a written survey or a telephone survey to collect the customer satisfaction data.

1.19 An experiment is any process that generates data as its outcome. The plan for performing the experiment in which the variable of interest is defined is referred to as an experimental design. In the experimental design one or more factors are identified to be changed so that the impact on the variable of interest can be observed or measured.

1.21. There will likely by a high rate of nonresponse bias since many people who work days will not be home during the 9-11 AM time slot. Also, the data collectors need to be careful where they get the phone number list as some people do not have listed phones in phone books and others have no phone or only a cell phone. This may result in selection bias.

1.23 The two types of validity mentioned in the section are internal validity and external validity. For this problem external validity is easiest to address. It simply means the sampling method chosen will be sufficient to insure the results based on the sample will be able to be generalized to the population of all students. Internal validity would involve making sure the data gathering method, for instance a questionnaire, accurately determines the respondent's attitude toward the registration process.

1.25 There are many potential sources of bias associated with data collection. If data is to be collected using personal interviews it will be important that the interviewer be trained so that interviewer bias, arising from the way survey questions are asked, is not injected into the survey. If the survey is conducted using either a mail survey or a telephone survey then it is important to be aware of nonresponse bias from those who do not respond to the mailing or refuse to answer your calls. You must also be careful when selecting your survey subjects so that selection bias is not a problem. In order to have useful, reliable data that is representative of the true student opinions regarding campus food service it is necessary that the data collection process be conducted in a manner that reduces or eliminates the potential for these and other sources of potential bias.

1.27 One advantage of this form of data gathering is the same as for mail questionnaires. That is low cost. Additional factors being speed of delivery and, with current software, with closed- ended questions, instant updating of data analysis. Disadvantages are also similar, in particular low response and potential confusion about questions. An additional factor might be the ability of competitors to "hack" into the database and analysis program.

1.29 Students should select some form of personal observation as the data gathering technique. In addition, there should be a discussion of a sampling procedure with an effort made to ensure the sample randomly selected both days of the week unless daily observations are made, and randomly selected times of the day since 24 hour observation would likely be impossible. A complete answer would also address efforts to reduce the potential bias of having an observer standing in an obvious manner by the displays.

1.31 The results of the survey are based on telephone interviews with 1,025 national adults, aged 18 and older. Students may also answer that the survey could have been conducted using personal interviews. Because telephone interviews were used to collect the survey data nonresponse biases associated with sampled adults who are not at home when phoned, or adults who refuse to participate in the survey. There is also the problem that some adults do not have a phone. If personal interviews are used to collect the data then it is important to guard against nonresponse bias from those sampled adults who refuse to be interviewed. There is also the problem of selection bias. In phone interviews we may miss the people who work evenings and nights. If personal interviews are used we must be careful to select a representative sample of the adult population, not just those who appear willing or interested in participating.

Section 1.3

1.33   To determine the range of employee numbers for the first employee selected in a systematic random sample use the following:

$$\text{Part range} = \frac{Population\ Size}{Sample\ Size} = \frac{18,000}{100} = 180$$

Thus, the first person selected will come from employees 1-180. Once that person is randomly selected, the second person will be the one numbered 100 higher than the first, and so on.

1.35 Statistical sampling techniques consist of those sampling methods that select samples based on chance. Nonstatistical sampling techniques consist of those methods of selecting samples using convenience, judgment, or other non-chance processes. In convenience sampling, samples are chosen because they are easy or convenient to sample. There is no attempt to randomize the selection of the selected items. In convenience sampling not every item in the population has a random chance of being selected. Rather, items are sampled based on their convenience alone. Thus, convenience sampling is not a statistical sampling method.

1.37 A census is an enumeration of the entire set of measurements taken from the population as a whole. While in some cases, the items of interest are obtained from people such as through a survey, in many instances the items of interest come from a product or other inanimate object. For example, a study could be conducted to determine the defect rate for items made on a production line. The census would consist of all items produced on the line in a defined period of time.

1.39 In stratified random sampling, the population is divided into homogeneous groups called strata. The idea is to make all items in a stratum as much alike as possible with respect to the variable of interest thereby reducing the number of items that will need to be sampled from each stratum. In cluster sampling, the idea is to break the population into heterogeneous groups called clusters (usually on a geographical basis) such that each cluster looks as much like the original population as possible. Then clusters are randomly selected and from the cluster, individual items are selected using a statistical sampling method.

1.41 These percentages would be parameters since it would include all U.S. colleges.

1.43
   a. Stratified random sampling
   b. Simple random sampling or possibly cluster random sampling
   c. Systematic random sampling
   d. Stratified random sampling

1.45
   a. Student answers will vary
   b. Cluster sampling could be used to ensure that you get all types of cereal. Make each cluster the area where certain cereals are located (i.e., isle, row, shelf, etc.)
   c. Cluster sampling would give you a better idea of the inventory of all types of food. Simple random sampling could possibly end up with only looking at 2 or 3 food types.

1.47
   a. The population should be all users of cross-country ski lots and trailheads in Colorado.
   b. Several sampling techniques could be selected. Be sure that some method of ensuring randomness is discussed. In addition, some students might give greater weight to frequent users of the lots. In which case the population would really be user days rather than individual users.
   c. Students using Excel should choose the Data tab, select Data Analysis from the Analysis group – Random Number Generation process. Students' answers may differ since Excel generates different streams of random numbers each time it is used. Since the application requires integer numbers, the Decrease Decimal option should be used.

Section 1.4

1.49.
   a. Time-series
   b. Cross-sectional
   c. Time-series
   d. Cross-sectional

1.51
   a. Ordinal – categories with defined order
   b. Nominal – categories with no defined order
   c. Ratio
   d. Nominal – categories with no defined order

1.53 Since the circles involve a ranking from best to worst, this would be ordinal data.

1.55
  a. Nominal Data
  b. Ratio Data
  c. Nominal Data
  d. Ratio Data
  e. Ratio Data
  f. Nominal Data
  g. Ratio Data

1.57   Vehicle Name – Nominal
        Sports Car – Nominal
        Sport Utility – Nominal
        Wagon – Nominal
        Minivan – Nominal
        Pickup – Nominal
        All-Wheel Drive – Nominal
        Rear-Wheel Drive – Nominal
        Suggested Retail Price – Ratio
        Dealer Cost – Ratio
        Engine Size – Ratio
        Number of Cylinders – Ratio
        Horsepower – Ratio
        City MPG – Ratio
        Highway MPG – Ratio
        Weight – Ratio
        Wheel base – Ratio
        Length - Ratio
        Width - Ratio

End of Chapter

1.59 Answers will vary with the student. But a good discussion should include the following factors:
        Sampling techniques and possible problems selecting a representative sample.
        Determining how to develop questions to measure approval.
        Structuring questions to avoid bias.
        The measurement scale associated with the questions.
        The fact these polls tend to develop time-series data.

1.61 Interval or ratio data.

1.63 Answers will vary with the student. But a good discussion should include the following factors:
        Sampling techniques and possible problems selecting a representative sample.
        Determining how to measure confidence.
        Structuring questions to avoid bias.
        The measurement scale associated with the questions.
        The fact this poll is specifically intended to develop time-series data.

1.65 Answers will vary with the student.

1.67
  a. They would probably want to sample the salsa jars as they come off the assembly line at the plant for a specified time period. They would want to use a random sample. One method would be to take a systematic random sample.
  b. The product is going to be ruined after testing it. You would not want to ruin the entire product that comes off the assembly line.

Chapter 2
Graphs, Charts, and Tables—Describing Your Data

Section 2.1

2.1 **Step 1:** List the possible values.

The possible values for the discrete variable are 0 through 12.

Step 2: Count the number of occurrences at each value.

The resulting frequency distribution is shown as follows:

x	Frequency
0	1
1	0
2	2
3	4
4	1
5	2
6	5
7	6
8	1
9	1
10	1
11	0
12	1
Total =	25

2.3

a. Given n = 1,000, the minimum number of classes for a grouped data frequency distribution determined using the $2^k \geq n$ guideline is:

$$2^k \geq n \quad \text{or} \quad 2^{10} = 1,024 \geq 1,000 \quad \text{Thus, use k = 10 classes.}$$

b. Assuming that the number of classes that will be used is 10, the class width is determined as follows:

$$w = \frac{High - Low}{Classes} = \frac{2,900 - 300}{10} = \frac{2,600}{10} = 260$$

Then we round to the nearest 100 points giving a class width of 300.

2.5

a. There are n = 60 observations in the data set. Using the $2^k \geq n$ guideline, the number of classes, k, would be 6. The maximum and minimum values in the data set are 17 and 0, respectively. The class width is computed to be: w = (17-0)/6 = 2.833, which is rounded to 3. The frequency distribution is

Class	Frequency
0-2	6
3-5	13
6-8	20
9-11	14
12-14	5
15-17	2
Total =	60

b. To construct the relative frequency distribution divide the number of occurrences (frequency) in each class by the total number of occurrences. The relative frequency distribution is shown below.

Class	Frequency	Relative Frequency
0-2	6	0.100
3-5	13	0.217
6-8	20	0.333
9-11	14	0.233
12-14	5	0.083
15-17	2	0.033
Total =	60	

c. To develop the cumulative frequency distribution, compute a running sum for each class by adding the frequency for that class to the frequencies for all classes above it. The cumulative relative frequencies are computed by dividing the cumulative frequency for each class by the total number of observations. The cumulative frequency and the cumulative relative frequency distributions are shown below.

Class	Frequency	Relative Frequency	Cumulative Frequency	Cumulative Relative Frequency
0-2	6	0.100	6	0.100
3-5	13	0.217	19	0.317
6-8	20	0.333	39	0.650
9-11	14	0.233	53	0.883
12-14	5	0.083	58	0.967
15-17	2	0.033	60	1.000
Total =	60			

d. To develop the histogram, first construct a frequency distribution (see part a). The classes form the horizontal axis and the frequency forms the vertical axis. Bars corresponding to the frequency of each class are developed.   The histogram based on the frequency distribution from part (a) is shown below.

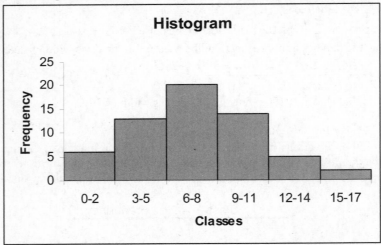

2.7
a. Proportion of days in which no shortages occurred = 1 – proportion of days in which shortages occurred = 1 – 0.24 = 0.76
b. Less than $20 off implies that overage was less than $20 and the shortage was less than $20 = (proportion of overages less $20) – (proportion of shortages at most $20) = 0.56 – 0.08 = 0.48
c. Proportion of days with less than $40 over or at most $20 short = Proportion of days with less than $40 over – proportion of days with more than $20 short = 0.96 – 0.08 = 0.86.

2.9

a. **Step 1** and **Step 2**. Group the data into classes and determine the class width:

The problem asks you to group the data. Using the $2^k \geq n$ guideline we get:

$$2^k \geq 60 \text{ so } 2^6 \geq 60$$

Class width is:

$$W = \frac{Maximum - Minumum}{\#Classes} = \frac{10 - 2}{6} = 1.33$$

which we round up to 2.0

Step 3: Define the class boundaries:

Since the data are discrete, the classes are:

Class
2-3
4-5
6-7
8-9
10-11

Step 4: Count the number of values in each class:

Class	Frequency	Relative Frequency
2-3	2	0.0333
4-5	25	0.4167
6-7	26	0.4333
8-9	6	0.1000
10-11	1	0.0167

b. The cumulative frequency distribution is:

Class	Frequency	Cumulative Frequency
2-3	2	2
4-5	25	27
6-7	26	53
8-9	6	59
10-11	1	60

c.

Class	Frequency	Relative Frequency	Cumu. Rel. Freq.
2-3	2	0.0333	0.0333
4-5	25	0.4167	0.4500
6-7	26	0.4333	0.8833
8-9	6	0.1000	0.9833
10-11	1	0.0167	1.000

The relative frequency histogram is:

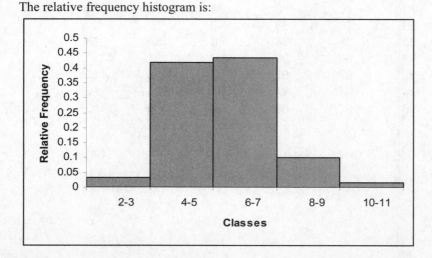

d.   The ogive is a graph of the cumulative relative frequency distribution.

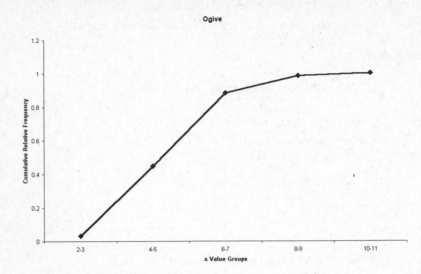

2.11

   a.

	Knowledge Level			
	Savvy	Experienced	Novice	Total
Online Investors	32	220	148	400
Traditional Investors	8	58	134	200
	40	278	282	600

   b.

	Knowledge Level		
	Savvy	Experienced	Novice
Online Investors	0.0533	0.3667	0.2467
Traditional Investors	0.0133	0.0967	0.2233

   c.   The proportion that were both on-line and experienced is 0.3667.
   d.   The proportion of on-line investors is 0.6667

2.13

   a.   The weights are sorted from smallest to largest to create the data array.

77	79	80	83	84	85	86
86	86	86	86	86	87	87
87	88	88	88	88	89	89
89	89	89	90	90	91	91
92	92	92	92	93	93	93
94	94	94	94	94	95	95
95	96	97	98	98	99	101

b.

Weight (Classes)	Frequency
77-81	3
82-86	9
87-91	16
92-96	16
97-101	5
Total =	49

c.   The histogram can be created from the frequency distribution. The classes are shown on the horizontal axis and the frequency on the vertical axis. The histogram is shown below.

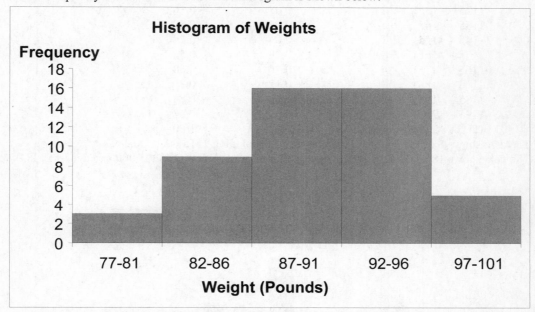

d.   Convert the frequency distribution into relative frequencies and cumulative relative frequencies as shown below.

Weights (Classes)	Frequency	Relative Frequency	Cumulative Relative Frequency
77-81	3	0.0612	0.0612
82-86	9	0.1837	0.2449
87-91	16	0.3265	0.5714
92-96	16	0.3265	0.8980
97-101	5	0.1020	1.0000
Total =	49		

The percentage of sampled crates with weights greater than 96 pounds is 10.20%.

2.15

a. $w = \dfrac{Largest - smallest}{number\ of\ classes} = \dfrac{214.4 - 105.0}{11} = 9.945 \rightarrow w = 10$. The salaries in the first class are (105, 105

+ 10) = (105, 115). The frequency distribution follows

Classes	Frequency	Relative Frequency	Cumulative Relative Frequency
(105 – <115)	1	0.04	0.04
(115 – <125)	1	0.04	0.08
(125 – <135)	2	0.08	0.16
(135 – <145)	1	0.04	0.20
(145 – <155)	1	0.04	0.24
(155 – <165)	7	0.28	0.52
(165 – <175)	4	0.16	0.68
(175 – <185)	3	0.12	0.80
(185 – <195)	2	0.08	0.88
(195 – <205)	0	0.00	0.88
(205 – <215)	3	0.12	1.00

b.   The data shows 8 of the 25, or 0.32 of the salaries including 175,000
c.   The data shows 18 of the 25, or 0.72 having salaries that are at most $205,000 and a least $135,000.

2.17
a.

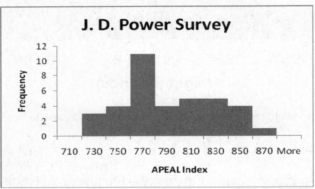

b.   The 2008 average is 782 which is less than the 2005 average of 866. This could indicate that the new models are less appealing to automobile customers, or customers could simply have rising expectations.

2.19.

a.   There are n = 294 values in the data. Then using the $2^k \geq n$ guideline we would need at least k = 9 classes.
b.   Using k = 9 classes, the class width is determined as follows:

$$w = \dfrac{High - Low}{Classes} = \dfrac{32 - 10}{9} = \dfrac{22}{9} = 2.44$$

Rounding this up to the nearest 1.0, the class width is 3.0.

c.

Rounds	Frequency
10, 11, 12	10
13, 14, 15	31
16, 17, 18	65
19, 20, 21	90
22, 23, 24	64
25, 26, 27	26
28, 29, 30	6
31, 32, 33	2
34, 35, 36	0
Total	294

Students should recognize that by rounding the class width up from 2.44 to 3.0, and by starting the lowest class at the minimum value of 10, the 9th class is actually not needed.

d.   Based on the results in part c, the frequency histogram is shown as follows:

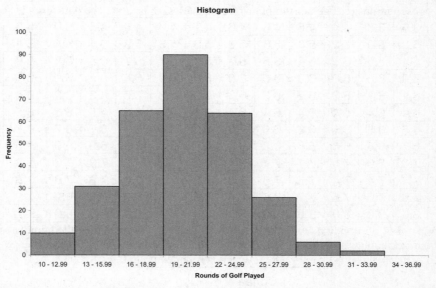

The distribution for rounds of golf played is mound shaped and fairly symmetrical. It appears that the center is between 19 and 22 rounds per year, but the rounds played is quite spread out around the center.

2.21

a.   Using the $2^k \geq n$ guideline, the number of classes should be 6. There are 38 airlines in the Total column. Solving finds that $2^5 = 32$ and $2^6 = 64$. Therefore, 6 classes are chosen.

b.   Class width is equal to the maximum - minimum. The maximum value is 690,628 and the minimum value is 439. The difference is 690,628 - 439 = 690,189. The class width is 690,189/6 classes = 115,031.5. Rounding up to the nearest 1,000 passengers results in a class width of 116,000.

c.

Classes	Frequency
0 < 116,000	29
116,000 < 232,000	3
232,000 < 347,000	4
347,000 < 462,000	1
462,000 < 577,000	0
577,000 < 692,000	1

d.

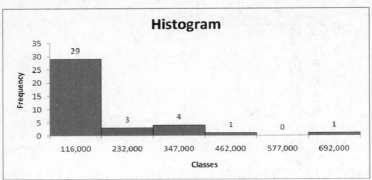

Based on the data from the Orlando International Airport, we see that far and away more airlines have less that 116,000 passengers at the airport,

2.23

a. Order the observations (coffee consumption) from smallest to largest. The data array is shown below:

3.5	3.8	4.4	4.5	4.6	4.6	4.7	4.7	4.8	4.8	5.0	5.0
5.0	5.0	5.2	5.3	5.3	5.3	5.3	5.3	5.3	5.4	5.4	5.4
5.4	5.5	5.5	5.6	5.6	5.7	5.7	5.7	5.7	5.8	5.8	5.9
5.9	6.0	6.0	6.0	6.0	6.0	6.0	6.0	6.0	6.1	6.1	6.1
6.1	6.1	6.2	6.2	6.2	6.3	6.3	6.3	6.3	6.3	6.3	6.4
6.4	6.4	6.4	6.4	6.4	6.4	6.5	6.5	6.5	6.5	6.5	6.5
6.5	6.5	6.5	6.6	6.6	6.6	6.6	6.6	6.7	6.7	6.7	6.7
6.7	6.8	6.8	6.8	6.8	6.8	6.8	6.8	6.8	6.9	6.9	7.0
7.0	7.0	7.0	7.1	7.1	7.1	7.2	7.2	7.2	7.2	7.2	7.3
7.4	7.4	7.4	7.5	7.5	7.5	7.5	7.5	7.6	7.6	7.6	7.6
7.6	7.6	7.6	7.7	7.7	7.8	7.8	7.8	7.9	7.9	7.9	7.9
8.0	8.0	8.0	8.0	8.0	8.3	8.4	8.4	8.4	8.6	8.9	10.1

b. There are n = 144 observations in the data set. Using the $2^k \geq n$ guideline, the number of classes, k, would be 8. The maximum and minimum values in the data set are 10.1 and 3.5, respectively. The class width is computed to be: w = (10.1-3.5)/8 = 0.821, which is rounded up to 0.9.

Coffee Consumption (kg.)	Frequency
3.5 - 4.3	2
4.4 - 5.2	13
5.3 - 6.1	35
6.2 - 7.0	49
7.1 - 7.9	33
8.0 – 8.8	10
8.9 - 9.7	1
9.8 – 10.6	1

Most observations fall in the class of 5.9 – 6.6 kg of coffee.

c. The histogram can be created from the frequency distribution. The classes are shown on the horizontal axis and the frequency on the vertical axis. The histogram is shown below.

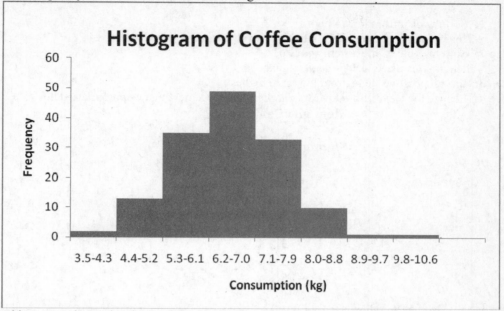

The histogram shows the shape of the distribution. This histogram is showing that fewer people consume small and large quantities and that most individuals consume between 5.3 and 8.0 kg of coffee, with the most individuals consuming between 6.2 and 7.0.

d. Convert the frequency distribution into relative frequencies and cumulative relative frequencies as shown below.

Consumption	Frequency	Relative Frequency	Cumulative Relative Frequency
3.5-4.3	2	0.0139	0.0139
4.4-5.2	13	0.0903	0.1042
5.3-6.1	35	0.2431	0.3472
6.2-7.0	49	0.3403	0.6875
7.1-7.9	33	0.2292	0.9167
8.0-8.8	10	0.0694	0.9861
8.9-9.7	1	0.0069	0.9931
9.8-10.6	1	0.0069	1

8.33% (100 - 91.67) of the coffee drinkers sampled consumes 8.0 kg or more annually.

Section 2-2

2.25

Step 1: Sort the data from low to high.
This is done on the problem. The lowest value is 0.7 and the highest 6.4.
Step 2: Split the values into a stem and leaf.
Stem = units place   leaf = decimal place
Step 3: List all possible stems from lowest to highest.
Step 4: Itemize the leaves from lowest to highest and place next to the appropriate stems.

Stem-and-Leaf Display		
Stem unit: 1		
0	7 8	
1	0 1 4 7 8	
2	0 0 1 4 8	
3	0 3 8	
4	3 4	
5	3 4 4	
6	3 4	

2.27.   One possible bar chart is shown as follows:

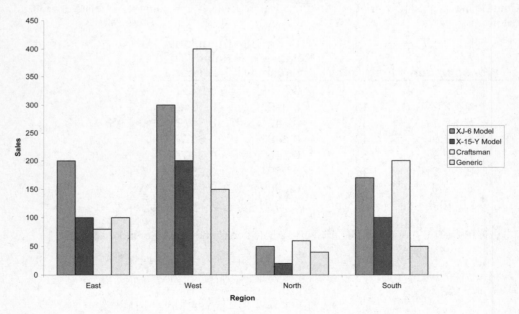

Another way to present the same data is:

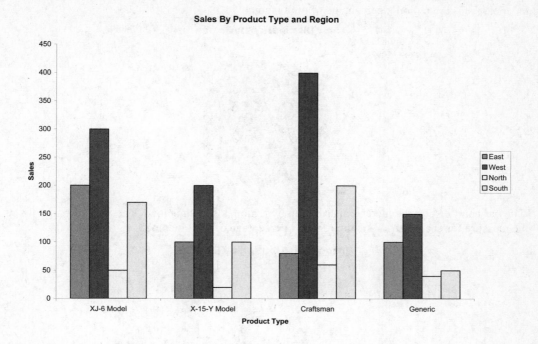

Still another possible way is called a "stacked" bar chart.

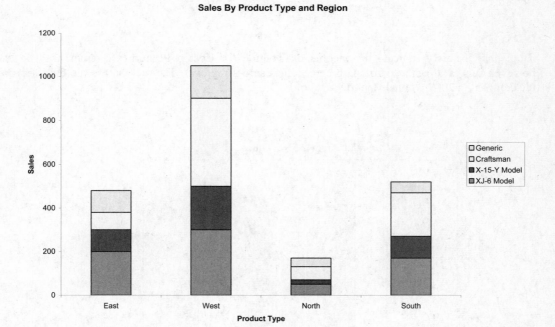

2.29

    a. A pie chart displaying income distribution by region is shown below. The categories are the regions and the measure is the region's percentage of total income.

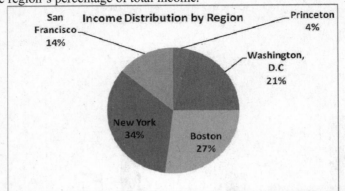

    b. The bar chart displaying income distribution by region is shown below. The categories are the regions and the measure for each category is the region's percentage of total income.

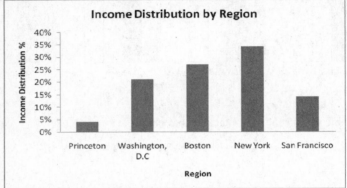

    c. Both charts clearly indicate the income distribution for Boston Properties by region. The bar chart, however, makes it easier to compare percentages across regions. The pie chart is the format presented in the company's 2007 Annual Report.

2.31

    a.

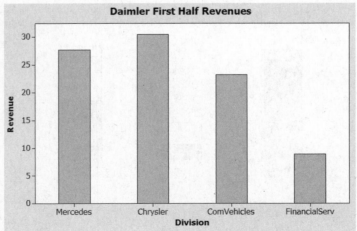

    b. Proportion of Vehicle Revenue = 1 – proportion of financial services

$$= 1 - 8.9/90.3$$
$$= 1 - 0.0985 = 0.9015$$

2.33. The bar chart is skewed below indicating that number of $1 Million houses is growing rapidly. It also appears that that growth is exponential rather than linear.

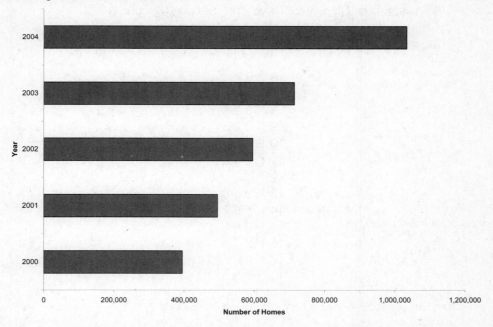

The bar chart is skewed below indicating that number of $1 Million houses is growing rapidly. It also appears that that growth is exponential rather than linear.

2.35 A bar chart can be used to make the comparison. Shown below are two examples of bar charts which compare North America to the United Kingdom.

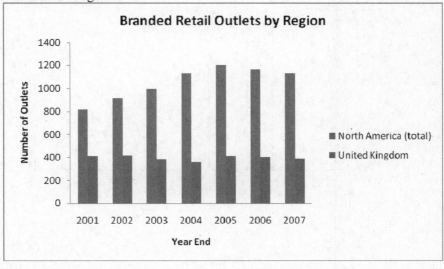

2.37

    a.   The following stem and leaf diagram was created using PhStat. The stem unit is 10 and the leaf unit is 1.

         Stem-and-Leaf Display for Drive-Thru Service (Seconds)

Stem unit: 10

```
 6 | 8
 7 | 1 3 4 6 9
 8 | 3 5 8
 9 | 0 2 3
10 | 3 5
11 | 0 6 9
12 |
13 | 0 4 8
14 | 5 6 7
15 | 6 6
16 | 2
17 | 8
18 | 1
```

    b.   The most frequent speed of service is between 70 and 79 seconds.

2.39

    a.   The bar graph is

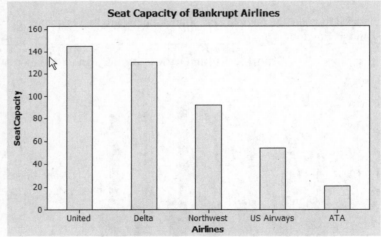

b. The percent equals the individual capacity divided by the total, e.g. United → percent = (145/858)100% = 16.90%, etc. This produces the following pie chart:

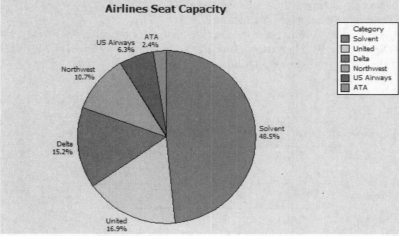

c. The percent of seat capacity of those in bankruptcy = 16.9 + 15.2 + 10.7 + 6.3 + 2.4 = 51.5%. Since this is larger than 50%, their statement was correct.

2.41

a.

Stem-and-Leaf Display: Days

```
Stem-and-leaf of Days   N  = 50
Leaf Unit = 1.0


    1    0  4
    2    0  7
    6    1  0344
   15    1  566677889
   23    2  00012244
  (13)   2  5666777888999
   14    3  000122344
    5    3  5669
    1    4  0
```

b. The shape of the data is slightly skewed to the left. The center of the data appears to be between 24 and 26.

c. $\bar{x} = \dfrac{2428}{50} = 24.28$. This and the data indicates that the mean is larger than indicated by J.D. Power. The difference is that the data set is only a sample of the data. Each sample will produce different results but approximately equal to the population average calculated by J.D. Power.

2.43

a. The following are the averages for each hospital computed by summing the charges and dividing by the number of charges:

University Related	Religious Affiliated	Municipally Owned	Privately Held
$6,398	$3,591	$4,613	$5,191

b.   The following steps are used to construct the bar chart:

   Step 1: Define the categories.
   The categories are the four hospital types

   Step 2: Determine the appropriate measure.
   The measure of interest is the average charge for outpatient gall bladder surgery.

   Step 3: Develop the bar chart using computer software such as Excel or Minitab.
   The bar chart is shown as follows:

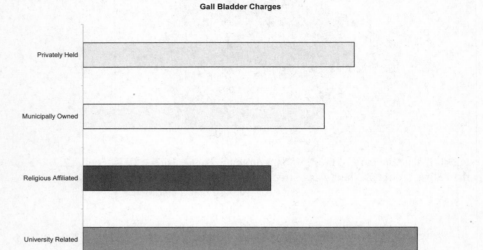

Gall Bladder Charges

   Step 4: Interpret the results.
   The largest average charges occurred for gall bladder surgery appears to be in University Related hospitals and the lowest average appears to be in Religious Affiliated hospitals.

c.   A pie chart is used to display the parts of a total. In this case the total charges of the four hospital types is not a meaningful number so a pie chart showing how that total is divided among the four hospital types would not be useful or appropriate.

2.45

   a.

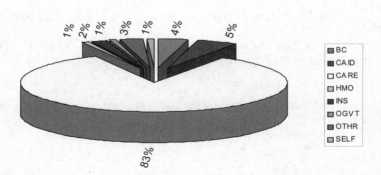

Health Insurance Payer

b.

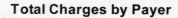

Total Charges by Payer

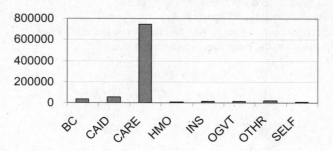

c.   Using PHStat the stem & leaf diagram is shown as follows.

Stem-and-Leaf Display for Length of Stay		
Stem unit: 1		
1	0 0 0 0 0 0 0 0	
2	0 0 0 0 0 0 0 0 0 0 0 0 0 0 0 0 0 0	
3	0 0 0 0 0 0 0 0 0 0 0 0 0 0 0 0 0 0 0 0 0 0 0 0 0 0 0 0 0 0 0 0 0 0 0 0 0 0 0 0 0	
4	0 0 0 0 0 0 0 0 0 0 0 0 0 0 0 0 0 0 0 0 0 0 0 0	
5	0 0 0 0 0 0 0 0 0 0 0 0 0 0 0 0 0	
6	0 0 0 0 0 0 0 0 0	
7	0 0 0 0 0 0 0 0 0 0	
8	0 0 0 0 0	
9	0 0 0 0	
10		
11	0 0	
12	0	
13		
14		
15	0	
16	0	

d.   Excel's pivot table can be used to develop a bar chart. The chart showed is a stacked bar chart.

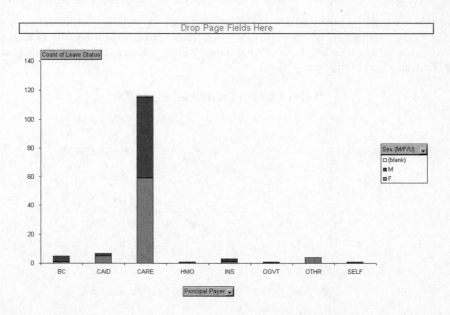

Section 2-3

2.47   **Step 1:** Identify the time-series variable
                      The variable of interest is the monthly sales.
          Step 2: Layout the Horizontal and Vertical Axis
                      The horizontal axis will be month and the vertical axis is sales .
          Step 3: Plot the values on the graph and connect the points

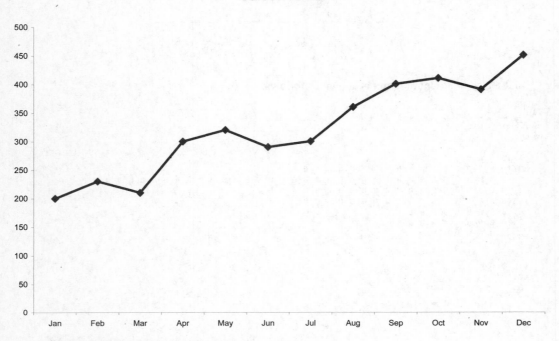

Sales Trend

The sales have trended upward over the past 12 months.

2.49   The time-series variable is Year-End Dollar Value Deposits   ($ in millions) measured over 8 years with a maximum value of 1,380 (million). The horizontal axis will have 8 time periods equally spaced. The vertical axis will start at 0 and go to a value exceeding 1,380. We will use 1,600. The vertical axis will also be divided into 200-unit increments. The line chart of the data is shown below.

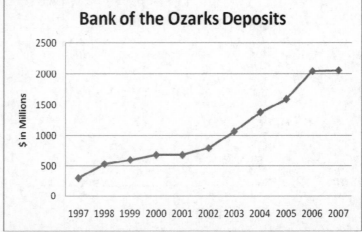

Bank of the Ozarks Deposits

The line chart shows that Year-End Deposits have been increasing since 1997, but have increased more sharply since 2002 and leveled off between 2006 and 2007.

2.51

a.

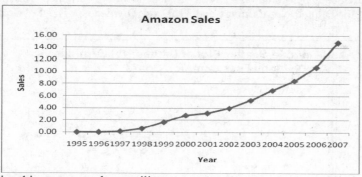

b. The relationship appears to be curvilinear.

c. The largest difference in sales occurred between 2006 and 2007. That difference was 14.835 − 10.711 = 4.124 $billions.

2.53

a. The time-series variable is diluted net earnings per common share measured over 10 years with a maximum value of $2.66. The horizontal axis will have 10 time periods equally spaced. The vertical axis will start at 0 and go to a value exceeding $2.66. We will use $3.00. The vertical axis will also be divided into $0.50-unit increments. The line chart of the data is shown below.

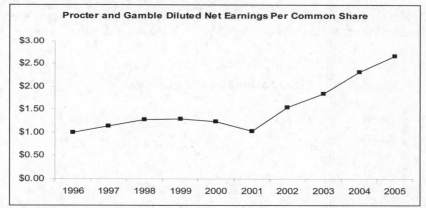

b. The time-series variable is dividends per common share measured over 10 years with a maximum value of $1.03. The horizontal axis will have 10 time periods equally spaced. The vertical axis will start at 0 and go to a value exceeding $1.03. We will use $1.20. The vertical axis will also be divided into $0.20-unit increments. The line chart of the data is shown below.

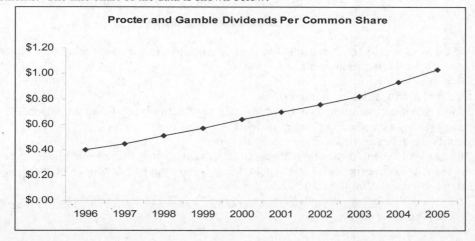

c.   One variable is Diluted Net Earnings per Common Share and the other variable is Dividends per Common Share. The variable dividends per common share is the dependent (y) variable. The maximum value for each variable is $2.66 for Diluted Net Earnings and $1.03 for Dividends. The XY Scatter Plot is shown below.

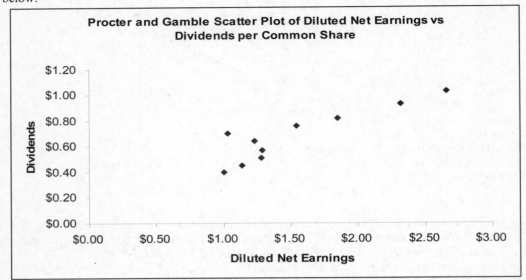

There is a relatively strong positive relationship between the two variables, which is as one would expect. That is, one might expect to see the two variables move in the same direction.

2.55.

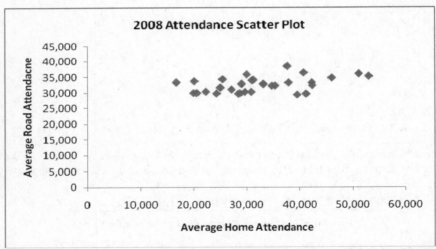

Based on the scatter diagram, it appears that there is a positive linear relationship between home and road attendance. However, the relationship is not perfect.

2.57. **Step 1:** Identify the two variables of interest

In this situation, there are two variables, fuel consumption per hour, the dependent variable, and passenger capacity, the independent variable.

Step 2: Identify the dependent and independent variables.

The analyst is attempting to predict passenger capacity using fuel consumption per hour. Therefore, the capacity is the dependent variable and the fuel consumption per hour is the independent variable.

Step 3: Establish the scales for the vertical and horizontal axes

The y variable (fuel consumption) ranges from 631 to 3,529 and the x variable (passenger capacity) ranges from 78 to 405.

Step 4: Plot the joint values for the two variables by placing a point in the x,y space shown as follows:

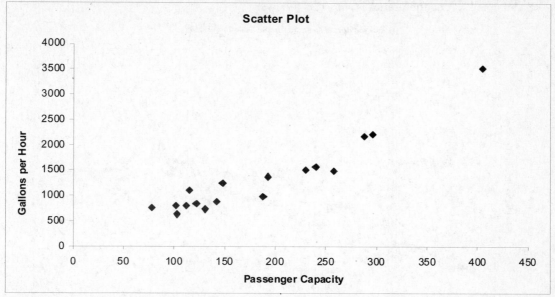

Based on the scatter diagram we see there is a strong positive linear relationship between passenger capacity and fuel consumption per hour.

2.59

a.   **Step 1:** Identify the time-series variable
          The variable of interest is annual average price of gasoline in California
      Step 2: Layout the Horizontal and Vertical Axis
          The horizontal axis will be the year and the vertical axis is average price (See Step 3)
      Step 3: Plot the values on the graph and connect the points

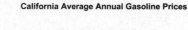

Gasoline prices have trended upward over the 36 year period with some short periods of decline. However, prices rises have been very steep since 1999.

b.   Adding the inflation adjusted prices to the graph does not require that we use a different scale. The results of adding the second time-series is shown as follows:

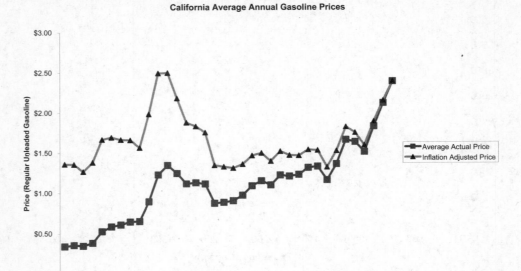

California Average Annual Gasoline Prices

c.   The graph in part b. shows an interesting result. That is, although the price of gasoline has risen quite steadily since 1970, when the value of the dollar is taken into account, the overall trend has been more level. In fact, the highest prices (when the inflation index is considered) occurred in 1980 and 1981 at the equivalent of slightly more than $2.50. This exceeds the prices during the 2000-2005 years. Thus, while gasoline prices were high in California in 2005, it is not the worst that has occurred in that state.

2.61
a.

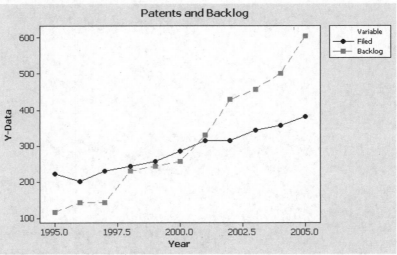

b.   Both relationships seem to be linear in nature.
c.   This occurred in 1998, 1999, and 2001.

End of Chapter

2.63 A relative frequency distribution deals with the percentage of the total observations that fall into each class rather than the number that fall into each class. Sometimes decision makers are more interested in percentages than numbers. Politicians, for instance, are often more interested in the percentage of voters that will vote for them (more than 50%) than the total number of votes they will get. Relative frequencies are also valuable when comparing distributions from two populations that have different total numbers.

2.65 Pie charts are effectively used when the data set is made up of parts of a whole, and therefore each part can be converted to a percentage. For instance, if the data involves a budget, a pie chart can represent the percentage of budget each category represents. Or, if the data involves total company sales, a pie chart can be used to represent the percentage contribution to sales for each major product line.

2.67
   a.

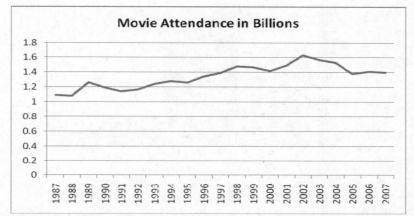

   b. It appears that there is a positive linear relationship between the attendance and the year. However, there does appear to be a sharp decline in the last five years. It could be evidence of a normal cycle since a similar decline occurred in 1990/91 which was followed by a steady climb in attendance for six of the next seven years.

2.69
   a.

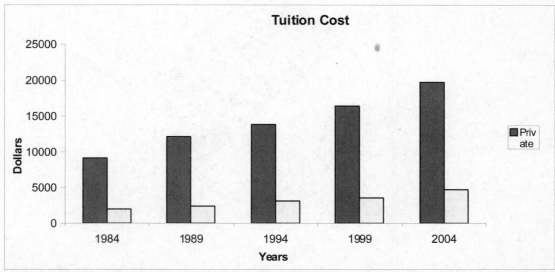

   b. Student answers will vary but should include identifying that both private and public college tuition costs have more than doubled in the 20 years of data.

2.71

a.   The frequencies can be calculated by multiplying the relative frequency times the sample size of 1,000.

Class Length (Inches)	Frequency	Relative Frequency
8 < 10	220	0.22
10 < 12	150	0.15
12 < 14	250	0.25
14 < 16	240	0.24
16 < 18	60	0.06
18 < 20	50	0.05
20 < 22	30	0.03

Frequency Distribution of Walleyes

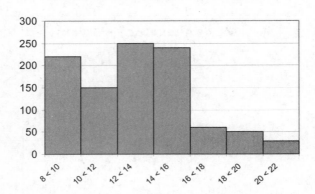

b.   The histogram is probably a better representation of the fish length data.

Pie Chart of Walleyes

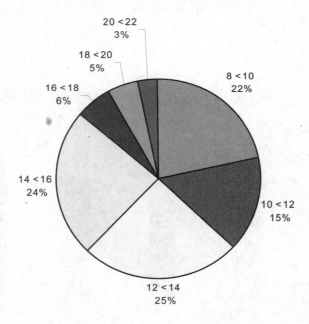

2.73

   a.   The independent variable is hours and the dependent variable is sales

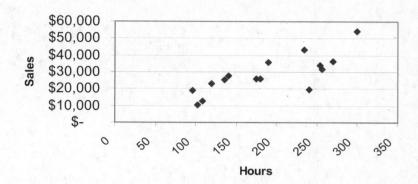

   b.   It appears that there is a positive linear relationship between hours worked and weekly sales. It appears that the more hours worked the greater the sales. No stores seem to be substantially different in terms of the general relationship between hours and sales.

2.75

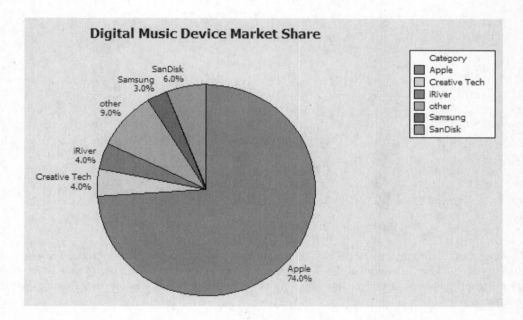

2.77

a.

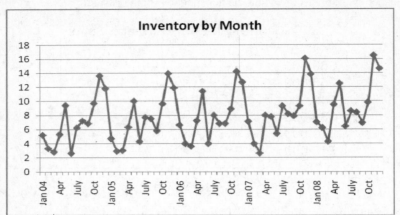

Inventory has been trending slightly up over the five years, but appears to be highly seasonal with predictable highs at certain points each year.

b.

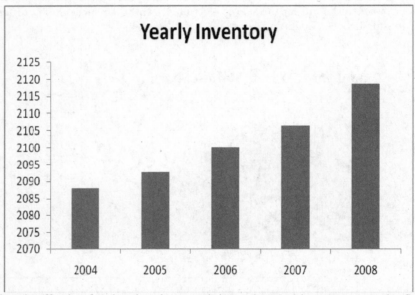

This bar chart is effective for showing the growth in total annual inventory over the five years. However, students should keep in mind that the sum of monthly inventory does not equate to how much inventory the store had on hand at the end of the year. Students might question why the store would graph the total inventory

Chapter 3
Describing Data Using Numerical Measures

Section 3.1

3.1 The sample mean is computed using the following steps:

    Step 1: Collect the sample data.

    Step 2: Add the values in the sample:

$$\sum x = 74349$$

    Step 3: Divide the sum by the sample size.

$$\bar{x} = \frac{74349}{15} = 4956.60$$

The quartiles are found using the following steps.

    Step 1: Sort the data from low to high.

4132	4188	4209	4423	4568
4573	4983	5002	5052	5176
5310	5381	5611	5736	6005

    Step 2: Determine the percentile location index.

To determine the location index for the 1st quartile (p=25) we do the following:

i = 25/100(n) = (25/100)*15 = 3.75.

    Step 3: Find the percentile.

Because the index is not an integer it is rounded up to 4. The first quartile is the fourth value in the sorted array and is equal to 4423.

        The median (or second quartile) is found by sorting the data from lowest to highest (see below). The index point, i , for the median is found by i = ½(n) = ½(15) = 7.5. Because i is not an integer it is rounded up to 8. The median is located by counting 8 values into the sorted data. The median is 5002.

        The location index for the 3rd quartile is:

        75/100(n) = 75/100(15) = 11.25.

Because *i* is not an integer it is rounded up to 12. The third quartile is the 12th value in the sorted array and is equal to 5381.

3.3.

    Step 1: Sort the data from low to high.

11.5	12.8	13.1	13.2	13.5	13.6	13.8	14.2	14.2	14.3
14.4	14.4	14.7	15.1	15.5	15.9	16.2	16.3	17.1	18.7

    Step 2: Determine the quartile location index and find the quartile value.

To determine the location index for the 1st quartile (p=25) we do the following:

$$i = \frac{p}{100}(n) = \frac{25}{100}(20) = 5$$

Since the index, 5, is an integer, the 1st quartile is determined by finding the average of the 5th and 6th values from the lower end of the sorted data. This is:

$$Q1 = \frac{13.5 + 13.6}{2} = 13.55$$

The location index for the 3rd quartile is:

$$i = \frac{p}{100}(n) = \frac{75}{100}(20) = 15$$

Since the index, 15, is an integer, the 3rd quartile is determined by finding the average of the 15th and 16th values from the lower end of the sorted data. This is:

$$Q3 = \frac{15.5 + 15.9}{2} = 15.7$$

Thus, the 1st quartile value is 13.55 meaning that 25 percent of the data values fall below 13.55. The third quartile is 15.7 meaning that 75% of the data values fall below 15.7.

3.5

Step 1: Sort the data from low to high.
The sorted data are shown below:

35	50	50	50
60	75	75	75
80	85	85	90
90	100	100	100
100	125	125	150

Step 2: Calculate the 25th percentile (Q_1), the 50th percentile (median), and the 75th percentile (Q_3).
The 25th percentile location is $(25/100)*20 = 5$. So Q_1 is the average of the values in the 5th and 6th position of the sorted array. $Q_1 = (60+75)/2 = 67.5$.
The median location is $(50/100)*20 = (1/2)*20 = 10$. Because the location point is an integer the median is the average of the values in the 10th and 11th location. Median $= (85 + 85)/2 = 85$.
The 75th percentile location is $(75/100)*20 = 15$. So Q3 is the average of the values in the 15th and 16th position of the sorted array. $Q_3 = (100 + 100)/2 = 100$.

Step 3: Draw the box so the ends correspond to Q_1 and Q_3.
Step 4: Draw a vertical line through the box at the median.
Step 5: Compute the upper and lower limits:
Lower limit = Q_1 - 1.5(Q_3-Q_1) = 67.5- 1.5*32.5 = 18.75
Upper Limit = Q_3 + 1.5 (Q_3-Q_1) = 100 + 1.5*32.5 = 148.75
Any value outside these limits will be labeled an outlier.
Step 6: Draw the whiskers.
Step 7: Plot the outliers. Outliers are typically indicated by an asterisk, *.
The box and whisker plot is shown below.

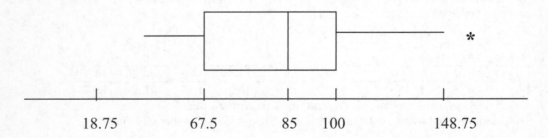

3.7

a.   The index is (p/100)n = (80/100)20 = 16 = integer. Therefore, an 80th percentile is obtained by calculating the average of the 16th and 17th data value = (31.2 + 32.2)/2 = 31.7.

b.   The 25th percentile: The index is (p/100)n = (25/100)20 = 5 = integer. Therefore, the 25th percentile is obtained by calculating the average of the 5th and 6th data value = (12.1 + 13)/2 = 12.55. The 75th percentile: The index is (p/100)n = (75/100)20 = 15 = integer. Therefore, the 75th percentile is obtained by calculating the average of the 15th and 16th data value = (26.7 + 31.2)/2 = 28.95.

c.   The median is the 50th percentile. The index is (p/100)n = (50/100)20 = 10 = integer. Therefore, a 50th percentile is obtained by calculating the average of the 10th and 11th data value = (20.8 + 22.8)/2 = 21.8.

3.9

a.

$$\bar{x} = \frac{\sum\limits_{i=1}^{n} x_i}{n} = 456/24 = 19$$

To compute the median, rank the observations and find the average of the middle two values.

10 12 14 14 17 17 18 .18 19 19 19 19

19 20 20 21 21 21 21 22 22 23 25 25

Median = (19 + 19)/2 = 19

Mode = 19

b. This data is symmetrical since the mean = median = mode

c.

Box-and-whisker Plot

Five-number Summary

Minimum	10
First Quartile	17.5
Median	19
Third Quartile	21
Maximum	25

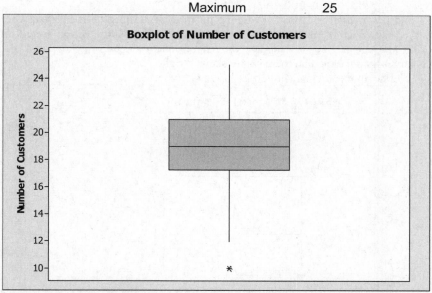

The box plot does support the idea that the distributions are symmetric although the median is not directly in the center between the Q_1 and Q_3.

3.11
- a.   The weighted mean is computed using:

$$\bar{x}_W = \frac{\sum w_i x_i}{\sum w_i} =$$

$$\frac{(7,400)(123) + (14,400)(402) + (12,300)(256) + (6,200)(109) + (3,100)(67)}{123 + 402 + 256 + 109 + 67} = 11,213.48$$

- b.   It is reasonable that plants with more employees would have more medical issues. The weighted average takes into account the number of employees and is a more reasonable measure of the average payments than would be an unweighted average that treats all plants as equals.

3.13
- a.   The sorted data are shown below.

68	85	110	146
71	88	116	147
73	90	119	156
74	92	130	156
76	93	134	162
79	103	138	178
83	105	145	181

The mean is 114.21 and the median is 107.50. Note the position of the median is $(1/2)(n)$ where $n = 28$. Because the median's position is 14, the average of the 14th and 15th position in the sorted array is the median, which is $(105+110)/2 = 107.50$. The mode is the most frequently occurring value and is 156.
- b.   Because the mean is larger than the median the data are skewed right.
- c.   The box and whisker plot developed using Minitab is shown below.

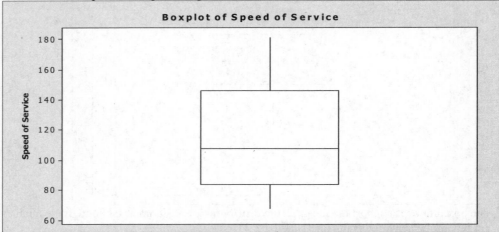

Note that the median is not in the center of the box and that the whiskers are not of equal length. The whisker going up is longer than the whisker going down which indicates that the data are skewed to the right. This supports the conclusion that the data are not symmetric, but skewed.

3.15

a.   Average $= \dfrac{\Sigma x_i}{n} = \dfrac{11259.9}{20} = 562.99$

b.   The 17th observation is quite larger than the rest of the data, an *outlier*. Averages, but not medians, are highly affected by outliers. Therefore, the median would be an appropriate measure for this data set. Arranged in numerical order, the data is

400.56	464.37	474.86	475.87	511.15	528.78	531.64	533.70	538.20	545.25
558.12	564.71	567.46	588.39	589.15	606.70	610.32	625.82	632.14	912.68

Calculating the index produces (p/100)n = (50/100)20 = 10. This is an integer. The rule says to average the 10th and 11th observation = (545.25 + 558.12)/2 = 551.685.

c.   The outlier will have the largest effect. Deleting it, produces the average

$= \dfrac{\Sigma x_i}{n} = \dfrac{11259.9 - 912.68}{20 - 1} = 544.59$. The observation closest to the original mean would have the

least effect. That number is 564.71. Deleting it, produces the average

$= \dfrac{\Sigma x_i}{n} = \dfrac{11259.9 - 564.71}{20 - 1} = 562.90$.

3.17

a.   FDIC Average $= \dfrac{\Sigma x_i}{n} = \dfrac{6826804000000}{8885} = 768351603.83$

Bank of America Average $= \dfrac{\Sigma x_i}{n} = \dfrac{681570000000}{6000} = 113595000$

b.   The ratio between the FDIC and BA averages is $768351603.83 / 113595000 = 6.76$. The discrepancy may be due to the use of the word "bank." The FDIC in referring to "bank" may consider a corporation such as BA to be a "bank." Whereas the BA term "banking center" refers to its branches. There may also be a small difference due to the fact that information was available for 2005 for the FDIC and for 2004 for BA.

c.   The answer to this question depends upon the intent of the measurements. If they were attempting to characterize only the specified years, they would be considered to be parameters. If, however, these data were considered "typical" and were to be used to describe past, current averages, they would be considered statistics.

3.19   Software such as Excel or Minitab can be used to compute these values. For instance, using the Descriptive Statistics Tool in Excel we get the following.

Processing Duration	
Mean	0.33
Standard Error	0.01
Median	0.31
Mode	0.24
Standard Deviation	0.09
Sample Variance	0.01
Kurtosis	-1.10
Skewness	0.44
Range	0.28
Minimum	0.22
Maximum	0.50
Sum	15.63
Count	48

Thus, the mean time is .33 minutes. The median is .31 minutes and the mode is .24 minutes. The data are slightly right skewed.

The 80th percentile is computed using the Percentile function in Excel to be .40 minutes.

3.21

a. $\bar{x} = \dfrac{2448.30}{20} = 122.465$ i = (50/100)20 = 10. Therefore, use average of the 10th and 11th number: median = (123.2 + 123.7)/2 = 123.45. Since the mean < median, this suggests that the distribution is left-skewed.

b. The average monthly increase would equal the difference in the PHSI between Jan 04 and Aug 05 divided by the number of months (20). Thus, the average = (129.5 – 111)/20 = 0.925.

c. Assuming the PHSI increases by 0.925 each month, then each month's weight should be the amount of increase since Dec 04. Thus, the weights would be: $w_1 = 0.925$, $w_2 = 2(0.925)$, . . ., $w_8 = 8(0.925)$. Therefore, the weighted average is

$$\bar{x}_w = \frac{0.925(120.6) + 2(0.925)(123.2) + ... + 8(0.925)(129.5)}{0.925 + 2(0.925) + ... + 8(0.925)} = \frac{4207.825}{33.3} = 126.36$$

d. The weighted average does seem more appropriate since the PHSI continues to increase each month. We expect that the most recent observations give a better appraisal as to the current, average PHSI.

3.23

a. The mean and median were computed using Minitab. The box and whisker plot was constructed using Minitab.

Descriptive Statistics: Expenditures

Variable	N*	Mean	Minimum	Q1	Median	Q3	Maximum	IQR
Expenditures	0	3061.6	2522.2	2901.0	3065.0	3235.6	3734.5	334.6

b. The mean is 3061.6 and the median is 3065.0. Because the mean and median are close in value the data are symmetric. The box and whisker plot also shows that the data are symmetric.

c. The first quartile is approximately 2901 and the third quartile is approximately 3236. Thus, approximately the middle 50% of the data values are between $2900 and $3250.

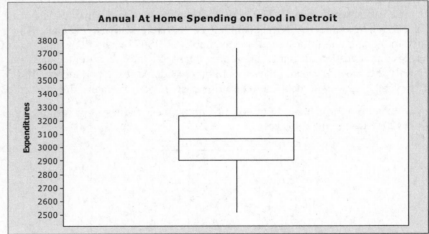

Section 3-2

3.25

a. The range is the difference between the high value and the low value in the set of data.

Range = High – Low

Range = $8 - 0 = 8$

b. The steps required to compute the sample variance are:

Step 1: Select the sample and record the data.

3	0	2	0	1	3	5	2
5	1	3	0	0	1	3	3
4	3	1	8	4	2	4	0

Step 2: Select the desired equation for computing the sample variance:

$$s^2 = \frac{\sum (x - \overline{x})^2}{n - 1}$$

Step 3: Compute the sample mean.

$$\overline{x} = \frac{\sum x}{n} = \frac{58}{24} = 2.42$$

Step 4: Determine the sum of the squared deviations of each x and $\overline{x}$.

x	$(x - \overline{x})$	$(x - \overline{x})^2$
3	0.58	0.3364
5	2.58	6.6564
4	1.58	2.4964
0	-2.42	5.8564
1	-1.42	2.0164
3	0.58	0.3364
2	-0.42	0.1764
3	0.58	0.3364
1	-1.42	2.0164
0	-2.42	5.8564
0	-2.42	5.8564
8	5.58	31.1364
1	-1.42	2.0164
0	-2.42	5.8564
4	1.58	2.4964
3	0.58	0.3364
1	-1.42	2.0164
2	-0.42	0.1764
5	2.58	6.6564
3	0.58	0.3364
4	1.58	2.4964
2	-0.42	0.1764
3	0.58	0.3364
0	-2.42	5.8564
	0	91.8

Step 5: Compute the sample variance.

$$s^2 = \frac{\sum (x - \overline{x})^2}{n - 1} = \frac{91.8}{24 - 1} = 3.99$$

c.   The sample standard deviation is the square root of the variance.

$$s = \sqrt{\frac{\sum (x - \bar{x})^2}{n-1}} = \sqrt{3.99} = 1.998$$

3.27

a.   The population variance is computed using the following steps. Note Equation 3.9 is used in this solution.

Step 1: Collect the data for the population.

16	15	17	15	15	15
14	9	16	15	13	10
8	18	20	17	17	17
18	23	7	15	20	10
14	14	12	12	24	21

Step 2: Select Equation 3.10 as the population variance's calculation formula.

Step 3: Calculate the population mean.

$$\mu = \frac{\sum x}{N} = \frac{457}{30} = 15.23$$

Step 4: Compute the sum of squared deviations from the mean.

$$\sum (x - \mu)^2 = (16 - 15.23)^2 + (15 - 15.23)^2 + ... (21 - 15.23)^2$$
$$= 506.24$$

Step 5: Compute the population variance.

$$\sigma^2 = \frac{\sum (x - \mu)^2}{N} = \frac{506.24}{30} = 16.87$$

b.   The population standard deviation is the square root of the population variance.

$$\sigma = \sqrt{\frac{\sum (x - \mu)^2}{N}} = \sqrt{\frac{506.24}{30}} = \sqrt{16.87} = 4.11$$

3.29 The sorted data is shown below.

5.4	6.6	7.5	7.8
8.5	8.9	10.3	11.5
12	12.2	13	14.4

The range is equal to the maximum value minus the minimum value = 14.4-5.4 = 9.

The first quartile's position is (25/100)*12 = 3. Therefore Q_1 is the average of the data values in the 3rd and 4th position = (7.5+7.8)/2 = 7.65.

The third quartile's position is (75/100)*12 = 9. Therefore Q_3 is the average of the data values in the 9th and 10th position = (12+12.2)/2 = 12.1.

The IQR = $Q_3 - Q_1$ = 12.1 - 7.65 = 4.45.

The variance is 7.86 and the standard deviation is 2.8.

$$\text{The variance} = \frac{\sum x^2 - \frac{(\sum x)^2}{n}}{n-1} = \frac{1,248.81 - (118.1^2)/12}{12-1} = 7.86$$

The standard deviation = $\sqrt{7.86} = 2.8$

3.31

a.   Range = largest − smallest = 30 − 6 = 24,

$$s^2 = \frac{\sum(x_i - \bar{x})^2}{n-1} = \frac{727.33}{14} = 51.95, \; s = \sqrt{s^2} = \sqrt{51.95} = 7.21 \;,$$

The index for Q_1 is: i = (p/100)n = (25/100)15 = 3.75. i = 4. Therefore, Q_1 = 12.
For Q_3 the index is (p/100)n = (75/100)15 = 11.25. i = 12. Therefore, Q_3 = 24. So the IQR = $Q_3 - Q_1$ = 24 − 12 = 12

b.   Range = largest − smallest = 30 − 6 = 24,

$$\sigma^2 = \frac{\sum(x_i - \mu)^2}{N} = \frac{727.33}{15} = 48.49, \; \sigma = \sqrt{48.49} = 6.96 \;,$$

The index for Q_1 is: i = (p/100)n = (25/100)15 = 3.75. i = 4. Therefore, Q_1 = 12.
For Q_3 the index is (p/100)n = (75/100)15 = 11.25. i = 12. Therefore, Q_3 = 24. So the IQR = $Q_1 - Q_3$ = 24 − 12 = 12

c. σ^2 is smaller than s^2 by a factor of (N − 1)/N. σ is smaller than s by a factor of $\sqrt{(N-1)/N}$. The range is not affected.

3.33

a.   The sorted data is shown below.

35	50	50	50
60	75	75	75
80	85	85	90
90	100	100	100
100	125	125	150

The range is equal to the maximum value minus the minimum value = 150−35 = 115.
The first quartile's position is (25/100)*20 = 5. Therefore Q_1 is the average of the data values in the 5th and 6th position = (60+75)/2 = 67.5.
The third quartile's position is (75/100)*20 = 15. Therefore Q_3 is the average of the data values in the 15th and 16th position = (100+100)/2 = 100.
The IQR = $Q_3 - Q_1$ = 100 − 67.5 = 32.5.
The variance is 815.79 and the standard deviation is 28.56.

$$\text{The variance} = \frac{\sum x^2 - \frac{(\sum x)^2}{n}}{n-1} = \frac{160,000 - (1.700^2)/20}{20-1} = 815.79$$

The standard deviation = $\sqrt{815.79} = 28.56$

b.   The range is computed by taking the difference between the two extreme values in a data set. That is the difference between the maximum and the minimum. The interquartile range looks at the middle 50% of the data values by taking the difference between the 75th and the 25th percentile. Both are measures of variability but the interquartile range overcomes the susceptibility of the range to being highly influenced by extreme values.

3.35

X	$X - \bar{x}$	$(X - \bar{x})^2$
32	5.9	34.81
22	-4.1	16.81
24	-2.1	4.41
27	0.9	0.81
27	0.9	0.81
33	6.9	47.61
28	1.9	3.61
23	-3.1	9.61
24	-2.1	4.41
21	-5.1	26.01
261		148.9

a. range = 33 – 21 = 12

$$\bar{x} = \frac{\sum_{i=1}^{n} x_i}{n} = 261/10 = 26.1$$

$$S^2 = \frac{\sum_{i=1}^{n}(x - \bar{x})^2}{n-1} = 148.9/(10\text{-}1) = 16.5444$$

$$S = \sqrt{S^2} = \sqrt{16.5444} = 4.0675$$

the 1st quartile is equal to the 25th percentile

$$i = \frac{p}{100}(n) = (25/100)(10) = 2.5 \text{ or the 3}^{rd} \text{ observation} = 23$$

the 3rd quartile is equal to the 75th percentile

$$i = \frac{p}{100}(n) = (75/100)(10) = 7.5 \text{ or the 8th observation} = 28$$

Interquartile Range = 28 – 23 = 5

b. Student answers will vary but they should look at the number of standard deviations the Whitworth mean is from the U. S. mean. U.S. Mean (37.8) – Whitworth Mean (26.1) = 11.7 which is 11.7/4.0657 = 2.8 or almost 3 standard deviations from the U.S. mean. Given this, although we are working with a small sample, there appears to be evidence to suggest that the ages are lower at Whitworth than for the U.S. Colleges and Universities as a group.

3.37

a. The range, interquartile range, variance, and standard deviation are shown below (calculated using Minitab).

```
Variable                StDev   Variance   Range   IQR
Speed of Exit           34.89   1217.14    113.00  62.25
```

The range is 113.0, the IQR is 62.25, the variance is 1217.14, and the standard deviation is 34.89.

b. No, the interquartile range looks at the middle 50% of the values so it is not affected by changes to the extreme values.

c. Adding a constant to all the data values leaves the variance unchanged.

3.39

a.   2004: $\bar{x} = \dfrac{\sum x_i}{n} = \dfrac{3.8}{9} = 0.422.$

$$s^2 = \frac{\sum (x_i - \mu)^2}{n-1} = \frac{7.992}{8} = 0.999, \ \ s = \sqrt{s^2} = \sqrt{0.999} = 1.000$$

For the first quartile for 2004, the index is (p/100)n = (25/100)9 = 2.25. The index is, therefore, 3. Therefore, $Q_1 = -0.2$. Similarly, For the third quartile, the index is (p/100)n = (75/100)9 = 6.75. Thus, i = 7. Therefore, $Q_2 = 1.5$. Therefore, the IQR is 1.5 – (-0.2) = 1.7.

2005: $\bar{x} = \dfrac{\sum x_i}{n} = \dfrac{4.03}{4} = 1.075.$

$$s^2 = \frac{\sum (x_i - \mu)^2}{n-1} = \frac{1.188}{3} = 0.396, \ \ s = \sqrt{s^2} = \sqrt{0.396} = 0.629$$

For the first quartile for 2005, the index is (p/100)n = (25/100)4 = 1 = integer. Therefore, $Q_1 = 25^{th}$ percentile is obtained by calculating the average of the 1st and 2nd value = 0.7. Similarly, For the third quartile, the index is (p/100)n = (75/100)4 = 3 = integer. Therefore, $Q_2 = 75^{th}$ percentile is obtained by calculating the average of the 3rd and 4th rank = 1.45. Therefore, the IQR is 1.45 – 0.7 = 0.75.

b.   b. $\bar{x}_2 = 1.075$ and $\bar{x}_1 = 0.422$. The second mean is more than twice that of the first indicating that the index has risen substantially.

c. $s_1 = 1.000$ and $s_2 = 0.629$. This indicates that the standard deviation for 2004 is approximately 60% (1/0.629 = 1.59) larger than that for 2005. We could say that the price indices for 2005 do not fluctuate as much as those in 2004.

3.41.   Software such as Excel or Minitab can be used to do the computations required in parts a. and b. We have used Excel's pivot table feature to provide the desired calculations.

a.   The mean and standard deviation for male and female customer phone purchase prices are shown as follows:

Data	F	M
Average of Price	98	117
StdDev of Price	36.14	68.06

In this sample, males spent an average of $117 while females spent an average of $98 for their phones. The standard deviation for males was nearly twice that for females.

b.   The mean and standard deviation for home and business use customer phone purchase prices are shown as follows:

Data	Business	Home
Average of Price	166.67	105.74
StdDev of Price	57.74	56.40

In this sample, business users spent an average of $166.67 on their phone while home users spent an average of $105.74. The variation in phone costs for the two groups was about equal.

3.43. Software such as Excel or Minitab can be used to compute the descriptive statistics in this exercise. Excel's descriptive statistics tool under Tools – Data Analysis has been used here.

List Price	
Mean	178465
Median	173000
Mode	148500
Standard Deviation	63271.22
Sample Variance	4E+09
Range	307000
Minimum	54100
Maximum	361100
Sum	56930400
Count	319

a.   The population mean is: $\mu = \dfrac{\sum x}{N} = \$178,465$

b.   The population median is: $\tilde{\mu} = \$173,000$

c.   The range is:
$$R = \text{High} - \text{Low}$$
$$R = \$361,100 - \$54,100$$
$$= \$307,000$$

d.   The population standard deviation is:

$$\sigma = \sqrt{\frac{\sum (x-\mu)^2}{N}} = \$63,172$$

Note, when using Excel, the function STDEVP is used to find the population mean. The Descriptive Statistics tool under Tools – Data Analysis returns the sample standard deviation.

e.   Student reports will vary but should include a discussion of the measures of the center and the measures of spread. Top students will think of attaching a histogram of the list prices to show graphically the distribution. They will use annotation to add the mean, median and standard deviation to the graph.

3.45
a.   The index is (p/100)n = (20/100)25 = 5. Therefore, the 20th percentile is obtained by calculating the average of the 5th and 6th rank = 5.5. Similarly, the 40th, 60th, and 80th percentiles are 10.5, 15.5, and 20.5, respectively.

b.   Since the data represents only the ranking of the institutions for the year 2005, the measurements are

parameters: $\mu_1 = \dfrac{\sum x_i}{N} = \dfrac{515279}{5} = 103056.$

$\sigma^2 = \dfrac{\sum (x_i - \mu)^2}{N} = \dfrac{3095924785}{5} = 619184957, \ \sigma = \sqrt{\sigma^2} = \sqrt{619184957} = 24883$. The

parameters were calculated to be:

	Top Ranked	2nd Ranked	3rd Ranked	4th Ranked	5th Ranked
μ	103056	82678	84300	87725	71047
σ^2	616184957	641965420	360030000	570233125	78214458
σ	24883	25337	18975	23880	8844

c.   The ranking of the first and fifth ranked subgroup appears to coincide to their average tuition. However, the rankings of the middle three ranked subgroup seemed to be the inverse of their average tuitions. The last ranked subgroup has a significantly smaller standard deviation than do the rest of the subgroups. This reflects the fact that it has no outliers. Each of the other subgroups have at least one outlier which increases their variability.

Section 3-3

3.47

a. Since the shape of the distribution is unknown, we can use Tchebysheff's theorem to determine the solution. Since $\sigma = 200$ and $\mu = 3,000$, then the range 2,600 to 3,400 is $\mu \pm 2(\sigma)$. According to Tchebysheff's theorem, at least 75% of the data in a distribution will fall within $\mu \pm 2(\sigma)$.

b. The range $\mu \pm 3(\sigma)$ should include at least 8/9 (89%) of the data values. That means that the range 2,400 to 3,600 should contain at least 89 percent of the data values. However, since we don't know the shape of the population, we can't say for sure what percentage will be greater than 3,600. We do know that the percentage will be less than 11% and most likely it will be considerably less.

c. The same issue is present here as in part b. We can't say with any certainty what the percentage will be. We do know that it will be less than 11 percent but we don't know how much less.

3.49

a. The sample mean is computed by summing the data values and dividing the sum by the number of observations. The mean = 1487/14 = 106.21. The sample standard deviation is found as follows. Add the x values and square the sum = 1487^2 = 2,211,169. Divide this value by the number of observations, 14, which gives 2,211,169/14 = 157,940.643. Square each of the x values and sum those squares = 166,071. Subtract 157,940.643 from 166,071 and divide the difference by n-1 or 13. The sample standard deviation is the square root of this result. $\sqrt{8130.3571 \big/ 13} = 25.008$.

b. The coefficient of variation is the ratio of the standard deviation to the mean expressed as a percentage. Here the coefficient of variation is (25.008/106.21)*100% = 23.55%. The coefficient of variation is a measure of the relative variation in the data.

c. The range of values that should include at least 89% of the data values according to Tchebysheff's Theorem is computed as being within 3 standard deviations of the mean. Thus, the range from 31.19 to 181.24 should contain 89% of the data values. In this instance the range contains all the data values. The interval range using Tchebysheff's Theorem was conservative.

3.51 The coefficient of variation is used to measure the relative variability of two or more distributions. It is computed using:

$$CV = \frac{\sigma}{\mu}(100)$$

For Distribution A we get: $CV = \frac{\sigma}{\mu}(100) = \frac{100}{500}(100) = 20\%$

For Distribution B we get: $CV = \frac{\sigma}{\mu}(100) = \frac{4.0}{10.0}(100) = 40\%$

Thus, even though distribution B has a standard deviation that is only 4 percent the size of A's standard deviation, distribution B is relatively more variable because the mean of A is so much greater than the mean of B.

3.53

a. The standardized value is $z = \dfrac{800 - \bar{x}}{s} = \dfrac{800 - 1000}{250} = -0.80$

b. The standardized value is $z = \dfrac{1200 - \bar{x}}{s} = \dfrac{1200 - 1000}{250} = 0.80$

c. The standardized value is $z = \dfrac{1000 - \bar{x}}{s} = \dfrac{1000 - 1000}{250} = 0.00$

3.55

a. $\bar{x} = \dfrac{1530}{30} = 51 \quad s^2 = \dfrac{\sum(x_i - \bar{x})^2}{n-1} = \dfrac{14812.04}{29} = 510.76, \quad s = \sqrt{s^2} = \sqrt{510.76} = 22.60.$

b.   Therefore, $\bar{x} \pm s$, $\bar{x} \pm 2s$, $\bar{x} \pm 3s$ are, respectively, 51 ± 22.60, $51 \pm 2(22.60)$, $51 \pm 3(22.60)$, i.e., (28.4, 73.6), (5.8, 96.2), and (-16.8, 118.8). There are (19/30)100% = 63.3%, of the data within (28.4, 73.6), (30/30)100% = 100%, of the data within (5.8, 96.2), (30/30)100% = 100%, of the data within (-16.8, 118.8).

c.   The Empirical indicates that the percentages should be approximately 68%, 95%, and 100% in these intervals. It does seem plausible that this data came from a bell-shaped population.

3.57

a.   The sample mean and sample standard deviation of the effect times for each drug are shown below. Calculations were performed using Excel.

	Drug A	Drug B
Mean	234.75	270.92
Standard Deviation	13.92	19.90

b.   Based on the sample means of the time each drug is effective, Drug B appears to be effective longer than Drug A.

c.   Based on the standard deviation of effect time, Drug B exhibits a higher variability in effect time than Drug A.

d.   d. The sample coefficient of variation is the ratio of the sample mean to the sample standard deviation expressed as a percentage. For Drug A, the sample coefficient of variation is (13.92/234.75)*100% = 5.93%. For Drug B the sample coefficient of variation is (19.90/270.92)*100% = 7.35%. The coefficient of variation is a measure of the relative variation in the effectiveness of the drugs. The larger the coefficient of variation the more variable the data is relative to its mean. Since Drug B has a higher coefficient of variation it has the greater relative spread.

3.59   At issue is relative variability. To assess this, the proper measure is the coefficient of variation computed as follows:

For a population: $CV = \dfrac{\sigma}{\mu}(100)$

For a sample: $CV = \dfrac{s}{\bar{x}}(100)$

For the existing supplier, we treat the mean and standard deviation as population values giving:

Existing Supplier: $CV = \dfrac{\sigma}{\mu}(100)$

$$CV = \dfrac{0.078}{3.75}(100) = 2.08\%$$

New Supplier: $CV = \dfrac{s}{\bar{x}}(100)$

We begin by computing the mean and standard deviation from the sample data giving:

$$\bar{x} = \dfrac{\sum x}{n} = \dfrac{360.586}{20} = 18.029$$

$$s = \sqrt{\dfrac{\sum(x-\bar{x})^2}{n-1}} = \sqrt{\dfrac{(18.018-18.029)^2 + (17.856-18.029)^2 + ... + (17.799-18.029)^2}{20-1}}$$

$$s = 0.135$$

Then the coefficient of variation for the new supplier is:

$$CV = \frac{s}{\overline{x}}(100)$$

$$CV = \frac{0.135}{18.029}(100) = 0.75\%$$

Student reports will differ. However, students should show the results of the coefficient of variation computations and conclude that the new supplier has the potential to produce parts with less variation than the existing supplier. The key is whether Lockheed-Martin managers believe they can effectively compare the two companies when different size products are being compared. The students should point out that the purpose of the coefficient of variation is to compare variability when the means of the two groups are different.

3.61   The Empirical Rule can be used to determine the cut-offs for this new test. For instance, this rule states that approximately 68 percent of the data will fall within one standard deviation either side of the mean. That means that 34% will fall on either side of the mean between the mean and one standard deviation. Thus, 16 percent of the data lie outside one standard deviation from the mean. Likewise, about 95% of the data will fall within two standard deviations of the mean. Thus, 2.5 percent will fall above two standard deviations from the mean.

We start by computing the mean and standard deviation.

$$\overline{x} = \frac{\sum x}{n} = \frac{2{,}157}{30} = 71.9$$

$$s = \sqrt{\frac{\sum (x-\overline{x})^2}{n-1}} = \sqrt{\frac{(76-71.9)^2 + (75-71.9)^2 + \ldots + (67-71.9)^2}{30-1}}$$

$$s = 10.04$$

Using the Empirical Rule:

68% within $\overline{x} \pm 1(s)$

$71.9 \pm 1(10.04)$

61.86 --------------81.94

Anyone scoring below 61.86 (rounded to 62) will be rejected without an interview.

95% within $\overline{x} \pm 2(s)$

$71.9 \pm 2(10.04)$

51.82 -----------------91.98

Anyone scoring higher than 91.98 (rounded to 92) will be sent directly to the company.

3.63.   Student reports will vary. However, they should weave in some or all of the following statistics based on the sample data. Students will use software such as Excel and Minitab to do the computations.

Taxes Owed	
Mean	11144.48
Median	10938.5
Mode	#N/A
Standard Deviation	3083.453
Sample Variance	9507680
Range	12960
Minimum	3677
Maximum	16637
Sum	557224
Count	50

The coefficient of variation is:

$$CV = \frac{s}{\bar{x}}(100)$$

$$CV = \frac{3,083.45}{11,144.48}(100) = 27.67\%$$

The following percentiles/quartiles have been computed:

Percentile	Value
20	$8,874
25	$9,127
40	$10,135
50	$10,939
60	$12,144
75	$13,413
80	$13,853
90	$14,875

Based on Tchebysheff's theorem, we know that at least 75 percent of CPA firms will compute a tax owed between:

$$\bar{x} \pm 2(s)$$

$$\$11,144.48 \pm 2(\$3,083.45)$$

$$\$4,977.58 \text{----------} \$17,311.38$$

The key is that we would expect all CPA firms to arrive at basically the same taxes owed. The fact that there is such a large variation by these experts exemplifies the difficulty that individuals have with the tax code.

3.65

a.

```
Variable    Mean  StDev  Variance     Q1   Median     Q3    IQR
Scores    94.780  4.130    17.056  93.000   96.000  98.000  5.000
```

The answer depends upon the way in which the scores were obtained. If there were some objective way that these scores were obtained then measures such as the mean, standard deviation, and variance would be applicable. However, if these scores, were judgments and represented categories rather than data on a ratio scale, then the median and the IQR would be applicable.

b.

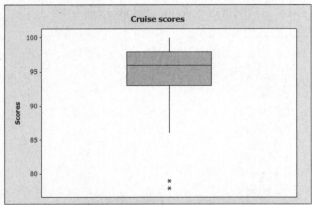

The box and whisker plot shows this data set is a left skewed distribution. Since the Empirical Rule only applies to bell-shaped distributions, Tchebysheff's Theorem would be preferable.

c. i = (p/100)n = (90/100)173 = 155.7 rounding up, i = 156. This score is 99.

3.67 Probably the most effective way to deal with this exercise is to covert the growth rates to standardized z-values. To do this, we use:

$$z = \frac{x - \mu}{\sigma}$$

Excel or Minitab can be used to calculate the z-values. In this case, we have used Excel's STANDARDIZE function. First, we need to compute the mean and standard deviation for the growth rate in population. This is done as follows:

$$\mu = \frac{\sum x}{N} = \frac{118.8}{74} = 1.6\%$$

$$\sigma = \sqrt{\frac{\sum (x - \mu)^2}{N}} = \sqrt{\frac{(5.9 - 1.6)^2 + (2.3 - 1.6)^2 + ... + (1.5 - 1.6)^2}{74}}$$

$$\sigma = 1.12$$

Now we calculate the z-values for each country and sort the countries by z-value. Only one country, Afghanistan, had a growth rate more than two standard deviations above the mean. This country was 3.84 standard deviations above the mean. No countries were more than 2 standard deviations below the mean. The closest was the Ukraine and z = -1.96.

End of Chapter Exercises

3.69 The first interval is $\mu \pm \sigma$. It contains 68% of the data. The remainder (100 − 68 = 32) is divided between the two tails. So a half of the area in the left hand tail is 32/2. Therefore, the lower endpoint is the 16th perecentile. 68 + (32/2) of the data is to the left of the upper endpoint. It is the 84th percentile. The second interval is $\mu \pm 2\sigma$. It contains 95% of the data. The remainder (100 − 95 = 5) is divided between the two tails. So a half of the area in the left hand tail is 5/2. Therefore, the lower endpoint is the 2.5th perecentile. 95 + (5/2) of the data is to the left of the upper endpoint. It is the 97.5th percentile. The third interval is $\mu \pm 3\sigma$. It contains 100% of the data. Therefore, the lower endpoint is the 0th perecentile. The upper endpoint is the 100th percentile.

3.71 Some problems are that it does not look at total hours taken. One student could have taken one class on campus and got an A so would have a 4.0 grade point average. Another student could have taken many hours and got all A's except one or two B's and would have lower than a 4.0 grade point average and people might conclude that the first student is a better student than the second based only upon grade point average. It also does not look at the difficulty of the classes taken. Comparing across two universities has the same problems as mentioned previously along with the fact that all universities are different and the type of classes and difficulty level of classes will be completely different. None of this is accounted for in calculating a grade point average.

3.73 The mode is a useful measure of location of a set of data if the data set is large and involves nominal or ordinal data. For example, if the Labor Department is interested in the category of employment that will generate the most new jobs over the next decade, the modal class would be important. The buyer for a large department store chair wold be interested in the category of shoe size most commonly bought.

3.75
  a. To determine how many standard deviations the data points are from the mean, calculate the standardized sample data: $Z = \frac{X - \overline{X}}{S}$.
     Z = (19 − 28)/9 = -1. The Empirical Rule indicates that 68% of the data is within one standard deviation from the mean. This area is half of that. So the proportion of players between 19 and 28 is 0.68/2 = 0.34.
  b. To determine how many standard deviations the data points are from the mean, calculate the standardized sample data: $Z = \frac{X - \overline{X}}{S}$. Z = (37 − 28)/9 = 1. This is the same area as in part a. except it is on the right hand side of the mean. Thus, the proportion of players between 28 and 37 is 0.68/2 = 0.34.

c. Sixty eight percent of the players are between 19 and 37. Therefore, $100 - 68 = 32$ percent are outside of this interval half of which are greater than 37. Thus, the proportion of players greater than 37 is $0.32/2 = 0.16$.

3.77

a.

$$\bar{x} = \frac{\sum_{i=1}^{n} x_i}{n} = 4373/12 = 364.42$$

b. $s^2 = \dfrac{\sum_{i=1}^{n} (x - \bar{x})^2}{n-1} = 183{,}288.9167/(12\text{-}1) = 16{,}662.63$

$$s = \sqrt{s^2} = \sqrt{16{,}662.6288} = 129.08$$

3.79

Student answers will vary but one approach would be to standardize the results for each manager
Plant 1: $(810 - 700)/200 = .55$ standard deviations
Plant 2: $(2600 - 2300)/350 = .86$ standard deviations
Plant 3: $(1320 - 1200)/30 = 4$ standard deviations
Based upon this the manager of Plant 3 performed far better than the other plants on a relative basis.

3.81

a. Comparing only the mean bushels/acre you would say that Seed Type C produces the greatest average yield per acre. Student answers will vary but may include things such as making sure soil type is the same, make sure watering and fertilizing is the same, etc.

b. Students need to calculate the coefficient of variation for each Seed Type.
CV of Seed Type A = 25/88 = 0.2841 or 28.41%
CV of Seed Type B = 15/56 = 0.2679 or 26.79%
CV of Seed Type C = 16/100 = 0.1600 or 16%
Seed Type C shows the least relative variability.

c. Seed Type A
Approximately 68% will be within 1 standard deviation
$88 \pm 25 = $ 63 to 113
Approximately 95% will be within 2 standard deviations
$88 \pm 2(25) = 38$ to 138
Approximately 100% will be within 3 standard deviations
$88 \pm 3(25) = 13$ to 163
Seed Type B
Approximately 68% will be within 1 standard deviation
$56 \pm 15 = $ 41 to 71
Approximately 95% will be within 2 standard deviations
$56 \pm 2(15) = 26$ to 86
Approximately 100% will be within 3 standard deviations
$56 \pm 3(15) = 11$ to 101
Seed Type C
Approximately 68% will be within 1 standard deviation
$100 \pm 16 = $ 84 to 116
Approximately 95% will be within 2 standard deviations
$100 \pm 2(16) = 68$ to 132
Approximately 100% will be within 3 standard deviations
$100 \pm 3(16) = 52$ to 148

    d.   Student answers will vary but students should say Seed Type A because the 135 is within 2 standard deviations. Since it has higher variability there is a greater chance that it will produce135.

    e.   Seed type C because 115 is included within one standard deviation.

3.83 Student answers will vary, but one approach to analyzing the data would be to calculate the mean and standard deviation for the three investments and from that calculate the coefficient of variation.

Calculation of the average return and the standard deviation of the returns for each investment are shown below:

IDACORP

X	$X - \bar{x}$	$(X - \bar{x})^2$
$100.00	($44.31)	$1,963.38
128.86	($15.45)	$238.70
137.11	($7.20)	$51.84
136.92	($7.39)	$54.61
186.71	$42.40	$1,797.76
176.26	$31.95	$1,020.80
$865.86		$5,127.09

Sample mean, $\bar{x}$ = $865.86/6 = $144.31

Sample standard deviation, s = $\sqrt{5127.09/5}$ = $32.02

S&P 500

X	$X - \bar{x}$	$(X - \bar{x})^2$
$100.00	($46.17)	$2,131.82
128.67	($17.50)	$306.31
142.65	($3.52)	$12.40
149.66	$3.49	$12.17
173.27	$27.10	$734.32
182.78	$36.61	$1,340.17
$877.03		$4,537.19

Sample mean, $\bar{x}$ = $877.03/6 = $146.17

Sample standard deviation, s = $\sqrt{4537.19/5}$ = $30.12

EEI Electric Utilities Index

X	$X - \bar{x}$	$(X - \bar{x})^2$
$100.00	($68.58)	$4,703.67
123.48	($45.10)	$2,034.31
151.68	($16.90)	$285.72
176.02	$7.44	$55.30
212.56	$43.98	$1,933.95
247.76	$79.18	$6,268.94
$1,011.50		$15,281.90

Sample mean, $\bar{x}$ = $1,011.5/6 = $168.58

Sample standard deviation, s = $\sqrt{15281.9/5}$ = $55.28

Investment	Coefficient of Variation
IDACORP	(32.02/144.31)*100% = 22.19%
S&P 500	(30.12/146.17)*100% = 20.61%
EEI Electric Utility Index	(55.28/168.58)*100% = 32.79%

Based on the sample means, we find that IDACORP has a smaller sample mean than either the S&P 500 or the EEI Electric Utilities Index. The coefficient of variation shows that IDACORP is slightly more variable than the S&P 500, but much less variable than the EEI Electric Utility Index.

Students could also have performed a similar analysis on the percentage returns for each investment by converting the original values into percentage returns.

3.85 Students should use Excel or Minitab to answer this question.

a.   Note, the students are free to select their own class limits. Below is one example. Students might consider having an open-end class on the upper end to better convey the data.

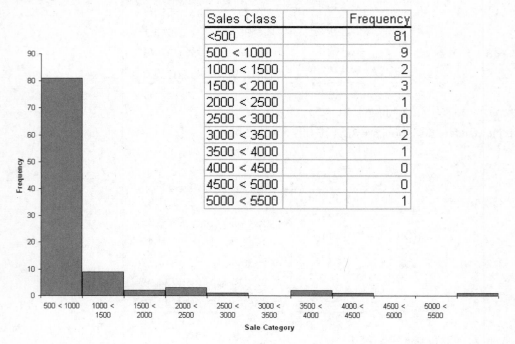

Sales Class		Frequency
<500		81
500 < 1000		9
1000 < 1500		2
1500 < 2000		3
2000 < 2500		1
2500 < 3000		0
3000 < 3500		2
3500 < 4000		1
4000 < 4500		0
4500 < 5000		0
5000 < 5500		1

b.

Sales	
Mean	468.89
Standard Error	80.81745
Median	184.95
Mode	131.8
Standard Deviation	808.1745
Sample Variance	653146.1
Kurtosis	16.77128
Skewness	3.823796
Range	5284.2
Minimum	90.3
Maximum	5374.5
Sum	46889
Count	100

c.   Using Excel's QUARTILE function

Q 3	Q 1	Interquartile Range
395.8	128.7	267.1

d.

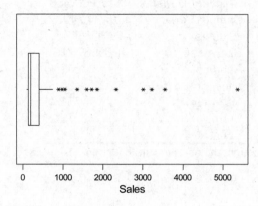

The upper limit is 395.8 + 1.5(267.1) = 796.45. Any value exceeding 796.45 will be considered an outlier.
The following sales values are outliers:

884.5
963.1
965.9
1044.8
1342.7
1586
1708.9
1843.4
2319.4
3011.3
3221.3
3553
5374.5

Deleting these 13 sales value, gives the following revised descriptive statistics:

Sales	
Mean	219.1977011
Standard Error	15.34834684
Median	170.9
Mode	131.8
Standard Deviation	143.1598488
Sample Variance	20494.74232
Kurtosis	2.500681936
Skewness	1.699896517
Range	641.1
Minimum	90.3
Maximum	731.4
Sum	19070.2
Count	87

e.   Using Excel's PERCENTILE function, the 65th percentile is found using Excel to be $246.20

3.87

a.
```
Variable    Mean  StDev
Price     22.000  3.813
```

b. $\bar{x} \pm 1s = 22 \pm (3.813) = (18.187, 25.813)$, $\bar{x} \pm 2s = (14.374, 29.626)$
$\bar{x} \pm 3s = (10.561, 33.439)$

c.   The Empirical Rule indicates that 95% of the data is contained within $\bar{x} \pm 2s$. This would mean that each tail has $(1 - 0.95)/2 = 0.025$ of the data. Therefore, the costume should be priced at $14.37.

3.89

a.
```
Variable       Mean   StDev   Median
Close-Open  -0.0354  0.2615  -0.0600
```

b.   It means that the closing price for GE stock is an average of approximately four ($0.0354) cents lower than the opening price.

c.
```
Variable       Mean   StDev   Median
Open         33.947  0.503   33.980
Close-Open  -0.0354  0.2615  -0.0600
```

On the servface it appears that the dispersion of the opening stock prices (0.503) is larger than that of the difference between the closing and opening stock prices (0.2615). However, the mean for the opening stock prices is approximately 959 times (33.947/0.0354) larger than that of the difference between closing and opening stock prices. The coefficient of variation should be used here.

```
Variable    CoefVar
Open           1.48
Close-Open   738.47
```

Here the relative dispersion is approximately 499 times (738.47/1.48) as large for the difference between closing and opening stock prices.

3.91 Students should use Excel or Minitab to answer questions a-c.

a.

CPA Firm	Taxes Owed	Difference	CPA Firm	Taxes Owed	Difference
1	$16,637	-$5,077	26	$6,087	$5,473
2	$11,804	-$244	27	$8,711	$2,849
3	$8,915	$2,645	28	$9,753	$1,807
4	$9,915	$1,645	29	$10,282	$1,278
5	$14,787	-$3,227	30	$13,385	-$1,825
6	$11,058	$502	31	$11,326	$234
7	$15,662	-$4,102	32	$16,183	-$4,623
8	$13,293	-$1,733	33	$14,232	-$2,672
9	$15,970	-$4,410	34	$8,482	$3,078
10	$9,103	$2,457	35	$16,274	-$4,714
11	$13,223	-$1,663	36	$12,758	-$1,198
12	$7,852	$3,708	37	$9,411	$2,149
13	$9,200	$2,360	38	$14,632	-$3,072
14	$13,607	-$2,047	39	$12,655	-$1,095
15	$13,793	-$2,233	40	$6,403	$5,157
16	$9,048	$2,512	41	$11,260	$300
17	$14,487	-$2,927	42	$8,478	$3,082
18	$9,409	$2,151	43	$11,586	-$26
19	$13,342	-$1,782	44	$10,299	$1,261
20	$14,093	-$2,533	45	$7,805	$3,755
21	$12,836	-$1,276	46	$13,422	-$1,862
22	$9,376	$2,184	47	$10,628	$932
23	$10,819	$741	48	$9,300	$2,260
24	$10,473	$1,087	49	$5,429	$6,131
25	$3,677	$7,883	50	$6,064	$5,496

b.

Classes	Frequency
-6928.42 to -5077.00	1
-5076.99 to -3225.57	5
-3225.56 to -1374.14	11
-1374.13 to 477.29	7
477.30 to 2328.72	12
2328.73 to 4180.15	9
4180.16 to 6031.58	3
6031.59 to 7883.01	2

c.

Difference	
Mean	415.52
Standard Error	436.0660531
Median	621.5
Mode	#N/A
Standard Deviation	3083.452632
Sample Variance	9507680.132
Kurtosis	-0.501771097
Skewness	0.177525892
Range	12960
Minimum	-5077
Maximum	7883
Sum	20776
Count	50

d.   The value of \$11,560 would be between the 28th (\$11,326) and 29th (\$11,586)observation. This is found by sorting the values for the "tax owed" variable. Since \$11,500 is closer to the 29th value than it is the to the 28th value, we will use i = 29 and solve for the percentile as follows:

$$i = \frac{p}{100} n \quad \text{so } 29 = (p/100)(50) \quad p = 58 \text{ or the 58th percentile.}$$

This shows that 58% of the tax consultants in this study showed less tax owed than did the IRS.

CHAPTERS 1—3
SPECIAL REVIEW SECTION

SR.1   a-c. Student answers will vary but class limits should be set so that classes are mutually exclusive and all-inclusive. Class intervals should be of equal size and chosen so that observations are approximately equally distributed over the interval.

SR.3.   Student reports will vary. We look for effective use of visual tools indicating trends, not just reliance on tables and numbers. Superior students might compare Intel graphs with competitors or benchmark companies.

SR.5.

a.

	Revenues	Profits	Employees
Mean	6354.71	803.43	21530.3
Median	3428	401	11000
Std Deviation	7457.66	881.812	21269.35

b.   The standardized z-values need to be computed using Equation 3-17 and can be done in either Excel or Minitab. Based on these z-values, the Mellon Bank Corporation is slightly below the average for profits ($z = -.03$) and revenues ($z = -.16$) and slightly above the average for number of employees ($z = .28$).

c.   You need to calculate the coefficient of variance for each variable.

	Revenues	Profits	Employees
Coefficient of variation	1.173564	1.097558	0.9878812

Revenues has the largest relative variation.

Chapter 4
Introduction to Probability

Section 4-1

4.1. The concept that allows the player to know that the probability of the next spin being black is 0.5 is the concept of independent events. If events are independent, then the probability of one event occurring is not influenced by the occurrence of the other events. In this case, since the wheel is deemed to be fair, the chance of a red or a black is 0.5 for any spin regardless of what has occurred on previous spins.

4.3.   The sample space is listed by following these steps:
Step 1: Define the experiment
The experiment consists of asking people to express their choice among three flavors of ice cream
Step 2: Define the possible outcomes for one trial of the experiment
$$V = \text{Vanilla}$$
$$C = \text{Chocolate}$$
$$S = \text{Strawberry}$$

Step 3: Define the sample space.
For two customers, the sample space is:
$$V, V$$
$$V, C$$
$$V, S$$
$$C, V$$
$$C, C$$
$$C, S$$
$$S, V$$
$$S, C$$
$$S, S$$

4.5.
   a.   Subjective probability based on expert opinion.
   b.   b Relative frequency based on previous customer return history
   c.   1/5 = .20

4.7.
Step 1: Define the experiment.
Students are randomly assigned to one of three dining halls.
Step 2: Determine whether the possible outcomes are equally likely.
In this case students purchasing a meal plan are randomly assigned to one of three dining halls. Thus, any dining hall has the same probability of being assigned as any other.
Step 3: Determine the total number of possible outcomes.
There are three dining halls on campus.
Step 4: Define the event of interest.
The event of interest is the next student being assigned to the Commons dining hall.
Step 5: Determine the number of outcomes associated with the event of interest. There is only one Commons dining hall.
Step 6: Compute the classical probability using equation 4.1.
P(Commons) = Number of Ways Commons Can Occur/Total Number of Possible Outcomes = 1/3 = 0.333333.

4.9.
a.   P(Brown) = # Brown/Total = 310/982 = 0.3157
b.   P(YZ-99) = #YZ-99/Total = 375/982 = 0.3819
c.   P(YZ-99 and Brown) = 205/982 = 0.2088
d.   The two events are not mutually exclusive since their joint probability is 0.1324. It is possible to choose a White YZ-99 product. To be mutually exclusive the outcome for one event (e.g., White) means the other outcome (YZ-99) cannot occur.

4.11.   Probability, using the classical probability assessment method, is computed using the following steps
a.   **Step 1:** Define the experiment:
Observing whether or not each of the three consumers purchases an HDTV constitutes the experiment
Step 2: Determine whether the outcomes are equally likely:
Since each decision is assumed to be equally likely, each outcome is equally likely. $P(e_i) = (1/2)^3 = 1/8$
b.   **Step 3:** Determine number of outcomes:
There are 8 equally likely events: e_1 = BBB, e_2 = BBD, e_3 = BDB, e_4 = DBB, e_5 = BDD, e_6 = DBD, e_7 = DDB, e_8 = DDD
c.   **Step 4:** Define the events of interest:
The events of interest are (1) only two consumers buy an HDTV (E_1), (2) at most two consumers buy HDTV's (E_2), and (3) at least two consumers buy HDTV's (E_3).
d.   **Step 5:** Determine the number of outcomes associated with the event of interest:
The events of interest are comprised of (1) $E_1 = \{e_2, e_3, e_4\}$, (2) $E_2 = \{e_2, e_3, e_4, e_5, e_6, e_7, e_8\}$, and $E_3 = \{e_1, e_2, e_3, e_4\}$
e.   **Step 6:** Compute the classical probability using Equation 4-1:

$$P(E_1) = \frac{Number\ of\ ways\ E_i\ can\ occur}{Total\ number\ of\ elementary\ events} = \frac{3}{8} = 0.375,$$

4.13.   The idea is to have unique assignments of three doctors. The following tree starts with Doctor 1 and shows how many unique assignments can involve Dr 1. It then moves on to Doctor 2 and so on. Finally, Doctors 4 and 5 have already been considered and so no assignments can start with them.

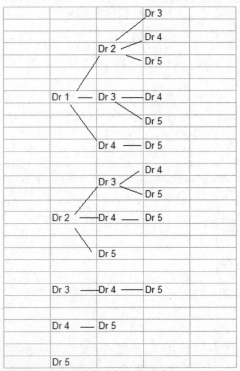

Ten weeks can be covered with this schedule.

4.15.

Type of Ad	Occurrences
Help Wanted Ad	204
Real Estate Ad	520
Other Ad	306
Total	1,030

a. P(help wanted ad) = number of help-wanted ads/total number of ads.
There are 204+520+306 = 1,030 total newspaper ads. Of this total 204 are help-wanted ads. Thus, the probability of a help-wanted ad being selected is 204/1,030 = 0.1981.
b. Relative frequency
c. Yes. Since the newspaper is choosing only one ad, it is impossible for them to select a help-wanted ad and another ad. Since the occurrence of a help-wanted ad being chosen precludes any other ad from being chosen, the events are mutually exclusive.

4.17.

a. Because data exists from past production, the manager would use the relative frequency assessment method.
b. Using the relative frequency assessment method, the probability is:

$$P(\#1) = \frac{4,100}{5,900} = 0.69$$

Thus, there is a 0.69 chance that a board produced by Welco Lumber will receive the #1 grade.

4.19.

a. Total number of orders last year = 12,753 + 5,893 + 3,122 = 21,768. Number of carry out orders = 3,122. Probability of a carry out order = 3,122/21,768 = 0.1434.
b. Relative frequency assessment method.
c. The sample space for two randomly selected customers is shown below:

Outcome	Customer 1	Customer 2
e_1	Dine-In	Dine-In
e_2	Dine-In	Delivery
e_3	Dine-In	Carry Out
e_4	Delivery	Dine-In
e_5	Delivery	Delivery
e_6	Delivery	Carry Out
e_7	Carry Out	Dine-In
e_8	Carry Out	Delivery
e_9	Carry Out	Carry Out

4.21.

a. Software such as Excel or Minitab could be used to assess the probability using the relative frequency assessment method. The following table from Excel's pivot table tool shows the breakdown of Caesarean versus normal births at this hospital.

Count of Delivery Method	
Delivery Method ▼	Total
Caesarean	22
Normal	28
Grand Total	50

Thus, using the relative frequency assessment method we get:

$$P(Caesarean) = \frac{22}{50} = 0.44$$

The probability of a Caesarean birth is 0.44 based on the data from past births at this hospital.

b. The concerns would be the number of births observed (50) is not very large. Second, in many cases there are specific reasons for a Caesarean delivery and not all births are alike. Thus, any new birth may not exactly match the 50 in this study.

4.23. The following joint frequency table (developed using Excel's pivot table feature) summarizes the data.

	Electrical	Mechanical	Total
Lincoln	28	39	67
Tyler	64	69	133
Total	92	108	200

a. The probability the scooter was assembled in the Tyler plant is found by dividing the row total for Tyler (133) by the overall total (200), 133/200 = 0.665.

b. The probability that a scooter breakdown was due to a mechanical failure is found by dividing the column total for Mechanical (108) by the overall total (200), 108/200 = 0.54.

c. The joint probability that a scooter with an electrical problem was assembled at the Lincoln plant is found by dividing the 28 electrical problems traced back to the Lincoln plant by the total of 200 breakdowns, (28/200) = 0.14.

4.25. The probabilities required to produce the answers to exercise are given by the following table:

a.

```
        Rows: Age    Columns: Preference

              Coke  Pepsi  All

        17        6      6   12
        18        6      6   12
        19        6      5   11
        20       12      7   19
        21       10      6   16
        22        6      8   14
        23       11      5   16
        All      57     43  100

        Cell Contents:       Count
```

$$\text{Relative frequency of E}_i = \frac{Number\ of\ times\ E_i\ occurs}{N} = \frac{43}{100} = 0.43$$

b. $$\text{Relative frequency of E}_i = \frac{Number\ of\ times\ E_i\ occurs}{N} = \frac{5+6+6}{100} = 0.17$$

c. $$\text{Relative frequency of E}_i = \frac{Number\ of\ times\ E_i\ occurs}{N}.$$

$$\text{For Pepsi, Probability} = \frac{5+6+6}{12+12+11} = \frac{17}{35} = 0.486.$$

$$\text{For Coke, Probability} = \frac{6+6+6}{12+12+11} = \frac{18}{35} = 0.514.$$

d. $$\text{Relative frequency of E}_i = \frac{Number\ of\ times\ E_i\ occurs}{N}.$$

$$\text{For Pepsi, Probability} = \frac{7+6+8+5}{19+16+14+16} = \frac{26}{65} = 0.4.$$

$$\text{For Coke, Probability} = \frac{12+10+6+11}{19+16+14+16} = \frac{39}{65} = 0.6$$

Section 4-2

4.27.
   a.   P(soft drink)*P(no fries) = (0.9)(1-0.5) = 0.45
   b.   P(Hamburger & FF) = $P(Hamburger)P(FF|Hamburger) = (0.6)(0.8) = 0.48$

4.29. The multiplication rule for dependent events is used since we are interested in the first player being a senior *and* the second player being a senior. The events are dependent since we are selecting the players without replacement. We are looking for:

$$P(senior1 \text{ } and \text{ } senior2) = P(senior1)P(senior2|senior1)$$

$$P(senior1 \text{ } and \text{ } senior2) = (\frac{5}{10})(\frac{4}{9}) = \frac{20}{90} = 0.22$$

4.31.
   a.   P(E_1 and B) = P(E_1|B) P(B) = 0.25(0.30) = 0.075
   b.   P(E_1 or B) = P(E_1) + P(B) - P(E_1 and B) = 0.35 + 0.30 - 0.075 = 0.575
   c.   P(E_1 and E_2 and E_3) = P(E_1)P(E_2) P(E_3) = 0.35(0.15)(0.40) = 0.021

4.33.
   a.   The probability of a disk drive coming from company B can be found using the relative frequency assessment method as:

$$P(B) = \frac{number \text{ } of \text{ } drives \text{ } from \text{ } B}{total \text{ } drives} = \frac{195}{700} = 0.28$$

   b.   The probability of a defective disk drive is:

$$P(Defect) = \frac{number \text{ } of \text{ } defective \text{ } drives}{total \text{ } drives} = \frac{50}{700} = 0.07$$

   c.   The probability of a defect *given* that company B supplied the disk drive is found using the following steps. The key word here is *given* which means that we are dealing with conditional probability.
   d.   **Step 1:**   Define the experiment.
              A quality manager for a Dell Computers has collected the following data on the quality status of disk drives by supplier.
       Step 2:   Define the events of interest
              The two events of interest are:

$$E_1 = Company \text{ } B = B$$

$$E_2 = Defective \text{ } Drive = Defect$$

       Step 3:   Define the probability statement of interest
              We are interested in the following:

$$P(Defect|B) = ? = \text{probability of a defective drive } given \text{ company B}$$

       Step 4:   Convert the data to probabilities using the relative frequency assessment method

$$P(B) = \frac{number \text{ } of \text{ } drives \text{ } from \text{ } B}{total \text{ } drives} = \frac{195}{700} = 0.28$$

$$P(Defect) = \frac{number \text{ } of \text{ } defective \text{ } drives}{total \text{ } drives} = \frac{50}{700} = 0.071$$

$$P(Defect \text{ } and \text{ } B) = \frac{number \text{ } of \text{ } defective \text{ } drives \text{ } from \text{ } B}{total \text{ } drives} = \frac{15}{700} = 0.021$$

Step 5: Use the rule for conditional probability

$$P(Defect \mid B) = \frac{P(Defect \ and \ B)}{P(B)} = \frac{0.02}{0.28} = 0.076$$

Note, you can also find the conditional probability from the data table by

$$P(Defect \mid B) = \frac{number \ of \ defective \ drives \ from \ B}{number \ of \ drives \ from \ B} = \frac{15}{195} = 0.076$$

4.35.
  a.   **Step 1:** Define events of interest: Let E_1 = the driver is a woman; E_2 = the driver stops to ask for directions.

  Step 2: Determine the probability of each event: $P(E_1) = 0.518$, $P(\overline{E}_1) = 1\text{-}0.518 = 0.482$, $P(E_2 \mid E_1) = 0.61$
  Step 3: Assess the joint probability: $P(E_1 \ and \ E_2) = P(E_2 \mid E_1) \ P(E_1) = (0.61)(0.518) = 0.316$.

  b.   **Step 1:** as in part a.

  Step 2: Determine the probability of each event: $P(E_1) = 0.518$, $P(\overline{E}_1) = 1\text{-}0.518 = 0.482$, $P(E_2 \mid E_1) = 0.61$, $P(E_2 \mid E_1') = 0.42$.
  Step 3: Determine if the two events are mutually exclusive. Calculate the joint probabilities: If the driver is a woman and stops to ask for directions, she cannot also be a man who is stopping to ask for directions. Therefore, (E_1 and E_2) or ($\overline{E}_1$ and E_2) are mutually exclusive. $P(E_1 \ and \ E_2) = 0.316$ from part a., and $P(\overline{E}_1 \ and \ E_2) = P(E_2 \mid \overline{E}_1) \ P(\overline{E}_1) = (0.42)(0.482) = 0.202$.

  Step 4: Compute the probability using Rule 5. $P[(E_1 \ and \ E_2) \ or \ (\overline{E}_1 \ and \ E_2)] = P(E_1 \ and \ E_2) + P(\overline{E}_1 \ and \ E_2) = 0.316 + (0.42)(0.482) = 0.316 + 0.202 = 0.518$.

  c. $P(\overline{E}_1 \mid E_2) = P(\overline{E}_1 \ and \ E_2)/P(E_2) = 0.202/0.518 = 0.39$

4.37.   If they purchase 4 black-and-white copiers, their probability of being able to provide a color copy is 0.0. Their probability of being able to provide a black-and-white copy on demand is $1 - [(0.1)(0.1)(0.1)(0.1)] = 0.9999$. If they buy all color copiers the probability of providing a black-and-white copy is the same as providing a color copy since color copiers can make black-and-white copies. This probability is $1 - [(0.2)(0.2)(0.2)(0.2)] = 0.9984$. They cannot get to 99.9% on color copies regardless of the configuration.

4.39   The probability from 4.38 is 0.00015. There are 1000 possible gas totals between $20.01 and $30.00 There are 9 possible winning totals in this range. This probability becomes 9/1000 = 0.009. Since 65% of the customers fall into this range the probability of these customers winning free gas is 0.65(0.009) = 0.00585. The remaining 5% customers = (1/100)(0.05) = 0.0005 . P(free gas) = 0.00015 + 0.00585 + 0.0005 = 0.0065

4.41.
  a.   Probability that a randomly selected participant prefers the NFL is a marginal probability and is equal to the number of times NFL preference was observed (105) divided by the total number of survey participants (200). Thus, P(NFL) = 105/200 = 0.5250.
  b.   The probability that a randomly selected survey participant has a college degree and prefers the NBA is a joint probability. P(College Degree and NBA) = 40/200 = 0.20.
  c.   This is a conditional probability. The probability that the man prefers the NFL given that he has a college degree and is equal to 10/50 = 0.20.
  d.   A survey participant's preference for the NBA is independent of having a college degree if P(NBA) = P(NBA given College Degree). Because P(NBA) = (95/200) = 0.475 does not equal P(NBA given College Degree) = (40/50) = 0.80, the two events are not independent. The two events are dependent. The probability of NBA preference is not the same for college degree and non-college degree participants.

4.43.   P(Line 1) = 0.4
P(Line 2) = 0.35
P(Line 3) = 0.25
P(Defective|Line 1) = 0.05
P(Defective|Line 2) = 0.10
P(Defective|Line 3) = 0.07
You need to calculate the probability of each line given you know the cases are defective. Use Bayes' Rule to calculate this.
P(Defective) = P(Defective|Line1)P(Line1) + P(Defective|Line2)P(Line2) + P(Defective|Line3)P(Line3) = (0.05)(0.4) + (0.1)(0.35)+(0.07)(0.25) = 0.0725
P(Line1|Defective) = (0.05)(0.4)/0.0725 = 0.2759
P(Line2|Defective) = (0.10)(0.35)/0.0725 = 0.4828
P(Line3|Defecitve) = (0.07)(0.25)/0.0725 = 0.2413
The unsealed cans probably came from Line 2

4.45.   P(Supplier A) = 0.3
P(Supplier B) = 0.7
P(Defective|Supplier A) = 0.15
P(Defective|Supplier B) = 0.10

Want to find the P(Supplier A|Defective) and the P(Supplier B|Defective) and see which probability is higher. Use Bayes' Rule to make these calculations.

P(Supplier A|Defective) = [P(Defective|Supplier A)P(Supplier A)]/P(Defective) and
P(Supplier B|Defective) = [P(Defective|Supplier B)P(Supplier B)/P(Defective)
so need to calculate the P(Defective)
P(Defective) = P(Defective|Supplier A)P(Supplier A) + P(Defective|Supplier B)P(Supplier B)
= (0.15)(0.3) + (0.10)(0.7) = 0.115
P(Supplier A|Defective) = (0.15)(0.3)/0.115 = 0.3913
P(Supplier B|Defective) = (0.10)(0.7)/0.115 = 0.6087
Supplier B is the most likely to have supplied the defective parts.

4.47.
a.   Let B = voted for Pres. Bush, V = voted in the election, R = registered to vote. P(B and V) = P(B|V)P(V) = 0.508(0.607) = 0.308.
Step 1: Define events of interest:
Let E_1 = an individual voted for Pres. Bush; E_2 = an individual voted in the election.
Step 2: Determine the probability of each event:
$P(E_2)$ = 0.607, $P(E_1|E_2)$ = 0.508.
Step 3: Determine if the two events are independent:

Since $P(E_1|E_2)$ = 0.508 and $P(E_1|\overline{E}_2)$ = 0, E_1 and E_2 are not independent.
Step 4: Compute the probability using Rule 8.
$P(E_1$ and $E_2)$ = $P(E_1|E_2)P(E_2)$ = 0.508(0.607) = 0.308.
b.   Since one cannot vote without registering P(V) = P(V and R) = 0.607. Since P(V|R) = P(V and R)/P(R), P(R) = P(V and R)/P(V|R) = 0.607/0.853 = 0.712.
Step 1: Define events of interest:
Let E_1 and E_2 be defined as in part a. Let E_3 = an individual registered to vote.
Step 2: Determine the probability of each event:
$P(E_2)$ = 0.607, $P(E_1|E_2)$ = 0.508. Since one cannot vote without registering $P(E_2)$ = $P(E_2$ and $E_3)$ = 0.607. $P(E_1|E_3)$ = 0.853
Step 3: Determine if the two events are independent:

Since $P(E_1|E_3)$ = 0.853 and $P(E_1|\overline{E}_3)$ = 0, E_1 and E_3 are not independent.
Step 4: Compute the probability using Rule 8.
Since $P(E_1|E_3)$ = $P(E_1$ and $E_3)/P(E_3)$, $P(E_3)$ = $P(E_1$ and $E_3)/P(E_1|E_3)$ = 0.607/0.853 = 0.712

4.49

a. Let E_1 = bladder-cancer patient survives; E_2 = surgery performed at a high-volume hospital. P (E_1 and E_2) = P($E_1|E_2$) P(E_2) = (1 - 0.007)(0.77) = 0.76.

b. **Step 1:** Define the experiment:

A randomly chosen bladder-cancer patient that has had surgery at either a low- or high-volume hospital is selected. It is determined whether or not the patient survived the first two weeks after surgery.

Step 2: Define events of interest:

Let E_1 = bladder-cancer patient survives; E_2 = surgery performed at a high-volume hospital.

Step 3: Determine the probability of each event:

$P(E_2) = 0.77$, $P(\overline{E}_2) = 1 - 0.77 = 0.23$, $P(E_1|\overline{E}_2) = 0.031$, $P(E_1|\overline{E}_2) = 1 - 0.031 = 0.969$, and $P(\overline{E}_1|E_2) = 0.007$.

Step 4: Determine if the two events are mutually exclusive.

Calculate the joint probabilities: If a patient survived an operation in a high-volume hospital, that patient could not also have survived that operation in a low-volume hospital. Therefore, (E_1 and E_2) or (E_1 and $\overline{E}_2$)] are mutually exclusive. $P(E_1$ and $E_2) = 0.76$ from part a. P (E_1 and $\overline{E}_2$) = $P(E_1|\overline{E}_2)$ P($\overline{E}_2$) = (1 - 0.031)(0.23) = 0.223.

Step 5: Compute the probability using Rule 5.

$P[(E_1$ and $E_2)$ or (E_1 and $\overline{E}_2$)] = P (E_1 and E_2) + P (E_1 and $\overline{E}_2$) = 0.765 + 0.223 = 0.988.

c. **Step 1:** Define the experiment.

Two randomly chosen bladder-cancer patients that have had surgery at either a low- or high-volume hospital are selected. It is determined whether or not the patients survived the first two weeks after surgery.

Step 2: Define the overall event of interest.

Only one of two bladder cancer patients would survive the first two weeks after surgery.

Step 3: Define the elementary events:

Let E_3 = the first bladder-cancer patient will survive the first two weeks after surgery; $\overline{E}_3$ = the first bladder-cancer patient will not survive the first two weeks after surgery. Let E_4 = the second bladder-cancer patient will survive the first two weeks after surgery; $\overline{E}_4$ = the second bladder-cancer patient will not survive the first two weeks after surgery.

Step 4: List the sample space for the events of interest:

The sample space of interest is (E_3 and $\overline{E}_4$) and ($\overline{E}_3$ and E_4).

Step 5: Compute the probabilities for the events of interest:

Since E_3 and E_4 are independent, $P(E_3$ and $\overline{E}_4) = P(E_3)P(\overline{E}_4) = 0.988(1 - 0.988) = 0.012$. $P(\overline{E}_3$ and $E_4) = P(E_3)P(\overline{E}_4) = (1 - 0.988)(0.988) = 0.012$

Step 6: Determine the probability for the overall event of interest:

P [(E_3 and $\overline{E}_4$) or ($\overline{E}_3$ and E_4)] = P (E_3 and $\overline{E}_4$) + P($\overline{E}_3$ and E_4) = $P(E_3)P(\overline{E}_4)$ + $P(\overline{E}_3)P(E_4)$ = 0.012 + 0.012 = 0.024.

d. P(at least one) = 1 − P(none) = 1 − [1 - P(E_3)] [1 - P(E_4)] = 1 − $(1 - 0.988)^2$] = 1 − 0.0001 = 0. 9999.

4.51 Student can use Excel's pivot table feature to answer this question.
  a.   P(both business) = (27/62)(26/61) = 0.1856

Type of Trip	Total
Business	27
Pleasure	26
Combination	9
Grand Total	62

  b.   P(business or hotel problem) = 27/62 + 14/62 – 10/62 = 31/62 = 0.50

| | Any Problems | | |
Type of Trip	Problems	No Problems	Grand Total
Business	10	17	27
Pleasure	3	23	26
Combination	1	8	9
Grand Total	14	48	62

  c.   P(business and in-state area code) = 2/62 = 0.0323

| | Phone | | | |
Type of Trip	No Response	In-State	Out-State	Grand Total
Business	3	2	22	27
Pleasure	9	2	15	26
Combination	1	1	7	9
Grand Total	13	5	44	62

  d.   If they are independent 22/62 which equals 0.3548 should equal (52/62)(27/62) which equals (0.8387)(0.4355) = 0.3653 since they are not equal they are not independent

| | Attentive | | | |
Type of Trip	No Response	Pass	Fail	Grand Total
Business	1	22	4	27
Pleasure	1	22	3	26
Combination		8	1	9
Grand Total	2	52	8	62

4.53. The probabilities required to produce the answers to exercise are given by the following table:

Rows: Response   Columns: Age Group

	15-25	26-35	36-45	46-55	56-65	66-75	All
1	53	52	53	51	45	29	283
	26.37	25.37	27.04	25.00	24.46	29.59	26.01
	4.871	4.779	4.871	4.688	4.136	2.665	26.011
2	39	39	41	47	36	16	218
	19.40	19.02	20.92	23.04	19.57	16.33	20.04
	3.585	3.585	3.768	4.320	3.309	1.471	20.037
3	19	25	24	21	29	13	131
	9.45	12.20	12.24	10.29	15.76	13.27	12.04
	1.746	2.298	2.206	1.930	2.665	1.195	12.040
4	13	19	16	16	11	1	76
	6.47	9.27	8.16	7.84	5.98	1.02	6.99
	1.195	1.746	1.471	1.471	1.011	0.092	6.985
5	13	15	9	12	8	8	65
	6.47	7.32	4.59	5.88	4.35	8.16	5.97
	1.195	1.379	0.827	1.103	0.735	0.735	5.974
6	64	55	53	57	55	31	315
	31.84	26.83	27.04	27.94	29.89	31.63	28.95
	5.882	5.055	4.871	5.239	5.055	2.849	28.952
All	201	205	196	204	184	98	1088
	100.00	100.00	100.00	100.00	100.00	100.00	100.00
	18.474	18.842	18.015	18.750	16.912	9.007	100.000

Cell Contents: Count
                   % of Column
                   % of Total

a. Let E_1 = the respondents 36 or older; E_2 = would not use a wireless phone exclusively because of some type of difficulty in placing and receiving calls. $P(E_2|E_1) = P(E_1 \text{ and } E_2)/P(E_1) = (16+16+11+1+9+12+8+8)/1088]/[(196+204+184+98)]/1088 = 0.074/0.627 = 0.119$

b. For ease of typing, let not E_1 be the complement of E_1. Then: $P(E_2| \text{ not } E_1) = P(\text{ not } E_1 \text{ and } E_2)/P(E_2) = (13+19+13+15)/1088]/[(201+205)]/1088 = 0.55/0.373 = 0.148$

c. Let A_i = the ith respondent stated that the most important reason for not using a wireless exclusively was that they need a line for Net access. $P(\text{at least one}) = 1 - P(\text{none}) = 1 - P(\text{ not } A_1 \text{ and not } A_2 \text{ and not } A_3) = 1 - P(\text{not } A_1)P(\text{ not } A_2) P(\text{ not } A_3) = 1 - [1- P(A_1)][1- P(A_2)] [1- P(A_3)] = 1 - (1 - 0.148)(1 - 0.148) (1 - 0.148) = 1 - 0.6186 = 0.3814$

4.55 The probabilities required to produce the answers to exercise are given by the following table:

Rows: Time   Columns: Cost

	0-2000	2001-4000	4001-6000	6001-8000	All
0-50	3	16	9	1	29
	50.00	50.00	81.82	100.00	58.00
	6	32	18	2	58
051-100	3	15	2	0	20
	50.00	46.88	18.18	0.00	40.00
	6	30	4	0	40
151-200	0	1	0	0	1
	0.00	3.13	0.00	0.00	2.00
	0	2	0	0	2
All	6	32	11	1	50
	100.00	100.00	100.00	100.00	100.00
	12	64	22	2	100

Cell Contents: Count
                   % of Column
                   % of Total

a. Let E_1 = vacancy took at most 100 days. E_2 = cost at most \$4000 to fill. $P(E_1 \text{ or } E_2) = P(E_1) + P(E_2) - P(E_1 \text{ and } E_2) = (20+29)/100 + (6+32)/100 - (3+16+3+15)/100 = 0.49 + 0.38 - 0.37 = 0.50$

b. $P(E_2|E_1) = P(E_1 \text{ and } E_2)/P(E_1) = [(3+16+3+15)/100]/[(20+29)]/100 = 0.37/0.49 = 0.755$

c. For ease of typing, let not E_1 be the complement of E_1. Let E_i = the ith vacancy cost at most \$4000 to fill. $P(\text{two}) = P[(E_1 \text{ and } E_2 \text{ and not } E_3) \text{ or } (E_1 \text{ and not } E_2 \text{ and } E_3) \text{ or } (\text{not } E_1 \text{ and } E_2 \text{ and } E_3)] = P(E_1 \text{ and } E_2 \text{ and not } E_3) + P(E_1 \text{ and not } E_2 \text{ and } E_3) + P(\text{not } E_1 \text{ and } E_2 \text{ and } E_3)] = P(E_1)P(E_2) P(\text{not } E_3) + P(E_1)P(\text{not } E_2) P(E_3) + P(\text{not } E_1)P(E_2) P(E_3) = 3(0.38)(0.38)(1 - 0.38) = 0.269.$

End of Chapter Exercises

4.57. Classical probability assessment, sometimes referred to as *a priori* probability, is the method of determining probability based on the ratio of the number of ways the event of interest can occur to the total number of ways any event can occur when the individual elementary events are equally likely. In most business situations, it is often not possible for the decision-maker to enumerate all the possible ways an event can occur. Furthermore, it is unlikely that the individual elementary events are equally likely. Therefore, classical probability assessment is rarely applied

4.59. Students' examples will vary. Subjective probability is defined as the expert opinion. Someone determines the probability based on judgment rather than mathematically calculated.

4.61.
a. $P(A|B) = P(A \text{ and } B)/P(B) = (800/2000)/[(800 + 200)/2000] = 0.80$,

$P(\overline{A}|B') = P(\overline{A} \text{ and } B')/P(\overline{B}) = (400/2000)/[(600 + 400)/2000] = 0.40$,

$P(\overline{A}|B) = P(\overline{A} \text{ and } B)/P(B) = (200/2000)/[(800 + 200)/2000] = 0.20$,

and $P(A|\overline{B}) = P(A \text{ and } \overline{B})/P(\overline{B}) = (600/2000)/[(600 + 400)/2000] = 0.60$.

b. You determined that $0.80 = P(A|B) = 1 - P(\overline{A}|B) = 1 - 0.20$ and, therefore, $\overline{A}|B$ and $A|B$ are complements. You determined that $0.60 = P(A|\overline{B}) = 1 - P(\overline{A}|\overline{B}) = 1 - 0.40$ and, therefore, $A|\overline{B}'$ and $\overline{A}|\overline{B}$ are complements.

4.63. The probability of correctly guessing on any one question is .25. The questions are independent.
a. $P(C \text{ and } C \text{ and } C) = .25 \times .25 \times .25 = 0.0156$
b. Sample space is:

$$P(C \text{ and } C \text{ and } C) = .25 \times .25 \times .25 = 0.0156$$
Or
$$P(C \text{ and } C \text{ and } W) = .25 \times .25 \times .75 = 0.0469$$
Or
$$P(C \text{ and } W \text{ and } C) = .25 \times .75 \times .25 = 0.0469$$
Or
$$P(W \text{ and } C \text{ and } C) = .75 \times .25 \times .25 = 0.0469$$

The probability of interest is found by summing these probabilities:
$P(\text{Passing}) = .0156 + .0469 + .0469 + .0469 = 0.1563$
Thus, the chances of passing a three question multiple choice exam if two or more correct answers are required is only 0.1563. Moral of the story is that you had better plan on studying.

c. For a. $P(C \text{ and } C \text{ and } C) = .5 \times .5 \times .5 = 0.125$
For b. Sample space is:

$$P(C \text{ and } C \text{ and } C) = .5 \times .5 \times .5 = 0.125$$
Or
$$P(C \text{ and } C \text{ and } W) = .5 \times .5 \times .5 = 0.125$$
Or
$$P(C \text{ and } W \text{ and } C) = .5 \times .5 \times .5 = 0.125$$
Or
$$P(W \text{ and } C \text{ and } C) = .5 \times .5 \times .5 = 0.125$$

The probability of interest is found by summing these probabilities:
$P(\text{Passing}) = .0125 + .125 + .125 + .125 = 0.50$
Thus, the chances of passing a three question multiple choice exam if two or more correct answers are required is increased to 0.50. Moral of the story is that you still better plan on studying on a more regular basis.

4.65. In this solution E' = not E.
a. Let E_1 = a randomly selected wealthy individual is audited. $P(E_1) = 1/63 = 0.016$ and $P(E_1') = 1 - P(E_1) = 1 - 0.016 = 0.984$. $P(\text{at least one}) = 1 - P(\text{none}) = 1 - P(E_1' \text{ and } E_1' \text{ and } \ldots \text{ and } E_1') = 1 - P(E_1')P(E_1') \ldots P(E_1') = 1 - (0.984)(0.984) \ldots (0.984) = 1 - 0.851 = 0.149$

b. Let E_2 = a randomly selected corporation with assets of at least \$250 million would be audited. $P(E_2) = 0.44$ and $P(E_2') = 1 - P(E_2) = 1 - 0.44 = 0.56$. P(at least one) = $1 - P(none) = 1 - P(E_2'$ and E_2' and . . . and $E_2')$ = $1 - P(E_2')P(E_2')$ . . . $P(E_2') = 1 - (0.56)(0.56)$ . . . $(0.56) = 1 - 0.003 = 0.997$

c. $P(E_1$ or $E_2) = P(E_1) + P(E_2) - P(E_1$ and $E_2) = P(E_1) + P(E_2) - P(E_1)P(E_2) = 0.016 + 0.44 - (0.016)(0.44)$ = 0.449.

4.67.

a. The relative frequency assessment approach was most likely used. A sample of customers who purchase gasoline at the pump are observed and the relative frequency of those that pay using a credit or debit card is calculated.

b. Let E_1 = a randomly selected customer who purchases gasoline pays using a credit or debit card. $P(E_1)$ = 0.70. $P(E_1$ and E_1 and . . . and $E_1) = P(E_1)P(E_1)$ . . . $P(E) = (0.70)(0.70)$ . . . $(0.70) = 0.028$

c. Let E_1 = a randomly selected customer who purchases gasoline pays using a credit or debit card. $P(E_1)$ = 0.90. $P(E_1$ and E_1 and . . . and $E_1) = P(E_1)P(E_1)$ . . . $P(E) = (0.90)(0.90)$ . . . $(0.90) = 0.349$

d. It is more than 12 times $(0.349/0.028 = 12.45)$ as likely that the sample result would occur if the proportion of customers who purchase gasoline pays using a credit or debit card 90% of the time than if they do so 70% of the time. Therefore, it does appear that a larger percentage of individuals use credit or debit cards at the local pump than is true for the nation as a whole

4.69. $P(\text{Clerk 1}) = 0.4$
$P(\text{Clerk 2}) = 0.3$
$P(\text{Clerk 3}) = 0.3$
$P(\text{Defective}|\text{Clerk 1}) = 0.02$
$P(\text{Defective}|\text{Clerk 2}) = 0.025$
$P(\text{Defective}|\text{Clerk 3}) = 0.015$
You need to calculate the probability of each clerk given you know the chocolates are defective.
Use Bayes' Rule to calculate this

$P(\text{Defective}) = P(\text{Defective}|\text{Clerk 1})P(\text{Clerk 1}) + P(\text{Defective}|\text{Clerk 2})P(\text{Clerk 2}) + P(\text{Defective}|\text{Clerk 3})P(\text{Clerk 3}) = (0.02)(0.4) + (0.025)(0.3) + (0.015)(0.3) = 0.02$
$P(\text{Clerk 1}|\text{Defective}) = (0.02)(0.4)/0.02 = 0.4$
$P(\text{Clerk 2}|\text{Defective}) = (0.025)(0.3)/0.02 = 0.375$
$P(\text{Clerk 3}|\text{Defective}) = (0.015)(0.3)/0.02 = 0.225$

Clerk 1 is most likely responsible for the boxes that raised the complaints.

4.71. The following table can be used to answer the questions.

```
Rows: Type   Columns: Location

            MW      NE      SE      SW       W      All

C           24      18      13      17      28      100
          32.00   36.00   52.00   34.00   28.00   33.33
          8.000   6.000   4.333   5.667   9.333   33.333

E           15      15       5      10      30       75
          20.00   30.00   20.00   20.00   30.00   25.00
          5.000   5.000   1.667   3.333  10.000   25.000

F           21      12       4      15      23       75
          28.00   24.00   16.00   30.00   23.00   25.00
          7.000   4.000   1.333   5.000   7.667   25.000

M           15       5       3       8      19       50
          20.00   10.00   12.00   16.00   19.00   16.67
          5.000   1.667   1.000   2.667   6.333   16.667

All         75      50      25      50     100      300
         100.00  100.00  100.00  100.00  100.00  100.00
          25.000  16.667   8.333  16.667  33.333  100.000

Cell Contents:      Count
                    % of Column
                    % of Total
```

a.   Relative frequency of W = $\dfrac{Number\ of\ times\ W\ occurs}{N} = \dfrac{100}{300} = 0.33$

b.   Relative frequency of (W and E) = $\dfrac{Number\ of\ times\ W\ \&\ E\ occurs}{N} = \dfrac{30}{300} = 0.10$

c.   Note: East = NE + SE. Relative frequency of East = $\dfrac{Number\ of\ times\ NE\ +\ SE\ occurs}{N} =$

$\dfrac{50 + 25}{300} = 0.25$

Relative frequency of C = $\dfrac{Number\ of\ times\ C\ occurs}{N} = \dfrac{100}{300} = 0.333$. Relative frequency of

(East and C) = $\dfrac{Number\ of\ times\ East\ +\ C\ occurs}{N} = \dfrac{18 + 13}{300} = 0.103$.

Therefore, P(East or C) = P(East) + P(C) – P(East and C) = 0.25 + 0.333 - 0.103 = 0.48.

d.   P(C|East) = P(C and East)/P(East) = 0.103/0.25 = 0.41

4.73. Students can use Excel's pivot table feature to answer this question.

a.   P(Wiring/Salt lake) = P(Wiring and Salt Lake)/P(Salt Lake) = (8/110)/(24/110) = 0.3333

	Manufacturing Plant			
Complaint Code	Boise	Salt Lake	Toronto	Grand Total
Corrosion	30	3	2	35
Cracked Lens	31	11	3	45
Wiring	13	8	2	23
Sound	4	2	1	7
Grand Total	78	24	8	110

b.   Using the table from above and the information in the problem you know:

P(Boise/return) = 78/110 = 0.7091

P(Salt lake/return) = 24/110 = 0.2182

P(Toronto/return) = 8/110 = 0.0727

Assuming the sample represents the population of returned products, the cost assignment should be based on the conditional probability of a city given that the product was returned. Thus, Boise will get 70.91% of the cost, Salt Lake will get 21.82% and Toronto will get 7.27% regardless of production volume.

4.75

a.

	Boomer	GenX	GenY	Silent
email	13	13	10	10
	13.00	13.00	10.00	10.00
	3.250	3.250	2.500	2.500
Face-to-face	39	38	52	39
	39.00	38.00	52.00	39.00
	9.750	9.500	13.000	9.750
Gp Meeting	41	42	36	40
	41.00	42.00	36.00	40.00
	10.250	10.500	9.000	10.000
Other	7	7	2	11
	7.00	7.00	2.00	11.00
	1.750	1.750	0.500	2.750
All	100	100	100	100
	100.00	100.00	100.00	100.00
	25.000	25.000	25.000	25.000

Cell Contents: Count
                        % of Column
                        % of Total

b.   Let E_1 = a member of the silent generation, E_2 = boomer generation, E_3 = X generation, E_4 = Y generation, and B = prefers face-to-face communication.

$$P(E_1)P(B|E_1) + P(E_2)P(B|E_2) + ... + P(E_4)P(B|E_4) = 0.39(0.075) + 0.39(0.42) +$$

$$0.38(0.295) + 0.52(0.21) = 0.4144.$$

c. $P(E_1|B) = \dfrac{P(E_i)P(B|E_i)}{P(E_1)P(B|E_1) + P(E_2)P(B|E_2) + ... + P(E_k)P(B|E_k)} =$

For Silent Generation:

$$\frac{(0.39)(0.075)}{(0.39)(0.075) + (0.39)(0.42) + (0.38)(0.295) + 0.52(0.21)} = \frac{0.0281}{0.4144} = 0.0678$$

For Baby Boomers:

$$\frac{(0.39)(0.42)}{(0.39)(0.075) + (0.39)(0.42) + (0.38)(0.295) + 0.52(0.21)} = \frac{1638}{0.4144} = 0.3953$$

For X generation:

$$\frac{(0.38)(0.295)}{(0.39)(0.075) + (0.39)(0.42) + (0.38)(0.295) + 0.52(0.21)} = \frac{0.1121}{0.4144} = 0.2705$$

For Y generation:

$$\frac{(0.52)(0.21)}{(0.39)(0.075) + (0.39)(0.42) + (0.38)(0.295) + 0.52(0.21)} = \frac{0.1092}{0.4144} = 0.2635$$

The most likely generation of which the individual is a member is the Baby Boomers.

Chapter 5
Discrete Probability Distributions

Section 5-1 Exercises

5.1
    a.   The variable, x, is a discrete random variable because x can take on only specific integer values.
    b.   The possible values for x are:
$$x = \{0, 1, 2, 3, 4, 5, 6\}$$

5.3
    a.   The random variable is x, the number of children under 22 living in a household.
    b.   The random variable is discrete since the values for x can take on only specific integer values such as 0, 1, 2, 3, 4, …

5.5   The expected value of a discrete probability distribution is determined using:
$$E(x) = \sum xP(x)$$

The calculations are:

x	P(x)	xP(x)
0	0.05	0
1	0.10	0.1
2	0.10	0.2
3	0.20	0.6
4	0.20	0.8
5	0.15	0.75
6	0.15	0.9
7	0.05	0.35
	Sum =	3.7

Thus, the expected number of days per week that a boat will leave port during poor weather is 3.7 days.

5.7
    a.   The expected value of x is calculated using equation 5-1, $E(x) = \sum xP(x)$.
        $E(x) = (100)(0.25) + (125)(0.30) + (150)(0.45) = 130$.
    b.   The variance of x is calculated using the following equation, $\sum[x-E(x)]^2P(x)$. The calculations are shown below

x	P(x)	xP(x)	[x-E(x)]	$[x-E(x)]^2P(x)$
100	0.25	25	-30	225
125	0.3	37.5	-5	7.5
150	0.45	67.5	20	180

The variance of x is equal to $225 + 7.5 + 180 = 412.50$.
    c.   The standard deviation is computed using equation 5-2. The standard deviation is the positive square root of the variance calculated in (b) above.
$$\sigma_x = \sqrt{412.50} = 20.31$$

5.9

a. $E(x) = \Sigma xP(x) = 5(0.10) + \ldots + 20(0.50) = 15.75$,

b. The probability distribution of y is

y	P(y)
10	0.10
15	0.15
20	0.25
25	0.50.

$E(y) = \Sigma yP(y) = 10(0.10) + \ldots + 25(0.50) = 20.75$

c. The probability distribution of Z is

z	P(z)
25	0.10
50	0.15
75	0.25
100	0.50.

$E(z) = \Sigma zP(z) = 25(0.10) + \ldots + 100(0.50) = 78.75$,

d. Adding a constant (in this case 5) increases both the expected value by an amount equal to the constant added.

e. Multiplying by a constant (in this case 5) results in both the expected value being multiplied by that same constant.

5.11

a. $E(X) = \Sigma xP(x) = 2(0.27) + \ldots + 7(0.03) = 3.51$.

b. $\sigma^2 = \Sigma(x - E(x))^2\, P(x) = (-1.51)^2(0.27) + \ldots + 3.49^2(0.03) = 1.6499$,

$$\sigma = \sqrt{\sigma^2} = \sqrt{1.6499} = 1.2845.$$

5.13

a. The expected value of a discrete probability distribution is determined using:

$$E(x) = \sum xP(x)$$

The calculations are shown as follows:

x	P(x)	xP(x)
1	0.15	0.15
2	0.25	0.5
3	0.3	0.9
4	0.18	0.72
5	0.12	0.6
	Sum =	2.87

Thus, the expected number of days that will be required to repair HDTVs is 2.87 days.

b. The variance for a discrete random variable is computed using the following equation:

$$\sigma^2 = \sum [x - E(x)]^2\, P(x)$$

The calculations are shown as follows:

x	P(x)	xP(x)	[x - E(x)]	[x-E(x)]²	[x-E(x)]²P(x)
1	0.15	0.15	-1.87	3.4969	0.5245
2	0.25	0.5	-0.87	0.7569	0.1892
3	0.3	0.9	0.13	0.0169	0.0051
4	0.18	0.72	1.13	1.2769	0.2298
5	0.12	0.6	2.13	4.5369	0.5444
	Sum =	2.87			1.4931

The variance is 1.4931 days squared. The standard deviation is the square root of the variance as follows:

$$\sigma = \sqrt{\sum [x - E(x)]^2 \, P(x)}$$
$$\sigma = \sqrt{1.4931} = 1.22$$

The standard deviation is 1.22 days.

c.   Based on the probability distribution, the chances of exceeding 4 days for repair time is 0.12. Thus, not all repair times can be expected to be done in 4 days or less. However, using the Empirical rule from Chapter 3, if the distribution is approximately bell shaped, about 68% of the occurrences will be within one standard deviation of the mean so the manager can expect about two-thirds of the time to repairs within the range:

   2.87 ± 1.22
   1.65 days to 4.09 days.

5.15

a.   To determine the total expected cost, you would first find the expected proportion of defects based on the discrete probability distribution that was assessed based on historical data. The expected value of a discrete probability distribution is determined using:

$$E(x) = \sum xP(x)$$

The calculations are shown as follows:

Proportion Defective	Probability	
x	P(x)	xP(x)
0.01	0.4	0.004
0.02	0.3	0.006
0.05	0.2	0.01
0.10	0.1	0.01
	E(x) =	0.03

Thus, Rossmore Brothers, Inc. can expect that when they order 2,000 faucets that 0.03 of the faucets will be defective. This means that 2000(0.03) = 60 of the faucets will be defective. The total expected cost for the order is:

   Total Expected Cost = 2,000($29.00) + 60($5.00) = $58,300

b.   For the new supplier, the total expected cost is calculated by first finding the expected proportion of defects as follows:

Proportion Defective	Probability	
x	P(x)	xP(x)
0.01	0.1	0.001
0.02	0.1	0.002
0.05	0.7	0.035
0.10	0.1	0.010
	E(x) =	0.048

Thus, Rossmore Brothers, Inc. can expect that when they order 2,000 faucets that 0.048 of the faucets will be defective. This means that 2000(0.048) = 96 of the faucets will be defective. The total expected cost for the order is:

   Total Expected Cost = 2,000($28.50) + 96($5.00) = $57,480

Then, comparing this expected cost with the expected cost of $58,300 found in part a., the best decision based on cost alone is to switch to the new supplier. The $0.50 per unit cost savings on the purchase price offsets the cost associated with the higher expected defect proportion from the new supplier.

5.17

   a.   Profit = Sales – Costs

       Small firm profits: 0.75(300000) – 150000 = 75000,

                                  0.75(400000) – 150000 = 150000 (can't sell more than produced)

                                  0.75(400000) – 150000 = 150000

       E(X) = ΣxP(x) = 75000(0.2) + 150000(0.5) + 150000(0.3) = \$135,000.

       Mid-sized profits: 0.75(300000) – 250000 = -25000,

                                   0.75(600000) – 250000 = 200000 (can't sell more than produced)

                                   0.75(600000) – 250000 = 200000

       E(X) = ΣxP(x) = -25000(0.2) + 200000(0.5) + 200000(0.3) = \$155,000

       Large firm profits: 0.75(300000) – 350000 = -125000,

                               0.75(700000) – 350000 = 175000

                               0.75(900000) – 350000 = 325000

        E(X) = ΣxP(x) = -125000(0.2) + 175000(0.5) + 325000(0.3) = \$160,000.

   b. $\sigma^2 = \Sigma(x - E(X))^2 P(x)$

       Small firm: σ^2 = $(-60000)^2(0.\,2) + 15000^2(0.\,5) + 15000^2(0.3)$ = 900000000,

$$\sigma = \sqrt{\sigma^2} = \sqrt{900000000} = \$30,000$$

       Mid-sized firm: σ^2 = $(-180000)^2(0.\,2) + 45000^2(0.\,5) + 45000^2(0.3)$ = 8.1×10^9,

$$\sigma = \sqrt{\sigma^2} = \sqrt{8.1 x 10^9} = \$90,000.$$

       Large firm: σ^2 = $(-285000)^2(0.\,2) + 15000^2(0.\,5) + 165000^2(0.3)$ = 2.45×10^{10},

$$\sigma = \sqrt{\sigma^2} = \sqrt{2.45 x 10^{10}} = \$156,604.60.$$

   c.   The large firm has the largest expected profit. This would be the choice unless the corporate board was risk adverse. In which case, the mid-sized firm has almost as large an expected profit and a standard deviation that is 43% (1 – 90000/156604.60) smaller than that of the large firm's.

5.19

   a.   The frequency distribution is

```
Sold   Count   Percent
   1       2      1.33
   2       7      4.67
   3      18     12.00
   4      30     20.00
   5      44     29.33
   6      24     16.00
   7      15     10.00
   8       6      4.00
   9       4      2.67
 N=      150
```

   b.   Let X = the number of magazines sold, then the probability distribution is

x	0	1	2	3	4	5	6	7	8	9	10
P(x)	0	0.013	0.047	0.120	0.200	0.293	0.160	0.100	0.040	.027	0

       E(X) = ΣxP(x) = 0(0) + 1(0.013) + . . . + 10(0) = 4.955

       E(Profit) = E(sales) – cost = 3.49E(X) – 10(1.95) = 3.49E(X) – 19.50 = 3.49(4.955) – 19.50 = -\$2.21

   c.   Since the expected loss is \$2.21 for the ten magazine to obtain a positive expected profit, the salvage value per magazine would have to be = 2.21/10 = \$0.221 or \$0.23.

5.21

a.   **Step 1:** Convert the frequency distribution into a probability distribution using the relative frequency of occurrence method. The frequency distribution is

Months	Count	Percent
14	1	0.80
15	3	2.40
16	8	6.40
17	6	4.80
18	23	18.40
19	27	21.60
20	30	24.00
21	16	12.80
22	9	7.20
23	2	1.60
N=	125	

x	14	15	16	17	18	19	20	21	22	23
P(x)	0.008	0.024	0.064	0.048	0.184	0.216	0.240	0.128	0.072	0.016

b.   **Step 2:** Compute the expected value using Equation 5-1.

$E(x) = \Sigma x P(x) = 14(0.008) + 15(0.024) + \ldots + 23(0.016) = 19.168$.

Step 3: Compute the standard deviation using 5-2.

$\sigma^2 = \Sigma (x - E(x))^2 P(x) = (-4.168)^2(0.008) + (-3.168)^2(0.024) + \ldots + 3.832(0.016) = 3.1634$, (2) $\sigma =$

$\sqrt{\sigma^2} = \sqrt{3.1634} = 1.7787$.

c.   For the majority of the covers to last longer than 19 months, the median would have to be at most 19. Here, $P(x \leq 19) = 0.544 > 0.50$ and $P(x \geq 19) = 0.672 > 1 - 0.50$. Therefore, the median is 19 and the quality control department is correct.

Section 5-2 Exercises

5.23   The following steps are used to solve this problem:

Step 1: Define the characteristics of the binomial distribution.

$n = 10, p = .30, x = 3$

Step 2: Determine the probability of x successes in n trials using the binomial formula.

$$P(x = 3) = \frac{n!}{x!(n-x)!} p^x (1-p)^{n-x}$$

$$P(x = 3) = \frac{10!}{3!(10-3)!} 0.30^3 (1-0.30)^{10-3}$$

$$P(x = 3) = (120)(0.027)(0.082)$$

$$P(x = 3) = 0.2668$$

There is a 0.2668 chance of observing 3 successes in a sample of ten items selected randomly from a population in which the probability of a success is 0.30.

5.25   Use binomial table for $n = 20$

a. $P(x = 5) = .0746$

b. $P(x \geq 7) = .1124 + .0609 + .0271 + .0099 + .0030 + .0008 + .0002 = .2143$

c. $E[x] = np = 20(.20) = 4$

d. $\sigma = \sqrt{npq} = \sqrt{20(.20)(.80)} = 1.7889$

5.27   This problem can be solved using the following steps:
    Step 1: Define the characteristics of the binomial distribution.
           $n = 10$, $p = .70$, $x = 5$
    Step 2: Go to the binomial table in Appendix B. Locate the appropriate section of the table for a sample size of $n = 10$ and the column with $q = 0.70$ at the bottom. This is:

X	p = 0.15	p = 0.20	p = 0.25	p = 0.30	p = 0.35	p = 0.40	p = 0.45	p = 0.50	n-X
0	0.0874	0.0352	0.0134	0.0047	0.0016	0.0005	0.0001	0.0000	15
1	0.2312	0.1319	0.0668	0.0305	0.0126	0.0047	0.0016	0.0005	14
2	0.2856	0.2309	0.1559	0.0916	0.0476	0.0219	0.0090	0.0032	13
3	0.2184	0.2501	0.2252	0.1700	0.1110	0.0634	0.0318	0.0139	12
4	0.1156	0.1876	0.2252	0.2186	0.1792	0.1268	0.0780	0.0417	11
5	0.0449	0.1032	0.1651	0.2061	0.2123	0.1859	0.1404	0.0916	10
6	0.0132	0.0430	0.0917	0.1472	0.1906	0.2066	0.1914	0.1527	9
7	0.0030	0.0138	0.0393	0.0811	0.1319	0.1771	0.2013	0.1964	8
8	0.0005	0.0035	0.0131	0.0348	0.0710	0.1181	0.1647	0.1964	7
9	0.0001	0.0007	0.0034	0.0116	0.0298	0.0612	0.1048	0.1527	6
10	0.0000	0.0001	0.0007	0.0030	0.0096	0.0245	0.0515	0.0916	5
11	0.0000	0.0000	0.0001	0.0006	0.0024	0.0074	0.0191	0.0417	4
12	0.0000	0.0000	0.0000	0.0001	0.0004	0.0016	0.0052	0.0139	3
13	0.0000	0.0000	0.0000	0.0000	0.0001	0.0003	0.0010	0.0032	2
14	0.0000	0.0000	0.0000	0.0000	0.0000	0.0000	0.0001	0.0005	1
15	0.0000	0.0000	0.0000	0.0000	0.0000	0.0000	0.0000	0.0000	0
	q = 0.85	q = 0.80	q = 0.75	q = 0.70	q = 0.65	q = 0.60	q = 0.55	q = 0.50	

    Step 3: Define the event of interest and obtain the desired probabilities from the binomial table.
    The event of interest is:
    $P(x \leq 6) - P(x \leq 5) = 0.1029$
    Hint: The value of x is found on the right side of the table when you are getting the probability of a success from the bottom of the column.
    There is a 0.1029 probability that exactly five successes will be observed in a sample of 10 items if the probability of a success is 0.70.

5.29
  a.   **Step 1:** Define the characteristics of the binomial distribution.
    In this case the characteristics are $n = 7$, $p = 0.65$, and $q = 1-p = 0.35$.
    Step 2: Define the probability of the event of interest in terms of the binomial probabilities given in Appendix B.
    $P(x = \underline{3}) = P(x \leq 3) - P(x \leq 2)$
    Step 3: Locate the appropriate section (e.g., sample size, n) and column (e.g., probability of success, p) in Appendix B.
    The sample size is $n = 7$, and the probability of a success is $p = 0.65$.
    Step 4: Locate the desired probability (probabilities) in the Appendix B and calculate the probability of the event of interest.
    We are interested in the probability of exactly 3 successes. $P(x = 3) = P(x \leq 4) - P(x \leq 3) = 0.1998 - .0556 = 0.1442$.
  b.   **Steps 1 and 2** are identical to (a) above.
    Step 3: the event of interest is the probability of four or more successes.
    $P(x \geq 4) = 1 - P(x \leq 3)$
  c.   **Steps 1, 2 and 3** are identical to (a) above.
    Step 4: the event of interest is the probability of exactly 7 successes. $P(x = 7) = P(x \leq 7) - P(x \leq 6) = 1 - 0.9510 = 0.0490$.
  d.   The expected value of the random variable can be found using the equation 5-5, $E(x) = np = (7)(0.65) = 4.55$

5.31

    a. $P(x = 2) = 0.0688$.

    b. $P(x < 4) = P(x \leq 3) = 0.0031$.

    c. $P(2 < x \leq 5) = P(x \leq 5) - P(x \leq 2) = 0.1487 - 0.0020 = 0.1467$.

    d. $P(x \geq 13) = 1 - P(x \leq 12) = 1 - 0.1530 = 0.8470$.

    e. $P(x > 3) = 1 - P(x \leq 3) = 1 - 0.0013 = 0.9987$

5.33

    a. $E(x) = np = 8(0.40) = 3.2$

    b. $\sigma = \sqrt{npq} = \sqrt{8(0.4)(1 - 0.4)} = \sqrt{1.92} = 1.386$

    c. $P(x > 3.2) = P(x \geq 4) = 1 - P(x \leq 3) = 0.4060$.

    d. $P(\mu - 2\sigma \leq x \leq \mu + 2\sigma) = P[3.2 - 2(1.386) \leq x \leq 3.2 - 2(1.386)] = P(0.428 \leq x \leq 5.972) = P(1 \leq x \leq 5)$
        $= P(x \leq 5) - P(x = 0) = 0.9502 - 0.0168 = 0.9334$

5.35

    a.   **Step 1:** Define the characteristics of the binomial distribution:
           $n = 10$, $p = 0.308$, $q = 1 - p = 1 - 0.308 = 0.692$.
       Step 2: Use equation 5-4 to find the expected value:
           $\mu_X = E(X) = np = 10(0.308) = 3.08$

    b.   **Step 1:** Define the characteristics of the binomial distribution:
           $n = 10$, $p = 0.607$, $q = 1 - p = 1 - 0.607 = 0.393$.
       Step 2: Determine the probability of x successes in n trials using the binomial formula, Equation 5-4:

$$P(X = 10) = \binom{10}{10} 0.607^{10}(0.393)^{10-10} = 0.0068$$

    c.   **Step 1:** Define the characteristics of the binomial distribution:
           $n = 10$, $p = 0.308$, $q = 1 - p = 1 - 0.308 = 0.692$.
       Step 2: Determine the probability of x successes in n trials using the binomial formula, Equation 5-4:
       $P(X \geq 8) = P(X = 8) + P(X = 9) + P(X = 10)$

$$= \binom{10}{8} 0.308^{8}(0.692)^{10-8} + \binom{10}{9} 0.308^{9}(0.692)^{10-9} + \binom{10}{10} 0.308^{10}(0.692)^{10-10}$$

$$= \frac{10!}{8!(10-8)!} 0.308^{8} 0.692^{2} + \frac{10!}{9!(10-9)!} 0.308^{9} 0.692^{1} + \frac{10!}{10!(10-10)!} 0.308^{10} 0.692^{0}$$

$$= 0.0017 + 0.0002 + 0.0000 = 0.0019.$$

    d.   It is quite unlikely that the employees followed the national trend. The probability of such an occurrence is very small, for voting only .0068, and for voting for President Bush, only 0.0019, assuming they were following the national trend.

5.37

    a. The sampling process meets the characteristics of a binomial distribution with n = 20, p = 0.04. We are interested in the event that x = 0 defective dowel holes are observed in the sample. The binomial table can be used to find this probability by going to the section of the table for n = 20 and the column headed p = 0.04 shown as follows:

X	n = 20									
	p = 0.01	p = 0.02	p =0.03	p =0.04	p =0.05	p =0.06	p =0.07	p =0.08	p =0.09	p =0.10
0	0.8179	0.6676	0.5438	0.4420	0.3585	0.2901	0.2342	0.1887	0.1516	0.1216
1	0.1652	0.2725	0.3364	0.3683	0.3774	0.3703	0.3526	0.3282	0.3000	0.2702
2	0.0159	0.0528	0.0988	0.1458	0.1887	0.2246	0.2521	0.2711	0.2818	0.2852
3	0.0010	0.0065	0.0183	0.0364	0.0596	0.0860	0.1139	0.1414	0.1672	0.1901
4	0.0000	0.0006	0.0024	0.0065	0.0133	0.0233	0.0364	0.0523	0.0703	0.0898
5	0.0000	0.0000	0.0002	0.0009	0.0022	0.0048	0.0088	0.0145	0.0222	0.0319
6	0.0000	0.0000	0.0000	0.0001	0.0003	0.0008	0.0017	0.0032	0.0055	0.0089
7	0.0000	0.0000	0.0000	0.0000	0.0000	0.0001	0.0002	0.0005	0.0011	0.0020
8	0.0000	0.0000	0.0000	0.0000	0.0000	0.0000	0.0000	0.0001	0.0002	0.0004
9	0.0000	0.0000	0.0000	0.0000	0.0000	0.0000	0.0000	0.0000	0.0000	0.0001
	q = 0.99	q = 0.98	q = 0.97	q = 0.96	q = 0.95	q = 0.94	q = 0.93	q = 0.92	q = 0.91	q = 0.90

The event of interest is:

$$P(x = 0)$$

The probability from the table is:

$$P(x = 0) = 0.4420$$

Thus, the probability that the sampling plan will properly lead the company to let the process continue operating when the defect rate is at the acceptable level of 0.04 is 0.4420. Note, however, that

$$P(x \geq 1) = 1 - 0.4420 = 0.5580$$

There is over a 55% chance that the sample will provide a result that causes the managers to stop the drilling process for re-calibration even though the process is working correctly. That would be a costly mistake.

    b. The sampling process meets the characteristics of a binomial distribution with n = 20, p = 0.10. We are interested in the event that x ≥ 1 defective dowel holes are observed in the sample. The binomial table can be used to find this probability by going to the section of the table for n = 20 and the column headed p = 0.10 shown as follows:

X	n = 20									
	p = 0.01	p = 0.02	p =0.03	p =0.04	p =0.05	p =0.06	p =0.07	p =0.08	p =0.09	p =0.10
0	0.8179	0.6676	0.5438	0.4420	0.3585	0.2901	0.2342	0.1887	0.1516	0.1216
1	0.1652	0.2725	0.3364	0.3683	0.3774	0.3703	0.3526	0.3282	0.3000	0.2702
2	0.0159	0.0528	0.0988	0.1458	0.1887	0.2246	0.2521	0.2711	0.2818	0.2852
3	0.0010	0.0065	0.0183	0.0364	0.0596	0.0860	0.1139	0.1414	0.1672	0.1901
4	0.0000	0.0006	0.0024	0.0065	0.0133	0.0233	0.0364	0.0523	0.0703	0.0898
5	0.0000	0.0000	0.0002	0.0009	0.0022	0.0048	0.0088	0.0145	0.0222	0.0319
6	0.0000	0.0000	0.0000	0.0001	0.0003	0.0008	0.0017	0.0032	0.0055	0.0089
7	0.0000	0.0000	0.0000	0.0000	0.0000	0.0001	0.0002	0.0005	0.0011	0.0020
8	0.0000	0.0000	0.0000	0.0000	0.0000	0.0000	0.0000	0.0001	0.0002	0.0004
9	0.0000	0.0000	0.0000	0.0000	0.0000	0.0000	0.0000	0.0000	0.0000	0.0001
	q = 0.99	q = 0.98	q = 0.97	q = 0.96	q = 0.95	q = 0.94	q = 0.93	q = 0.92	q = 0.91	q = 0.90

The event of interest is:

$$P(x \geq 1) = 1 - P(x = 0)$$
$$P(x \geq 1) = 1 - 0.1216 = 0.8784$$

Thus, there is over an 87% chance that the sample will correctly tell the managers to stop the process when the defect rate is 0.10. This is a high probability, which is good.

    c. Individual letters will differ but should conclude that the sampling plan does a good job of detecting when the defect rate is higher than acceptable (p = 0.10) but is not effective at allowing the process to continue operating when the defect rate is at the acceptable rate of 0.04. An increase in sample size would be required to improve this.

5.39   n=8, p=0.37
    a.   Expected number = 8(0.37) = 2.96
    b.   Variance = 8(0.37)(0.63) = 1.8648, standard deviation = 1.3656
    c. $P(x \leq 2) = 0.0248 + 0.1166 + 0.2397 = 0.3811$

5.41
    a.   If 5 or more confirmed guests do not show then no guests will be sent to another hotel. Therefore, we find the probability of 5 or more successes, where a success is defined as a confirmed reservation that does not show. In this case n = 25, p = 0.15 and x = number of no shows. The $P(x \geq 5) = 1 - P(\leq 4) = 1 - 0.6821 = 0.3179$.
    b.   The probability that exactly two confirmed guests will be sent to another hotel is the probability of there being exactly 3 successes. That is there are 3 no shows from the 25 confirmed reservations leaving 22 guests for only 20 rooms. The probability is found to be $P(x = 3) = 0.2174$.
    c.   The probability that three or more guests will be sent to another hotel means that there are two or fewer no shows. If x = number of no shows is defined as a success then x = 0 implies that 5 guests must be sent to another hotel. If x = 1 then four guests must be sent to another hotel. If x = 2 then three guests must be sent to another hotel. Thus, we find $P(x \leq 2) = 0.25374$.

5.43
    a.   The characteristics of the binomial distribution are p = 0.69, q = 1-p = 0.31, and n = 30. The event of interest is the probability that from a sample of 30, fewer than 17 workers and/or their spouses have saved any money for retirement, $P(x < 17) = P(x \leq 16)$. This probability can be found using Excel = binomdist (16, 30, 0.69, true) = 0.051987.
    b.   The characteristics of the binomial distribution are p = 0.69, q = 1-p = 0.31, and n = 50. The event of interest is the probability that in a random sample of 50 workers more than 40 workers and/or their spouses have saved for retirement.
$P(x > 40) = P(x \geq 41) = 1-P(x \leq 40)$. This probability can be found using Excel's binomdist function as follows: =1- binomdist(40, 50, 0.69, true) = 1-0.971011 = 0.028989.

5.45
    a. $$\bar{x}_w = \frac{\sum w_i x_i}{\sum w_i} = \frac{30(0.50) + 10(0.10) + 50(0.35)}{30 + 10 + 50} = 0.372.$$
If Vericours is correct (i.e., that 40% don't redeem their rebates) this would suggest that 60% do redeem their rebates. It appears that TCA Fulfillment's redemption rate is much smaller that indicated by Vericours.
    b.   **Step 1:** Define the characteristics of the binomial distribution:
         n = 20, p = 0.60, q = 1 – p = 1 – 0.60 = 0.40.
Step 2: Use equation 5-4 to find the expected value:
$\mu_x = E(x) = np = 20(0.60) = 12$.
Given that the average obtained is 12, 4 seems to be extremely small. It would seem that Vericours' estimate may be too high.

c.   **Step 1:** Define the characteristics of the binomial distribution:
$n = 20$, $p = 0.372$, $q = 1 - p = 1 - 0.372 = 0.628$.
Step 2: Determine the probability of x successes in n trials using the binomial formula, Equation 5-4:
$P(x \le 4) = P(x = 0) + P(x = 1) + P(x = 2) + P(x = 3) + P(x = 4)$

$$= \binom{20}{0}0.372^0(0.628)^{20-0} + \binom{20}{1}0.372^1(0.628)^{20-1} + \binom{20}{2}0.372^2(0.628)^{20-2} +$$

$$\binom{20}{3}0.372^3(0.628)^{20-3} + \binom{20}{4}0.372^4(0.628)^{20-4}$$

$$= \frac{20!}{0!(20-0)!}0.372^0 0.628^{20} + \frac{20!}{1!(20-1)!}0.372^1 0.628^{20-1} + \frac{20!}{2!(20-2)!}0.372^2 0.628^{20-2} +$$

$$\frac{20!}{3!(20-3)!}0.372^3 0.628^{20-3} + \frac{20!}{4!(20-4)!}0.372^4 0.628^{20-4}$$

$= 0.0001 + 0.0011 + 0.0061 + 0.0216 + 0.0543 = 0.0832.$

d.   Substituting $p = 0.60$ for 0.372 in the calculations for part c., the resulting answer for Vericours is 0.0003.

e.   Given the probabilities in part c. and d., it would seem that the redemption rate is lower than either Vericours or TCA Fulfillment estimate.

5.47

a.   Minitab output

Tabulated statistics: Male-Female

Columns: Male-Female (M-F > 0) = "0" (M-F ≤ 0) = "1"

0	1	All
113	37	150
75.33	24.67	100.00

Cell Contents: Count
% of Row

b. $E(x) = np = 135(0.325) = 43.875.$

c.   Minitab output

Cumulative Distribution Function

Binomial with n = 135 and p = 0.325

$P(x \le 36) = 0.086047$

$P(x \ge 37) = 1 - P(x \le 36) = 1 - 0.086047 = 0.913953.$

d.   Since there is a very large probability that the outcome we observed or something larger would occur, it seems quite plausible that the Utah percentage agrees with that obtained by the Bureau of Labor Statistics.

5.49

a.   Minitab output

Columns: Months

0	1	All
26	9	35
74.29	25.71	100.00

Cell Contents: Count
% of Row

There were nine corporations that recovered their investment in analytics in 6 months or less.

b.   Minitab output

Binomial with n = 35 and p = 0.29

$P(x \le 9) = 0.414324$

c. Minitab output
     Inverse Cumulative Distribution Function
     Binomial with n = 35 and p = 0.29
          P(x ≤ 11) = 0.414324   P(x ≤ 12) = 0.811031
     From the output P(x ≤ 12) = 0.8110 > 0.70 and P(x ≥ 12) = 1 – P(x ≤ 11) = 1 – 0.6991 = 0.3009 > 1 – 0 > 70.
     Therefore by definition, the 70th percentile is 12.

Section 5-3 Exercises
5.51
a. You can find the desired probability using the following steps:
   Step 1: Define the segment unit.
         Because the mean was stated to be 3 arrivals per 15 minutes, the segment unit is 15 minutes or .25 hours.
   Step 2: Determine the mean of the random variable.
         The mean is $\lambda = 3$
   Step 3: Determine the segment size, t and then calculate λt.
         The issue in the problem asks for the probability of no customers arriving in 15 minutes which is one segment so t = 1. Thus, $\lambda t = (3)(1) = 3$
   Step 4: Define the event of interest and use the Poisson table to find the desired probability.
         The event of interest is:
              P(x = 0)
         To use the Poisson table, go to the column headed $\lambda t = 3$. Then find the value of x from the left hand column. The desired probability is:
              P(x = 0) = 0.0498
b. To determine the desired probability, you can use the following steps.
   Step 1: Define the segment unit.
         Because the mean was stated to be 3 arrivals per 15 minutes, the segment unit is 15 minutes or .25 hours.
   Step 2: Determine the mean of the random variable.
         The mean is $\lambda = 3$
   Step 3: Determine the segment size, t and then calculate λt.
         The issue in the problem asks for the probability of fewer than 3 customers arriving in 30 minutes which is two segments so t = 2. $\lambda t = (3)(2) = 6$
   Step 4: Define the event of interest and use the Poisson table to find the desired probability.
         We are asked to calculate the probability that fewer than 4 customers will arrive. Thus, the event of interest is:
              P(x ≤ 3)
         To use the Poisson table, go to the column headed $\lambda t = 6$. Then find the values of x from the left hand column. The desired probability is:
              P(x ≤ 3) = 0.1512

5.53   To determine this probability we recognize that because the sampling is without replacement and the sample size is large relative to the size of the population, the hypergeometric distribution applies. The following steps can be used:

Step 1: Define the population size and the combined sample size.

The population size is $N = 10$ and the combined sample size is $n = 3$

Step 2: Define the event of interest.

We are interested in the event described by getting

$$P(x = 2 \text{ } red \text{ } and \text{ } n - x = 1 \text{ } green) = ?$$

Step 3: Determine the number of each category in the population.

The population contains $X = 3$ red and $N-X = 7$ green.

Step 4: Compute the desired probability using the hypergeometric distribution.

$$P(x = 2) = \frac{C_{n-x}^{N-X} * C_x^X}{C_n^N} = \frac{C_{3-2}^{10-3} * C_2^3}{C_3^{10}} = \frac{C_1^7 * C_2^3}{C_3^{10}} = \frac{(7)(3)}{120} = \frac{21}{120} = 0.175$$

Thus, the probability of selecting 2 red and 1 green from a population with 3 red and 7 green is 0.175.

5.55

a.   **Step 1:** Determine the population size, N, and the sample size, n. The population size, N, is the number of manufacturing plants and is equal to 11. The sample size, n, is the number of plants selected for a performance evaluation and is equal to 4.

Step 2: Define the event of interest. The event of interest is the probability that exactly four plants outside the United States are included in the performance evaluation $P(x = 4)$

Step 3: Determine the number of successes in the population and the number of successes in the sample. In this case the number of successes in the population is the number of plants located outside the United States, which is 4. Therefore $X = 4$. The number of successes in the sample is the number of plants outside the United States included in the performance evaluation and is equal to 1. Therefore, $x = 1$.

Step 4: Compute the desired probability using the following equation:

$$P(x) = \frac{C_{n-x}^{N-X} * C_x^X}{C_n^N} = P(x = 1) = \frac{C_{4-1}^{11-4} * C_1^4}{C_4^{11}} = 0.4242$$

b.   **Step 1:** Determine the population size, N, and the sample size, n. The population size, N, is the number of manufacturing plants and is equal to 11. The sample size, n, is the number of plants selected for a performance evaluation and is equal to 4.

Step 2: Define the event of interest. The event of interest is the probability that exactly three plants in the United States are included in the performance evaluation $P(x = 3)$

Step 3: Determine the number of successes in the population and the number of successes in the sample. In this case the number of successes in the population is the number of plants located in the United States, which is 7. Therefore $X = 7$. The number of successes in the sample is the number of plants in the United States included in the performance evaluation and is equal to 3. Therefore, $x = 3$.

Step 4: Compute the desired probability using the following equation:

$$P(x) = \frac{C_{n-x}^{N-X} * C_x^X}{C_n^N} = P(x = 3) = \frac{C_{4-3}^{11-7} * C_3^7}{C_4^{11}} = 0.4242$$

c.   **Step 1:** Determine the population size, N, and the sample size, n. The population size, N, is the number of manufacturing plants and is equal to 11. The sample size, n, is the number of plants selected for a performance evaluation and is equal to 4.

Step 2: Define the event of interest. The event of interest is the probability that two or more plants outside the United States are included in the performance evaluation $P(x \geq 2)$

Step 3: Determine the number of successes in the population and the number of successes in the sample. In this case the number of successes in the population is the number of plants located outside the United States, which is 4. Therefore $X = 4$. The number of successes in the sample is the number of plants outside the United States included in the performance evaluation and is equal to 2 or more. Therefore, $x \geq 2$.

Step 4: Compute the desired probability using the following equation:
$P(x \geq 2) = P(x = 2) + P(x = 3) + P(x = 4)$, where

$$P(x) = \frac{C_{n-x}^{N-X} * C_x^X}{C_n^N}$$

$$P(x = 2) = \frac{C_{4-2}^{11-4} * C_2^4}{C_4^{11}} = 0.3818$$

$$P(x = 3) = \frac{C_{4-3}^{11-4} * C_3^4}{C_4^{11}} = 0.0848$$

$$P(x = 4) = \frac{C_{4-4}^{11-4} * C_4^4}{C_4^{11}} = 0.0030$$

Therefore, the $P(x \geq 2) = 0.4696$

5.57

a. $P(x = 3) = \frac{C_{n-x}^{N-X} C_x^X}{C_n^N} = \frac{C_{4-3}^{10-7} C_3^7}{C_4^{10}} = \frac{3(35)}{210} = 0.5$;

b. $P(x = 5) = 0$ since the sample size, n, is 4, the maximum number of successes is 4.

c. $P(X \geq 4) = P(X = 3) + P(X = 4) = 0.5 + \frac{C_{4-4}^{10-7} C_4^7}{C_4^{10}} = 0.5 + \frac{1(35)}{210} = 0.5 + 0.1667 = 0.6667$

d. Since $P(x > 3) = 0.1667$, $P(x > 2) = 0.5 + 0.1667 = 0.6667 > 0.25$; then x' = 2.

5.59 If the quality standards are being satisfied, the mean defects per sheet is 3.5. Thus the segment size is 1 sheet. However, the customer inspected 2 sheets (2 segments) so we have $\lambda t = (3.5)(2) = 7$. They discovered 10 defects in the two sheets and we are interested in the probability of ten or more defects as follows:

$$P(x \geq 10) = 1 - P(x \leq 9)$$

We go to the Poisson table and the column headed $\lambda t = 7$. Then find the values of x from the left-hand column as follows:

$$P(x \geq 10) = 1 - 0.8305 = 0.1695$$

There is a 0.1695 chance that 10 or more defects would be found in two sheets even though the average is supposed to be 7 defects in two sheets. Although this is not a high probability, it is certainly possible to see this result when the quality standards are being made. Thus, there is no cause to say that the quality does not meet the standards.

5.61 This is a situation in which the sampling will be performed without replacement from a finite population when the sample size is large relative to the population size. As such, the desired probability can be computed using the hypergeometric distribution. The event of interest is:

$$P(x_1 = 7, x_2 = 0, x_3 = 0) = \frac{C_{x_1}^{X_1} * C_{x_2}^{X_2} * C_{x_3}^{X_3}}{C_n^N} = \frac{C_7^{10} * C_0^5 * C_0^5}{C_7^{20}} = \frac{(120)(1)(1)}{77,520} = \frac{120}{77,520} = 0.0015$$

The probability of all seven stocks being "large caps" is 0.0015. This means that in only 15 chances in ten thousand would this happen due to chance so it is very likely that the sampling was not done using random selection as directed by the customer.

5.63

a. **Step 1:** Determine the population size and the combined sample size.
The population size and sample size are
N = 20 and n = 5.

Step 2: Define the event of interest.
The technician needs to determine
$P(x = 4)$.

Step 3: Determine the number of successes in the population and the number of successes in the sample.
In this situation, a success is the event that the technician selects a non-defective processor. There are $20 - 4 = 16$ ($= x$) successes in the population and 4 ($5 - 1 = x$) in the sample.

Step 4: Compute the desired probabilities using Equation 5-9.

$$P(x = 4) = \frac{C_{n-x}^{N-X} C_x^{SX}}{C_n^N} = \frac{C_{5-4}^{20-16} C_4^{16}}{C_5^{20}} = \frac{4(1820)}{15504} = 0.4696$$

b. $$P(x = 3) = \frac{C_{n-x}^{N-X} C_x^{X}}{C_n^N} = \frac{C_{5-3}^{20-16} C_3^{16}}{C_5^{20}} = \frac{6(560)}{15504} = 0.2167$$

c. The technician will have enough processors if he selects 3 or more non-defective processors. Thus, noting that

$$P(x = 5) = \frac{C_{5-5}^{20-16} C_5^{16}}{C_5^{20}} = \frac{1(4368)}{15504} = 0.2817$$

The probability is
$P(x \geq 3) = 0.4696 + 0.2167 + P(X = 5) = 0.6863 + 0.2817 = 0.9680$

5.65

a. The desired event can occur is they all select fruit trees or pine trees or maple trees. The probabilities of these outcomes are:

$$P(4,0,0) = \frac{C_4^{10} \bullet C_0^8 \bullet C_0^{14}}{C_4^{32}} = \frac{210 \bullet 1 \bullet 1}{35,960} = .0058$$

$$P(0,4,0) = \frac{C_0^{10} \bullet C_4^8 \bullet C_0^{14}}{C_4^{32}} = \frac{1 \bullet 70 \bullet 1}{35,960} = .0019$$

$$p(0,0,4) = \frac{C_0^{10} \bullet C_0^8 \bullet C_4^{14}}{C_4^{32}} = \frac{1 \bullet 1 \bullet 1,001}{35,960} = .0278$$

The overall probability is found by summing these: $.0058 + .0019 + .0278 = .0355$

b. $$P(0,3,1) = \frac{C_0^{10} \bullet C_3^8 \bullet C_1^{14}}{C_4^{32}} = \frac{1 \bullet 56 \bullet 14}{35,960} = .0218$$

c. $$P(0,2,2) = \frac{C_0^{10} \bullet C_2^8 \bullet C_2^{14}}{C_4^{32}} = \frac{1 \bullet 28 \bullet 91}{35,960} = .0709$$

5.67

    a.   The average demand for one hour is Poisson distributed with a mean of 50. Therefore the average demand over a two hour period is 2*50 = 100 which is also Poisson distributed. The probability that demand will exceed 115 is equal to 1-Probability (Demand $\leq$ 115) = 1-0.9368 = 0.0632.

    b.   The probability of running out of spicy hot dogs when 115 are stocked is 0.0632. Thus, the owner will have to stock more than 115. As the number stocked increases the probability of stocking out decreases. By stocking 120 spicy hot dogs the probability that demand will exceed supply is 0.02267, which is less than the desired probability of a stockout of 0.025. Note that the Probability (Demand $\leq$ 120) = 0.97733. The probability that demand will be greater than 120 is 1-0.97733 = 0.02267. By stocking 120 Spicy Dogs the probability of being out of hot dogs is less than 0.025.

5.69

    a. $P(x_1, x_2, x_3) = \dfrac{C_{x_1}^{S_1} C_{x_2}^{S_2} C_{x_3}^{S_3}}{C_n^N} = \dfrac{C_5^{15} C_3^{26} C_2^9}{C_{10}^{50}} = \dfrac{3003(2600)(36)}{10272278170} = 0.0274$

    b. $P(10,0,0) = \dfrac{C_{x_1}^{S_1} C_{x_2}^{S_2} C_{x_3}^{S_3}}{C_n^N} = \dfrac{C_{10}^{15} C_0^{26} C_0^9}{C_{10}^{50}} = \dfrac{3003(1)(1)}{10272278170} = 0.0000$

    c. $P(6,0,4) = \dfrac{C_{x_1}^{S_1} C_{x_2}^{S_2} C_{x_3}^{S_3}}{C_n^N} = \dfrac{C_6^{15} C_0^{26} C_4^9}{C_{10}^{50}} = \dfrac{5005(1)(126)}{10272278170} = 0.0001$

5.71

    a.   Minitab output
        Sum of Scratches
        Sum of Scratches = 8

    b.   **Step 1:** Define the segment unit. Since the company's goal is to have no more than an average of one scratch per set of pocket billiard balls and that sixteen balls are in a set, the segment unit is 16 balls.

        Step 2: Determine the mean of the random variable. One scratch per set of balls is the company's goal. Therefore, the mean will be $\lambda = 1$.

        Step 3: Determine the segment size t and then calculate λt. Since there are 16 balls per set, the 48 balls were that were selected is the same as 3 (48/16) sets of balls. So t = 3.

        So the average number per set would be $\lambda t = 1(3) = 3$.

    c.   **Step 4:** Define the event of interest and use the Poisson formula or the Poisson tables to find the probability.

        Here 8 scratches were observed. Since the 8 exceeds the expected number ($\lambda t = 1(3) = 3$), Cliff would want to find $P(X \geq 8)$ which we will obtain from Minitab:

            Cumulative Distribution Function
            Poisson with mean = 3
            x   P(X <= x)
            7   0.988095
            $P(X \geq 8) = 1 - P(X \leq 7) = 1 - 0.9881 = 0.0119$.

    d.   It is very unlikely that as many or more than 8 scratches would occur in 48 balls if the company's goal had been met. Therefore, we believe that the goal has not been met.

End of Chapter Exercises

5.73   As the sample size is increased for a given level of the probability of success, p, the probability distribution becomes more symmetric, or bell-shaped.

5.75
a. Let S_i = a success is obtained on the ith trial and F_i = a failure is obtained on the ith trial. $P(S_2|S_1) = \frac{1}{2}$. $P(S_2|F_1) = 2/2 = 1$. Thus, the probability of getting a success on the second trial depends upon what occurs on the first trial. This means the trials are dependent.
b. $P(S_1) = 2/3$.
    $P(S_2) = P[(S_1 \text{ and } S_2) \text{ or } (F_1 \text{ and } S2)] = P(S_1 \text{ and } S_2) + P(F_1 \text{ and } S2) = P(S_2|S_1)P(S_1) + P(S_2|F_1)P(F_1) = (1/2)(2/3) + (2/2)(1/3) = 2/3$, and
    $P(S_3) = P[(S_3 \text{ and } S_2 \text{ and } F_1) \text{ or } P(S_3 \text{ and } F_2 \text{ and } S_1)] = P(S_3 \text{ and } S_2 \text{ and } F_1) + P(S_3 \text{ and } F_2 \text{ and } S_1) = P(S_3| F_2 \text{ and } S_1)P(F_2 \text{ and } S_1) + P(S_3| S_2 \text{ and } F_1)P(S_2 \text{ and } F_1) = P(S_3| F_2 \text{ and } S_1)P(F_2| S_1)P(S_1) + P(S_3| S_2 \text{ and } F_1)P(S_2| F_1)P(F_1) = (1/1)(1/2)(2/3) + (1/1)(2/2)(1/3) = 2/3$.
    Therefore, the probability of a success is the same (2/3) for all three trials. This indicates that the probability of a success being constant does not imply that the trials are independent.

5.77
a. This means that the managing editor should expect to see 0.80 errors per ad. While most ads will not have an error, some will have as many as 4 errors.

X	P(x)	xP(x)
0	0.56	0.00
1	0.21	0.21
2	0.13	0.26
3	0.07	0.21
4	0.03	0.12
		0.80

b. standard deviation = 1.0954   Variance = 1.20

x	P(x)	xP(x)	x-E(x)	$[x-E(x)]^2$	$[x-E(x)]^2P(x)$
0	0.56	0.00	-0.8000	0.6400	0.3584
1	0.21	0.21	0.2000	0.0400	0.0084
2	0.13	0.26	1.2000	1.4400	0.1872
3	0.07	0.21	2.2000	4.8400	0.3388
4	0.03	0.12	3.2000	10.2400	0.3072
		0.80			1.2000

These values measure the variation in the number of printing errors from ad to ad in the newspaper.

5.79   n = 9 cans; p = .50 (if in control)
$P(x = 9) = P(x \le 9) - P(x \le 8) = 0.0020$
Thus, there is a 0.002 chance that this sample result would occur from a process that is in control. Because this is such a small probability, we would likely conclude that the process is not in control. The filling process tends to overfill.

5.81   Use the Hypergeometric distribution with: $P(x) = \dfrac{C_{n-x}^{N-X} \bullet C_x^X}{C_n^N}$

Then with N = 20; n = 4; X = 4; x = 0

$P(x \ge 1) = 1 - P(x = 0)$. $P(0) = \dfrac{C_{4-0}^{20-4} \bullet C_0^4}{C_4^{20}} = \dfrac{1,820 \bullet 1}{4,845} = .3756$.

1-0.3756 =0.6244.

5.83

x	P(x)	xP(x)
0	0.2	0
1	0.2	0.2
2	0.2	0.4
3	0.2	0.6
4	0.2	0.8
		2.0

a. The expected number of defectives is equal to 2. This means that on the average of several shipments Stafford Productions should expect the number of defectives to be 2. It does not mean that each shipment will have exactly 2 defects.

b.

X	P(x)	xP(x)	x-E(x)	$[x-E(x)]^2$	$[x-E(x)]^2P(x)$
0	0.2	0	-2	4	0.8
1	0.2	0.2	-1	1	0.2
2	0.2	0.4	0	0	0
3	0.2	0.6	1	1	0.2
4	0.2	0.8	2	4	0.8
		2			2

The standard deviation is equal to 1.4142. This is the square root of the average squared deviation from the mean. It is a measure of average deviation from the mean number of defective products based on the probability distribution.

c. This probability distribution is called a Uniform Distribution since the probability of each outcome is equally likely (0.2). Often times if there is no estimate or past history to base the probability on people will use the uniform distribution.

5.85

x	P(x)	xP(x)	x-E(x)	$[x-E(x)]^2$	$[x-E(x)]^2P(x)$
-1000	0.1	-100	(1,750)	3,062,500	306,250
0	0.1	0	(750)	562,500	56,250
500	0.3	150	(250)	62,500	18,750
1000	0.3	300	250	62,500	18,750
2000	0.2	400	1,250	1,562,500	312,500
		750			712,500

y	P(y)	yP(y)	y-E(y)	$[y-E(y)]^2$	$[y-E(y)]^2P(y)$
-1000	0.2	-200	(1,100)	1,210,000	242,000
0	0.4	0	(100)	10,000	4,000
500	0.3	150	400	160,000	48,000
1000	0.05	50	900	810,000	40,500
2000	0.05	100	1,900	3,610,000	180,500
		100			515,000

a. E(x) = 750; E(y) = 100
b. StDev(x) = 844.0972; StDev(y) = 717.635
c. CV(x) = 844.0972/750 = 1.1255
    CV(y) = 717.635/100 = 7.1764
d. Student answers will vary but they should comment on the fact that you cannot compare standard deviations of datasets with different means. They should be standardized by calculating the coefficient of variation. In this case it shows that the 2nd stock is actually more risky than the 1st stock.

5.87

a. Let x = the number of non-smoking rooms given to the tour guide.

$$P(x = 6) = \frac{C_{10-6}^{20-12} C_6^{12}}{C_{10}^{20}} = \frac{70(924)}{184756} = 0.3501$$

b. $P(x \leq 5) = 1 - P(x \geq 6) = 1 - P(x = 6) - P(x = 7) - P(X = 8) - P(X = 9) - P(x = 10)$

$$= 1 - 0.3501 - \frac{C_{10-7}^{20-12} C_7^{12}}{C_{10}^{20}} - \frac{C_{10-8}^{20-12} C_8^{12}}{C_{10}^{20}} - \frac{C_{10-9}^{20-12} C_9^{12}}{C_{10}^{20}} - \frac{C_{10-10}^{20-12} C_{10}^{12}}{C_{10}^{20}}$$

$$= 1 - 0.3501 - 0.2400 - 0.075 - 0.0095 - 0.0004 = 0.3250.$$

5.89

a. Minitab output

Sum of Defectives

Sum of Defectives = 38

So then proportion of defectives is 38/[20(90)] = 0.02.

b. $E(X) = \mu = np = 20(0.02) = 0.4$; $\sigma = \sqrt{npq} = \sqrt{20(0.02)(1-0.02)} = 0.6261$.

c. $\mu \pm \sigma = 0.4 \pm 3(0.6261) = (-1.4783, 2.2783)$. Since it is impossible to have a negative number here the limits are (0, 2.2783)

d. $P(0 \leq X \leq 2.2783) = P(0 \leq X \leq 2)$. So the probability that the number of defectives is beyond the control limits equals $1 - P(X \leq 2)$.

Using Minitab

Cumulative Distribution Function

Binomial with n = 20 and p = 0.02

x P(X <= x)

2   0.992931

So $1 - P(X \leq 2) = 1 - 0.9929 = 0.0071$.

Chapter 6
Introduction to Continuous Probability Distributions

Section 6-1 Exercises

6.1. The following steps are used to compute the z-values
   Step 1: Determine the mean and standard deviation
   Step 2: Determine the event of interest.
   Step 3: Convert the random variable to a standardized z-value using:

$$z = \frac{x - \mu}{\sigma}$$

   a. We are given the mean and standard deviation as follows: $\mu = 200$ and $\sigma = 20$
      The event of interest is x = 225

      We find the z-value using: $z = \frac{x - \mu}{\sigma} = \frac{225 - 200}{20} = \frac{25}{20} = 1.25$

   b. We are given the mean and standard deviation as follows: $\mu = 200$ and $\sigma = 20$
      The event of interest is x = 190

      We find the z-value using: $z = \frac{x - \mu}{\sigma} = \frac{190 - 200}{20} = \frac{-10}{20} = -0.50$

   c. We are given the mean and standard deviation as follows: $\mu = 200$ and $\sigma = 20$
      The event of interest is x = 240

      We find the z-value using: $z = \frac{x - \mu}{\sigma} = \frac{240 - 200}{20} = \frac{40}{20} = 2.00$

6.3.
   a. Use the normal distribution table
      $P(0.00 < z \leq 2.33) = .4901$
   b. $P(-1.00 < z \leq 1.00) = .3413 + .3413 = .6826$
   c. $P(1.78 < z < 2.34) = (.4904) - (.4625) = .0279$

6.5.
   a. $P(0 < z < 1.96) = 0.4750.$

   b. $P(z > 1.645) = 0.5 - \dfrac{0.4495 + 0.4505}{2} = 0.5 - 0.4500 = 0.05.$

   c. $P(1.28 < z \leq 2.33) = P(0 < z \leq 2.33) - P(0 < z \leq 1.28) = 0.4901 - 0.3997 = 0.0904$
   d. $P(-2 \leq z \leq 3) = P(-2 < z \leq 0) + P(0 < z \leq 3) = P(0 < z \leq 2) + P(0 < z \leq 3) = 0.4772 + 0.49865 = 0.97585.$
   e. $P(z > -1) = P(-1 < z \leq 0) + P(Z \geq 0) = P(0 < z \leq 1) + P(z \geq 0) = 0.3413 + 0.5000 = 0.8513.$

6.7.

   a. $P(0 < x < 8) = P\left(\dfrac{0-5}{2} < z < \dfrac{8-5}{2} \right) = P(-2.5 < z < 1.5) = P(-2.5 < z \leq 0) + P(0 \leq z < 1.5) = P(0 \leq z < 2.5) + P(0 \leq z \leq 1.5) = 0.4938 + 0.4332 = 0.9270.$

   b. $P(0 < x < 8) = P\left(\dfrac{0-5}{4} < z < \dfrac{8-5}{4} \right) = P(-1.25 < z < 0.75) = P(-1.25 < z \leq 0) + P(0 \leq z < 0.75) = P(0 \leq z < 1.25) + P(0 \leq z < 0.75) = 0.3944 + 0.2734 = 0.6678.$

c. $P(0 < x < 8) = P\left(\dfrac{0-3}{2} < z < \dfrac{8-3}{2}\right) = P(-1.50 < z < 2.50) = P(-1.50 < z \le 0) + P(0 \le z < 2.50) = P(0 \le z$

$< 1.50) + P(0 \le Z < 2.50) = 0.4322 + 0.4938 = 0.9260.$

d. $P(x > 1) = P\left(z > \dfrac{1-4}{3}\right) = P(z > -1) = P(-1 < z \le 0) + P(z \ge 0) = P(0 \le z \le 1) + P(z \ge 0) = 0.3413 + 0.5 =$

$0.8413.$

e. $P(x > 1) = P\left(z > \dfrac{1-0}{3}\right) = P(z > 0.33) = P(z \ge 0) - P(0 < z \le 0.33) = 0.5 - 0.1293 = 0.3707.$

6.9.

a. The following steps are used to compute the desired value of x
   Step 1: Determine the mean and standard deviation
   The mean and standard deviation are $\mu = 5.5$ and $\sigma = .50$
   Step 2: Determine the event of interest.
   We are interested in determining the value of x such that the probability of a value exceeding x is at most 0.10.
   Step 3: Determine the z-value corresponding to the known probability.
   The area in the upper tail of the distribution above x is defined to be 0.10. That means that the area between x and the population mean of 5.5 is 0.40. In Appendix D, we go to the inside of the table and locate the value 0.40 or just larger and determine the z-value associated with this probability. The closest probability is 0.4015. The z-value corresponding to this probability is z = 1.29.
   Step 4: Substitute the known values into the following equation:
   $$z = \dfrac{x - \mu}{\sigma}$$
   $$1.29 = \dfrac{x - 5.5}{.50}$$
   Step 5: Solve for x:
   $$x = 1.29(.50) + 5.5 = 6.145$$

b. We are asked to determine what the population mean must be if we want the following:
   $$P(x > 6.145) \le 0.05$$
   The following steps can be used to solve for the new population mean:
   Step 1: Determine the mean and standard deviation
   The mean and standard deviation are $\mu = 5.5$ and $\sigma = .50$
   Step 2: Determine the event of interest.
   We are interested in determining the value of μ such that the probability of a value exceeding 6.145 is at most 0.05: $P(x > 6.145) \le 0.05$.
   Step 3: Determine the z-value that corresponds to an upper tail area equal to 0.05.
   From the standard normal distribution table, we look for a probability on the inside of the table equal to 0.45 (or slightly larger) and determine the corresponding z-value. The closest probability is .4505. The z-value corresponding to this probability is 1.65. (Note, students could interpolate between 0.4495 and 0.4505 giving a z=1.645.)
   Step 4: Substitute the known values into the following equation:
   $$1.65 = \dfrac{6.145 - \mu}{.50}$$
   Step 5: Solve for μ
   $$\mu = 6.145 - (1.65)(.50) = 5.32$$
   Thus, the population mean must be reduced from 5.5 to 5.32 in order for the probability of a value exceeding 6.145 to be reduced from 0.10 to 0.05.

6.11.

a. $P(z > 2.78) = 0.5 - 0.4973 = 0.0027$

b. $P(z < -0.83) = 0.5 - 0.2967 = 0.2033$

   therefore, $P(x < 1,485) = 0.2033$

c. $P(z < -1.39) = 0.5 - 0.4177 = 0.0823$

   $P(z > 1.94) = 0.5 - 0.4738 = 0.0262$

   $P(x < 1,475 \text{ or } x > 1,535) = 0.0823 + 0.0262 = 0.1085$

6.13.

a. $P(z < -1.5) = 0.5 - 0.4332 = 0.0668$

   therefore, $P(x < 46.5) = 0.0668$

b. $P(z > 2.00) = 0.5 - 0.4772 = 0.0228$

   therefore, $P(x > 78) = 0.0228$

c. $P(-1 < z < 1.5) = 0.3413 + 0.4332 = 0.7745$

   therefore, $P(51 < x < 73.5) = 0.7745$

6.15. The mean and standard deviation of the random variable are 50 and 1.25, respectively.

a. $P(x < 49.5) = P(z < (49.5 - 50)/1.25 = P(z < -0.40) = 0.5 - 0.1554 = 0.3446$

b. $P(48.5 < z < 51) = P((48.5 - 50)/1.25 < z < (51 - 50)/1.25) = P(-1.2 < z < 0.8) = 0.3849 + 0.2881 = 0.6730$

c.   You want 15% in the upper tail of the standard normal distribution. Go to the body of the standard normal table and find the probability as close to 0.35 (0.5 - .15) as possible. This is 0.3508, therefore, z=1.04. Substituting known values into Formula 6.2 gives

$$1.04 = \frac{x - 50}{1.25}$$

Solving for x,

   $x = 50 + 1.04(1.25) = 51.30$

Therefore, the minimum weight a bag of dog food could be and remain in the top 15% of all bags filled is 51.3 kilograms.

d.   You want 2% in the upper tail of the standard normal distribution. Go to the body of the standard normal table and find the probability as close to 0.48 (0.5 - .02) as possible. This is essentially between 0.4798 and 0.4803, therefore, z is approximately 2.055. Substituting known values into Formula 6.2 gives

$$2.055 = \frac{52 - 50}{\sigma}$$

Solving for σ,

   $\sigma = (52-50)/2.055 = 0.9732$

Therefore, the standard deviation would need to be approximately 0.9732.

6.17.

a. $P(x>5000) = P(z > (5000 - 4300)/750) = P(z > 0.93) = 0.5 - 0.3238 = 0.1762$

b. $P(x<4000) = P(z < (4000 - 4300)/750) = P(z < -0.40) = 0.5 - 0.1554 = 0.3446$

c. $P(2500 < x < 4200) = P[(2500 - 4300)/750 < z < (4200 - 4300)/750] = P(-2.40 < z < -0.13) = 0.4918 - 0.0517 = 0.4401$

d. $P(x>5500) = P(z > (5500 - 4300)/750) = P(z > 1.6) = 0.5 - 0.4452 = 0.0548$

6.19. The mean and standard deviation of the random variable are 15,000 and 1,250, respectively.

a. $P(x \leq 13,000) = P(z < (13000-15000)/1250) = P(z < -1.6) = 0.5 - 0.4452 = 0.0548$

b. $P(x > 17,500) = P(z > (17500-15000)/1250) = P(z > 2) = 0.5 - 0.4772 = 0.0228$

c. You want 1% in the lower tail of the standard normal distribution. Go to the body of the standard normal table and find the probability as close to 0.49 (0.5 - .01) as possible. This is essentially between 0.4901, therefore, z is approximately -2.33.

Substituting known values into Formula 6.2 gives

$$-2.33 = \frac{13000 - \mu}{1,250}$$

Solving for μ,

μ = 13,000 + 2.33(1,250)

μ = 15,912 (approximately).

6.21. The objective here is to compute the population standard deviation. We start by using the information that tells us that:

$$P(x > 13,000) = 0.025$$

Assuming that the distribution is normal, we can determine the z-value associated with x = \$13,000 by going to the standard normal distribution table, looking to the inside where the probabilities are located and finding the value closest to $0.5000 - 0.025 = 0.475$. The z-value is z = 1.96.

Next, we solve for the population standard deviation using:

$$z = \frac{x - \mu}{\sigma}$$

Substituting for the values we know, we get:

$$1.96 = \frac{13,000 - 6,400}{\sigma}$$

Now, we solve for σ as follows:

$$\sigma = \frac{x - \mu}{z} = \frac{13,000 - 6,400}{1.96} = 3,367.35$$

Thus, the population standard deviation must be about \$3,367.35 indicating that there is substantial differences between teachers in terms of how much they contribute to the 403-B Annuity program.

6.23.

a. $P(x > 1500) = P\left(z > \frac{1500 - 1200}{350}\right) = P(z > 0.86) = 0.50 - P(0 \leq z \leq 0.86) = 0.5 - 0.3051 = 0.1949.$

b. $\mu \pm 2\sigma = 1200 \pm 2(350) = (500, 1900). P(500 \leq x \leq 1900) = P\left(\frac{500 - 1200}{350} \leq z \leq \frac{1900 - 1200}{350}\right) = P(-2$

$\leq z \leq 2) = P(-2 \leq z \leq 0) + P(0 \leq z \leq 2) = 2 P(0 \leq z \leq 2) = 2(0.4772) = 0.9544$

c. The median is the value, x_0, such that $P(x \leq x_0) = 0.5$. For a symmetric distribution such as the normal, this is also the characteristic of the mean. That is to say, that the mean and the median are the same for a normal distribution. Here the mean is \$1,200 and so is the median.

6.25. We are interested in the percentage of users who require less than 1 GB of storage capacity. This is:

$$P(x < 1.0) = ?$$

To find this probability, we start by converting the value x = 1.0 to its corresponding z-value using the following:

$$z = \frac{x - \mu}{\sigma} = \frac{1.0 - 1.95}{0.48} = -1.98$$

Next, we go to the standard normal distribution table in Appendix D to find the probability associated with z =-1.98. This is 0.4761. This is the probability between x = 1.0 and the mean. To find the desired probability, we subtract this probability from 0.50 as follows:

$$P(x < 1.0) = 0.5000 - 0.4761 = 0.0239$$

Thus, there is only a .0239 chance that a current I-Pod user would be currently storing less that 1.0 GB on their I-Pod player. This low probability compounded with the natural desire on the part of users to be sure they have enough capacity make this proposed new product a risky idea.

6.27.

a. The population is assumed to be normally distributed with a mean equal to 0.751 and a standard deviation equal to 0.004 inches. We are interested in the following:

$$P(0.747 \le x \le 0.753) = ?$$

We will use Excel's NORMDIST function to determine the probability of interest. We use the function as follows:

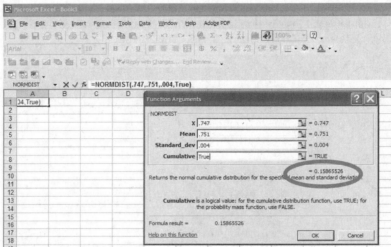

The circled value represents P(x < .747) = 0.1587. Next we use the NORMDIST function again as follows:

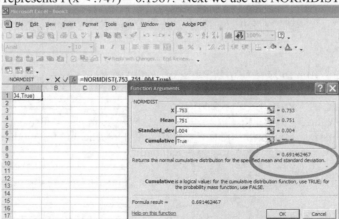

The circled value is P(x <0.753) = 0.6915. Now, to find the desired probability, we subtract the probabilities as follows:

$$P(0.747 \le x \le 0.7530 = 0.6915 - 0.1587 = 0.5378$$

Thus, the manager can expect approximately 53 percent of his product to meet the quality specifications. It is clear why he is worried.

b. First, it assumed that the population mean has been shifted to 0.75 inches. The question is, what must happen to the population standard deviation if the probability of meeting specifications is to be increased from 0.5328 to 0.98. To answer this question, we know that the lower specification limit equal to 0.747 and the upper specification of 0.753 are equidistant from the mean of 0.75 inches. Thus, the lower tail area and upper tails are equal have a probability of 0.01.

First, we determine the lower tail z-value that cuts off an area equal to 0.01 in the lower tail. We do this using Excel's NORMSINV function as follows:

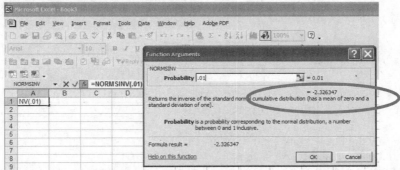

The z-value is -2.33. We know that the upper z-value will be a positive 2.33. Now we can solve for the population standard deviation using:

$$z = \frac{x - \mu}{\sigma}$$

Then:

$$2.33 = \frac{.753 - .75}{\sigma}$$

Solving for σ, we get:

$$\sigma = \frac{0.753 - 0.75}{2.33} = 0.001$$

Thus, the population standard deviation will have to be reduced from 0.004 to 0.001. This will be a challenge and require serious process improvement efforts.

6.29.

a.

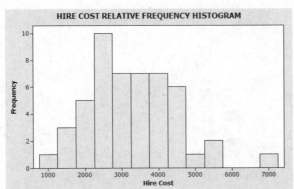

The histogram seems to be "bell shaped" with the exception of three or four observations. These could be due to sampling error.

b.

Descriptive Statistics: Hire Cost

```
Variable    Mean   StDev
Hire Cost   3270   1181
```

c.   The $P(2000 < x < 3000) = P\left(\dfrac{2000 - 3270}{1181} < z < \dfrac{3000 - 3270}{1181} \right) =$

$P(-1.08 < z < -0.23) = P(-1.08 \le z \le 0) - P(-0.23 \le z < 0) =$
$P(0 \le z < 1.08) - P(0 \le z \le 0.23) = 0.3599 - 0.0910 = 0.2689.$

d.   We wish to find the $P(x > 2500| \, 2000 < x < 3000).$
Using conditional probability, we have

$$\frac{P[(x > 2500) \text{ and } (2000 < x < 3000)]}{P(2000 < x < 3000)} = \frac{P(2500 < x < 3000)}{P(2000 < x < 3000)}.$$

We obtain $P(2500 < x < 3000) = P\left(\dfrac{2500 - 3270}{1181} < z < \dfrac{3000 - 3270}{1181} \right) =$

$P(-0.65 < z < -0.23) = P(-0.65 \le z \le 0) - P(-0.23 \le z < 0) =$
$P(0 \le z < 0.65) - P(0 \le z \le 0.23) = 0.2422 - 0.0910 = 0.1512.$

Then $P(x > 2500| \, 2000 < x < 3000) = \dfrac{P(2500 < x < 3000)}{P(2000 < x < 3000)} = \dfrac{0.1512}{0.2689} = 0.5623.$

6.31.

a.

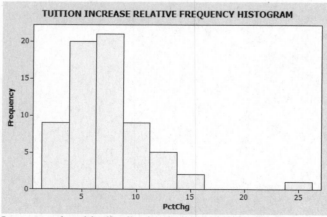

It appears that this distribution is skewed right.

b.

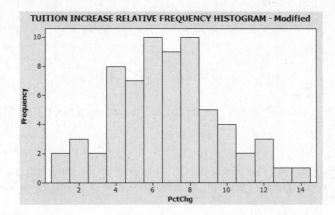

The histogram now seems to represent an approximate normal distribution.

c. $P(x > 10) = P\left(z > \dfrac{10 - 6.712}{2.842} \right) = P(z > 1.16) = 0.50 - P(0 \le z \le 1.16) =$

0.5 − 0.3770 = 0.1230.

Descriptive Statistics: PctChg

```
Variable   Mean   StDev
PctChg     6.712  2.842
```

d. $P(0 \le z \le 1.645) = P(-1.645 \le z \le 0) = 0.4500.$ $x_o = \mu + z_o \sigma$;
so $x_o = 6.712 + (-1.645)(2.842) = 2.034\%$.

Section 6-2

6.33.

a. $f(x) = \dfrac{1}{b-a} = \dfrac{1}{30-10} = 0.05$. $P(10 \le x \le 20) = f(x)(d- c) = 0.05(20 - 10) = 0.5$ and $P(15 \le x \le 25) =$
   $f(x)(d- c) = 0.05(25 - 15) = 0.5$ Using the Addition Rule for two events $P[(10 \le x \le 20)$ or $(15 \le x \le 25)] =$
   $P(10 \le x \le 20) + P(15 \le x \le 25) - P[(10 \le x \le 20)$ and $(15 \le x \le 25)] = P(10 \le x \le 20) + P(15 \le x \le 25) -$
   $P[(15 \le x \le 20)] = 0.5 + 0.5 - 0.05(20 - 15) = 0.75$.

b. $f(x) = \dfrac{1}{b-a} = \dfrac{1}{20-4} = 0.0625$.

   For the first quartile $.0625(Q_1 - 4) = .25$
                          $Q_1 = 4.25/.0625 = 8$
   For the second quartile $.0625(Q_2 - 4) = .50$
                          $Q_2 = 4.50/.0625 = 12$
   For the third quartile $.0625(Q_3 - 4) = .75$
                          $Q_3 = 4.75/.0625 = 16$

c.   The mean time between events equals $1/\lambda$. $P(0 \le x \le a) = 1 - e^{-\lambda a}$, so the median (Q_2) is derived from 0.50
   $= 1 - e^{-\lambda Q_2} = 1 - e^{-\lambda 10}$. Therefore $\lambda = [\ln(1 - 0.50)]/(-10) = 0.069$. So the mean time between events equals
   $1/\lambda = 1/0.069 = 14.43$.

   d.   The mean time between events = $1/\lambda$ = 0.4. Therefore, λ = 1/0.4 = 2.5. The 90th percentile is such that 0.90 = $1 - e^{-2.5x}$. Therefore x = $[\ln(1 - 0.90)]/(-2.5)$ = 0.92.

6.35.

   a.   Since $P(0 \leq x \leq a) = 1 - e^{-\lambda a}$, $P(x < 5) = P(0 \leq x \leq 5) = 1 - e^{-0.5(5)} = 1 - 0.0821 = 0.9179$

   b. $P(x > 6) = 1 - P(0 \leq x \leq 6) = 1 - [1 - e^{-0.5(6)}] = e^{-3} = 0.0498$.

   c. $P(5 \leq x \leq 6) = P(0 \leq x \leq 6) - P(0 \leq x \leq 5) = (1 - e^{-0.5(6)}) - (1 - e^{-0.5(5)})] = 0.9502 - 0.9179 = 0.0323$

   d. $P(x \geq 2) = 1 - P(0 \leq x \leq 2) = 1 - (1 - e^{-0.5(2)}) = 0.368$.

         The probability that x is at most 6 = $P(0 \leq x \leq 6)$ which was calculated in part c. to be $1 - e^{-0.5(6)}$ = 1 - 0.0498 = 0.9502

6.37.

   a.   Lambda is equal to 1/mean, so λ = 1/1.5 = 0.6667. The probability that the time between the next two calls is 45 seconds or less is computed by converting the 45 seconds to minutes (45/60) = 0.75. Therefore, a = 0.75. Probability $(x \leq 0.75) = 1 - e^{-(0.6667)(0.75)}$ = 1-0.6065 = 0.3935

   b.   In this case a = 112.5 seconds which is 112.5/60 = 1.875 minutes. Probability $(x \geq 112.5$ seconds$) = e^{-\lambda a} = e^{-(0.0.6667)(1.875)} = e^{-1.25} = 0.2865$.

6.39.

   a. $P(x>10) = (15-10)/(15-8) = 5/7 = 0.7143$

   b. $P(x<9) = (9-8)/(15-8) = 1/7 = 0.1429$

   c. $(0.1429)(0.1429) = 0.0204$

6.41. Students can use Excel's EXPONDIST function to solve this problem.

   a. λ = 1/4000 = .00025; $P(x<2100)$ = EXPONDIST(2100,0.00025,true) = 0.4084; Yes because this is a pretty high probability of a failure at less than 2100.

   b.   100,000(0.4084) = 40,840

6.43.

   a.   The average cost = $1/\lambda$ = 8,166. Therefore, λ = 1/8166 = 0.000122. Since $P(0 \leq X \leq a) = 1 - e^{-\lambda a}$, $P(x > 10,000) = 1 - P(0 \leq x \leq 10,000) = 1 - [1 - e^{-0.000122(10000)}]$ = 0.2939

   b. $P(X < 5,000) = P(0 \leq X \leq 5,000) = 1 - e^{-0.000122(5000)}$ = 1 - 0.5421 = 0.4579.

   c. $P(8,000 \leq x \leq 12,000) = P(0 \leq X \leq 12,000) - P(0 \leq X \leq 8,000) = [1 - e^{-0.000122(12000)}] - [1 - e^{-0.000122(8000)}] = (1 - 0.2313) - (1 - 0.3768) = 0.1455$.

6.45.

   a.   The average amount spent = $1/\lambda$ = 1,250. Therefore, λ = 1/1250 = 0.0008 = Since $P(0 \leq x \leq a) = 1 - e^{-\lambda a}$, $P(x > 5,000) = 1 - P(0 \leq x \leq 5,000) = 1 - [1 - e^{-0.0008(5000)}]$ = 0.0183

   b. $P(x > 1,250) = 1 - P(0 \leq x \leq 1,250) = 1 - [1 - e^{-0.0008(1250)}]$ = 0.3679.

   c.   For the exponential distribution the average = standard deviation = $1/\lambda$. Therefore, one standard deviation below the mean = 1,250 − 1,250 = 0. So this exercise is requiring $P(x > 0)$ = 1.

6.47.

   a.   Lambda is 0.75 and a is 4. Therefore, probability that the plant would run for 4 or more consecutive shifts without a knife related shutdown is equal to Probability $(x \geq 4) = e^{-\lambda a} = e^{-(0.75)(4)}$ = 0.0498.

   b.   With the computer decision model lambda becomes 0.20. Probability of operating 4 or more consecutive shifts without a knife related shutdown becomes: Probability $(x \geq 4) = e^{-\lambda a} = e^{-(0.2)(4)}$ = 0.4493. The decision model has drastically improved the probability of operating 4 or more consecutive shifts without a knife related shutdown over the current process. Without the decision model the process is very unlikely to operate 4 or more shifts without a knife related shutdown (0.0498). The decision model improves the probability to 0.4493. While this might seem low, it is substantially better than the current process.

   c.   The probability that the exponentially distributed random variable x is greater than or equal to a is $P(x \geq a) = e^{-\lambda a}$. Setting $e^{-\lambda a}$ = 0.70 and solving for x (given that a is 4) is approximately λ = 0.08917. The answer could also be found through trial and error using a spreadsheet, or a spreadsheet tool such as Goal Seek.

6.49.

a. Minitab output

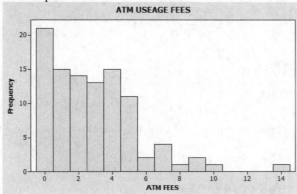

This histogram definitely has the shape of an exponential distribution being positively skewed, no data below 0, and a "ski slope" shape.

b. Minitab output

Descriptive Statistics: ATM FEES

```
Variable    Mean   StDev
ATM FEES    2.907   2.555
```

c.

Cumulative Distribution Function

```
Exponential with mean = 2.91

x    P( X <= x )
3       0.643324
```

Using the above Minitab results, P(X >3) = 1 – P(X ≤ 3) = 1 – 0.6433 = 0.3567.

Chapter Exercises

6.51.   A discrete distribution allows you to list the individual outcomes. A continuous distribution can take on any value over some range of values. It is impossible to list these values. One variable of interest that may be considered either continuous or discrete would be dollar values.

6.53.   The exponential distribution is defined by a sample parameter, its mean. It is not a symmetric distribution. Example will vary by student.

6.55.

a. The average = $1/\lambda$ = 0.5. Therefore, λ = 1/(0.5) = 2. Since P(0 ≤ X ≤ a) = $1 - e^{-\lambda a}$. P(X > 1) = 1 - P(0 ≤ X ≤ 1) = $1 - [1 - e^{-2(1)}] = e^{-2} = 0.1353$.

b. This is a conditional probability P(X > 1 + 2|X > 2) =
$$\frac{P[(X>3) \text{ and } (X>2)]}{P(X>2)} = \frac{P(X>3)}{P(X>2)} = \frac{1-[1-e^{-2(3)}]}{1-[1-e^{-2(2)}]} = \frac{e^{-2(3)}}{e^{-2(2)}} = e^{-2} = 0.1353.$$ So we see that the exponential distribution does have a "memoryless" property.

6.57. λ = 12/hour = 0.2 per minutes; P(x<4) = $1 - e^{-(.2)(4)}$ = 1 - 0.4493 = 0.5507

6.59.

Machine #1: P(11.9 $\leq$ x $\leq$ 12.0) = $P\left(\dfrac{11.9 - 11.9}{0.07} \leq z \leq \dfrac{12.0 - 11.9}{0.07} \right)$ =

P(0 $\leq$ z $\leq$ 1.43) = 0.4236.

Machine #2: P(11.9 $\leq$ x $\leq$ 12.0) = $P\left(\dfrac{11.9 - 12.0}{0.05} \leq z \leq \dfrac{12.0 - 12.0}{0.05} \right)$ =

P(-2 $\leq$ z $\leq$ 0) = P(0 $\leq$ z $\leq$ 2) = 0.4772.
There is a larger probability of producing acceptable amounts of dispensed liquid with Machine #2. It should be selected.

6.61.
a.   The average = 1/λ = 1. Therefore, λ = 1. Since P(0 $\leq$ x $\leq$ a) =
     $1 - e^{-\lambda a}$ P(x > 3) = 1 - P(0 $\leq$ x $\leq$ 3) = $1 - [1 - e^{-1(3)}] = e^{-3}$ = 0.0498.
b.   Let x = the number of products that last longer than 3 years = binomial random variable with p = 0.0498 and n = 2.

So (x $\geq$ 1) = 1 - P(x = 0) = $1 - \left(\dfrac{2!}{0!2!} \right) 0.0498^{0} (1 - 0.0498)^{2-0}$ =

   1 - 1(1.0)(0.9502)^2 = 1- 0.9029 = 0.0971.
c.   P(x > 1) = 1 - P(0 $\leq$ x $\leq$ 1) = $1 - [1 - e^{-1(1)}] = e^{-1}$ = 0.3679.

$$P(x > 3 | x > 1) = \frac{P[(x > 3) \text{ and } (x > 1)]}{P(x > 1)} = \frac{P(x > 3)}{P(x > 1)} = \frac{0.0498}{0.3679} = 0.1354$$

6.63.
a.   The range is 0.25 $\pm$ 0.10 = (0.15, 0.35). We calculate f(x) = 1/(b − a) = 1/(0.35 − 0.15) = 5.
b.   "More than 0.05 of an inch below the mean" means less than 0.20. Therefore, P(0.15 $\leq$ x $\leq$ 0.20) = f(x)(d - c) = 5(0.20 − 0.15) = 0. 25.
c.   "More than 0.075 above the mean" means more than 0.25 + 0.075 = 0.325. Therefore, P(x > 0.325) = P(0.325 $\leq$ x $\leq$ 0.35) = f(x)(d - c) = 5(0.35 − 0.325) = 0.125.

d. $P(x > 0.325 | x > 0.2) = \dfrac{P[(x > 0.325) \text{ and } (x > 0.2)]}{P(x > 0.2)} = \dfrac{P(x > 0.325)}{P(x > 0.2)} = \dfrac{0.125}{0.75} = 0.167$

6.65.

P(x>74) = P(z > (74 − 58)/14) = P(z > 1.14) = 0.5 − 0.3729 = 0.1271
P(x>90) = P(z > (90 − 58)/14) = P(z > 2.29) = 0.5 − 0.489 = 0.011
Only 1.1 percent of the employees could be expected to take more sick leave than the second employee. That employee has taken excessive sick leave. The first employee took more sick leave than 87.29 percent of the employees. The office manager would have to decide whether this is to be considered excessive.

6.67.
  a.

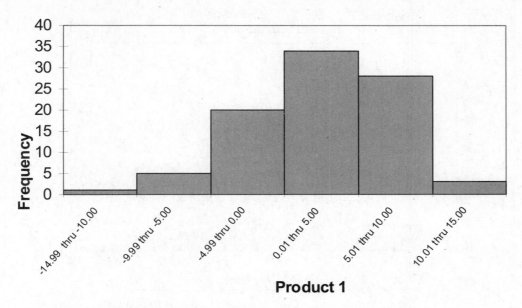

Product 1

It does appear that the distribution is approximately normally distributed.

b.   Students can use Excel's descriptive statistics to determine the mean and standard deviation.

Product # 1	
Mean	2.452747253
Standard Error	0.500820671
Median	2.6
Mode	0.9
Standard Deviation	4.777524711
Sample Variance	22.82474237
Kurtosis	1.325755364
Skewness	-0.643107821
Range	29.2
Minimum	-15.5
Maximum	13.7
Sum	223.2
Count	91

c.   Remember that positive values indicate weight gain so students need to determine the Probability that the weight loss is more than negative 12.
$P(x<-12) = P(z < (-12 - 2.4527)/4.7775) = P(z < -3.03) = 0.5 - 0.4988 = 0.0012$

d.   No, this would not be an appropriate claim. The probability of losing 12 or more pounds is only 0.12%. In fact the average for this product in a weight gain of 2.45 pounds.

6.69.
   a.   Minitab output

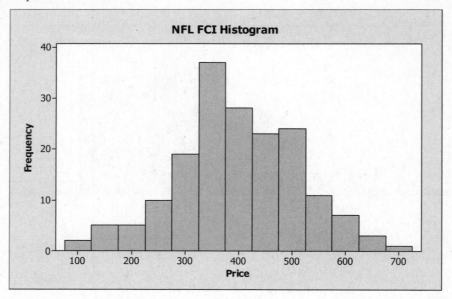

The histogram seems to be "bell shaped" with the exception of a few observations. These could be due to sampling error.
   b.   Minitab output:
   Descriptive Statistics: Price
```
Variable     Mean    StDev
Price      396.36   112.41
```

   c.   Minitab output:
   Inverse Cumulative Distribution Function

```
Normal with mean = 396.36 and standard deviation = 112.41
P( X <= x )        x
        0.9   540.419
```

   The 90th percentile is 540.419
   d.   Minitab output:
   Cumulative Distribution Function

```
Normal with mean = 396.36 and standard deviation = 112.41


       x  P( X <= x )
  376.71     0.430616
```

   So 376.71 is the 43rd percentile.

6.71. Minitab is used to solve this problem.

    a.   Minitab output:

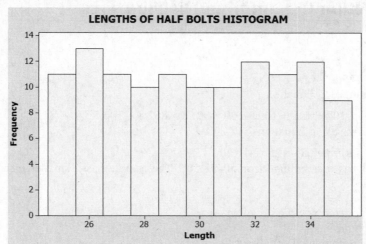

        The frequency for each difference seems to be very close to the same, a characteristic of a uniform distribution. Sampling error could account for differences in this sample.

    b.   The range of values are from 24.8 to 35. In minutes,

$$f(x) = \frac{1}{b-a} = \frac{1}{35-24.8} = 0.098.$$

    c.   The amount of cloth required is 8(3.8) = 30.4.

        Minitab output:

            Continuous uniform on 24.8 to 35

             x P(X <= x)

          30.4   0.549020

        Therefore, the $P(X \geq 30.4) = 1 - 0.549 = 0.451$.

Chapter 7
Introduction to Sampling Distributions

Section 7-1 Exercises

7.1. **Step 1:** The population mean of 125 is given

Step 2: Compute the sample mean using Equation 7-3

$$\bar{x} = (103 + 123 + 99 + 107 + 121 + 100 + 100 + 99)/8 = 852/8 = 106.5$$

Step 3: Compute the sampling error using Equation 7-1

Sampling Error = $\bar{x} - \mu = 106.5 - 125 = -18.50$

The sample of eight has a sampling error of -18.50. The sample has a smaller mean than the population as a whole.

7.3. The following steps can be used to determine the sampling error:

Step 1: Determine the population mean.

The population mean is computed as follows:

$$\mu = \frac{\sum x}{N} = \frac{273}{24} = 11.38$$

Step 2: Compute the sample mean.

$$\bar{x} = \frac{\sum x}{n} = \frac{61}{6} = 10.17$$

Step 3: Compute the sampling error.

Sampling error = $\bar{x} - \mu = 10.17 - 11.38 = -1.21$

7.5.

a. **Step 1:** Compute the population mean using Equation 7-2.

μ= 10+14+32+9+34+19+31+24+33+11+14+30+6+27+33+32+28+30+ 10+31+19+13+6+35)/24 = 531/24 = 22.125

Step 2: Compute the sample mean using Equation 7-3

$$\bar{x} = (32+19+6+11+10+19+28+9+13+33)/10 = 180/10 = 18$$

Step 3: Compute the sampling error using Equation 7-1

Sampling Error = $\bar{x} - \mu = 18 - 22.125 = -4.125$

The sample of ten has a sampling error of -4.125. The sample has a smaller mean than the population as a whole.

For parts (b) and (c), the population rank order is shown below.

6	6	9	10	10	11	13	14
14	19	19	24	27	28	30	30
31	31	32	32	33	33	34	35

b. In order to calculate the extreme sampling error, the data needs to be rank-ordered from lowest to highest. Use the rank-order table shown above. Calculate the sample mean for the 6 smallest values and the 6 largest values. Compute the sampling error for each.

Lowest Possible Sample Mean = (6+6+9+10+10+11)/6 = 52/6 = 8.667

The population mean is 22.125 from part (a).

Sampling Error = 8.667 - 22.125 = -13.458

Highest Possible Sample Mean = (32+32+33+33+34+35)/6 = 199/6 = 33.167

Sampling Error = 33.167 - 22.125 = 11.042

The range of extreme sampling error for a sample of size n = 6 is -13.458 to 11.042.

c. In order to calculate the extreme sampling error, the data needs to be rank-ordered from lowest to highest. Use the rank-order table shown above. Calculate the sample mean for the 12 smallest values and the 12 largest values. Compute the sampling error for each.
Lowest Possible Sample Mean = (6+6+9+10+10+11+13+14+14+
19+19+24)/12 = 155/12 = 12.917
The population mean is 22.125 from part (a).
Sampling Error = 12.917 - 22.125 = -9.208
Highest Possible Sample Mean = (27+28+30+30+31+31+32+32+33+33+34+35)/12 = 376/12 = 31.333
Sampling Error = 31.333 – 22.125 = 9.208
The range of extreme sampling error for a sample of size n = 12 is –9.208 to 9.208.
As the sample size increases, the range of sampling error decreases.

7.7.

a. $\mu = \dfrac{\sum x_i}{N} = \dfrac{18}{3} = 6.$

b.

Data		Mean
3	3	3
3	6	4.5
3	9	6
6	3	4.5
6	6	6
6	9	7.5
9	3	6
9	6	7.5
9	9	9

c.

Means	3	4.5	6	4.5	6	7.5	6	7.5	9
Sampling Error	-3	-1.5	0	-1.5	0	1.5	0	1.5	3

d. Each sample, and, therefore, each sampling error, is equally likely with probability 1/9.Thus, P(SE = -3) = P(SE = 3) = 1/9, P(SE = -1/5) = P(SE = 1.5) = 2/9, and P(SE = 0) = 3/9. The distribution is, therefore,

SE	Prob.
-3	.1111
-1.5	.2222
0	.3333
1.5	.2222
3	.1111

7.9. **Step 1:** Determine the population mean:
μ = 6.16 (from CDC)
Step 2: Compute the sample mean using Equation 7-3:

$$\bar{x} = \frac{\sum x_i}{n} = \frac{340}{50} = 6.8.$$

Step 3: Compute the sampling error using Equation 7-1:
Sampling error = $\bar{x} - \mu$ = 6.8 – 6.16 = 0.64.

7.11.

a. $\mu = \dfrac{\sum x}{N} = \dfrac{864}{20} = 43.20$ days

b. $\bar{x} = \dfrac{\sum x}{n} = \dfrac{206}{5} = 41.20$ days
Sampling error = 41.20 - 43.20 = -2 days

    c.   The smallest 5 values that could be in a sample are:

$$7 \quad 15 \quad 16 \quad 17 \quad 19 \qquad \bar{x} = \frac{\sum x}{n} = \frac{74}{5} = 14.8$$

The sampling error = 14.8 - 43.20 = -28.4 days
The largest 5 values that could be in a sample are:

$$107 \quad 88 \quad 80 \quad 77 \quad 66 \qquad \bar{x} = \frac{\sum x}{n} = \frac{418}{5} = 83.6$$

The sampling error = 83.6 – 43.2 = 40.4 days
The range in sampling error is from – 28.4 days to 40.4 days.

7.13.

    a. $\bar{x} = \dfrac{\sum x_i}{n} = \dfrac{68906}{20} = \$3445.30.$

    b.   Sampling error = $\bar{x} - \mu$ = 3445.30 – 3475 = -\$29.70

    c.   The sample mean (3445.30) is smaller than the presumed population mean (3475). If there is not sampling error, the average cruise fare has been reduced by the mentioned discounters. If not, an increase has not occurred. To determine which is correct, the entire population would have to be censused.

7.15.

    a. μ = 35,802/25 = 1,432.08

    b. $\bar{x}$ = 7,596/5 = 1,591.2
       Sampling error = 1,591.2 – 1,432.08 = 87.12

    c.   The population rank-order is shown below

1093	1134	1216	1291	1347
1350	1362	1362	1365	1371
1378	1410	1446	1447	1453
1480	1500	1522	1532	1534
1552	1575	1601	1647	1834

Lowest Possible Sample Mean = 8,793/7 = 1,256.143
Sampling Error = 1,256.143 – 1,432.08 = -175.937
Highest Possible Sample Mean = 11,275/7 = 1,610.714
Sampling Error = 1,610.714 – 1,432.08 = 178.634
The range of extreme sampling error for a sample of size n = 7 is -175.937 to 178.634.

7.17.

    a.   Minitab output:

Mean of Sales

`Mean of Sales = 2764.83`

    b.   Minitab output:

Mean of Sample

`Mean of Sample = 2797.16`

    c.   The sampling error = $\bar{x} - \mu$ = 2797.16 – 2764.83 = \$32.33 million.

d. The 25 smallest sales figures yields the following mean (in millions $)

Mean of Small Data

```
Mean of Small Data = 2594.36
```

Therefore, the smallest sampling error = $\bar{x} - \mu$ = 2594.36 – 2764.83 = -$170.47

The 25 largest sales figures yields the following mean (in millions $)

Mean of Large Data

```
Mean of Large Data = 2983.24
```

Therefore, the largest sampling error = $\bar{x} - \mu$ = 2983.24 – 2764.83 = $218.41

7.19

a. Either Excel or Minitab could be used to compute the sample mean potential value for each log diameter. We have used Excel's pivot table feature to get the following:

Diameter	Mean Value
6	$7.90
7	$11.13
8	$16.55
9	$21.54
10	$28.87
11	$35.40
12	$41.80
13	$48.54
14	$58.86
15	$65.97
16	$76.48
17	$85.33
18	$93.63
19	$105.01
20	$109.89
21	$120.31

b. assuming that the sample means calculated in part a. are based on a random sample from the population of all logs to be used by the company, there is no way to predict with any certainty what the sampling error is. To do so would require that we know the true population mean. Also, we cannot predict with accuracy whether the sample means are higher or lower than the true population mean.

7.21.

a. The first step is compute the sample mean based on the data in the file called Badke, Either Excel or Minitab can be used to get:

$$\bar{x} = \frac{\sum x}{n} = \frac{\$2,629}{166} = \$15.84$$

Because the consultant claimed that the mean would be $20.00, we use that as the population mean. If that number is correct, then this sample has a sampling error of:

Sampling error = $\bar{x} - \mu = \$15.84 - \$20.00 = -\$4.16$

b. It is possible that this sample constitutes a random sample. However, there is no was to be assured of that. We don't have any way of knowing if the people who contributed are a random selection of all those who would eventually contribute. We don't know what process was used to distribute the letter and materials in the first place. However, that being said, the computation of sampling error does not depend on whether the sample is a random sample. Random and non-random samples can produce sampling error and the error is computed the same way.

Section 7-2 Exercises

7.23. Because the population is normally distributed, the sampling distribution for the mean will also be normally distributed. Thus, the following steps can be used to answer this question:

   Step 1: Determine the sample mean.

   The sample mean is given to be $\overline{x} = 2,100$

   Step 2: Define the sampling distribution.

   The sampling distribution will be normally distributed and will have $\mu_{\overline{x}} = \mu = 2000$ and a

standard deviation equal to $\sigma_{\overline{x}} = \dfrac{\sigma}{\sqrt{n}} = \dfrac{230}{\sqrt{8}} = 81.32$

   Step 3: Define the event of interest.

   We are interested in the following:
   $$P(\overline{x} > 2,100) = ?$$

   Step 4: Convert the sample mean to a standardized z value.

   $$z = \frac{\overline{x} - \mu}{\dfrac{\sigma}{\sqrt{n}}} = \frac{2,100 - 2,000}{\dfrac{230}{\sqrt{8}}} = \frac{100}{81.32} = 1.23$$

   Step 5: Use the standard normal distribution to find the desired probability.

   The probability associated with a z-value of 1.23 from the standard normal table is 0.3907. Then
   $$P(\overline{x} > 2,100) = 0.5000 - 0.3907 = 0.1093$$

Thus, there is slightly more than a 0.10 chance that a sample mean exceeding 2,100 would come from this population if a sample size of n = 8 is selected.

7.25. The sampling distribution of $\overline{x}$ will be normally distributed with $\mu_{\overline{x}} = \mu = 250$ and a standard deviation

equal to $\sigma_{\overline{x}} = \dfrac{\sigma}{\sqrt{n}} = \dfrac{40}{\sqrt{25}} = 8$

7.27. $P(\overline{x} > 200) = P(z > (200 - 195)/[(20/\sqrt{100})\sqrt{(350-100)/(350-1)}] = P(z > 2.95) = 0.5 - 0.4984 = 0.0016$

7.29.

   a. $P(\overline{x} > 36) = P(x > 36)$ when n = 1. Therefore, $P(\overline{x} > 36) = P(x > \dfrac{36 - 12}{90}) = P(z > P(z > 0.27) = 0.5 -$

   $P(0 \leq z \leq 0.27) = 0.5 - 0.1064 = 0.3936$

   b. $P(\overline{x} > \overline{x}_0) = P\left(z > \dfrac{\overline{x}_0 - \mu}{\sigma/\sqrt{n}}\right)$. So $P(\overline{x} > 36) = P\left(z > \dfrac{36 - 12}{90/\sqrt{9}}\right) = P(z > 0.8) = 0.5 - P(0 \leq z \leq 0.8) =$

   $0.5 - 0.2881 = 0.2119.$

   c. $P(\overline{x} > 36) = P\left(z > \dfrac{36 - 12}{90/\sqrt{16}}\right) = P(z > 1.07) = 0.5 - P(0 \leq z \leq 1.07) = 0.5 - 0.3577 = 0.1423.$

   d. $P(\overline{x} > 36) = P\left(z > \dfrac{36 - 12}{90/\sqrt{25}}\right) = P(z > 1.33) = 0.5 - P(0 \leq z \leq 1.33) = 0.5 - 0.4082 = 0.0918.$

7.31.

a. **Step 1:** Compute the sample mean. The sample mean is $\bar{x} = \dfrac{\Sigma x}{n} = \dfrac{450}{36} = 12.5$.

Step 2: Define the sampling distribution. If the population is approximately normally distributed with a mean of 12 and a standard deviation of 3, the sampling distribution is also approximately normally distributed with

$$\mu_{\bar{x}} = \mu = 12 \text{ and } \sigma_{\bar{x}} = \frac{\sigma}{\sqrt{n}} = \frac{3}{\sqrt{36}} = 0.50.$$

Step 3: Define the event of interest. The event of interest is: $P(\bar{X} \le 12.5)$

Step 4: Convert the sample mean to a standardized z value.

$$z = \frac{\bar{x} - \mu}{\dfrac{\sigma}{\sqrt{n}}} = \frac{12.5 - 12}{\dfrac{3}{\sqrt{36}}} = 1.00 \,.$$

Step 5: Use the standard normal distribution to find the desired probability. From the standard normal table $P(0 \le z \le 1.00) = 0.3413$. Therefore, $P(\bar{X} \le 12.5) = P(z \le 1.00) = 0.50 + 0.3413 = 0.8413$.

b. **Step 1:** Compute the sample mean. The sample mean is $\bar{x} = \dfrac{\Sigma x}{n} = \dfrac{450}{36} = 12.5$.

Step 2: Define the sampling distribution. If the population is approximately normally distributed with a mean of 12 and a standard deviation of 3, the sampling distribution is also approximately normally distributed with

$$\mu_{\bar{x}} = \mu = 12 \text{ and } \sigma_{\bar{x}} = \frac{\sigma}{\sqrt{n}} = \frac{3}{\sqrt{36}} = 0.50.$$

Step 3: Define the event of interest. The event of interest is: $P(\bar{X} > 12.5)$

Step 4: Convert the sample mean to a standardized z value.

$$z = \frac{\bar{x} - \mu}{\dfrac{\sigma}{\sqrt{n}}} = \frac{12.5 - 12}{\dfrac{3}{\sqrt{36}}} = 1.00 \,.$$

Step 5: Use the standard normal distribution to find the desired probability. From the standard normal table $P(0 \le z = 1.00) = 0.3413$. Therefore, $P(\bar{X} > 12.5) = P(z > 1.00) = 0.50 - 0.3413 = 0.1587$.

c. Although the population of returns processed daily is not normally distributed, the sample size is sufficiently large so that the sampling distribution of $\bar{X}$ is normally distributed. In other words, the Central Limit Theorem applies here because the sample size, n=36, is sufficiently large so that the distribution of sample means $\bar{X}$ will be approximately normally distributed.

7.33.

a. **Step 1:** Compute the sample mean. In this case there are two sample means: $\bar{x} = 70$ and $\bar{x} = 80$.

Step 2: Define the sampling distribution. The population is approximately normally distributed with a mean of 75 and a standard deviation of 10. Therefore, the sampling distribution is also approximately normally distributed with

$$\mu_{\bar{x}} = \mu = 75 \text{ and } \sigma_{\bar{x}} = \frac{\sigma}{\sqrt{n}} = \frac{10}{\sqrt{1}} = 10.$$

Step 3: Define the event of interest. The event of interest is: $P(70 \le \bar{x} \le 80)$

Step 4: Convert the sample mean to a standardized z value.

$$z = \frac{\bar{x} - \mu}{\dfrac{\sigma}{\sqrt{n}}} = \frac{70 - 75}{\dfrac{10}{\sqrt{1}}} = -0.50 \text{ , and } \frac{\bar{x} - \mu}{\dfrac{\sigma}{\sqrt{n}}} = \frac{80 - 75}{\dfrac{10}{\sqrt{1}}} = 0.50 .$$

Step 5: Use the standard normal distribution to find the desired probability. From the standard normal table

$P(0 \le z \le 0.50) = 0.1915$. Therefore, $P(70 \le \bar{x} \le 80) = P(-0.50 \le z \le 0.50) = 0.1915 + 0.1915 = 0.3830$.

b. **Step 1:** Compute the sample mean. In this case there are two sample means: $\bar{x} = 70$ and $\bar{x} = 80$.

Step 2: Define the sampling distribution. The population is approximately normally distributed with a mean of 75 and a standard deviation of 10. Therefore, the sampling distribution is also approximately normally distributed with

$$\mu_{\bar{x}} = \mu = 75 \text{ and } \sigma_{\bar{x}} = \frac{\sigma}{\sqrt{n}} = \frac{10}{\sqrt{16}} = 2.5.$$

Step 3: Define the event of interest. The event of interest is: $P(70 \le \bar{x} \le 80)$

Step 4: Convert the sample mean to a standardized z value.

$$z = \frac{\bar{x} - \mu}{\dfrac{\sigma}{\sqrt{n}}} = \frac{70 - 75}{\dfrac{10}{\sqrt{16}}} = -2.00 \text{ , and } \frac{\bar{x} - \mu}{\dfrac{\sigma}{\sqrt{n}}} = \frac{80 - 75}{\dfrac{10}{\sqrt{16}}} = 2.00 .$$

Step 5: Use the standard normal distribution to find the desired probability. From the standard normal

table $P(0 \le z \le 2.00) = 0.4772$. Therefore, $P(70 \le \bar{x} \le 80) = P(-2.00 \le z \le 2.00) = 0.4722 + 0.4722 = 0.9444$.

c. **Step 1:** Compute the sample mean. In this case there are two sample means: $\bar{x} = 70$ and $\bar{x} = 80$.

Step 2: Define the sampling distribution. The population is approximately normally distributed with a mean of 75 and a standard deviation of 9. Therefore, the sampling distribution is also approximately normally distributed with

$$\mu_{\bar{x}} = \mu = 75 \text{ and } \sigma_{\bar{x}} = \frac{\sigma}{\sqrt{n}} = \frac{9}{\sqrt{16}} = 2.25.$$

Step 3: Define the event of interest. The event of interest is: $P(70 \le \bar{x} \le 80)$

Step 4: Convert the sample mean to a standardized z value.

$$z = \frac{\bar{x} - \mu}{\dfrac{\sigma}{\sqrt{n}}} = \frac{70 - 75}{\dfrac{9}{\sqrt{16}}} = -2.22 \text{ , and } \frac{\bar{x} - \mu}{\dfrac{\sigma}{\sqrt{n}}} = \frac{80 - 75}{\dfrac{9}{\sqrt{16}}} = 2.22 .$$

Step 5: Use the standard normal distribution to find the desired probability.

From the standard normal table $P(0 \le z \le 2.22) = 0.4868$. Therefore, $P(70 \le \bar{x} \le 80) = P(-2.22 \le z \le 2.22) = 0.4868 + 0.4868 = 0.9736$.

7.35. The following steps can be used to answer this question:
  Step 1: Determine the sample mean.
    The sample mean was calculated to be 4.2 minutes
  Step 2: Define the sampling distribution.
    The sampling distribution will be normally distributed and will have $\mu_x = \mu = 4.2$ and a standard deviation equal to

$$\sigma_x = \frac{\sigma}{\sqrt{n}} = \frac{1.0}{\sqrt{25}} = 0.2$$

  Step 3: Define the event of interest.
    We are interested in the following:

$$P(\overline{x} > 4.2) = ?$$

  Step 4: Convert the sample mean to a standardized z value.

$$z = \frac{\overline{x} - \mu}{\dfrac{\sigma}{\sqrt{n}}} = \frac{4.2 - 3.5}{\dfrac{1}{\sqrt{25}}} = \frac{0.7}{0.2} = 3.5$$

  Step 5: Use the standard normal distribution to find the desired probability.
    The probability associated with a z-value of 3.5 from the standard normal table is approximately 0.4989. Then

$$P(\overline{x} \geq 4.2) = 0.5000 - 0.4989 = 0.0011$$

Thus, there virtually no chance that a random sample of size 25 could produce a sample mean equal to 4.2 or greater if the sample came from a population with mean equal to 3.5 and standard deviation equal to 1.0. Either sample was not randomly selected, or the population parameters are misstated. The manager should be concerned that the waiting time has increased.

7.37. The following steps can be used to answer this question:
  Step 1: Determine the sample mean.

$$\overline{x} = \frac{\sum x}{n} = \frac{469}{14} = 33.5$$

  Step 2: Define the sampling distribution.
    The sampling distribution will be normally distributed and will have $\mu_{\overline{x}} = \mu = 34.3$ and a

standard deviation equal to $\sigma_x = \dfrac{\sigma}{\sqrt{n}} = \dfrac{5.7}{\sqrt{14}} = 1.52$

  Step 3: Define the event of interest.
    We are interested in the following:

$$P(\overline{x} \leq 33.5) = ?$$

  Step 4: Convert the sample mean to a standardized z value.

$$z = \frac{\overline{x} - \mu}{\dfrac{\sigma}{\sqrt{n}}} = \frac{33.5 - 34.3}{\dfrac{5.7}{\sqrt{14}}} = \frac{-0.8}{1.52} = -0.53$$

  Step 5: Use the standard normal distribution to find the desired probability.
    The probability associated with a z-value of -0.53 from the standard normal table is 0.2019 Then

$$P(\overline{x} \leq 33.5) = 0.5000 - 0.2019 = 0.2981$$

Thus, there is slightly less than a 30% chance that a random sample of size 14 could produce a sample mean equal to 33.5 or less if the sample came from a population with mean equal to 34.3 and standard deviation equal to 5.7.   The organization would probably agree the average weight of bags has not changed.

7.39.

    a.   Minitab output

Descriptive Statistics: Video Price

```
Variable        Mean  StDev
Video Price   45.580  2.528
```

    b.   Minitab output using $\sigma_{\bar{x}} = \dfrac{2.528}{\sqrt{200}} = 0.179$

Cumulative Distribution Function

```
Normal with mean = 46 and standard deviation = 0.179

     x   P( X <= x )
  45.58    0.0094787
```

    c.   Minitab output with $\mu = 45.75$:
        Cumulative Distribution Function
```
Normal with mean = 45.75 and standard deviation = 0.179

     x   P( X <= x )
  45.58     0.171127
```

    d.   It is more than 18 (0.1711/0.00948) times as likely that a sample mean no larger than 45.58 would come from a distribution with a mean of 45.75 than from one with a mean of 46. Therefore, it appears that the average retail price has declined.

7.41.

    a.   Minitab output:

Median of HD Costs   Mean of HD Costs

Median of HD Costs = 144.89   Mean of HD Costs = 141.99

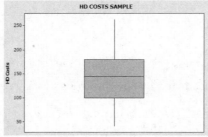

The box plot indicates that the median is somewhat larger than the sample mean. This indicates that the sample is negatively skewed. The upper whisker appears to be longer than the lower whisker suggesting a positive skewness of the sample. These two would seem to offset each other and allow that the population from which the sample was drawn could, in fact, be normally distributed.

b. More than $5 away from the obtained sample mean would be beyond $141.99 – $5 = $136.99 and beyond $141.99 + $5 = $146.99. We first calculate the standard deviation of the sample means:

$$\sigma_{\bar{x}} = \frac{\sigma}{\sqrt{n}} = \frac{50}{\sqrt{150}} = 4.082$$

$$P(\bar{x} < 136.99) = P(z < \frac{136.99 - 150}{4.082}) = P(z < -3.19) \cong 0$$

$$P(\bar{x} > 146.99) = P(z > \frac{146.99 - 150}{4.082}) = P(z > -0.74) = 0.5000 + 0.2704 = 0.7704$$

c. The box plot presents differing evidence indicating both positive and negative skewness. This could very well signal either sampling error or a non-normal distribution of the population. However, since the sample size is considerably larger than 30, there is not a requirement that the population is normally distributed in order to make these procedures valid.

7.43.
  a. We can use Excel's *Data –Data Analysis- Descriptive Statistics* option to find the population parameters shown as follows:

Age	
Mean	55.68
Standard Error	0.30
Median	56
Mode	56
Standard Deviation	6.75
Sample Variance	45.52
Kurtosis	0.43
Skewness	0.20
Range	42
Minimum	39
Maximum	81
Sum	27617
Count	496

Thus, the population mean is 55.68 years with a population standard deviation equal to 6.75 years.

  b. Student answers will vary depending on what sample is selected. One possible sample of 12 ages is the following:

63
61
55
59
55
57
52
46
49
51
47
60

The sample mean for this sample is:

$$\bar{x} = \frac{\sum x}{n} = \frac{655}{12} = 54.58$$

The sampling error for this sample is:

$$\bar{x} - \mu = 54.58 - 55.68 = -1.10$$

c.   We are asked to find the probability of a sample mean as large or larger than the one we found. This is:

$$P(\overline{x} \geq 54.58) = ?$$

To find this probability, we standardize as follows:

$$z = \frac{\overline{x} - \mu}{\dfrac{\sigma}{\sqrt{n}}} = \frac{54.58 - 55.68}{\dfrac{6.75}{\sqrt{12}}} = -0.56$$

From the standard normal distribution table, the probability associated with z = -0.56 is 0.2123. Thus:

$$P(\overline{x} \geq 54.58) = 0.2123 + 0.5000 = 0.7123$$

Student answers to parts b. and c. will vary depending on the sample selected but the methodology should follow that displayed in this solution.

Section 7-3 Exercises

7.45.

a.   **Step 1:** Determine the population proportion, π.

The population proportion was stipulated to be 0.30.

Step 2: Calculate the sample proportion.

The sample proportion was given as 0.35

Step 3: Determine the mean and standard deviation of the sampling distribution.

The mean of the sampling distribution is equal to π, the population proportion. So $\mu_p = 0.30$.

The standard deviation of the sampling distribution for π is computed using:

$$\sigma_p = \sqrt{\frac{\pi(1-\pi)}{n}} = \sqrt{\frac{0.30(1-0.30)}{100}} = \sqrt{0.0021} = 0.0458$$

Step 4: Define the event of interest.

$$p \leq 0.35$$

Step 5: If $n\pi$ and $n(1 - \pi)$ are both ≥ 5. then convert p to a standardized z-value.

Checking, we get

$n\pi = 100(0.30) = 30 > 5$ and $n(1 - \pi) = 100(0.70) = 0.70 > 5$ then we convert p to a standardized z-value

$$z = \frac{p - \pi}{\sqrt{\dfrac{\pi(1-\pi)}{n}}} = \frac{0.35 - 0.30}{\sqrt{\dfrac{0.30(1-0.30)}{100}}} = 1.09$$

Step 6: Use the standard normal distribution table in Appendix D to determine the probability for the event of interest. We want

$$P(p \leq 0.35) \text{ or } P(z \leq 1.09) = 0.50 + 0.3621. = 0.8621$$

b.   Using the same steps outlined above:

(1) $\pi = 0.30$,

(2) $p = 0.40$,

(3) $\mu_p = 0.30$, $\sigma_p = \sqrt{\dfrac{0.30(1-0.30)}{100}} = 0.0458$,

(4) $p \leq 0.40$,

(5) $n\pi = 100(0.30) = 30 > 5$ and $n(1 - \pi) = 100(0.70) = 0.70 > 5$ then

$$z = \frac{0.40 - 0.30}{\sqrt{\dfrac{0.30(1-0.30)}{100}}} = 2.18,$$

(6) $P(p > 0.40)$ or $P(z > 2.18) = 0.50 - 0.4854 = 0.0146$.

c. (1) $\pi = 0.30$,

    (2) $0.25 \le p \le 0.40$,

    (3) $\mu_p = 0.30$, $\sigma_p = \sqrt{\dfrac{0.30(1-0.30)}{100}} = 0.0458$,

    (4) $0.25 \le p \le 0.40$,

    (5) $n\pi = 100(0.30) = 30 > 5$ and $n(1 - \pi) = 100(0.70) = 0.70 > 5$ then

$$z = \frac{0.25 - 0.30}{\sqrt{\dfrac{0.30(1-0.30)}{100}}} = -1.09,$$

    (6) $P(0.25 \le p \le 0.40)$ or $P(-1.09 \le z \le 2.18) = 0.3621 + 0.4854 = 0.8475$.

d. (1) $\pi = 0.30$,

    (2) $p = 0.27$,

    (3) $\mu_p = 0.30$, $\sigma_p = \sqrt{\dfrac{0.30(1-0.30)}{100}} = 0.0458$,

    (4) $p \ge 0.27$,

    (5) $n\pi = 100(0.30) = 30 > 5$ and $n(1 - \pi) = 100(0.70) = 0.70 > 5$ then

$$z = \frac{0.27 - 0.30}{\sqrt{\dfrac{0.30(1-0.30)}{100}}} = -0.65,$$

    (6) $P(p \ge 0.27)$ or $P(z \ge -0.65) = 0.50 + 0.2422 = 0.7422$.

7.47.

a. The sampling error is computed as follows:

    Sampling error = $p - \pi = 0.65 - 0.70 = -0.05$

b. To find the probability that the sample proportion will be 0.65 or less, we rely on the fact that the sampling distribution for the sample proportion will be approximately normal so long as both $n\pi \ge 5$ and $n(1 - \pi) \ge 5$ which are satisfied in this situation. We can use the following steps:

Step 1: Determine the population proportion.

    The population proportion is $\pi = 0.70$

Step 2: Calculate the sample proportion.

    The sample proportion is calculated using $p = \dfrac{x}{n}$. In this case, we are given $p = 0.65$.

Step 3: Determine the mean and standard deviation of the sampling distribution.

    The mean is $\mu_p = \pi = 0.70$ and the standard deviation of the sampling distribution is

$$\sigma_p = \sqrt{\frac{\pi(1-\pi)}{n}} = \sqrt{\frac{0.70(1-0.70)}{100}} = 0.046$$

Step 4: Define the event of interest.

    We are interested in finding:

$$P(p \le 0.65) = ?$$

Step 5: Convert the sample proportion to a standardized z-value.

$$z = \frac{p - \pi}{\sqrt{\dfrac{\pi(1-\pi}{n}}} = \frac{0.65 - 0.70}{\sqrt{\dfrac{0.70(1-0.70)}{100}}} = \frac{-0.05}{0.046} = -1.09$$

Step 6: Use the standard normal distribution table to determine the probability for the event of interest. The probability associated with z = -1.09 is 0.3621. This, the desired probability is:
$$P(p \leq 0.65) = 0.5000 - 0.3621 = 0.1379$$
Thus, there is nearly a .14 chance that the sample proportion would be 0.70 or less.

7.49.

a. **Step 1:** The population proportion has been given as $\pi = 0.20$.
Step 2: In this case there are two sample proportions, p = 0.18 and p = 0.23.
Step 3: Determine the mean and standard deviation of the sampling distribution:
$$\mu_p = \pi = 0.20$$
$$\sigma_p = \sqrt{\frac{\pi(1-\pi)}{n}} = \sqrt{\frac{0.20(1-0.20)}{500}} = 0.0179$$
Step 4: Define the event of interest.
$$P(0.18 \leq p \leq 0.23) = ?$$
Step 5: If $n\pi$ and $n(1-\pi)$ are both ≥ 5, then convert p to a standardized z-value. Checking we get 500(0.20) = 100 $\geq$ 5 and 500(1-0.20) = 400 $\geq$ 5. Then we convert, p to a standardized z-value using
$$z = \frac{p-\pi}{\sigma_p} = \frac{0.18-0.20}{0.0179} = -1.12$$
$$z = \frac{p-\pi}{\sigma_p} = \frac{0.23-0.20}{0.0179} = 1.68$$
Step 6: Use the standard normal distribution table in Appendix D to determine the probability for the even of interest. We want
$$P(0.18 \leq p \leq 0.23) \text{ or } P(-1.12 \leq z \leq 1.68) = 0.3686 + 0.4535 = 0.8221$$

b. **Step 1:** The population proportion has been given as $\pi = 0.20$.
Step 2: In this case there are two sample proportions, p = 0.18 and p = 0.23.
Step 3: Determine the mean and standard deviation of the sampling distribution:
$$\mu_p = \pi = 0.20$$
$$\sigma_p = \sqrt{\frac{\pi(1-\pi)}{n}} = \sqrt{\frac{0.20(1-0.20)}{200}} = 0.0283$$
Step 4: Define the event of interest.
$$P(0.18 \leq p \leq 0.23) = ?$$
Step 5: If $n\pi$ and $n(1-\pi)$ are both ≥ 5, then convert p to a standardized z-value. Checking we get 200(0.20) = 40 $\geq$ 5 and 200(1-0.20) = 160 $\geq$ 5
Then we convert, p to a standardized z-value using
$$z = \frac{p-\pi}{\sigma_p} = \frac{0.18-0.20}{0.0283} = -0.71$$
$$z = \frac{p-\pi}{\sigma_p} = \frac{0.23-0.20}{0.0283} = 1.06$$
Step 6: Use the standard normal distribution table in Appendix D to determine the probability for the even of interest. We want
$$P(0.18 \leq p \leq 0.23) \text{ or } P(-0.71 \leq z \leq 1.06) = 0.2611 + 0.3554 = 0.6165$$

7.51.

a. $z = \dfrac{.42 - .40}{\sqrt{\dfrac{.40(1 - .40)}{1000}}} = 1.29$; $P(z < 1.29) = .50 + .4015 = .9015$

b. $z = \dfrac{.44 - .40}{\sqrt{\dfrac{.40(1 - .40)}{1000}}} = 2.58$; $P(z > 2.58) = .50 - .4951 = .0049$

7.53.

a. The sample proportion is computed using:

$$p = \frac{x}{n}$$

where x is the number of "YES" responses in the sample and n is the sample size. We get:

$$p = \frac{x}{n} = \frac{27}{60} = 0.45$$

b. To find the probability of a sample proportion as extreme or more extreme than that found in part a. we can use the following steps:

Step 1: Determine the population proportion.

The population proportion is $\pi = 0.40$

Step 2: Calculate the sample proportion.

The sample proportion is calculated using $p = \dfrac{x}{n}$. This was found in part a. to be

$$p = \frac{x}{n} = \frac{27}{60} = 0.45$$

Step 3: Determine the mean and standard deviation of the sampling distribution.   The mean is
$\mu_p = \pi = 0.40$ and the standard deviation of the sampling distribution is

$$\sigma_p = \sqrt{\frac{\pi(1-\pi)}{n}} = \sqrt{\frac{0.40(1-0.40)}{60}} = 0.063$$

Step 4: Define the event of interest.

We are interested in finding:
$$P(p \geq 0.45) = ?$$

Step 5: Convert the sample proportion to a standardized z-value.

$$z = \frac{p - \pi}{\sqrt{\dfrac{\pi(1-\pi)}{n}}} = \frac{0.45 - 0.40}{\sqrt{\dfrac{0.40(1-0.40)}{60}}} = \frac{0.05}{0.063} = 0.79$$

Step 6: Use the standard normal distribution table to determine the probability for the event of interest.

The probability associated with z = 0.79 is 0.2852. This, the desired probability is:
$$P(p \geq .45) = 0.5000 - 0.2852 = 0.2148$$

7.55. The population proportion is $\pi = 0.06$. The sample proportion is:

$$p = \frac{x}{n} = \frac{27}{300} = 0.09$$

The probability of finding 0.09 of the fries with dark ends given that the population contains only 0.06 fries with this attribute can be found by converting the sample proportion to a standardized z-value as follows:

$$z = \frac{p - \pi}{\sqrt{\dfrac{\pi(1-\pi)}{n}}} = \frac{0.09 - 0.06}{\sqrt{\dfrac{0.06(1-0.6)}{300}}} = \frac{0.03}{0.014} = 2.14$$

The probability associated with a z-value of 2.14 from the standard normal table is 0.4838. Thus, the probability of interest is:

$$P(p \geq 0.09) = 0.5000 - 0.4838 = 0.0162$$

There is less than a 2 percent chance that a sample of 300 would yield 27 fries with dark ends if the population of fries meets the 0.06 specification. Simplot managers would want to look into the situation and take corrective action.

7.57.
    a. $\pi = 0.105 \; p = 8/50 = 0.16$

$$P(p \geq 0.16) = P\left(z \geq \frac{0.16 - 0.105}{\sqrt{\dfrac{0.105(1-0.105)}{50}}}\right) = P(z \geq 1.27) = 0.5 - 0.3980 = 0.1020$$

    b. $\pi = 0.105, \; p = 5/50 = 0.10$

$$P(p \leq 0.10) = P\left(z \leq \frac{0.10 - 0.105}{\sqrt{\dfrac{0.105(1-0.105)}{50}}}\right) = P(z \leq -0.12) = 0.5 - 0.0478 = 0.4522$$

    c. $\pi = 0.105, \; p = 5/200 = 0.025$

$$P(p \leq 0.025) = P\left(z \leq \frac{0.025 - 0.105}{\sqrt{\dfrac{0.105(1-0.105)}{200}}}\right) = P(z \leq -3.69) = 0.5 - 0.5 \approx 0.0$$

7.59.
    a. $\pi = 0.96, \; p = 188/200 = 0.94$

$$P(p \leq 0.94) = P\left(z \leq \frac{0.94 - 0.96}{\sqrt{\dfrac{0.96(1-0.96)}{200}}}\right) = P(z \leq -1.44) = 0.5 - 0.4251 = 0.0749$$

    b. $\pi = 0.96, \; p = 197/200 = 0.985$

$$P(p \geq 0.985) = P\left(z \geq \frac{0.985 - 0.96}{\sqrt{\dfrac{0.96(1-0.96)}{200}}}\right) = P(z \geq 1.8) = 0.5 - 0.4641 = 0.0359$$

Perhaps. 197 on-time deliveries from a sample of 200 is a sample proportion of 0.985. The probability of a sample proportion greater than or equal to this is 0.0359. While this is not impossible it might be sufficiently small to be surprising.

c. $\pi = 0.96$, $p = 178/200 = 0.89$

$$P(p \le 0.89) = P(z \ge \frac{0.89 - 0.96}{\sqrt{\dfrac{0.96(1-0.96)}{200}}})=P(z \le -5.05) = 0$$

The probability of a sample proportion this small or smaller when the true proportion is 0.96 is essentially 0. This is indeed a rare event if the true population is as stated. You should be surprised by this result.

7.61.

a. Minitab output

Tally for Discrete Variables: Arrival

```
Arrival  Count  Percent
   LATE     49    28.00
ON TIME    126    72.00
    N=     175
```

The proportion equals 0.72.

b. Within ±0.06 of the population proportion would be 0.7808 ±0.06 = (0.7208, 0.8408). The standard error is given by $\sigma_p = \sqrt{\dfrac{\pi(1-\pi)}{n}} = \sqrt{\dfrac{0.7808(1-0.7808)}{175}} = \sqrt{0.000978} = 0.0313$.

Cumulative Distribution Function

```
Normal with mean = 0.7808 and standard deviation = 0.0313

      x    P( X <= x )
 0.7208      0.027623
 0.8408      0.972377
```

Therefore, proportion within ±0.06 equals 0.9724 – 0.0276 = 0.9448.

c. The sample proportion was 0.72 which is outside the interval for which the probability in part b. was calculated. There is only a 5.5% chance that a sample proportion would be outside this interval given that the population proportion was 0.7808. Therefore, it seems as though the proportion of on-time arrivals is smaller than in 2004.

7.63.

a. There are 131 1's which means 131 sampled subscribers have annual incomes over $100,000 and 65 0's which means 65 sampled subscribers have incomes of $100,000 or less.

b. $p = 131/196 = 0.668$

c. $P(p > 0.668) = P(z > \dfrac{0.668 - 0.65}{\sqrt{\dfrac{0.65(1-0.65)}{196}}} = 0.53) = 0.5 - 0.2019 = 0.2981$

d. d, It would be a judgment call. The sample proportion of 0.668 is higher than the claimed population proportion of 0.65. But because the chance of getting a sample proportion of 0.668 or higher if the true proportion is 0.65 is about almost 30%, the value seen could be due to sampling error.

Chapter Exercises

7.65. The finite population correction factor should be used if the sample size is greater than 5 percent of the population size and sampling is performed without replacement.

7.67. The sample means are measures of central location and would therefore, measure the centers of the samples. These averages cannot be as extreme as the values upon which they are based and, therefore, would be less variable than the population. Examples will vary.

7.69.
    a.   The true population mean is 405.55. According to the Central Limit Theorem the mean of the sample means should be the same as the population mean.

    b. $12.25 = [(\text{sigma}/\sqrt{150}\,)\sqrt{(1250-150)/(1250-1)}\,] = \text{sigma} = 159.83$

7.71. A sample size of 1 would be sufficient since the population itself is normal. Large samples would also produce normally distributed sampling distributions.

7.73.
    a. $P(\bar{x} > 16.00) = P(z > (16.00 - 15.30)/(7/\sqrt{40}\,) = P(z > 0.63) = 0.5 - 0.2357 = 0.2643$

    b. $P(15.10 < \bar{x} < 15.80) = P[(15.10\text{-}15.30)/(7/\sqrt{100}\,) < z < (15.80\text{-}15.30)/(7/\sqrt{100}\,)] = P(-0.29 < z < 0.71)$
        $= 0.2611 + 0.1141 = 0.3752$

    c. $P(\bar{x} \le 14.00) = P(z \le (14.00 - 15.30)/(7/\sqrt{50}\,) = P(z \le -1.31) = 0.5 - 0.4049 = 0.0951$
        The probability of getting an average of $14 or less for a sample of 50 is only 9.5%. Thus, there is a fairly low chance that this sample of fifty bikes would have an average repair cost of $14 or less. Thus, he would probably have been better off to charge a higher price per bike.

7.75.
    a.   In this population the median is $53,440 which is smaller than $115,260. This indicates that the population has a right skewed distribution which can not be a normal distribution which is symmetric. Thus, a normal distribution can not be used.

    b.   Since the sample size is equal to 5, which is much smaller, than the conservatively indicated 30 or more, the sampling distribution of the sample means cannot be approximated by a normal distribution.

    c.   This sample size, 35, is bigger than 30. So the calculation can be done as follows:

$$P(\bar{x} > 115{,}260) = P\left(z > \frac{115260 - 115260}{75000 / \sqrt{35}} \right) = P(z > 0) = 0.50.$$

7.77.
    a.   For a continuous uniformly distributed random variable the mean, $\mu = \dfrac{a+b}{2}$, where a is the lower limit and b is the upper limit. In this case, $\mu = \dfrac{3+6}{2} = 4.5$. The standard deviation for a continuous uniformly distributed random variable is $\sigma = \sqrt{\dfrac{(b-a)^2}{12}} = \sqrt{\dfrac{(6-3)^2}{12}} = 0.8660$

b. **Step 1:** Compute the sample mean. Here the sample mean is given: $\bar{x} = 4.25$.
Step 2: Define the sampling distribution. The population is uniformly distributed with a mean of 4.5 and a standard deviation of 0.8660. However, because the sample size, n = 49, is sufficiently large, the distribution of sample means is approximately normally distributed with

$$\mu_{\bar{x}} = \mu = 4.5 \text{ and } \sigma_{\bar{x}} = \frac{\sigma}{\sqrt{n}} = \frac{0.8660}{\sqrt{49}} = 0.1237.$$

Step 3: Define the event of interest. The event of interest is: $P(\bar{x} \geq 4.25)$
Step 4: Use the standard normal distribution to find the probability of interest. Convert the sample means

to corresponding z-values: $z = \dfrac{\bar{x} - \mu}{\dfrac{\sigma}{\sqrt{n}}} = \dfrac{4.25 - 4.5}{\dfrac{0.8660}{\sqrt{49}}} = -2.02$. From the standard normal table the

probability associated with z = -2.02 is 0.4783. Therefore, $P(\bar{x} \geq 4.25) = P(z \geq -2.02) = 0.4783 + 0.50 = 0.9783$.
Step 5: Use the standard normal distribution to find the desired probability. From the standard normal table $P(0 \leq z \leq 2.02) = 0.4783$. Although the population of service times is not normally distributed, but uniformly distributed, the sample size is sufficiently large so that the sampling

distribution of $\bar{x}$ is normally distributed. In other words, the Central Limit Theorem applies here

because the sample size, n=49, is sufficiently large so that the distribution of sample means $\bar{x}$ will be approximately normally distributed even though the original population is uniformly distributed.

7.79.
a. The desired probability is:
$$P(x > 16.10) = ?$$
Assuming that the population is normally distributed, the first step to find the desired probability is to standardize the value, x = 16.10 as follows:
$$z = \frac{x - \mu}{\sigma} = \frac{16.1 - 16}{0.25} = 0.40$$
From the standard normal distribution, the probability associated with z = 0.40 is 0.1554. Then:
$$P(x > 16.10) = 0.5000 - 0.1554 = 0.3446$$
Thus, there is nearly a 0.35 chance that a single bag of Cheetos will contain more than 16.10 ounces of product.
b. For a random sample of size 12 bags, the desired probability is:
$$P(\bar{x} > 16.10) = ?$$
The sampling distribution for $\bar{x}$ will be approximately normal with $\mu_{\bar{x}} = \mu = 16$ and

$$\sigma_{\bar{x}} = \frac{\sigma}{\sqrt{n}} = \frac{0.25}{\sqrt{12}} = 0.072$$

Now, standardize the sample mean as follows:
$$z = \frac{\bar{x} - \mu}{\dfrac{\sigma}{\sqrt{n}}} = \frac{16.1 - 16}{\dfrac{0.25}{\sqrt{12}}} = \frac{0.1}{0.072} = 1.39$$
From the standard normal distribution table, the probability associated with z = 1.39 is 0.4177. Then:
$$P(\bar{x} > 16.10) = 0.5000 - 0.4177 = 0.0823$$
The probability that a sample mean for a random sample of size 12 will exceed 16.1 ounces is just slightly larger than 0.08.

c.   The probability that the sample mean will exceeds 16.1 ounces is much smaller than the probability that an individual bag will contain more than 16.,1 ounces. This is because the sampling distribution is less variable that the population distribution. Thus, it is more likely that an extreme outcome will occur if one item is selected from the population compared with a sample mean of 12 items randomly selected from the same population.

7.81.

Note, because of the small population, the finite correction factor is used.

a. $P(\bar{x} \le 5.9) = P(z \le (5.9 - 6.2)/ [(3/\sqrt{100})\sqrt{(300-100)/(300-1)}] = P(z \le -1.22) = 0.5 - 0.3888 = 0.1112$

b.   Based on this low probability either the mean or the standard deviation or both may have changed.

c. $P(\bar{x} \le 5.9) = P(z \le (5.9 - 6.2)/ [(3/\sqrt{40})\sqrt{(300-40)/(300-1)}] = P(z \le -0.68) = 0.5 - 0.2517 = 0.2483$

d.   The probabilities differ because the spread of the sampling distribution is smaller for the larger sample. For a large sample, the distribution is more tightly grouped and the probability of observing an extreme value is smaller.

7.83.

a. $P(\bar{x} \le 88626) = P\left(\dfrac{88626 - 92500}{40000 / \sqrt{5829}} \ge z\right) = P(-7.39 \ge z) = 0.$

b.   A sample mean of at most \$88,626 from a population with a mean of \$92500 is highly unlikely, i.e., has a probability that is essentially 0. Therefore, the two years' means are highly unlikely to be equal to each other.

c.   Let X = the number of graduates who receive an annual base salary of at least \$92,500. X has a binomial distribution with n = 5 and p = 0.50 since the mean and median have the same value in a Normal distribution. Therefore, we capture $P(x \ge 5/2) = P(x \ge 3) = P(x = 3) + P(x = 4) = P(x = 5) =$

$\binom{5}{3}0.5^3(1-0.5)^{5-3} + \binom{5}{4}0.5^4(1-0.5)^{5-4} + \binom{5}{5}0.5^5(1-0.5)^{5-5} = 0.3125 + 0.1562 + 0.0312$

$= 0.4999.$

7.85. Students can use Excel's pivot table feature to group data by gender.

a. $\pi = 67/138 = 0.4855$

F	70
M	67
U	1
Grand Total	138

$P(p < 0.4855) = P(z < (0.4855 - 0.70)/ \sqrt{[0.70(1-0.70)]/138}) = P(z < -5.50) = 0$

Because there is essentially no chance of getting a sample proportion of .4855 if the true proportion of males is .70, then you can only conclude that the population proportion of male patients must be less than 70%.

b. Students can use Excel's pivot table feature to group by Medicare.
    P(Medicare) = 116/138 = 0.8406

BC	5
CAID	7
CARE	116
HMO	1
INS	3
OGVT	1
OTHR	4
SELF	1
Grand Total	138

P(p>0.8406) = P(z > (0.8406 − 0.80)/ $\sqrt{[0.80(1-0.80)]/138}$) = P(z > 1.19) = 0.5 − 0.383 = 0.117

Since the probability of finding a sample with a proportion of .8406 or greater if the true proportion is .80 is only 11.7% then you may reasonably assume that the proportion of people on Medicare is actually greater than 80%.

7.87.
a.

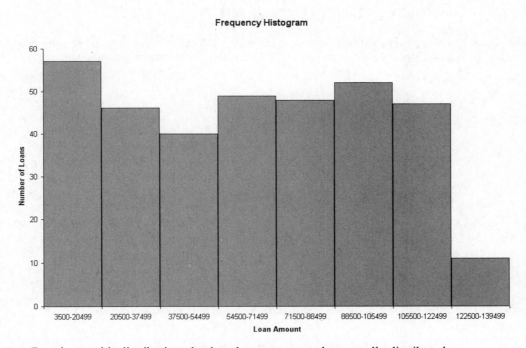

Based upon this distribution, the data do not appear to be normally distributed.
b. Using Excel's average function the mean = 63,668.57
c. Using Excel's STDEVP function the standard deviation = 35938.16
d. Student answers will vary depending upon the sample selected. Students should remember that the Central Limit Theorem shows that the sampling distribution will be approximately normally distributed as long as the sample size is greater than 30 even though the distribution of the underlying parent population is unknown.

7.89.

  a. Minitab output

Tally for Discrete Variables: 20/Over

```
20/Over  Count  Percent
      0     98    78.40
      1     27    21.60
    N=     125
```

Legend: 0 = at most 20, 1 = more than 20 months.

Thus, the P(p ≥ 20) = 0.216.

  b. $\pi = 0.2$, $\sigma = \sqrt{\dfrac{.2(1-.2)}{125}} = 0.0358$

      Minitab output

Cumulative Distribution Function

```
Normal with mean = 0.2 and standard deviation = 0.0358

    x   P( X <= x )
0.216      0.672536
```

P(p ≥ 0.216) = 1 − P(p ≤ 0.216) = 1 − 0.6725 = 0.3275.

  c. It appears likely that a sample proportion as least as large as 0.216 could occur if the population proportion of covers surpassing the 20-month warranty were 0.20. Reducing the warranty is a judgment call.

Chapter 8
Estimating Single Population Parameters

Section 8-1 Exercises

8.1. Since the population standard deviation is unknown, the following steps can be used to compute the confidence interval estimate.

Step 1: Define the population of interest and select a simple random sample.

The population of interest is the collection of all items of interest. A simple random sample of size n = 13 will be collected.

Step 2: Specify the confidence level.

The desired confidence level is 95%.

Step 3: Compute the sample mean and the sample standard deviation.

The sample mean and sample standard deviation are given to be:
$$\bar{x} = 18.4 \qquad s = 4.2$$

Step 4: Determine the standard error of the sampling distribution.

The sample standard deviation is computed to be $s = 4.2$. The standard error of the sampling distribution is:
$$\sigma_{\bar{x}} \approx \frac{s}{\sqrt{n}} = \frac{4.2}{\sqrt{13}} = 1.16$$

Step 5: Determine the critical value for the desired confidence level.

The critical value for 95% confidence from the student t-distribution table with degrees of freedom equal to n − 1 = 12 is
$t = 2.1788$.

Step 6: Compute the confidence interval estimate.

The 95% confidence interval estimate for the population mean is:
$$\bar{x} \pm t \frac{s}{\sqrt{n}}$$

Therefore the confidence interval is:
$$18.4 \pm 2.1788 \frac{4.2}{\sqrt{13}}$$

18.4 ± 2.54

15.86 -------------------------------- 20.94

8.3. Since the population standard deviation is known, the following steps can be used to develop the desired confidence interval estimate.

Step 1: Define the population of interest and select a simple random sample.

The population of interest is the collection of all items of interest. A simple random sample of size n = 250 will be collected.

Step 2: Specify the confidence level.

The desired confidence level is 95%.

Step 3: Compute the sample mean.

The sample mean is given to be $\bar{x} = 300$.

Step 4: Determine the standard error of the sampling distribution.

The population standard deviation is known to be $\sigma = 55$. The standard error of the sampling distribution is:
$$\sigma_{\bar{x}} = \frac{\sigma}{\sqrt{n}} = \frac{55}{\sqrt{250}} = 3.48$$

Step 5: Determine the critical value, z, from the standard normal distribution table.

The z value is 1.96.

Step 6: Compute the confidence interval estimate.

The 95% confidence interval estimate for the population mean is:

$$\bar{x} \pm z\frac{\sigma}{\sqrt{n}}$$

The critical value for 95% confidence from the standard normal distribution table is z = 1.96. Therefore the confidence interval is:

$$300 \pm 1.96\frac{55}{\sqrt{250}}$$

$$300 \pm 6.82$$

$$293.18 \text{ --------------------------------- } 306.82$$

8.5.   **Step 1:** Define the population of interest and select a simple random sample.

The population of interest is not precisely stated here. A simple random sample of n = 100 is selected.

Step 2: Specify the confidence level.

A 90% confidence interval estimate is to be constructed.

Step 3: Compute the sample mean.

The sample mean, $\bar{x}$, is given as being equal to 1,200.

Step 4: Determine the standard error of the sampling distribution.

The standard error of the sampling distribution is $\dfrac{\sigma}{\sqrt{n}} = \dfrac{121}{\sqrt{100}} = 12.1$

Step 5: Determine the critical value, z, from the standard normal table.

Because the sample size is large the sampling distribution will be normally distributed and the critical value will be a z-value from the standard normal distribution. Because a 90% confidence interval estimate is desired the z-value is 1.645.

Step 6: Compute the confidence interval estimate.

The 90% confidence interval estimate for the population mean is

$$\bar{x} \pm z\frac{\sigma}{\sqrt{n}} = 1200 \pm 1.645\frac{121}{\sqrt{100}} = 1200 \pm 19.90$$

$$1180.10 \text{ ------------- } 1219.90.$$

8.7.

a.   The 90% confidence interval estimate for the population mean is:

$$\bar{x} \pm t\frac{s}{\sqrt{n}}$$

Therefore the confidence interval is:

$$3 \pm 1.8331\frac{2.26}{\sqrt{10}}$$

$$3 \pm 1.31$$

$$1.69 \text{ --------------------------------- } 4.31$$

b.   If the confidence level is increased to 95%, the critical t from the t-distribution will change from 1.8331 to 2.2622. This will result in a wider confidence interval as follows:

$$3 \pm 2.2622\frac{2.26}{\sqrt{10}}$$

$$3 \pm 1.62$$

$$1.38 \text{ --------------------------------- } 4.62$$

For a higher confidence interval, the margin of error is greater causing the interval to be wider (less precise).

8.9. The 95% confidence interval estimate for the population mean is

$$\bar{x} \pm t\frac{s}{\sqrt{n}} = 102 \pm 2.201\frac{6.89}{\sqrt{12}} = 102 \pm 4.38$$

97.62 ------------- 106.38.

8.11.

  a. The 90% confidence interval estimate for the population mean is

$$\bar{x} \pm t\frac{s}{\sqrt{n}} = 13.4 \pm 1.8331(0.9804) = 13.4 \pm 1.7972 =$$

(11.6028, 15.1972)

  b. Using the same steps as part a:

$$\bar{x} = \frac{\sum x_i}{n} = \frac{3744}{120} = 31.2 \text{ and } s = 8.2.$$

$$s_{\bar{x}} = \frac{s}{\sqrt{n}} = \frac{8.2}{\sqrt{120}} = 0.7486.$$

The population has a normal distribution. However, the population standard deviation is unknown. Therefore, the critical value will come from the t-distribution. Using Excel, the critical value for 90% confidence is 1.6578. The 90% confidence interval estimate for the population mean is

$$\bar{x} \pm t\frac{s}{\sqrt{n}} = 31.2 \pm 1.6578(0.7486) = 31.2 \pm 1.241 = (29.9590, 32.4410)$$

  c. The population has a normal distribution whose mean is unknown but standard deviation is known.

$$\bar{x} = \frac{\sum x_i}{n} = \frac{40.5}{9} = 4.5 \text{ and } \sigma = 2.9.$$

$$\sigma_{\bar{x}} = \frac{\sigma}{\sqrt{n}} = \frac{2.9}{\sqrt{9}} = 0.9667.$$

The critical value will come from the standard normal distribution. The critical value for a 90% confidence interval is 1.645. The 90% confidence interval estimate for the population mean is

$$\bar{x} \pm z\frac{s}{\sqrt{n}} = 4.5 \pm 1.645(0.9667) = 4.5 \pm 1.5902 = (2.9098, 6.0902)$$

  d. The population has a normal distribution whose mean and standard deviation are unknown.

$$\bar{x} = \frac{\sum x_i}{n} = \frac{585.9}{27} = 21.7$$

$$s = \sqrt{\frac{\sum x^2 - \frac{(\sum x)^2}{n}}{n-1}} = \sqrt{\frac{15472.37 - \frac{(585.9)^2}{27}}{26}} = 10.3. \quad s_{\bar{x}} = \frac{s}{\sqrt{n}} = \frac{10.3}{\sqrt{27}} = 1.9822.$$

The population standard deviation is unknown, the sample size is less than 30, and the sample came from a population that is normally distributed. Therefore, the critical value will come from the t-distribution. The critical value for 90% confidence and 27 -1 = 26 degrees of freedom is 1.7056. The 90% confidence interval estimate for the population mean is

$$\bar{x} \pm t\frac{s}{\sqrt{n}} = 21.7 \pm 1.7056(1.9822) = 21.7 \pm 3.3808 = (18.3192, 25.0808)$$

8.13.

    a. $14.23 \pm 1.645(3.00/\sqrt{300})$; $14.23 \pm \$.2849$; 13.945 ------------ 14.515

          Based on the sample data and with 90 percent confidence, we believe that the mean prescription amount is between \$13.95 and \$14.52.

    b.   If we believe that the population mean is at the upper limit of the interval computed in part a., the expected total for 528 prescriptions would be \$7,663.92. If we believe that the population mean were on the low end of the confidence interval estimate in part a., the expected total for 528 prescriptions is \$7,362.96. Given that this outlet reported sales of \$7,392 for the 528 prescriptions, there is no reason to believe that this is out of line.

8.15.

    a.   a. $\bar{x} \pm z\dfrac{\sigma}{\sqrt{n}} = 5000 \pm 1.96(\dfrac{1500}{\sqrt{179}}) = 5000 \pm 219.75 = (4780.25,\ 5219.75)$

    b.   The margin of error is $z\dfrac{\sigma}{\sqrt{n}} = 1.96(\dfrac{1500}{\sqrt{179}}) = 219.75.$

    c.   Reducing the margin of error by 50 percent would produce a margin of error = 219.75/2 = 109.875. So

        $z\dfrac{\sigma}{\sqrt{n}} = 1.96(\dfrac{1500}{\sqrt{n}}) = 109.875.$

        Solving n $= \left(\dfrac{1.96(1500)}{109.875}\right)^{2} = 715.97 \approx 716.$

8.17.

    a.   Since the population standard deviation is unknown, the following steps can be used to compute the confidence interval estimate.

        The 95% confidence interval estimate for the population mean is:

$$\bar{x} \pm t\frac{s}{\sqrt{n}}$$

      Therefore the confidence interval is:

$$\$9.18 \pm 2.0452\frac{\$10.41}{\sqrt{30}}$$

$$\$9.18 \pm 3.89$$
$$\$5.29 \text{ -------------------------------- } \$13.07$$

      Based on the sample data, with 95% confidence, we can state that the true population mean error in hotel charges is between \$5.29 and \$13.07.

    b.   The interval includes the \$11.35 mean value determined in the American Express study. Therefore, these sample data do not dispute the American Express study. Any value in the confidence interval computed in part a. is equally likely to be the true population mean.

8.19.

    a.   a. $\bar{x} = \dfrac{\sum x_i}{n} = \dfrac{16101}{30} = 536.7$ $s = \sqrt{\dfrac{\sum(x-\bar{x})^2}{n-1}} = \sqrt{\dfrac{203577.86}{29}} = 83.785.$

    b.   b. $\bar{x} \pm t\dfrac{s}{\sqrt{n}} = 536.7 \pm 2.0452(\dfrac{83.785}{\sqrt{30}}) = 536.7 \pm 31.285 = (505.415,\ 567.985)$

    c.   The average number of minutes spent watching TV in 2007 was = 494 [8(60) + 14]. Since the plausible values for the mean did not include 494 and the entire confidence was above 494, it would appear that the average time spent watching TV has increased since 2007.

8.21.

a. The sample mean, $\bar{x}$ = 167.52. The population standard deviation is not known. The sample standard deviation, s, is used to estimate the population standard deviation. The sample standard deviation, s = 28.5179 . The critical value for a confidence interval when the population standard deviation is not known is the t-distribution. Here the sample size, n, is 196. The degrees of freedom are 196-1 = 195. The t-value for 95% level of confidence is 1.9722. The confidence interval is calculated as follows:

$$\bar{x} \pm t \frac{s}{\sqrt{n}} = 167.52 \pm 1.9722 \frac{28.5179}{\sqrt{196}} = 167.52 \pm 4.0174 = 163.5026 \text{----------------} 171.5374$$

b. The margin of error can be reduced by increasing the sample size, or by decreasing the level of confidence. The margin of error can also be reduced if the standard deviation can be reduced but this is not an option available to the study's authors in this case.

8.23.

a. The best estimate of average annual coffee consumption for German coffee drinkers is the sample mean,

$$\bar{x} = \sum \frac{x}{n} = \frac{941.3}{144} = 6.5368.$$ The value could have also been determined by using Excel's "average" function.

b. The population standard deviation is not known so the critical value is a t-value. The degrees of freedom are n-1 = 144-1 = 143. The sample standard deviation, s = 1.0775. The t-value of a 90% confidence interval with 143 degrees of freedom is 1.6556. The confidence interval is calculated as follows:

$$\bar{x} \pm t \frac{s}{\sqrt{n}} = 6.5368 \pm 1.6556 \frac{1.0775}{\sqrt{144}} = 6.5368 \pm 0.1487 = 6.3881 \text{----------------} 6.6855$$

Thus, based upon the sample data, with 90% confidence, the marketing research firm can conclude that the population mean annual coffee consumption of German coffee drinkers is between 6.3381 kilograms and 6.6855 kilograms.

8.25.

a. The sample mean is

$$\bar{x} = \frac{33,281}{130} = 256.01$$

The sample standard deviations, s, is 80.68 (calculated using Excel's STDEV function).

b. Assuming the population of pass times is normally distributed the 95% confidence interval is calculated as

$$\bar{x} \pm t \frac{s}{\sqrt{n}}$$

The t interval is used because the population standard deviation is unknown. There are 130-1 = 129 degrees of freedom. Using Excel's TINV function the interval coefficient is found to be 1.9785. The confidence interval is computed below:

$$256.01 \pm 1.9785 \frac{80.68}{\sqrt{130}}$$

$$256.01 \pm 14.00. \quad 242.01.............270.01$$

c. The margin of error is $\pm$ 14.00 seconds.

Section 8-2 Exercises

8.27.   **Step 1:** Specify the desired margin of error.
        The estimate is to be within $\pm$ 50 of the true mean, so the margin of error is e = 50.
        Step 2: Determine the population standard deviation.
        Based on previous studies or other knowledge, the population variance is known to be 122500.
        Therefore, the population standard is $\sigma = \sqrt{122500} = 350$.
        Step 3: Determine the critical value for the desired level of confidence.
        The critical value will be a z-value from the standard normal table for 95% confidence. This is z = 1.96.
        Step 4: Compute the required sample size using Equation 8-6.

$$\text{The required sample size is } n = \frac{z^2 \sigma^2}{e^2} = \frac{1.96^2 350^2}{50^2} = 188.24 = 189$$

8.29.   The equation for sample size is:

$$n = \frac{z^2 \sigma^2}{e^2} = \left(\frac{z\sigma}{e}\right)^2 = \left(\frac{(1.96)(680)}{44}\right)^2 = 917.54 \approx 918$$

The required sample size is 918 items from the population.

8.31.   In this problem we are told the sample size (n = 1,000) and the confidence level is constructed with a width of 600 (the difference between the upper and lower limit of the confidence interval). The margin of error is one half of the width, so the margin of error = 600/2 = 300. A 99% confidence interval was established so the z-value is 2.575. This provides the following:

$$n = \frac{z^2 \sigma^2}{e^2} = \frac{2.575^2 \sigma^2}{300^2} = 1000.$$

We are to solve for σ. Rearranging the equation we find $\sigma^2 = \frac{1000(300)^2}{2.575^2} = 13{,}573{,}381.09$. The square root of the variance will give us the standard deviation, thus, $\sqrt{13{,}573{,}381.09} = 3{,}684.21$.

8.33.

a. $n = \dfrac{z^2 \sigma^2}{e^2} = \dfrac{1.96^2 (16)^2}{4^2} = 61.47$, n = 62.

b.   Using the same steps as in part a. (1) e = 0.5, (2) σ = 23, (3) z = 1.645, (4) $n = \dfrac{1.645^2 (23)^2}{0.5^2} = 5725.95$, n = 5726.

c.   (1) e = 1, (2) σ = 0.5, (3) z = 2.575, (4) $n = \dfrac{2.575^2 (0.5)^2}{1^2} = 1.658$, n = 2.

d.   (1) e = 0.2, (2) σ = 1.5, (3) z = 2.33, (4) $n = \dfrac{2.33^2 (1.5)^2}{0.2^2} = 305.38$, n = 306.

e.   (1) e = 2, (2) σ = 6, (3) z = 1.96, (4) $n = \dfrac{1.96^2 (6)^2}{2^2} = 34.57$, n = 35.

8.35. The required sample size is $n = \dfrac{z^2\sigma^2}{e^2} = \dfrac{1.75^2 0.009^2}{0.001^2} = 248.06 = 249$ boxes must be sampled.

8.37.

a. The required sample size is 883 bags from the population. However, the 20 items in the pilot sample can be used so the net required sample is $883 - 20 = 863$.

b. If sampling an additional 863 bags is thought to be too much, the shipping company has the following general options for reducing the required sample size:
   1. Reduce the confidence level to something less than 95 percent
   2. Increase the margin of error beyond 0.25 pounds.
   3. Some combination of decreasing the confidence level and increasing the margin of error.

Note, decreasing the standard deviation would also result in a lower required sample size but it is doubtful that the airlines can do anything about the standard deviation.

8.39. The equation for sample size is:

$$n = \frac{z^2\sigma^2}{e^2} = \left(\frac{z\sigma}{e}\right)^2 = \left(\frac{(2.575)(1.4)}{.2}\right)^2 = 324.9 \cong 325$$

The required sample size is 325 customers from the population. However, the 50 items in the pilot sample can be used so the net required sample is $325 - 50 = 275$.

8.41.

a. The margin of error equals $1.25 = e$. Therefore,

$$n = \frac{z^2\sigma^2}{e^2} = \frac{1.96^2 10^2}{(1.25)^2} = 245.86, n = 246.$$

b. $$n = \frac{z^2\sigma^2}{e^2} = \frac{1.96^2 10^2}{(0.25)^2} = 6146.56, n = 6147.$$

c. For $n = 1{,}500$, $\sigma = 10$, 1.96, $e = \dfrac{z\sigma}{\sqrt{n}} = \dfrac{1.96(10)}{\sqrt{1500}} = 0.5061$

For $n = 2{,}000$, $\sigma = 10$, 1.96, $e = \dfrac{z\sigma}{\sqrt{n}} = \dfrac{1.96(10)}{\sqrt{2000}} = 0.4383$.

So the range of values for the margin of error is from \$0.44 to \$0.51.

8.43.

a. The required sample size is :

$$n = \frac{z^2\sigma^2}{e^2} = \frac{2.575^2 30^2}{5^2} = 238.70 = 239.$$

b. The manager is incorrect, the required sample size has nearly quadrupled.

8.45.

a. The desired margin of error is ± 25. Using Excel, the sample standard deviation is 263.8979, therefore, σ is assumed to be 263.8979. For 95% confidence, the critical value from the standard normal table is 1.96.

Using Equation 8-6, the required sample size is $n = \dfrac{z^2\sigma^2}{e^2} = \dfrac{1.96^2 263.8979^2}{25^2} = 428.06 = 429$ samples

must be taken. Since 137 households were sampled to estimate σ, $429 - 137 = 292$ additional households must be sampled.

b. The desired margin of error us $\pm$ 25. Using Excel, the sample standard deviation is 263.8979, therefore, σ is assumed to be 263.8979. For 90% confidence, the critical value from the standard normal table is 1.645.

Using Equation 8-6, the required sample size is n = $\dfrac{z^2\sigma^2}{e^2} = \dfrac{1.645^2 263.8979^2}{25^2} = 301.52 = 302$ samples

must be taken. Since 137 households were sampled to estimate σ, 302 – 137 = 165 additional households must be sampled.

8.47.

a. The equation for sample size is:

$$n = \frac{z^2\sigma^2}{e^2} = \left(\frac{z\sigma}{e}\right)^2 = \left(\frac{(1.96)(3.2)}{0.15}\right)^2 = 1,748.35 \approx 1,749$$

The required sample size is 1,749 customers from the population. However, the 150 calls in the pilot sample can be used so the net required sample is 1,749 – 150 = 1,599.

b. If an additional sample size of 1,599 is considered to be too many, the company has the option to reduce the confidence level (lowers the z-value) or increase the margin of error or some combination of the two.

Section 8-3 Exercises

8.49.   To determine the sample size.

$$n = \frac{z^2\pi(1-\pi)}{e^2} = \frac{2.575^2\ 0.2(1-0.2)}{0.025^2} = 1,697.44\ or\ 1,698$$

Total sample size needs to be 1,698, but the pilot sample of 75 can be used so 1,698-75 = 1,623 additional items must be randomly sampled.

8.51.   The format for the confidence interval is:

$$p \pm z\sqrt{\frac{p(1-p)}{n}}$$

$$0.28 \pm 1.96\sqrt{\frac{0.28(1-0.28)}{240}}$$

$$0.28 \pm 0.056$$

0.224 ---------------------------------- 0.336

Based on the sample data, with 95% confidence, we believe that the true population proportion of people that do not have health coverage is between 0.224 and 0.336.

8.53.

a. Here np = 150(0.35) = 52.5 > 5 and nq =150(1 – 0.35) = 97.5 > 5. The sample size is large enough so that the sampling distribution can be approximated by a normal distribution.

b. The   standard   error   of   sample   proportion   is   equal   to

$$p \pm z\sqrt{\frac{p(1-p)}{n}} = 0.35 + 1.645\sqrt{\frac{0.35(1-0.35)}{150}} = 0.35 \pm 0.064. = (0.286, 0.414)$$

c. Based on the sample data and with 90% confidence we believe that the population proportion is between 0.286 and 0.414.

d. The margin of error associated with this confidence interval is given by $e = z\sqrt{\dfrac{p(1-p)}{n}} = 0.064$ as

calculated in part b.

8.55.

a. $p = \dfrac{x}{n} = \dfrac{7}{40} = 0.175$

b.

$$p \pm z\sqrt{\dfrac{p(1-p)}{n}} = 0.175 + 1.96\sqrt{\dfrac{0.175(1-0.175)}{40}} = 0.175 \pm 0.118 =$$

(0.057, 0. 293)

c. The equation to calculate the required sample size is

$$n = \dfrac{z^2 p(1-p)}{e^2} = \dfrac{1.96^2(0.175)(1-0.175)}{(0.025)^2} = 887.4, \ n = 888.$$

8.57.

a. $0.38 \pm 2.575(\sqrt{[(0.38)(1-0.38]/499}$); 0.324 ----- 0.436

b. Since pilot sample information is not given, a conservative estimate must be made:
   $n = 1.96^2(0.5)(1-0.5)/(0.01)^2 = 9,604$

8.59.   p = 345/1000 = 0.345

a. $0.345 \pm 1.96(\sqrt{[(0.345)(1-0.345]/1000}$); 0.3155 ----- 0.3745

Based on the sample data and with 95% confidence we believe that the proportion of customers that carry more than one bag on the airline is between 0.3155 and 0.3745. The proportion of customers who would have been affected by the policy is thought to be in this range.

b. (0.3155)(568) ----- (0.3745)(568); 179.20 ----- 212.716

c. p = (280/690) = 0.4058

$$0.4058 \pm 1.96(\sqrt{[(0.4058)(1-0.4058]/690}$$); 0.3692 ---- 0.4424

Based on 95% confidence, the proportion of males that would be affected is between .3692 and .4424. So less that half would be affected. However, this might imply that men may be more affected than the population overall.

d. $n = \dfrac{z^2 p(1-p)}{e^2} = \dfrac{1.96^2(.15)(1-.15)}{.02^2} = 1,224.51 = 1,225$

8.61.   The format for the confidence interval is:

$$p \pm z\sqrt{\dfrac{p(1-p)}{n}}$$

$$0.91 \pm 1.645\sqrt{\dfrac{0.91(1-0.91)}{1,000}}$$

$$0.91 \pm 0.015$$

0.895 ---------------------------------- 0.925

Based on the sample data, with 95% confidence, Nike can conclude that the true proportion of women who are satisfied with their bodies is between 0.895 and 0.925. However, because Nike's target population is not "all" women, they should be careful in how they use the results of this survey. The proportions may overstate the true proportion of younger women who have a positive view of their bodies.

8.63.

a. The point estimate for the population proportion is given as 0.69. The sample size is given as n = 777. A 90% confidence level is desired. The critical value from the standard normal distribution table is z = 1.645. Compute the confidence interval using Equation 8-10

$$p \pm z\sqrt{\frac{p(1-p)}{n}} = 0.69 \pm 1.645\sqrt{\frac{0.69(1-0.69)}{777}} = 0.69 \pm 0.0273 = 0.6627 \text{--------- } 0.7173$$

b. The desired level of confidence is 95%. The z-value for the 95% confidence level is 1.96. The estimate is to be within ± 0.02 percentage points of the true proportion. Therefore, the margin of error is e = 0.02. The largest possible sample size assumes that you have no estimate for the value of population proportion, π, therefore, you use an estimate of 0.5. Compute the sample size required using Equation 8-12.

$$n = \frac{z^2 \pi(1-\pi)}{e^2} = \frac{1.96^2 \ 0.5(1-0.5)}{0.02^2} = 2401.$$ The required sample size is 2401.

c. From part (a), n = 777. The margin of error is given as 0.04, therefore, e = ± 0.04. With no knowledge of the proportion having the attribute of interest assume the most conservative sample size should be calculated which implies p = 0.50. Use Equation 8-12 to solve for the level of confidence.

$$n = \frac{z^2 \pi(1-\pi)}{e^2} \text{ therefore, } \frac{z^2 \ 0.5(1-0.5)}{0.04^2} = 777.$$ Solve for z and determine the level of confidence. z =

2.23, which implies a confidence level of 0.4871(2) = 0.9742.

8.65.

a. $p = \frac{x}{n} = \frac{35}{300} = 0.1167$. This is a characteristic of the sample. Even though it is smaller than the 14.1% attained by the population as a whole, this could be just a result of sampling error. An inference based upon a sample must incorporate probability in the analysis. Here, it is required to determine the probability that an event this extreme or more so has occurred. This is calculated in part b.

b. $n\pi = 300(0.141) = 42.3 > 5$; $n(1 - \pi) = 300(1 - 0.141) = 257.7 > 5$. Therefore, the sampling distribution of p can be approximated with a normal distribution.

$$P(p \le 0.1167) = P\left(z \le \frac{p - \pi}{\sqrt{\frac{\pi(1 - \pi)}{n}}}\right) = P\left(z \le \frac{0.1167 - 0.141}{\sqrt{\frac{0.141(1 - 0.141)}{300}}}\right) = P(z \le -1.21) = 0.5 - 0.3869 =$$

0.1131. This indicates that there is a somewhat significant probability that a result at most as large as our sample could occur from a population with a proportion = 0.141.

c. $p \pm z\sqrt{\frac{p(1 - p)}{n}} = 0.1167 \pm 2.33\sqrt{\frac{0.1167(1 - 0.1167)}{300}} = 0.1167 \pm 0.0431 = (0.0736, 0.1598)$. Since

0.141 is enclosed by this confidence interval, it is quite plausible that the proportion of students that pass at least one AP class in math and science is not different from those that pass at least one AP class.

8.67.

a. Use Excel to count the number of Miami households that have ever funded an IRA account with a rollover from an employer-sponsored retirement plan. The number is 67; therefore, the best point estimate for the population proportion is calculated from the sample information as x/n = 67/90 = 0.7444.

b. A 99% confidence level is desired. The critical value from the standard normal distribution table is z = 2.575. Compute the confidence interval using Equation 8-10

$$p \pm z \sqrt{\frac{p(1-p)}{n}} = 0.7444 \pm 2.575 \sqrt{\frac{0.7444(1-0.7444)}{90}} = 0.7444 \pm 0.1184 =$$

0.6260 --------- 0.8628.

c. The sample size could be increased. This would reduce the margin of error while leaving the confidence level unchanged.

8.69.

a. Minitab output

Test and CI for One Proportion: Males

```
Test of p = 0.5 vs p not = 0.5

Event = yes


Variable    X    N  Sample p          99% CI         Z-Value  P-Value
Males      48  100  0.480000  (0.351312, 0.608688)    -0.40    0.689
```

Test and CI for One Proportion: Females

```
Test of p = 0.5 vs p not = 0.5

Event = yes


Variable    X    N  Sample p          99% CI         Z-Value  P-Value
Females    22  100  0.220000  (0.113297, 0.326703)    -5.60    0.000
```

b. The largest ratio would be 0.6087/0.1133 = 5.37 and the smallest ratio would be 0.3513/0.3267 = 1.08.

c. One of the plausible ratios for these proportions is 2. Therefore, the analysis did not refute the assert made by Frank N. Magid Associates Inc. Any ratio in the range (1.08, 5.37) is possible.

Chapter Exercises

8.71. When estimating a population mean you always need to deal with the error associated with the point estimate based on the sample mean. If the population standard deviation is not known you now need to use the sample standard deviation to estimate the population standard deviation. Since you have added another source of error, the critical value is larger making the confidence interval wider to insure it will contain the population mean.

8.73 This is not correct. The average number of miles people commute is a single value. Therefore it has no probability. What the confidence interval is telling you is that if you want to produce all the possible confidence intervals using each possible sample mean from the population, 95% of these intervals would contain the population mean.

8.75.

   a. $0.76 \pm 1.645(\sqrt{[(0.76)(1-0.76]/441}$); 0.7265 ----- 0.7935

   b. 0.7265(35,000) ----- 0.7935(35,000); 25,427.50 ----- 27,772.50

8.77.

   a. $n = (1.96)^2 (200)^2/(50)^2 = 61.4656$ or 62 so you would need to sample 62-40 = 22 more

   b. cost of pilot with the 22 additional sampled = (62)($10) = $620

          without pilot:

          $n = (1.96)^2 (300)^2/(50)^2 = 138.29$ or 139 @ $10 = $1390;

          so savings of $1390 - $620 = $770

8.79

   a. $\bar{x} = \dfrac{\sum x_i}{n} = \dfrac{250,000}{48,000} = 5.21$

   b. $n = \dfrac{z^2 \sigma^2}{e^2} = \dfrac{1.645^2 1.5^2}{(1/8)^2} = 389.67$, n = 390

   c. $e = \dfrac{z\sigma}{\sqrt{n}} = \dfrac{1.645(1.5)}{\sqrt{100}} = 0.25$ work days = 2.00 work hours.

8.81.

   a.   p = 404/548 = 0.7372

Count of Current Cable Subscriber	
Current Cable Subscriber	Total
No	144
Yes	404
Grand Total	548

$0.7372 \pm 1.96(\sqrt{[(0.7372)(1-0.7372]/548}$); 0.7372 ± 0.0369 ;

0.7003 ----- 0.7741

b.

Household Annual Income	
Mean	32801.09489
Standard Error	266.1365661
Median	31000
Mode	30000
Standard Deviation	6230.097282
Sample Variance	38814112.14
Kurtosis	3.044243192
Skewness	1.481126946
Range	41000
Minimum	20000
Maximum	61000
Sum	17975000
Count	548

$32801.095 \pm 1.96(6230.097/\sqrt{548})$; 32,279.4674 ----- 33,322.7227

Based on the sample data, with 95% confidence the company can conclude that the mean income is between $32,279 and $33,323.

8.83.

a. Excel output:

Video Price	
Mean	45.580
Standard Error	0.179
Median	45.810
Mode	43.700
Standard Deviation	2.528
Sample Variance	6.388
Kurtosis	0.406
Skewness	-0.233
Range	15.320
Minimum	36.950
Maximum	52.270
Sum	9115.910
Count	200
Confidence Level(95.0%)	0.352

The 95% confidence interval is: 45.58 ± 0.35 or 45.23 to 45.93.

b. The entire confidence interval is below the mean of $46. It, therefore, seems plausible that the average price has decreased.

c. $n = [1.96(2.528)/1]^2 = 24.55 \approx 25$

8.85

a.   The population mean = 9987.44

b.

Classes	Frequency
5001 - 6000	0
6001 - 7000	1
7001 - 8000	4
8001 - 9000	24
9001 - 10000	100
10001 - 11000	79
11001 - 12000	40
12001 - 13000	2

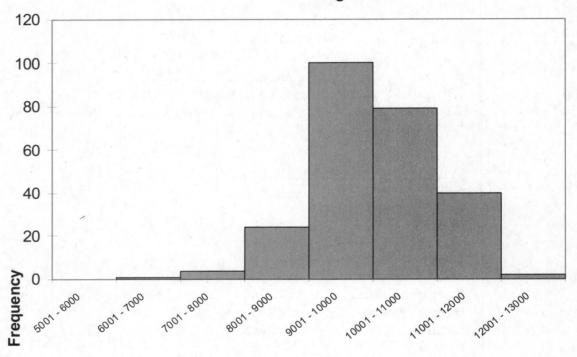

c.

Count of Sales	
Region	Total
East	39.60%
Midwest	17.60%
South	31.60%
West	11.20%
Grand Total	100.00%

d. e, and f. Student answers for d-f will vary depending upon the sample selected.

Chapter 9
Introduction to Hypothesis Testing

Section 9-1

9.1.
   a. $z = 1.96$
   b. $t = -1.6991$
   c. $t = \pm 2.4033$
   d. $z = \pm 1.645$

9.3.
   a. Use the standard normal distribution, $z_\alpha = 1.645$.
   b. Use the t-distribution with d.f. = n -1 = 22, $t_{\alpha/2} = \pm 2.5083$
   c. Use the standard normal distribution, $z_{\alpha/2} = \pm 2.575$.
   d. Use the t-distribution with d. f. = 4, $-t_\alpha = -1.5332$
   e. Invalid. Hypotheses concern population parameters and not sample statistics such as $\bar{x}$.

9.5.
   a. This is a two-tailed test of the population mean when the population standard deviation is known. Therefore, the decision rule is: reject the null hypothesis if the calculated value of the test statistic, z, is greater than 2.575 or less than -2.575. Otherwise, do not reject.
   b. $z = (196.5-200)/(9/\sqrt{64}) = -3.111$
   c. Because the calculated value of the test statistic, $z = -3.111$, is less than -2.575, reject the null hypothesis and conclude that the population mean is not equal to 200.

9.7.
   a. This is a one-tailed test of the population mean with σ unknown. Therefore, the decision rule is: reject the null hypothesis if the calculated value of the test statistic, t, is less than the critical value of -2.0639. Otherwise, do not reject.
   b. $t = (20-23)/(8/\sqrt{25}) = -1.875$
   c. Because the computed value of t = -1.875 is not less than the critical value of t = -2.0639, do not reject the null hypothesis and conclude that the mean is not less than 23.

9.9.
   a. This is a one-tailed test of the population mean with σ unknown. Therefore, the decision rule is: reject the null hypothesis if the calculated value of the test statistic, t, is greater than 1.3277. Otherwise, do not reject.
   b. $t = (71.2-70)/(6.9/\sqrt{20}) = 0.78$
   c. Because the computed value of t = 0.78 is not greater than 1.3277, do not reject the null hypothesis.

9.11.
   a. If the null hypothesis is rejected a Type I error would be committed.
   b. If the null hypothesis is not true a Type II error would be committed.
   c. If the null hypothesis is true a Type I error would be committed.
   d. No error is made.
   e. If the null hypothesis is not rejected a Type II error would be committed.
   f. No error is made.

9.13.

a. H_0: $\mu \geq 30,000$

   H_A: $\mu < 30,000$

b. For alpha = .05 and a one tailed , lower tail test, the critical value is z = -1.645. Solving for the critical x-bar: -1.645 = (x-bar – 30,000)/250, x-bar = $30,411.25

c. Since the sample value of $29,750 is less than the critical value of $30,411.25, do not reject the null hypothesis.

d. A Type II error could have been made since the null hypothesis was not rejected.

9.15.

a.

$$H_o : \mu \geq 3,600$$

$$H_A : \mu < 3,600$$

b. Since the population standard deviation is unknown, the appropriate test statistic to use is the t-distribution assuming that the population of miles between oil changes is approximately normal.

The sample provides the following statistics:

$$\overline{x} = \frac{\sum x}{n} = \frac{34,224}{10} = 3,422.4 \quad \text{and} \quad s = \sqrt{\frac{\sum (x - \overline{x})^2}{n-1}} = 658$$

The test statistic is:

$$t = \frac{\overline{x} - \mu}{\dfrac{s}{\sqrt{n}}} = \frac{3,422.4 - 3,600}{\dfrac{658}{\sqrt{10}}} = -0.85$$

From the t-distribution table for alpha = 0.05 and df = 9, the critical t-value for a one tail test is -1.8331. Since t = -0.85 > -1.8331, the null hypothesis is not rejected. Thus, based on these sample data, the franchise owner is unable to conclude that the marketing manager's claim does not apply to his franchise's customers.

9.17.

a.

$$H_o : \mu \geq 55$$

$$H_A : \mu < 55$$

b. Since the population standard deviation is unknown, the t-distribution should be used to conduct this test as long as you are willing to assume that the population is approximately normal.

The sample provides the following statistics:

$$\overline{x} = \frac{\sum x}{n} = \frac{1,562}{30} = 52.07 \quad \text{and} \quad s = \sqrt{\frac{\sum (x - \overline{x})^2}{n-1}} = 17.19$$

The test statistic is:

$$t = \frac{\overline{x} - \mu}{\dfrac{s}{\sqrt{n}}} = \frac{52.07 - 55}{\dfrac{17.19}{\sqrt{30}}} = -0.93$$

From the t-distribution table for alpha = 0.01 and df = 29, the critical t-value for a one tail test is –2.4620. Because t = -0.93 > -2.4620, the null hypothesis is not rejected. Thus, based on these sample data, we are unable to reject the null hypothesis. Thus, the statement that the mean age of millionaires in the United States is less than 55 years old is not supported by the data

9.19. With n = 137, s = $263.90, and $\bar{x}$ = $3,061.56, the calculated value of t is

$$\frac{3,061.56 - 3,417}{\dfrac{263.90}{\sqrt{137}}}$$

-15.7648.

Because t = -15.7648 is less than the critical t value of -2.0736, reject Ho.

The annual average consumer unit spending for food at home in Detroit is less than the 2006 national consumer unit average.

9.21.

a. The percentage growth rates selected in the sample are:

1.8
1
2
2.4
1.6
0.8
2.8
2.4
0.5
0.2
2.7
2.9
2.2
0.3

We now compute the sample mean and sample standard deviation either manually or with the help of software such as Excel or Minitab. These results are:

$$\bar{x} = 1.69$$

$$s = 0.958$$

If we assume that the population of percentage growth rates is approximately normally distributed, the t-distribution can be used to test the following null and alternative hypotheses:

$$H_o : \mu = 1.5$$

$$H_A : \mu \neq 1.5$$

The t-test statistic is:

$$t = \frac{\bar{x} - \mu}{\dfrac{s}{\sqrt{n}}} = \frac{1.69 - 1.5}{\dfrac{0.958}{\sqrt{14}}} = 0.74$$

The critical value for a two-tailed test with α = 0.05 and 14-1 = 13 degrees of freedom is 2.1604. Since t = 0.74 < 2.1604, we do not reject the null hypothesis based these sample data. This means we believe that the population mean growth rate could be 1.5 percent.

b. The mean growth rate for all 74 countries is:

$$\mu = 1.61 \text{ percent}$$

Thus, the null hypothesis that $\mu = 1.5$ is actually false. Therefore, because we did not reject the false null hypothesis, we committed a Type II statistical error. The small sample size and relatively large sample standard deviation have lead to this error.

Section 9-2

9.23.
    a. $z = 1.96$
    b. $z = -1.645$
    c. $z = \pm 2.33$
    d. $z = \pm 1.645$

9.25.   Begin by computing the sample proportion as:

$$p = \frac{x}{n} = \frac{105}{200} = 0.525$$

The z-test statistic is computed as follows:

$$z = \frac{p - \pi}{\sqrt{\dfrac{\pi(1 - \pi)}{n}}} = \frac{0.525 - 0.60}{\sqrt{\dfrac{(0.60)(0.40)}{200}}} = -2.17$$

From the standard normal table, the critical z-values for a one-tailed test with alpha = .05 is z = -2.33 Since -2.17 > -2.33, the null hypothesis is not rejected.

9.27.
    a.   This is a one-tailed test of the population proportion. The decision rule is: reject the null hypothesis if the calculated value of the test statistic, z, is less than the critical value of the test statistic z = -1.96. Otherwise, do not reject.

    b. $z = (0.66-0.75)/ (\sqrt{0.75*(1-0.75)/100}\,)=-2.0785$

    c.   Because the computed value of z= -2.0785 is less than the critical value of z =   -1.96, reject the null hypothesis and conclude that the population proportion is less than 0.75.

9.29.

    a. $z = \dfrac{0.12 - 0.30}{\sqrt{\dfrac{0.3(0.7)}{25}}} = -1.964$

           p-value = 2[P(z ≤ -1.964)] = 2(.5 − 0.475) = 0.05

    b. $z = \dfrac{0.35 - 0.30}{\sqrt{\dfrac{0.3(0.7)}{25}}} = .5454$

           p-value = 2[P(z ≥ 0.5454)] = 2(.5 − 0.2054) = 0.5892

    c. $z = \dfrac{0.42 - 0.30}{\sqrt{\dfrac{0.3(0.7)}{25}}} = 1.3093$

           p-value = 2[P(z ≥ 1.3093)] = 2(.5 − 0.4049) = 0.1902

    d. $z = \dfrac{0.50 - 0.30}{\sqrt{\dfrac{0.3(0.7)}{25}}} = 2.1822$

           p-value = 2[P(z ≥ 2.1822)] = 2(.5 − 0.4854) = 0.0292

9.31.   x= the number preferring stocks = 900-360 = 540
p = x/n = 540/900 =0.60

$$z = \frac{0.60 - 0.65}{\sqrt{\dfrac{0.65 * (1 - 0.65)}{900}}} = -3.145$$

Because z = -3.145 is less than -2.055, reject Ho.
A lower proportion of investors prefer stocks today than 10 years ago.

9.33.

$$p = \frac{x}{n} = \frac{40}{90} = 0.44$$

$$z = \frac{p - \pi}{\sqrt{\dfrac{\pi(1 - \pi)}{n}}} = \frac{0.44 - 0.39}{\sqrt{\dfrac{(0.39)(0.61)}{90}}} = 0.97$$

Since z = 0.97 < 1.645, we do not reject the null hypothesis.
There is insufficient evidence to conclude that the 0.39 rate quoted in the WSJ article is wrong.

9.35.   x =228

p = x/n = 228/300 = 0.76

$$z = \frac{0.76 - 0.72}{\sqrt{\dfrac{0.72 * (1 - 0.72)}{300}}} = 1.543$$

Because z = 1.543 is less than 1.96, do not reject Ho.
The proportion of college students at this university who are concerned about Internet theft is not greater than the general public.
p-value = P(z > 1.543)
            = 0.50 – 0.4382 = 0.0618

9.37.
   a.   The null and alternative hypotheses are:

$$H_o : \pi \le 0.40$$

$$H_A : \pi > 0.40$$

   b.   The sample proportion is:

$$p = \frac{x}{n} = \frac{174}{400} = 0.435$$

The z-test statistic is computed as follows:

$$z = \frac{p - \pi}{\sqrt{\dfrac{\pi(1 - \pi)}{n}}} = \frac{0.435 - 0.40}{\sqrt{\dfrac{(0.40)(0.60)}{400}}} = 1.43$$

The critical z-value from the standard normal table for a one-tailed test with alpha = 0.05 is 1.645. Since z = 1.43 < 1.645, we do not reject the null hypothesis. Therefore, the statement that population proportion exceeds .40 is not statistically supported by these sample data.

9.39.
- a. The null and alternative hypotheses are:

$$H_o : \pi \le 0.10$$

$$H_A : \pi > 0.10$$

- b. The sample proportion is:

$$p = \frac{x}{n} = \frac{24}{200} = 0.12$$

  The z-test statistic is computed as follows:

$$z = \frac{p - \pi}{\sqrt{\dfrac{\pi(1 - \pi)}{n}}} = \frac{0.12 - 0.10}{\sqrt{\dfrac{(0.10)(0.90)}{200}}} = 0.943$$

  p-value = 0.5 - .3264 = .1736

Since the p-value = .1736 is greater than .05, the null hypothesis is not rejected. So even though the sample proportion is greater than 0.10, the sample data is not sufficient to contradict the manager's contention.

9.41.
- a.

$$z = \frac{p - \pi}{\sqrt{\dfrac{\pi(1 - \pi)}{n}}} = \frac{0.36 - 0.26}{\sqrt{\dfrac{0.26(0.74)}{290}}} = 3.8824$$

Since z = 3.8824 > 1.96, reject H_O.

There is sufficient evidence to conclude that the proportion of men is not the same as the proportion of women who have had experience with a Global Positioning System device.

- b. p-value = 2(0.5 – 0.5) = 0.0

9.43. p = x/n = 67/90 = 0.7444

$$z = \frac{0.7444 - 0.72}{\sqrt{\dfrac{0.72 * (1 - 0.72)}{90}}} = 0.5155$$

Because z = 0.5155 is neither less than -1.645 nor greater than 1.645, do not reject Ho.

The proportion of Miami households that have funded an IRA account with rollovers is not different from the national proportion of households that have funded IRA accounts using rollovers.

9.45.

a. The null and alternative hypothesis are:

$$H_o : \pi \geq 0.50$$

$$H_A : \pi < 0.50$$

b. The sample size shown in the ECCO data file is 110. Of these 110 returns, 23 were coded as a wiring problem.

Next, we compute the sample proportion as:

$$p = \frac{x}{n} = \frac{23}{110} = 0.21$$

The z-test statistic is computed as follows:

$$z = \frac{p - \pi}{\sqrt{\frac{\pi(1-\pi)}{n}}} = \frac{0.21 - 0.50}{\sqrt{\frac{(0.50)(0.50)}{110}}} = -6.08$$

The z-critical values from the standard normal table for a one-tailed test with alpha = 0.02 is z = -2.05. Since z = -6.08 < -2.05, we reject the null hypothesis. Thus, based on these sample data, there is sufficient evidence to reject the null hypothesis and conclude that the operations manager's claim is correct.

9.47.

a. The appropriate null and alternative hypotheses are:

$$H_o : \pi \geq 0.95$$

$$H_A : \pi < 0.95$$

Note, the hypothesis is tested as a one tail test as Seadoo would only be interested in rejecting the hypothesis if the sample proportion of highly satisfied customers is too low.

b. Based on the sample data in the file called Seadoo, a total of 638 customers in the sample of 700 were highly satisfied.

Next, we compute the sample proportion as:

$$p = \frac{x}{n} = \frac{638}{700} = 0.91$$

The z-test statistic is computed as follows:

$$z = \frac{p - \pi}{\sqrt{\frac{\pi(1-\pi)}{n}}} = \frac{0.91 - 0.95}{\sqrt{\frac{(0.95)(0.05)}{700}}} = -4.85$$

The z-critical values from the standard normal table for a one-tailed test with alpha = 0.05 is z = -1.645. Since z = -4.85 < -1.645, we reject the null hypothesis. Thus, based on these sample data, there is sufficient evidence to reject the null hypothesis and conclude that less than 95 percent of Seadoo's customers are "Highly Satisfied"

Section 9-3

9.49.

a. $\bar{x}_{\alpha U} = 1.2 + 1.645(0.5/\sqrt{60}\,)$; $\bar{x}_{\alpha U} = 1.3062$

$\bar{x}_{\alpha L} = 1.2 - 1.645(0.5/\sqrt{60}\,)$; $\bar{x}_{\alpha L} = 1.0938$

Beta = $P[(1.0938 - 1.25)/(0.5/\sqrt{60}\,) < z < (1.3062 - 1.25)/(0.5/\sqrt{60}\,)] = P(-2.42 < z < 0.87) = 0.4922 + 0.3078 = 0.80$

b. Power of the test = $1 - 0.80 = 0.20$

c. The power increases, and beta decreases, as the sample size increases. We could also increase alpha since alpha and beta are inversely related.

d. If $\bar{x} > 1.3062$ or $\bar{x} < 1.0938$ reject H_o

Otherwise, do not reject H_o

Since $\bar{x} = 1.23$ then $1.0398 < 1.23 < 1.3062$ do not reject H_o

9.51. Given $\alpha = 0.01$ for an upper one-tailed test $z = + 2.33$

$$500 + 2.33*(36/\sqrt{64}\,) = 510.485$$

Type II Error = $\text{Prob}(z \le (510.485-505)/(36/\sqrt{64}\,))$

Type II Error = $\text{Prob}(z \le 1.22) = 0.5 + 0.3888 = 0.8888$

9.53. Given the one-tailed hypothesis test with alpha = 0.05, the critical z-value from the standard normal table is $z = 1.645$

Next, we compute the critical value which marks the cut-off for the rejection region as follows:

$$\bar{x}_\alpha = \mu + z_\alpha \frac{\sigma}{\sqrt{n}}$$

$$\bar{x}_\alpha = 100 + 1.645\frac{10}{\sqrt{49}} = 102.35$$

Next, we calculate the z-value associated with the "true" population mean as follows:

$$z = \frac{102.35 - 103}{\frac{10}{\sqrt{49}}} = -0.46$$

The probability from the standard normal table for a z-value of -0.46 is 0.1772. Then beta = 0.5000 – 0.1772 = 0.3228. Thus, there is over a 0.32 chance that a type II error will be made.

9.55.

   a. H_0: $\mu = 30$

       H_{A}: $\mu \neq 30$

       $\alpha = 0.05$

       $\pm z_{\alpha/2} = \pm 1.96$

$$\bar{x}_{L/U} = \mu \pm z_{\alpha/2}\frac{\sigma}{\sqrt{n}} = 30 \pm 1.96\frac{13}{\sqrt{50}}, \text{ so:}$$

$$\bar{x}_L = 26.3966 \text{ and } \bar{x}_U = 33.6034$$

$$\text{For } \mu = 22, \ z = \frac{\bar{x}_L - \mu}{\frac{\sigma}{\sqrt{n}}} = \frac{26.3966 - 22}{\frac{13}{\sqrt{50}}} = 2.3914$$

$$\text{and } z = \frac{\bar{x}_U - \mu}{\frac{\sigma}{\sqrt{n}}} = \frac{33.6034 - 22}{\frac{13}{\sqrt{50}}}$$

       $\beta = P(2.39 < z < 6.31) = 0.5 - 0.4916 = 0.0084$

   b. $\alpha = 0.05$

       $\pm z_{\alpha/2} = \pm 1.96$

$$\bar{x}_{L/U} = \mu \pm z_{\alpha/2}\frac{\sigma}{\sqrt{n}} = 30 \pm 1.96\frac{13}{\sqrt{50}}, \text{ so}$$

$$\bar{x}_L = 26.3966 \text{ and } \bar{x}_U = 33.6034$$

$$\text{For } \mu = 25, \ z = \frac{\bar{x}_L - \mu}{\frac{\sigma}{\sqrt{n}}} = \frac{26.3966 - 25}{\frac{13}{\sqrt{50}}} = 0.7596 \text{ and } z = \frac{\bar{x}_U - \mu}{\frac{\sigma}{\sqrt{n}}} = \frac{33.6034 - 25}{\frac{13}{\sqrt{50}}} = 4.6796$$

       $\beta = P(0.76 < z < 4.68) = 0.5 - 0.2764 = 0.2236$

   c. $\alpha = 0.05$

       $\pm z_{\alpha/2} = \pm 1.96$

$$\bar{x}_{L/U} = \mu \pm z_{\alpha/2}\frac{\sigma}{\sqrt{n}} = 30 \pm 1.96\frac{13}{\sqrt{50}} \text{ so}$$

$$\bar{x}_L = 26.3966 \text{ and } \bar{x}_U = 33.6034$$

$$\text{For } \mu = 29, \ z = \frac{\bar{x}_L - \mu}{\frac{\sigma}{\sqrt{n}}} = \frac{26.3966 - 29}{\frac{13}{\sqrt{50}}} = -1.4161 \text{ and } z = \frac{\bar{x}_U - \mu}{\frac{\sigma}{\sqrt{n}}} = \frac{33.6034 - 29}{\frac{13}{\sqrt{50}}} = 2.5039$$

       $\beta = P(-1.42 \leq z \leq 2.50) = 0.4222 + 0.4938 = 0.9160$

9.57.

a. Given the one-tailed hypothesis test with $\alpha = 0.01$, the critical z-value from the standard normal table is z = 2.33

Next, we compute the critical value which marks the cut-off for the rejection region as follows:

$$p_\alpha = \pi + z_\alpha \sqrt{\frac{\pi(1-\pi)}{n}} = 0.65 + 2.33\sqrt{\frac{0.65(1-0.65)}{500}}$$

$p_\alpha = 0.70$

Next, we calculate the z-value associated with the "true" population mean as follows:

$$z = \frac{0.70 - 0.68}{\sqrt{\frac{0.68(1-0.68)}{500}}} = 0.96$$

The probability from the standard normal table for a z-value of 0.96 is 0.3315. Then $\beta = 0.5000 + 0.3315 = 0.8315$. We then solve for the power as:

Power $= 1 - \beta$

$= 1 - 0.8315 = 0.1685$

Thus, there is only about a 17% chance that the hypothesis test will reject that the population mean is 0.65 or less if the true mean is actually 0.68.

b. Done like a. with different true π and critical z values.

$$p_\alpha = \pi + z_\alpha \sqrt{\frac{\pi(1-\pi)}{n}} = 0.65 + 1.96\sqrt{\frac{0.65(1-0.65)}{500}}$$

$p_\alpha = 0.692$

Next, we calculate the z-value associated with the "true" population mean as follows:

$$z = \frac{0.692 - 0.67}{\sqrt{\frac{0.67(1-0.67)}{500}}} = 1.06$$

The probability from the standard normal table for a z-value of 1.06 is 0.3554. Then $\beta = 0.5000 + 0.3554 = 0.8554$. We then solve for the power as:

Power $= 1 - \beta$

$= 1 - 0.8554 = 0.1446$

c. Done like a. with different true π and critical z values.

$$p_\alpha = \pi + z_\alpha \sqrt{\frac{\pi(1-\pi)}{n}} = 0.65 + 1.645\sqrt{\frac{0.65(1-0.65)}{500}}$$

$p_\alpha = 0.685$

Next, we calculate the z-value associated with the "true" population mean as follows:

$$z = \frac{0.685 - 0.66}{\sqrt{\frac{0.66(1-0.66)}{500}}} = 1.18$$

The probability from the standard normal table for a z-value of 1.18 is 0.3810. Then $\beta = 0.5000 + 0.3810 = 0.8810$. We then solve for the power as:

Power $= 1 - \beta$

$= 1 - 0.8810 = 0.1190$

9.59.

    a.   The appropriate null and alternative hypotheses are:

$$H_o : \mu \geq 243$$

$$H_a : \mu < 243$$

    b.   Given the one-tailed hypothesis test with alpha = 0.05, the critical z-value from the standard normal table is z = -1.645

Next, we compute the critical value which marks the cut-off for the rejection region as follows:

$$\bar{x}_\alpha = \mu + z_\alpha \frac{\sigma}{\sqrt{n}}$$

$$\bar{x}_\alpha = 243 - 1.645 \frac{40}{\sqrt{100}} = 236.42$$

Next, we calculate the z-value associated with the "true" population mean as follows:

$$z = \frac{236.42 - 230}{\frac{40}{\sqrt{100}}} = 1.61$$

The probability from the standard normal table for a z-value of 1.61 is 0.4463. Then beta = 0.5000 - 0.4463 = 0.0537. Thus, there is just over a 5 percent chance that a type II error will be made.

9.61.

    a.   The appropriate null and alternative hypotheses are:

$$H_o : \mu \geq 15$$

$$H_a : \mu < 15$$

    b.   Given the one-tailed hypothesis test with alpha = 0.01, the critical z-value from the standard normal table is z = -2.33

Next, we compute the critical value which marks the cut-off for the rejection region as follows:

$$\bar{x}_\alpha = \mu + z_\alpha \frac{\sigma}{\sqrt{n}}$$

$$\bar{x}_\alpha = 15 - 2.33 \frac{2}{\sqrt{60}} = 14.40$$

Next, we calculate the z-value associated with the "true" population mean as follows:

$$z = \frac{14.40 - 14}{\frac{2}{\sqrt{60}}} = 1.55$$

The probability from the standard normal table for a z-value of 1.55 is 0.4394. Then beta = 0.5000 − 0.4394 = 0.0606. Thus, there is just over a 6 percent chance that a type II error will be made.

9.63.

a. The appropriate null and alternative hypotheses are:
$$H_O = \mu \geq \$47,413$$
$$H_A = \mu < \$47,413$$
Note: we have put the claim in the alternate hypothesis

b. Given the one-tailed hypothesis test with alpha = 0.01, the critical z-value from the standard normal table is z = -2.33

Next, we compute the critical value which marks the cut-off for the rejection region as follows:

$$\bar{x}_\alpha = \mu + z_\alpha \frac{\sigma}{\sqrt{n}}$$

$$\bar{x}_\alpha = 47,413 + (-2.33)\frac{4,600}{\sqrt{200}} = 47,413 - 757.88 = 46655.12$$

Next, we calculate the z-value associated with the "true" population mean as follows:

$$z = \frac{46655.12 - 47,000}{\frac{4,600}{\sqrt{200}}} = 1.06$$

The probability from the standard normal table for a z-value of -1.06 is 0.3554. Then beta = 0.5000 - 0.3554 = 0.1446. Thus, there is just over a 14 percent chance that a type II error will be made.

9.65. Finding the critical value in terms of cost:

$$\bar{x}_\alpha = \mu + z_\alpha \frac{\sigma}{\sqrt{n}} = 10659.60 + (-2.33)\frac{750}{\sqrt{100}} = 10484.85$$

Assume $\mu = 10361$

$$z = \frac{\bar{x}_\alpha - \mu}{\frac{\sigma}{\sqrt{n}}} = \frac{10484.85 - 10361}{\frac{750}{\sqrt{100}}} = 1.6513$$

$$\beta = P(z > 1.6513) = 0.5 - 0.4505 = 0.0495$$

9.67.

a. H_O: $\mu \geq 11.35$
H_A: $\mu < 11.35$
$\alpha = 0.05$
Since σ is unknown, we use a t test statistic, and reject H_O if t < -1.6991

From the data set, $\bar{x} = \frac{\Sigma x}{n} = \frac{308.661}{30} = 10.2887$

$$s = \sqrt{\frac{\sum(x - \bar{x})^2}{n-1}} = \sqrt{\frac{62.0877}{29}} = \sqrt{2.1410} = 1.4632,$$

So $t = \frac{\bar{x} - \mu}{\frac{s}{\sqrt{n}}} = \frac{10.2887 - 11.35}{\frac{1.4632}{\sqrt{30}}} = -3.97$

Since t = -3.97 < -1.6991 we reject H_O and conclude there is sufficient evidence the average overpayment is smaller than that indicated by Corporate Lodging Consultants.

b. $\bar{x}_\alpha = \mu + z_\alpha \dfrac{\sigma}{\sqrt{n}} = 11.35 + (-1.645)\dfrac{1.50}{\sqrt{30}} = 10.8995$

Assuming $\mu = 11$

$z = \dfrac{\bar{x}_\alpha - \mu}{\dfrac{\sigma}{\sqrt{n}}} = \dfrac{10.8995 - 11}{\dfrac{1.50}{\sqrt{30}}} = -0.3670$

$\beta = P(z > -0.3670) = 0.5 + 0.1443 = 0.6443$
Power $= 1 - \beta = 1 - 0.6443 = 0.3557$

End of chapter Exercises

9.69.   The critical value is the cut-off point or demarcation between "acceptance" and rejection regions in a hypothesis test. It may be expressed in terms of a value of the sample mean, as a z value of as an alpha value.

9.71.   A Type I error occurs when the decision maker rejects a true null hypothesis. A Type II error occurs when a false null hypothesis is accepted. Business examples of these two types of error will vary.

9.73.   You use the population proportion to calculate the standard error. If you were testing that the population proportion were 0 then the standard error would be 0. This would make it impossible to make a logical calculation.

9.75.   The probability of committing a Type I error is denoted by alpha (α) and is usually specified by the decision maker. The choice of alpha reflects the cost of making a Type I error. If the cost is high, alpha will be set at a lower value than if the cost of committing the error is low.

9.77.
   a.   If α is decreased, the rejection region is smaller making it easier to accept H_0, so β is increased.
   b.   If n is increased, the test statistic is also increased making it harder to accept H_0, so β is decreased.
   c.   If n is increased, the test statistic is also increased making it harder to accept H_0, so β is decreased and power is increased.
   d.   If α is decreased, the rejection region is smaller making it easier to accept H_0, so β is increased and power is decreased.

9.79.

   a.   z (Standard normal) test statistic, $z = \dfrac{\bar{x} - \mu}{\dfrac{\sigma}{\sqrt{n}}}$

   b.   t (Student's t) test statistic, $t = \dfrac{\bar{x} - \mu}{\dfrac{s}{\sqrt{n}}}$

   c.   z (standard normal) test statistic, $z = \dfrac{p - \pi}{\sqrt{\dfrac{\pi(1 - \pi)}{n}}}$, should not be used since n(1-p) < 5.

   d.   A hypothesis test using a small (< 30) sample from a skewed distribution cannot be conducted using procedures in this text.

9.81.

a.
$$H_o : \mu \le 4,000$$
$$H_A : \mu > 4,000$$

b. The normality assumption can be examined by looking at a box and whiskers plot although with only 12 values, such a plot may not be conclusive. The box and whiskers plot is shown as follows:

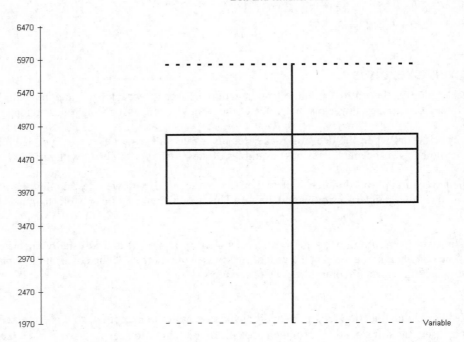

Box-and-whisker Plot

This plot is not all that consistent with what would be expected from a normal distribution, but the small sample size may be a problem. The t-test is fairly robust to the normality assumption so we will continue with it as a method for testing whether the population mean exceeds 4,000.

$$\bar{x} = 4,366 \text{ and } s = 1000.849$$

$$t = (4,366 - 4,000)/(1000.849/\sqrt{12}) = 1.2668$$

The critical t for a one-tailed test with alpha = .05 and 11 degrees of freedom is 1.7959. Since t = 1.2668 < 1.7959, there is insufficient evidence to reject the null hypothesis. Thus, they cannot make the claim that mean life of a component exceeds 4,000 hours. A larger sample would be desirable.

9.83.

a. H_o: $\pi \ge 0.50$
H_a: $\pi < 0.50$ (less than 50% believe there should be different equipment rules)

b. If 67% do not believe there should be different rules, then 33% believe there should be different rules. Therefore p = .33.

$$z = \frac{p - \pi}{\sqrt{\dfrac{\pi(1-\pi)}{n}}} = \frac{.33 - .50}{\sqrt{\dfrac{.50(1-.50)}{300}}} = -5.889$$

Since z = -5.889 < -1.645, reject the null hypothesis.
Since z = -5.889, the p-value is approximately zero.

9.85.

  a. H_o: $\pi \geq 0.70$
      H_a: $\pi < 0.70$
      $p = 63/100 = 0.63$
      $z = (0.63 - 0.70)/\sqrt{(0.70)(1-0.70)/100} = -1.5275$

      Decision Rule:
      If $z < -1.645$ reject H_o, otherwise do not reject
      Since $z = -1.5275 > -1.645$ do not reject and conclude that the difficulty of the test seems to be appropriate

  b. A Type II error in this problem would mean that the proportion of students passing the test is actually less than 0.70 but the sample results lead the administrators to believe that it is actually 70% or better. This would mean that a test that must be too difficult would continue to be administered.

9.87.

  a. $n\pi = 17346(0.175) = 3033.55 > 5$; $n(1-\pi) = 17346(1-0.175) = 14310.45 > 5$ The normal approximation to the binomial is warranted.

  b. H_O: $\pi \leq 0.175$
      H_A: $\pi > 0.175$
      $\alpha = 0.05$, reject H_O if p-value < 0.05

$$p = \frac{3470}{17346} = 0.2000$$

$$z = \frac{p-\pi}{\sqrt{\frac{\pi(1-\pi)}{n}}} = \frac{0.200-0.175}{\sqrt{\frac{0.175(0.825)}{17346}}} = 8.665$$

      p-value = $P(z \geq 8.665)$. From the standard normal distribution table, the p-value is less than $0.5 - 0.4990 = 0.001$, or certainly less than $\alpha = 0.05$. There is sufficient evidence to conclude that consumer interest was more than 17.5%. The self checkout machines should be installed.

9.89.

  a. $n\pi = 2500(0.75) = 1875 > 5$; $n(1-\pi) = 625 > 5$
      The normal approximation to the binomial is warranted.

  b. H_O: $\pi \geq 0.75$
      H_A: $\pi < 0.75$

      $\alpha = 0.025$, reject H_O if $z < -z_\alpha = -1.96$ $z = \dfrac{p-\pi}{\sqrt{\frac{\pi(1-\pi)}{n}}} = \dfrac{0.74-0.75}{\sqrt{\frac{0.75(0.25)}{2500}}} = -1.1547$

      Since $z = -1.1547 > -1.96$ do not reject H_O. There is not sufficient evidence to conclude that less than 75% of new mortgages had a loan amount at least 5% above the original mortgage balance.

9.91.

  a. The research hypothesis is that the parts do not have an average diameter of 6 inches.
      H_o: $\mu = 6$ inches
      H_a: $\mu \neq 6$ inches

  b. Reject H_o if $z > 2.58$ or $z < -2.58$; otherwise do not reject H_o
      $\bar{x}_{\alpha/2} = 6 \pm 2.58(.10/\sqrt{200}) = 5.9818$ and 6.0182

        If $\bar{x} < 5.9818$, reject the null hypothesis
        If $\bar{x} > 6.0182$, reject the null hypothesis
        Otherwise, do not reject

  c. Since $\bar{x} = 6.03 > 6.0182$, reject the null hypothesis. Thus, the average diameter appears to be higher than 6 inches.

9.93.

a. "more than the reported amount" becomes a research hypothesis:

H_O: $\mu \leq 50,000$

H_A: $\mu > 50,000$

$\alpha = 0.025$

Since σ is known, we can use a z test statistic and reject H_O if z > 1.96.

$$z = \frac{\bar{x} - \mu}{\dfrac{\sigma}{\sqrt{n}}} = \frac{51,035 - 50,000}{\dfrac{1734.23}{\sqrt{55}}} = 4.426$$

Because z = 4.426 > 1.96 we reject H_O. There is sufficient evidence to conclude that GM's workers average balance in 401(k) accounts is, in fact, exceeding that of other workers.

b. The statement ". . .average balance in which you have 90% confidence" implies a confidence interval.

$$\bar{x} \pm z_{\alpha/2} \frac{\sigma}{n} ;\text{ at the 90\% confidence level}$$

$$\bar{x} \pm z_{\alpha/2} \frac{\sigma}{\sqrt{n}} = 51035 \pm 1.645 \frac{1734.23}{\sqrt{55}} = 51035 \pm 384.67\ (50650.33,\ 51419.67).\quad \text{The largest}$$

plausible average balance in the GM workers' 401(k) in which you could have 90% confidence = $51419.67.

9.95. H_o: $\pi \leq 0.60$

H_a: $\pi > 0.60$

Of the 553 who rated overall satisfaction a 4 or 5, 394 were females. Using Excel's Pivot Table we get:

Count of Gender	Gender		
Overall Service Satisfaction	Male	Female	Grand Total
1-3	31.62%	68.38%	100.00%
4-5	28.75%	71.25%	100.00%
Grand Total	30.31%	69.69%	100.00%

$$z = (0.7125 - 0.60)/\sqrt{(0.60)(1 - 0.60)/553} = 5.40$$

p-value = 0 so reject H_o and conclude that of the customers who express overall service satisfaction, more than 60% of these are female. Should not initiate a new exercise program.

9.97.

a. H_o: $\mu = 0.75$ inch

H_a: $\mu \neq 0.75$ inch

b. Students can use Excel's AVERAGE and STDEV functions to determine the sample mean and standard deviation.

$\bar{x} = 0.7532$ s = 0.0337

$t = (0.7532 - 0.75)/(0.0337/\sqrt{100}) = 0.9496$

$t_{.01/2} = \pm 2.6264$ (using Excel) or approximately 2.6259 using the table with df = 100.

Since t = 0.9496 < 2.6264, do not reject H_o and conclude that the product is meeting the thickness specifications.

9.99.

a. H_O: $\mu \geq 6920$

H_A: $\mu < 6920$

$\alpha = 0.025$

Since σ is unknown, we use a t test statistic and reject H_O if p-value < 0.025. Using the data file

$$\bar{x} = \frac{\Sigma x}{n} = \frac{255128}{40} = 6378.20$$

$$s = \sqrt{\frac{\sum(x-\bar{x})^2}{n-1}} = \sqrt{\frac{77905873.09}{39}} = \sqrt{1997586.49},$$

$$t = \frac{\bar{x} - \mu}{\frac{s}{\sqrt{n}}} = \frac{6378.20 - 6920}{\frac{1413.36}{\sqrt{40}}} = -2.4233$$

The p-value = Prob(t ≤ -2.4233) with d.f. = 40 − 1. Using Excel's TDIST option the p-value is 0.01. Since the p-value is less than α we reject H_O. There is sufficient evidence to conclude that MBNA has a larger average annual spending per active account than the rest of the credit card industry.

b. We need to find Prob(x > 6920) from a normal distribution with a mean of 5560 and a standard deviation of 1140.

$$z = \frac{6920 - 5560}{1140} = 1.193$$

From the standard normal table, the probability z > 1.193 is = 0.5 − 0.3830 = 0.1170.

9.101.

a. Wanting to prove the machines can be paid for we hypothesize as:

H_O: $\mu \leq 750$

H_A: $\mu > 750$

$\alpha = 0.05$

Since σ is unknown we use a t test statistic with d.f. = 24 − 1. Reject H_O if p-value is less than 0.05.

From the data: $\bar{x} = \frac{\Sigma x}{n} = \frac{18671.74}{24} = 777.989$

$$s = \sqrt{\frac{\sum(x-\bar{x})^2}{n-1}} = \sqrt{\frac{174323.20}{23}} = \sqrt{7579.27} = 87.059,$$

$$t = \frac{\bar{x} - \mu}{\frac{s}{\sqrt{n}}} = \frac{777.989 - 750}{\frac{87.059}{\sqrt{24}}} = 1.5750$$

The p-value = Prob(t ≥ 1.575). Using Excel's TDIST option this probability is 0.0644. ;Since the p-value is greater than α we do not reject H_O. There is not sufficient evidence to conclude that an average monthly income of more than $750 can be obtained.

b. Trial has two outcomes: average monthly income of at least $ 750 or not with a fixed number of trials. But the probability on the second try depends on what happens on the first. We have a hypergeometric distribution. Using Equation 5-9 we find:

$$P(x \geq 2) = 1 - P(x \leq 1) = 1 - \left[\frac{C_4^6 x C_0^4}{C_4^{10}} + \frac{C_3^6 x C_1^4}{C_4^{10}} \right] = 1 - 95/210$$

$$= 1 - 0.4524 = 0.5476$$

Chapter 10
Estimation and Hypothesis Testing
for Two Population Parameters

Section 10-1 Exercises

10.1.

$$(\bar{x}_1 - \bar{x}_2) \pm ts_p \sqrt{\frac{1}{n_1} + \frac{1}{n_2}}$$

Then the interval estimate is

$$-3 \pm 1.7056(5.48)\sqrt{\frac{1}{15} + \frac{1}{13}} = -3 \pm 3.54 = -6.54 \leq (\mu_1 - \mu_2) \leq 0.54$$

10.3.

$$s_p = \sqrt{\frac{(n_1 - 1)s_1^2 + (n_2 - 1)s_2^2}{n_1 + n_2 - 2}} = \sqrt{\frac{(9-1)5.24^2 + (9-1)3.2^2}{9+9-2}} = 4.34$$

The critical value comes from a t-distribution with $df = n_1 + n_2 - 2$. The degrees of freedom is 9+9–2=16. The critical value from the t-distribution table is 1.7459.

When the population variances are assumed to be equal, the confidence interval estimate is computed using:

$$(\bar{x}_1 - \bar{x}_2) \pm ts_p \sqrt{\frac{1}{n_1} + \frac{1}{n_2}}$$

Then

$$-9.77 \pm 1.7459(4.34)\sqrt{\frac{1}{9} + \frac{1}{9}}$$

$$-9.77 \pm 3.57$$

$$-13.34 \leq \mu_1 - \mu_2 \leq -6.2$$

10.5.

The point estimate is the difference between the two sample means:

$$\text{Point estimate} = \bar{x}_1 - \bar{x}_2 = 400.67 - 375.33 = 25.34$$

The standard error of the sampling distribution.

$$s_1 = 42.5 \qquad \text{and} \qquad s_2 = 41.9$$

The standard error is: $\sqrt{\dfrac{42.5^2}{12} + \dfrac{41.9^2}{12}}$

Since we are unable to assume that the population variances are equal, we must first calculate the degrees of freedom for the t-distribution. This is done as follows:

$$df = \frac{\left(\frac{s_1^2}{n_1} + \frac{s_2^2}{n_2}\right)^2}{\left(\frac{\left(\frac{s_1^2}{n_1}\right)^2}{n_1 - 1} + \frac{\left(\frac{s_2^2}{n_2}\right)^2}{n_2 - 1}\right)} = \frac{\left(\frac{42.5^2}{12} + \frac{41.9^2}{12}\right)^2}{\left(\frac{\left(\frac{42.5^2}{12}\right)^2}{11} + \frac{\left(\frac{41.9^2}{12}\right)^2}{11}\right)} = \frac{88,103}{4,004.68} = 22$$

Thus, the degrees of freedom will be 22. For 95% confidence, using the t-distribution table the approximate t value is 2.0739

The confidence interval estimate is computed using:

$$(\bar{x}_1 - \bar{x}_2) \pm t\sqrt{\frac{s_1^2}{n_1} + \frac{s_2^2}{n_2}}$$

Then the interval estimate is:

$$(400.67 - 375.33) \pm 2.0739\sqrt{\frac{42.5^2}{12} + \frac{41.9^2}{12}}$$

$$25.34 \pm 25.27$$
$$0.07 \le (\mu_1 - \mu_2) \le 50.61$$

10.7.

$$\bar{x}_1 = \frac{\sum x}{n_1} = 56.7 \qquad \text{and} \quad \bar{x}_2 = \frac{\sum x}{n_2} = 70.4$$

The point estimate is: $\bar{x}_1 - \bar{x}_2 = 56.7 - 70.4 = -13.7 \; hours$

The standard error of the sampling distribution.

$$s_p = \sqrt{\frac{(n_1 - 1)s_1^2 + (n_2 - 1)s_2^2}{n_1 + n_2 - 2}} = \sqrt{\frac{(15-1)7.1^2 + (15-1)8.3^2}{15 + 15 - 2}} = 7.72$$

The critical value comes from a t-distribution with $df = n_1 + n_2 - 2$. The degrees of freedom are 15+15–2=28. The critical value from the t-distribution table is 2.0484.
When the population variances are assumed to be equal, the confidence interval estimate is computed using:

$$(\bar{x}_1 - \bar{x}_2) \pm ts_p\sqrt{\frac{1}{n_1} + \frac{1}{n_2}}$$

$$-13.7 \pm 2.0484(7.72)\sqrt{\frac{1}{15} + \frac{1}{15}}$$

$$-13.7 \pm 5.77$$
$$-19.47 \le \mu_1 - \mu_2 \le -7.93$$

Based on the sample data with 95% confidence the manager can conclude that the Denton Texas facility produces parts on average between 7.93 and 19.47 hours faster than the Lincoln plant. This may be due to the automation or some other factor such as plant layout.

10.9.

a. Point estimate for the difference between the two population means is

$$\bar{x}_1 - \bar{x}_2 = 24.96 - 25.01 = -0.05$$

b. Develop a confidence interval using equation 10-4.

$$(\bar{x}_1 - \bar{x}_2) \pm ts_p \sqrt{\frac{1}{n_1} + \frac{1}{n_2}}$$

$$s_p = \sqrt{\frac{(n_1 - 1)s_1^2 + (n_2 - 1)s_2^2}{n_1 + n_2 - 2}} = \sqrt{\frac{(19 - 1)0.07^2 + (23 - 1)0.08^2}{19 + 23 - 2}} = 0.0757$$

Then the interval estimate is

$$-0.05 \pm 2.0211(0.0757)\sqrt{\frac{1}{19} + \frac{1}{23}} = -0.05 \pm 0.0474 =$$

$$-0.0974 \le (\mu_1 - \mu_2) \le -0.0026$$

c. Since the interval does not contain zero, the managers can conclude the two lines do not fill bags with equal average amounts. However, the difference is at most about 0.1 lbs.

10.11.

a. $s_p = \sqrt{\dfrac{(14 - 1)2.5^2 + (14 - 1)1.8^2}{14 + 14 - 2}} = 2.1783$

$(17.2 - 15.9) \pm 1.7056(2.1783)\sqrt{(1/14) + (1/14)}$; -0.1043 ----- 2.7043; No because the interval contains the value 0 you cannot say that there is a difference setup time for the two additives.

b. No because again you cannot say that there is a difference in the setup time for the two additives.

10.13.

a. The ratio between the two variances is 200. It seems highly unlikely that sample variances that are so different would come from populations with the same variance.

b. $\sqrt{\dfrac{s_1^2}{n_1} + \dfrac{s_2^2}{n_1}} = \sqrt{\dfrac{64}{1442} + \dfrac{0.36}{1442}} = 0.211$

The degrees of freedom are derived as

$$df = \frac{(s_1^2/n_1 + s_2^2/n_2)^2}{\left(\dfrac{\left(s_1^2/n_1\right)^2}{n_1 - 1} + \dfrac{\left(s_2^2/n_2\right)^2}{n_2 - 1}\right)} = \frac{(64/1442 + 0.36/1442)^2}{\left(\dfrac{(64/1442)^2}{1442 - 1} + \dfrac{(0.36/1442)^2}{1442 - 1}\right)} = 1457.2 \approx 1457.$$

Therefore, the critical value = 2.5792.

$$(\bar{x}_1 - \bar{x}_2) \pm t_{\alpha/2}\sqrt{\frac{s_1^2}{n_1} + \frac{s_2^2}{n_1}} = (38.9 - 2) \pm 2.5792\sqrt{\frac{64}{1442} + \frac{0.36}{1442}} = 36.9 \pm 0.5449 =$$

$$(36.3551, 37.4449)$$

c. The confidence interval expresses the plausible values for the difference in the average number of job applications between 2002 and 2005. Since both 36.5 and 37 are in this interval, this indicates that both values are plausible values for the difference in the average number of job applications. This is not a contradiction. All values contained in the interval are plausible values for the difference in the means. Sampling error produces the uncertainty.

10.15. The confidence interval estimate can be computed using software such as Excel or Minitab. Using Excel's pivot table feature, we compute the following from the sample data:

Average of Years With the Club	2.7	2.6
StdDev of Years With the Club	1.6	1.6
Count of Years With the Club	368	846

Based on the population assumptions of normality and equal variances, we can use the t-distribution to obtain the critical value and the interval estimate is computed as follows:

$$(\bar{x}_1 - \bar{x}_2) \pm ts_p \sqrt{\frac{1}{n_1} + \frac{1}{n_2}}$$

where:

$$s_p = \sqrt{\frac{(n_1-1)s_1^2 + (n_2-1)s_2^2}{n_1 + n_2 - 2}} = \sqrt{\frac{(368-1)1.6^2 + (846-1)1.6^2}{368+846-2}} = 1.6$$

The degrees of freedom for the t-distribution is 368+846 – 2 = 1,212

Because df = 1,212 is not in the table, we can use Excel's TINV function as:
=TINV(0.05,1,212) = 1.961

Note, when the degrees of freedom gets large, the critical t-value approaches the critical z-value from a standard normal distribution. Some statisticians suggest using z when the degrees of freedom exceeds the table values.

Then

$$(2.7 - 2.6) \pm 1.961(1.6)\sqrt{\frac{1}{368} + \frac{1}{846}}$$

$$0.1 \pm 0.20$$

$$-0.10 \le \mu_1 - \mu_2 \le 0.30$$

This confidence interval indicates that based on the sample data with 95 percent confidence, the difference in mean years that males have been with the fitness club versus females is somewhere between -.10 year and 0.30 years. That is on the one end, females may have been the club on average slightly longer than males or on the other end, males may have been with the club slightly longer on average than the females. Since the interval estimated crosses over zero, we are unable to conclude that a difference exists.

10.17.
   a. Minitab output:

```
              N    Mean   StDev  SE Mean
INCOME01    100   72400   12879    1288
INCOME04    100   70700   14678    1468


Difference = mu (INCOME01) - mu (INCOME04)
Estimate for difference:  1699.75
```

The percentage decline is $= \dfrac{72400 - 70700}{72400}100\% = 2.35\%$.

   b. Minitab output:

Two-Sample T-Test and CI: INCOME01, INCOME04

```
Two-sample T for INCOME01 vs INCOME04

              N    Mean   StDev  SE Mean
INCOME01    100   72400   12879    1288
INCOME04    100   70700   14678    1468


Difference = mu (INCOME01) - mu (INCOME04)
Estimate for difference:  1699.75
90% CI for difference:  (-1527.32, 4926.82)
```

c. Since the confidence interval defines the plausible values for the difference in the average family incomes, one of the plausible values for this difference is 0. Indicating that is plausible that there is no difference. The measure this exercise alludes to is the margin of error. The margin of error for the two-sampled t is equal to the width of the confidence interval divided by 2.

Therefore, the margin of error $= \dfrac{4926.82 - (-1527.32)}{2} = 3227$

Section 10-2 Exercises

10.19. Since the population standard deviations are unknown and must be estimated from the sample data, the test statistic will be a t-value from the t distribution.

$$t = \frac{(\bar{x}_1 - \bar{x}_2) - (\mu_1 - \mu_2)}{s_p\sqrt{\dfrac{1}{n_1} + \dfrac{1}{n_2}}}$$

where:

$$s_p = \sqrt{\frac{(n_1 - 1)s_1^2 + (n_2 - 1)s_2^2}{n_1 + n_2 - 2}}$$

and

$$s = \sqrt{\frac{\sum(x - \bar{x})^2}{n-1}}$$

Then

$$\bar{x}_1 = \frac{\sum x}{n_1} = \frac{312}{9} = 34.67 \qquad \bar{x}_2 = \frac{\sum x}{n_2} = \frac{400}{9} = 44.44$$

and

$$s_1 = 5.2 \quad \text{and} \quad s_1 = 3.2$$

and

$$s_p = \sqrt{\frac{(n_1 - 1)s_1^2 + (n_2 - 1)s_2^2}{n_1 + n_2 - 2}} = \sqrt{\frac{(9-1)5.2^2 + (9-1)3.2^2}{9+9-2}} = 4.32$$

Substituting we get:

$$t = \frac{(34.67 - 44.44) - 0}{4.32\sqrt{\dfrac{1}{9} + \dfrac{1}{9}}} = -4.80$$

Since t = -4.80 < -2.1199, we reject
Based on the sample data, we conclude that the mean for population 1 is not equal to the mean for population 2.

10.21.

$$z = \frac{(\bar{x}_1 - \bar{x}_2) - (\mu_1 - \mu_2)}{\sqrt{\dfrac{\sigma_1^2}{n_1} + \dfrac{\sigma_2^2}{n_2}}}$$

Substituting we get:

$$z = \frac{(144 - 129) - 0}{\sqrt{\dfrac{11^2}{40} + \dfrac{16^2}{50}}} = 5.26$$

Since z = 5,26 > 1.645, we reject the null hypothesis.
Based on the sample data we conclude that the mean for population 1 exceeds the mean for population 2.

10.23.

a. The hypotheses are: H_0: $\mu_1 = \mu_2$
                             H_A: $\mu_1 \neq \mu_2$
   $$df = 125 + 120 - 2 = 243$$
   The Decision Rule is: If t > 1.9698 or t < -1.9698 (t found using Excel) reject H_0, otherwise do not reject H_0

b. $$s_p = \sqrt{\frac{(n_1 - 1)s_1^2 + (n_2 - 1)s_2^2}{n_1 + n_2 - 2}} = \sqrt{\frac{(125 - 1)31^2 + (120 - 1)38^2}{125 + 120 - 2}} = 34.61$$

   $$t = \frac{(130 - 105) - 0}{34.61\sqrt{\dfrac{1}{125} + \dfrac{1}{120}}} = 5.652$$

   Since 5.652 > 1.9698 reject H_0

10.25. $H_o : \mu_1 = \mu_2$

$H_A : \mu_1 \neq \mu_2$

The test statistic is

$$t = \frac{(\bar{x}_1 - \bar{x}_2) - (\mu_1 - \mu_2)}{s_p\sqrt{\dfrac{1}{n_1} + \dfrac{1}{n_2}}}$$

The pooled standard deviation is

$$s_p = \sqrt{\frac{(n_1 - 1)s_1^2 + (n_2 - 1)s_2^2}{n_1 + n_2 - 2}}$$

$$s_p = \sqrt{\frac{(25 - 1)425^2 + (20 - 1)415^2}{25 + 20 - 2}} = 420.611$$

Then the t-statistic is

$$t = \frac{(7200 - 7087) - (0)}{420.611\sqrt{\dfrac{1}{25} + \dfrac{1}{20}}} = 0.896$$

Because the calculated value of t = 0.896 is neither less than the lower tail critical value of t = -2.0167, nor greater than the upper tail critical value of t = 2.0167, do not reject the null hypothesis.
Based on these sample data, at the $\alpha = 0.05$ level of significance there is not sufficient evidence to conclude that the average tensile strength of ropes produced at the two plants is different.

10.27.

a. H_0: $\mu_C - \mu_R \geq 0.25$
   H_A: $\mu_C - \mu_R < 0.25$
   $df = 25 + 25 - 2 = 48$
   If $t < -1.677$ reject H_0, otherwise do not reject H_0

   $$s_p = \sqrt{\frac{(25-1)0.87^2 + (25-1)0.79^2}{25+25-2}} = 0.8310$$

   $t = ((3.74 - 3.26) - 0.25)/(0.8310\sqrt{(1/25)+(1/25)}) = 0.9785$

   Since $0.9785 > -1.677$ do not reject H_0 and conclude that the difference is at least $0.25

b. Since you accepted the null hypothesis the type of error that could occur is accepting a false null hypothesis that is a Type II error.

10.29. $H_0 : \mu_1 - \mu_2 \geq 0$

$H_A : \mu_1 - \mu_2 < 0$

The test statistic will be a t-value from the t distribution.

$$t = \frac{(\bar{x}_1 - \bar{x}_2) - (\mu_1 - \mu_2)}{s_p\sqrt{\dfrac{1}{n_1} + \dfrac{1}{n_2}}}$$

where:

$$s_p = \sqrt{\frac{(n_1-1)s_1^2 + (n_2-1)s_2^2}{n_1+n_2-2}} = \sqrt{\frac{(125-1)58.20^2 + (125-1)62.45^2}{125+125-2}} = 60.36$$

Substituting we get:

$$t = \frac{(45.68 - 78.49) - 0}{60.36\sqrt{\dfrac{1}{125} + \dfrac{1}{125}}} = -4.30$$

Since t = -4.30 < -1.6510, we reject the null hypothesis and conclude that the mean for population 2 exceeds the mean for population 1.
This means that the mean transaction at the self checkout is less than the mean transaction at the traditional checkout. If this has resulted in the overall decline in sales volume, there would be cause for concern.

10.31.

a. The ratio of these two standard deviations is 2084/2050 = 1.02. This, quite conceivably, could indicate that the population standard deviations are equal to each other.

b. **Step 1:** $\mu_1 - \mu_2$,
   Step 2: H_O: $\mu_1 - \mu_2 \geq 25,000$
            H_A: $\mu_1 - \mu_2 < 25,000$,
   Step 3: $\alpha = 0.01$,
   Step 4: Reject H_O if p-value $< \alpha = 0.01$,

Step 5: $s_p = \sqrt{\dfrac{(n_1-1)s_1^2 + (n_2-1)s_2^2}{n_1+n_2-2}}$

$= \sqrt{\dfrac{(75-1)(2050)^2 + (205-1)(2084)^2}{75+205-2}} = 2075.004$

$t = \dfrac{(\overline{x}_1 - \overline{x}_2) - (\mu_1 - \mu_2)}{s_p\sqrt{\dfrac{1}{n_1} + \dfrac{1}{n_2}}} = \dfrac{(38300-11800) - (25000)}{2075.004\sqrt{\dfrac{1}{75} + \dfrac{1}{205}}} = 5.36.$

$n_1 - n_2 - 2 = 75 + 205 - 2 = 278$. Therefore, the p-value = $P(t \le 5.36) \cong 1.00$ (from t-table).

Step 6: Because p-value = $P(t \le 5.36) \cong 1.00$, the null hypothesis is not rejected.

Step 7: Based on these sample data, there is evidence to conclude that the average college debt for bachelor of arts degree recipients is at least $25,000 more for graduates from private than for public college graduates.

10.33.

    a.   The ratio of the two means is 9.60/1.40 = 6.857. This is quite close to a ratio of 7. Since it was, perhaps, obtained from sample data, it is possible that the ratio is seven between the two population averages.

    b.   Minitab output

Descriptive Statistics: 94Salary, 04Salary

```
Variable   Mean   StDev
94Salary   1.398  1.468
04Salary   9.603  8.545
```

The ratio of the two standard deviations is 8.545/1.468 = 5.821. This seems to indicate that the two variances come from populations that do not have the same standard deviations.

    c.   Minitab output

Two-Sample T-Test and CI: 04Salary, 94Salary

```
Two-sample T for 04Salary vs 94Salary

          N  Mean  StDev  SE Mean
04Salary  100  9.60  8.55   0.85
94Salary  100  1.40  1.47   0.15


Difference = mu (04Salary) - mu (94Salary)
Estimate for difference:  8.20456
2.5% lower bound for difference:  9.92392
T-Test of difference = 9.8 (vs >): T-Value = -1.84  P-Value = 0.966  DF = 104
```

Since p-value = 0.966 > 0.25 do not reject the null. It appears that the difference in the average CEO salary between 1994 and 2004 is not more than $9.8 million.

10.35.

   a. Minitab output:

       Two-Sample T-Test and CI: Before, After

```
Two-sample T for Before vs After

          N    Mean   StDev   SE Mean
Before   75   110.3    19.0       2.2
After    75   117.7    20.5       2.4


Difference = mu (Before) - mu (After)
Estimate for difference:  -7.38200
95% CI for difference:  (-13.76438, -0.99962)
```

A difference of -10 or more would indicate the goal has been met. Since -10 is contained in this interval it is plausible the goal has been met.

   b. H_0: $\mu(\text{After}) - \mu(\text{Before}) \geq \$10.00$

       H_A: $\mu(\text{After}) - \mu(\text{Before}) < \$10.00$

       t-Test: Two-Sample Assuming Unequal Variances

	After	Before
Mean	117.6776	110.2956
Variance	420.0532	362.205
Observations	75	75
Hypothesized Mean Difference	10	
df	147	
t Stat	-0.81063	
P(T<=t) one-tail	0.209443	
t Critical one-tail	1.976233	
P(T<=t) two-tail	0.418886	
t Critical two-tail	2.264593	

Since the p-value is greater than 0.025, we do not reject the null hypothesis.

   c. You should be able to reach the same conclusion using either a confidence interval estimate of a hypothesis test. You have to be careful about how you formulate your null hypothesis however. In this problem, if the null had been an increase of $9.00 or less, you would not have rejected that hypothesis and seemingly reached a different conclusion.

Section 10-3 Exercises

10.37. The confidence interval estimate can be developed using the following steps.

Step 1: Define the population value of interest.

The samples are paired so the population value of interest is μ_d, the mean paired difference between the two populations.

Step 2: Specify the desired confidence level.

Step 3: Collect the sample data and compute the point estimate, $\overline{d}$ and the standard deviation of the paired differences, s_d.

The first thing we must do is compute the paired differences shown as follows:

Sample #	Sample 1	Sample 2	d
1	3693	4635	-942
2	3679	4262	-583
3	3921	4293	-372
4	4106	4197	-91
5	3808	4536	-728
6	4394	4494	-100
7	3878	4094	-216

Next, we compute the sample mean paired difference and the standard deviation for the sample paired differences:

$$\overline{d} = \frac{\sum d}{n} = \frac{-3032}{7} = -433.14$$

Step 4: Calculate the standard deviation, s_d.

$$s_d = \sqrt{\frac{\sum (d - \overline{d})^2}{n-1}} = 328.5$$

Step 5: Determine the critical value, t, from the t-distribution table

The confidence level is specified to be 90 percent. The critical value will be a t-value from the t distribution with 7-1 = 6 degrees of freedom. From the t-table we get t = 1.9432

Step 6: Compute the confidence interval estimate.

The confidence interval estimate is computed using the following format:

$$\overline{d} \pm t \frac{s_d}{\sqrt{n}}$$

substituting into this equation we get:

$$-433.14 \pm 1.9432 \frac{328.5}{\sqrt{7}}$$

$$-433.14 \pm 241.27$$

$$-674.41 \leq \mu \leq -191.87$$

10.39.
  a. If the difference is Sample 1 – Sample 2, the hypotheses are:
$$H_0: \ \mu_d \geq 0$$
$$H_A: \ \mu_d < 0$$
  b. The differences are:

Sample 1	Sample 2	Difference
4.4	3.7	0.7
2.7	3.5	-0.8
1	4	-3
3.5	4.9	-1.4
2.8	3.1	-0.3
2.6	4.2	-1.6
2.4	5.2	-2.8
2	4.4	-2.4
2.8	4.3	-1.5

Using these values find: $\overline{d}$ = -1.456

$$s_d = \ 1.2$$

The Decision Rule is: Reject if t < -1.3968. Using Equation 10-15:

$$t = \frac{-1.456 - 0}{\dfrac{1.2}{\sqrt{9}}} = -3.64$$

Since –3.64 < -1.3968, reject H_0.

Using the p-value approach, the calculated value of –3.64 is less than –3.3544, the smallest value in the t table (adjusting for a lower tail test). Therefore, the p-value < 0.01 < 0.10 = α and the null hypothesis is rejected.

  c. The 90% confidence interval is:

$$-1.456 \pm 1.8595(1.2/\sqrt{9} = -2.1998 \ - - - - - - \ -.7122$$

This confidence interval does not contain 0. Therefore, a value of 0 is not a plausible value for μ_d as was concluded by the hypothesis test.

10.41.
  a.

$$\overline{d} = \frac{\displaystyle\sum_{i=1}^{n} d_i}{n} = \frac{63.2}{6} = 10.5333$$

The standard deviation for the paired differences is computed using Equation 10.13.

$$s_d = \sqrt{\frac{\displaystyle\sum_{i=1}^{n}\left(d - \overline{d}\right)^2}{n-1}} = \sqrt{\frac{62.5733}{6-1}} = 3.5376$$

For a 90% confidence interval, the critical value is a t-value from the t-distribution with n-1 = 6 – 1 = 5. From the t-table , t = 2.015.

$$\overline{d} \pm t\frac{s_d}{\sqrt{n}} = 10.5333 \pm 2.015\frac{3.5376}{\sqrt{6}} =$$

$$10.5333 \pm 2.9101 = (7.6232, \ 13.4434)$$

b. H_O: $\mu_d \leq 10$

H_A: $\mu_d > 10$

$$t = \frac{\overline{d} - \mu_d}{\frac{s_d}{\sqrt{n}}} = \frac{10.5333 - 10.0}{\frac{3.5376}{\sqrt{6}}} = 0.37$$

Because t = 0.37< 1.459, the null hypothesis cannot be rejected.

10.43.

a. Since the same administrative assistant was used on both the ergonomic and the standard keyboards, the sampling was done dependently. The samples were matched pairs.

b.

$$\overline{d} = \frac{\sum\limits_{i=1}^{n} d_i}{n} = \frac{87}{10} = 8.7 \qquad s_d = \sqrt{\frac{\sum\limits_{i=1}^{n}\left(d - \overline{d}\right)^2}{n-1}} = \sqrt{\frac{678}{10-1}} = 8.68012$$

$t = \dfrac{8.7 - 0}{\dfrac{8.68012}{\sqrt{10}}} = 3.17$. Therefore, 0.005 < P-value < 0.01 (or from Minitab 0.006)

Because 0.005 < P-value < 0.01 = α , the null hypothesis should be rejected.

10.45.

a. H_0: $\mu_p - \mu_g = 0$

H_A: $\mu_p - \mu_g \neq 0$

Decision Rule:

Assuming the variances are equal, df = 70 + 50 – 2 = 118. Using Excel's TINV function :

If t > 1.98 or -t < -1.98 reject H_0, otherwise do not reject H_0

$s_p = [\{(70 - 1)\text{x}55.52^2 + (50 - 1)\text{x}61.75^2\}/(70 + 50 - 2)]^{1/2} = 58.19$

$$t = \frac{(230.25 - 309.45) - 0}{58.19\sqrt{\dfrac{1}{70} + \dfrac{1}{50}}} = -7.35$$

Since t = -7.35 < -1.98 reject H_0, and conclude that there is a difference in the mean amount employees give to United Way depending on whether the employer is a private business or a government agency.

b. $(230.25 - 309.45) \pm 1.98(58.19)\sqrt{\dfrac{1}{70} + \dfrac{1}{50}}$

-100.563 ------ -57.86

Yes they give compatible results. The hypothesis test concluded there was a difference and the confidence interval concludes the same thing because the interval does not contain the value 0.

10.47.

a. H_O: $\mu_d = 0$ H_A: $\mu_d \neq 0$,

$$\bar{d} = \frac{\sum\limits_{i=1}^{n} d_i}{n} = \frac{-28.3}{23} = -1.2304 \qquad s_d = \sqrt{\frac{\sum\limits_{i=1}^{n}\left(d - \bar{d}\right)^2}{n-1}} = \sqrt{\frac{8.97}{23-1}} = 0.63849$$

$$t = \frac{-1.2304 - 0}{\dfrac{0.63849}{\sqrt{23}}} = -9.24$$

Because t = -9.24 < -2.3646 the null hypothesis is rejected.

b. $s_1 = \sqrt{\dfrac{\sum(x - \bar{x})^2}{n-1}} = \sqrt{\dfrac{61.66}{22}} = 1.6741.$ $s_2 = \sqrt{\dfrac{70.87}{22}} = 1.7948.$

$$s_p = \sqrt{\frac{(n_1 - 1)s_1^2 + (n_2 - 1)s_2^2}{n_1 + n_2 - 2}} = \sqrt{\frac{(23-1)(1.6741)^2 + (23-1)(1.7948)^2}{23 + 23 - 2}} = 1.7355$$

$s_p\sqrt{\dfrac{1}{n_1} + \dfrac{1}{n_2}} = 1.7355\sqrt{\dfrac{1}{23} + \dfrac{1}{23}} = 0.5118,$ $\dfrac{s_d}{\sqrt{n}} = \dfrac{0.63849}{\sqrt{23}} = 0.13313.$ The ratio of the two standard

errors is 3.84 (= 0.5118/0.13313). Since the standard error is in the denominator of the t-statistic, a smaller standard error means that the test can detect smaller differences in the population means.

10.49. Looking at the difference between the new machines and the old machines, the null and alternative hypotheses are:

$$Ho: \mu_d \leq 0$$
$$H_A: \mu_d > 0$$

Using Excel's data analysis tool for t-Test: Paired Two Sample for Means, the following information is obtained:

t-Test: Paired Two Sample for Means

	New	Current
Mean	373.1428571	350.8285714
Variance	10663.36134	9577.087395
Observations	35	35
Pearson Correlation	0.245500253	
Hypothesized Mean Difference	0	
df	34	
t Stat	1.068010665	
P(T<=t) one-tail	0.146520185	
t Critical one-tail	2.135581318	

Since the test statistic of 1.068 is not greater than the critical value for a one-tail test of 2.136, do not reject the null hypothesis and conclude that the new machine does not have the desired result.

Section 10-4 Exercises

10.51.

a. $n_1p_1 = x_1 = 6 > 5$, $n_1q_1 = n_1 - x_1 = 15 - 6 = 9 > 5$; $n_2p_2 = x_2 = 16 > 5$, $n_2q_2 = n_2 - x_2 = 20 - 16 = 4 < 5$. The last test failed. Therefore, the sampling distribution cannot be approximated with a normal distribution.

b. $n_1p_1 = x_1 = 10(0.60) = 6 > 5$, $n_1q_1 = 10(.4) = 4 < 5$; $n_2p_2 = x_2 = 19 > 5$, $n_2q_2 = n_2 - x_2 = 30 - 19 = 11 > 5$. The second test failed. Therefore, the sampling distribution cannot be approximated with a normal distribution.

c. $n_1p_1 = x_1 = 6 > 5$, $n_1q_1 = n_1 - x_1 = 25 - 6 = 19 > 5$; $n_2p_2 = x_2 = 16(0.4) = 6.4 > 5$, $n_2q_2 = n_2 - x_2 = 16 - 6.4 = 9.6 > 5$. There were no tests that failed. Therefore, the sampling distribution can be approximated with a normal distribution.

d. $n_1p_1 = 100(0.05) = 5 \geq 5$, $n_1q_1 = 100(0.95) = 95 > 5$; $n_2p_2 = x_2 = 75(0.05) = 3.75 < 5$, $n_2q_2 = 75(0.95) = 71.25 > 5$. The third test failed. Therefore, the sampling distribution cannot be approximated with a normal distribution.

10.53. $H_o : \pi_1 = \pi_2$

$H_A : \pi_1 \neq \pi_2$

The sample proportions are

$$p_1 = \frac{42}{120} = 0.35 \text{ and } p_2 = \frac{57}{150} = 0.38$$

The test statistic is calculated using Equation 10-18

$$z = \frac{(p_1 - p_2) - (\pi_1 - \pi_2)}{\sqrt{\bar{p}(1 - \bar{p})(\frac{1}{n_1} + \frac{1}{n_2})}}$$

where, using Equation 10-17:

$$\bar{p} = \frac{n_1 p_1 + n_2 p_2}{n_1 + n_2} = \frac{120(0.35) + 150(0.38)}{120 + 150} = 0.367$$

Then:

$$z = \frac{(0.35 - 0.38) - (0)}{\sqrt{0.367(1 - 0.367)(\frac{1}{120} + \frac{1}{150})}} = -0.508$$

The probability of finding a z-value this small or smaller when the null hypothesis is true is approximately 0.5- 0.1950 =0.3050. Because this is a two-tailed test the p-value is twice this amount. Therefore, the p-value is 2*0.3050 = 0.61. There is evidence to reject the null hypothesis when the p-value is smaller than α. Here, because the p-value is greater than α, we do not reject the null hypothesis.
Conclude there is no difference in the two population proportions.

10.55.

a. $H_O: \pi_1 - \pi_2 = 0$
   $H_A: \pi_1 - \pi_2 \neq 0$

$$\bar{p} = \frac{x_1 + x_2}{n_1 + n_2} = \frac{35 + 35}{50 + 75} = \frac{70}{125} = 0.56$$

$$z = \frac{p_1 - p_2 - (\pi_1 - \pi_2)}{\sqrt{\bar{p}(1 - \bar{p})(\frac{1}{n_1} + \frac{1}{n_2})}} = \frac{0.70 - 0.47 - (0)}{\sqrt{0.56(0.44)(\frac{1}{50} + \frac{1}{75})}} = 2.538$$

Since z = 2.538 > 1.96, reject H_O
There is sufficient evidence to conclude that $\pi_1 - \pi_2 \neq 0$.

b.   Using the same steps found in part a, indicated in ( ). (1). π_1 - π_2, (2) H$_O$: π_1 - $\pi_2 \geq$ 0 vs. H$_A$: π_1 - $\pi_2 < 0$, (3) α = 0.05, (4) the critical value is - 1.645, Reject H$_O$ if z $<$ -1.645, (5) z = 2.538, (6) Since z = 2.538 $>$ - 1.645, fail to reject H$_O$, (7) There is not sufficient evidence to conclude that π_1 - $\pi_2 < 0$.

c.   Using the same steps found in part a, indicated in ( ). (1). π_1 - π_2, (2) H$_O$: π_1 - $\pi_2 =$ 0 vs. H$_A$: π_1 - $\pi_2 > 0$, (3) α = 0.025, (4) the critical value is 1.96, Reject H$_O$ if z $>$ 1.96, (5) z = 2.538, (6) Since z = 2.538 $>$ 1.96, reject H$_O$, (7) There is sufficient evidence to conclude that π_1 - $\pi_2 > 0$.

d.   Using the same steps found in part a, indicated in ( ). (1). π_1 - π_2, (2) H$_O$: π_1 - $\pi_2 = 0.05$ vs. H$_A$: π_1 - $\pi_2 \neq$ 0.05, (3) α = 0.02, (4) the critical values are $\pm$ 2.33, Reject H$_O$ if z $<$ -2.33 or z $>$ 2.33, (5)

$$z = \frac{p_1 - p_2 - (\pi_1 - \pi_2)}{\sqrt{\bar{p}(1-\bar{p})(\frac{1}{n_1} + \frac{1}{n_2})}} = \frac{0.70 - 0.47 - (0.05)}{\sqrt{0.56(0.44)(\frac{1}{50} + \frac{1}{75})}} = 1.987$$

(6) Since z = 1.987 $<$ 2.33, fail to reject H$_O$, (7) There is not sufficient evidence to conclude that π_1 - $\pi_2 \neq$ 0.05.

10.57. $H_o : \pi_S = \pi_M$

$H_A : \pi_S \neq \pi_M$

Using an α = 0.01, the critical value is z = $\pm$ 2.575. The decision rule based on the z-statistic is: If z calculated $<$ -2.575 or z calculated $>$ 2.575, reject the null hypothesis; Otherwise, do not reject.

$$p_S = \frac{66}{200} = 0.33 \text{ and } p_M = \frac{63}{180} = 0.35$$

Using Equation 10-17:

$$= \frac{n_1 p_1 + n_2 p_2}{n_1 + n_2} = \frac{200(0.33) + 180(0.35)}{200 + 180} = 0.3395$$

Using Equation 10-18

$$z = \frac{(p_1 - p_2) - (\pi_1 - \pi_2)}{\sqrt{\bar{p}(1-\bar{p})(\frac{1}{n_1} + \frac{1}{n_2})}} = \frac{(0.33 - 0.35) - (0)}{\sqrt{0.3395(1 - 0.3395)(\frac{1}{200} + \frac{1}{180})}} = -0.4111$$

Since the test statistic, -0.4111, is not less than the critical value of -2.575, do not reject the null hypothesis and conclude that there is no difference between the population proportions of adults between the ages of 27 and 35 in the two cities with college degrees.

10.59.

a.   **Step 1:** π_1 - π_2

Step 2: H$_O$: π_1 - $\pi_2 \leq 0.04$ vs. H$_A$: π_1 - $\pi_2 > 0.04$

Step 3: α = 0.05

Step 4: Reject H$_O$ if p-value $<$ 0.05

Step 5:

$$\bar{p} = (.103 + .149) / 2) = 0.126$$

$$z = \frac{p_1 - p_2 - (\pi_1 - \pi_2)}{\sqrt{\bar{p}(1-\bar{p})(\frac{1}{n_1} + \frac{1}{n_2})}} = \frac{0.149 - 0.103 - (0.04)}{\sqrt{0.126(0.874)(\frac{1}{23601} + \frac{1}{23601})}} = 1.964$$

p-value = P(z $>$ 1.96) = 0.5 - 0.475 = 0.025

Step 6: Since p-value = 0.025 $<$ 0.05 reject H$_O$

Step 7:   There is sufficient evidence to conclude that there has been more than a 0.04 increase in the proportion of students that indicate they have been diagnosed with depression.

b. The margin of error is given by $\pm z \sqrt{\dfrac{p_1 q_1}{n_1} + \dfrac{p_2 q_2}{n_2}} = \pm 1.96 \sqrt{\dfrac{0.149(0.851)}{23601} + \dfrac{0.103(0.897)}{23601}} = 0.00597.$

c. This is testing to see if the student understand what the margin of error represents. As such, the smallest difference equals the margin of error = 0.00597.

10.61.

a. $n_1 p_1 = 400(60/400) = 60 \geq 5$, $n_1 q_1 = 400(340/400) = 340 > 5$; $n_2 p_2 = x_2 = 300(63/300) = 63 > 5$, $n_2 q_2 = 300(237/300) = 237 > 5$. There was no test that failed. Therefore, the sampling distribution can be approximated with a normal distribution.

b. b.

```
Test and CI for Two Proportions: USAPriority, ASIAPriority

Event = yes


Variable      X    N  Sample p
USAPriority   60  400  0.150000
ASIAPriority  63  300  0.210000


Difference = p (USAPriority) - p (ASIAPriority)
Estimate for difference:  -0.06
95% CI for difference:  (-0.117869, -0.00213125)
Test for difference = 0 (vs not = 0):  Z = -2.06  P-Value = 0.039
```

Since the p-value = 0.039 < 0.05, the null hypothesis is rejected. There is sufficient evidence that there is a difference in the proportion of USA and Asian executives that feel as though innovation is their top priority.

10.63.

a. $n_1 p_1 = 147(72/147) = 72 > 5$, $n_1 q_1 = 147(75/147) = 75 > 5$; $n_2 p_2 = 120(48/120) = 48 > 5$, $n_2 q_2 = 120(72/120) = 72 > 5$. There was no test that failed. Therefore, the sampling distribution can be approximated with a normal distribution.

b. Minitab output:

```
Test and CI for Two Proportions: UpperIncome, LowIncome

Event = Male


Variable     X    N  Sample p
UpperIncome  72  147  0.489796
LowIncome    48  120  0.400000


Difference = p (UpperIncome) - p (LowIncome)
Estimate for difference:  0.0897959
99% lower bound for difference:  -0.0517098
Test for difference = 0.01 (vs > 0.01):  Z = 1.31  P-Value = 0.095
```

Since the p-value = 0.095 > 0.01. The null hypothesis is not rejected. There is not sufficient evidence to indicate that the proportion of male undergraduates in the upper income category is more than 1% greater than that of the low income category.

c. The difference, $p_1 - p_2 = 0.49 - 0.40 = 0.09$, is greater than the hypothesized value 0.01. However, the difference "0.09" is the difference between the sample proportions. The hypothesis test is testing the difference between the population proportions. Given the sample sizes, the difference, 0.09, is not large enough to support the assertion that the difference in the population proportions is more than 0.01. Incidentally, the sample sizes cannot support an assertion that the population proportion are not equal to each other. Larger sample sizes would be required to detect a difference in the two population proportions.

Chapter Exercises

10.65. Variability in the measured value of any characteristics of interest is often caused by many factors. For instance, variability in mileage the same model of tire will get is determined in variation in the tire's construction, but also by factors such as weather, road conditions, type of driving and type of driver. Independent random samples would not only find variability in tire manufacture but also variability in the other factors mentioned. Paired samples of tires would tend to subject pairs to the same other factors, controlling for their effects.

10.67.

a.

$$s_P = \sqrt{\frac{(n_1-1)s_1^2 + (n_2-1)s_2^2}{n_1+n_2-2}} = \sqrt{\frac{(15-1)(3)^2 + (10-1)(4)^2}{15+10-2}}$$

$$s_P = 3.4262, \quad (\overline{x}_1 - \overline{x}_2) \pm t_{\alpha/2}\, s_P \sqrt{\frac{1}{n_1} + \frac{1}{n_2}} = (12 - 7) \pm (2.0687)(3.4262)\sqrt{\left(\frac{1}{15} + \frac{1}{10}\right)} = 5 \pm 2.8936 =$$

$(2.1064, 7.8936)$.

b. $$t = \frac{(\overline{x}_1 - \overline{x}_2) - (\mu_1 - \mu_2)}{s_P \sqrt{\frac{1}{n_1} + \frac{1}{n_2}}} = \frac{(12-7)-(7.8936)}{3.4262\sqrt{\frac{1}{15} + \frac{1}{10}}} .= -2.0687$$

Any value specified in H_O larger than the upper confidence limit would result in a test statistic smaller than the lower critical value and a rejection of H_O

c. $$t = \frac{(\overline{x}_1 - \overline{x}_2) - (\mu_1 - \mu_2)}{s_P \sqrt{\frac{1}{n_1} + \frac{1}{n_2}}} = \frac{(12-7)-(2.1064)}{3.4262\sqrt{\frac{1}{15} + \frac{1}{10}}} .= 2.0687$$

Any value specified in H_O smaller than the lower confidence limit would result in a test statistic larger than the upper critical value and a rejection of H_O

d. To conduct a two-tailed hypothesis test using a confidence interval, simply compare the value stated in H_O. If that value is contained in the confidence interval, do not reject H_O. If that value is not contained in the confidence interval, reject H_O.

10.69. Develop a confidence interval for the difference in the means. A 90% confidence interval would be:

Mean of A = 362.7273   Mean of B = 375.3636

$$s_p = \sqrt{\frac{(11-1)134.9919^2 + (11-1)218.2298^2}{11+11-2}} = 181.4484$$

$(375.3636 - 362.7273) \pm 1.7247(181.4484) \sqrt{(1/11) + (1/11)}$;

-120.8035 ----- 146.0761

10.71.

a. $n_1 p_1 = (19/300)(300) = 19 > 5$; $n_1(1-p_1) = 300(1-0.0633) = 281 > 5$

$n_2 p_2 = (12/250)(250) = 12 > 5$; $n_2 p_2(1-p_2) = 250(1-0.048) = 238 > 5$: The normal distribution is appropriate.

b. H_0: $\pi_1 - \pi_2 = 0$

H_A: $\pi_1 - \pi_2 \neq 0$

Decision Rule:

If $z > 2.17$ or $z < -2.17$ reject H_0, otherwise do not reject H_0

$p_1 = 19/300 = 0.0633$

$p_2 = 12/250 = 0.048$

$\bar{p} = (19+12)/(300+250) = 0.0564$

$z = [(0.0633 - 0.048) - 0] / \sqrt{(0.0564)(1 - 0.0564)[(1/300) + (1/250)]} = 0.7745$

Since $0.7745 < 2.17$ do not reject H_0 and conclude that there is no difference in the packing materials.

10.73.

Individual	Turbo Tax	Tax-Cut	d
1	70	88	-18
2	56	71	-15
3	79	89	-10
4	94	66	28
5	93	78	15
6	101	64	37
7	42	74	-32
8	71	99	-28
9	91	79	12
10	59	68	-9
11	65	93	-28
12	50	93	-43
13	47	86	-39
14	60	86	-26
15	63	81	-18
16	43	83	-40

Next, we compute the sample mean paired difference and the standard deviation for the sample paired differences:

$$\bar{d} = \frac{\sum d}{n} = \frac{-214}{16} = -13.38$$

$$s_d = \sqrt{\frac{\sum (d - \bar{d})}{n-1}} = 24.4$$

The critical value will be a t-value from the t distribution with $16-1 = 15$ degrees of freedom. From the t-table we get $t = 2.1315$

The confidence interval estimate is computed using the following format:

$$\bar{d} = \pm t \frac{s_d}{\sqrt{n}}$$

Substituting into this equation we get:

$$-13.38 \pm 2.1315 \frac{24.4}{\sqrt{16}}$$

-13.38 ± 13.02

$-26.40 \leq \mu_d \leq -0.36$

Based on the sample data, with 95% confidence we conclude that the Turbo tax software requires on average between 26.40 minutes and 0.36 minutes less to use than does the Tax-Cut software.

10.75.

a. Since the medications were administered to the same patients, the sampling is dependent. That is to say, it is a paired samples experiment.

b. Minitab output:

Paired T-Test and CI: AmbienHrs, SonataHrs

```
Paired T for AmbienHrs - SonataHrs

              N     Mean    StDev    SE Mean
AmbienHrs    245   7.97143  0.79538  0.05081
SonataHrs    245   7.25143  0.99204  0.06338
Difference   245   0.720000 1.251347 0.079946


95% lower bound for mean difference: 0.588000
T-Test of mean difference = 0 (vs > 0): T-Value = 9.01  P-Value = 0.000
```

Since the p-value = 0.000 < 0.05 = α, the null hypothesis is rejected. It appears that the researchers were correct in Ambien patients sleeping longer.

c. Since no hypothesis exists here, the procedure of choice is the confidence interval.

Minitab output:

Paired T-Test and CI: AmbienHrs, SonataHrs

```
Paired T for AmbienHrs - SonataHrs

              N     Mean    StDev    SE Mean
AmbienHrs    245   7.97143  0.79538  0.05081
SonataHrs    245   7.25143  0.99204  0.06338
Difference   245   0.720000 1.251347 0.079946


95% CI for mean difference: (0.562528, 0.877472)
```

The plausible values are (0.5625, 0.8775). The 95% confidence interval indicates Ambien patients sleep from 33.75 to 52.56 minutes longer.

10.77.

a. The "gap" between private and public 4-year colleges for the 1980 – 81 academic year in 2005 dollars was $8,180 - $1,818 = $6362. Doubling this would yield 2(6362) = 12724.

H_0: μ(2005-2006) - μ(1980-19811) $\leq$ 12724

H_A: μ(2005-2006) - μ(1980-19811) > 12724

t-Test: Two-Sample Assuming Equal Variances

	Private05	Public05
Mean	21234.59	5490.938
Variance	23168591	3601780
Observations	81	81
Pooled Variance	13385186	
Hypothesized Mean Difference	12724	
df	160	
t Stat	5.252578	
P(T<=t) one-tail	2.36E-07	
t Critical one-tail	2.34988	
P(T<=t) two-tail	4.72E-07	
t Critical two-tail	2.606903	

The critical values for the one tailed test is 2.3499. the calculated t value is 5.25. The null hypothesis is rejected. The gap between the average tuition and fees at private and public colleges has more than doubled.

b. Since the null hypothesis was rejected, the only statistical error that could have been made is a type I error = rejecting H_O when in fact H_O was true.

Chapter 11
Hypothesis Tests and Estimation for Population Variances

Section 11-1 Exercises

11.1. No statistical method exists for developing a confidence interval estimate for a population standard deviation directly. Instead we must first convert to variances. This, we get a sample variance equal to $s^2 = 360^2 = 129,600$.

Now we compute the interval estimate using:

$$\frac{(n-1)s^2}{\chi_U^2} \le \sigma^2 \le \frac{(n-1)s^2}{\chi_L^2}$$

where

s^2 = sample variance
n = sample size
χ_L^2 = Lower Critical Value
χ_U^2 = Upper Critical Value

The denominators come from the chi-square distribution with n -1 degrees of freedom. In an application in which the sample size is n = 20 and the desired confidence level is 95%, from the chi-square table in Appendix G we get the critical value

$$\chi_U^2 = \chi_{0.025}^2 = 32.8523$$

Likewise, we get:

$$\chi_L^2 = \chi_{0.975}^2 = 8.9065$$

Now given that the sample variance computed from the sample of n = 20 values is $s^2 = 360^2 = 129,600$. Then, we construct the 95% confidence interval as follows:

$$\frac{(20-1)129,600}{32.8523} \le \sigma^2 \le \frac{(20-1)129,600}{8.9065}$$

$$74,953.7 \le \sigma^2 \le 276,472.2$$

Thus, at the 95% confidence level, we conclude that the population variance will fall in the range 74,953.7 to 276,472.2. By taking the square root, you can convert to an interval estimate of the population standard deviation as the interval 273.78 to 525.81.

11.3. $H_0 : \sigma^2 \ge 16,900$

$H_A : \sigma^2 < 16,900$

If $\chi^2 < 10.1170$, reject the null hypothesis
Otherwise, do not reject the null hypothesis
The random sample of n = 20 items provided a sample standard deviation equal to 105. Thus, $s^2 = 11,025$. The test statistic is:

$$\chi^2 = \frac{(n-1)s^2}{\sigma^2} = \frac{(20-1)11,025}{16,900} = 12.39$$

Since $\chi^2 = 12.39 > 10.1170$, do not reject the null hypothesis.

Based on the test results, the data do not present sufficient evidence to justify concluding that the population standard deviation has dropped below 130.

11.5

a. The random sample consists of n = 12 observations. The sample variance is $s^2 = 9^2 = 81$. The test statistic is

$$\chi^2 = \frac{(n-1)s^2}{\sigma^2} = \frac{(12-1)81}{50} = 17.82$$

Because $\chi^2 = 17.82 < \chi^2_{0.05} = 19.6752$ and because $\chi^2 = 17.82 > \chi^2_{0.95} = 4.5748$ do not reject the null hypothesis based on these sample data.

Based on the sample data and the hypothesis test conducted we do not reject the null hypothesis at the $\alpha = 0.10$ level of significance and we conclude the population variance is not different from 50.

b. The decision rule is:

If the test statistic, $\chi^2 > \chi^2_{0.25} = 31.5264$, reject the null hypothesis

If the test statistic, $\chi^2 < \chi^2_{0.975} = 8.2307$, reject the null hypothesis

Otherwise, do not reject the null hypothesis

The random sample consists of n = 19 observations. The sample variance is $s^2 = 6^2 = 36$. The test statistic is

$$\chi^2 = \frac{(n-1)s^2}{\sigma^2} = \frac{(19-1)36}{50} = 12.96$$

Because $\chi^2 = 12.96 < \chi^2_{0.025} = 31.5264$ and because $\chi^2 = 12.96 > \chi^2_{0.975} = 8.2307$ we do not reject the null hypothesis.

Based on the sample data and the hypothesis test conducted we do not reject the null hypothesis at the $\alpha = 0.05$ level of significance and conclude the population variance is not different from 50.

11.7

a. H_O: $\sigma^2 \leq 39.69$
H_A: $\sigma^2 > 39.69$

$$\chi^2 = \frac{(n-1)s^2}{\sigma^2} = \frac{(28-1)66.2}{(6.3)^2} = 45.03 ,$$

p-value = $P(\chi^2 \geq 45.03)$. Therefore, $0.01 < $ p-value < 0.025.

Since p-value $< \alpha$, reject H_O.

b. **Step 1:** The parameter of interest is the population variance, σ^2,
Step 2: H_O: $\sigma^2 \geq 39.69$ H_A: $\sigma^2 < 39.69$,
Step 3: $\alpha = 0.025$,

Step 4: $\chi^2 = \frac{(n-1)s^2}{\sigma^2} = \frac{(8-1)9.02}{(6.3)^2} = 1.591$,

Step 5: The critical value is obtained from a χ^2 distribution with n − 1 = 7 degrees of freedom, i.e., 1.6899,

Step 6: Since the test statistic = 1.591 < the χ^2 critical value = 1.6899, reject the null hypothesis,
Step 7: Conclude that the variance has decreased.

c.   **Step 1:** The parameter of interest is the population variance, σ^2
     Step 2: H_O: $\sigma^2 = 39.69$ H_A: $\sigma^2 \neq 39.69$.
     Step 3: $\alpha = 0.10$

   Step 4: Since $\chi^2 = \dfrac{(n-1)s^2}{\sigma^2} = \dfrac{(18-1)62.9}{(6.3)^2} = 26.94$,

   p-value = $P(s^2 \geq 62.9) = P(\chi^2 \geq 26.94)$.

   Step 5: $\alpha = 0.10 <$ p-value = 0.94
            From Minitab:
            Cumulative Distribution Function
            Chi-Square with 17 DF

            x P(X <= x)
            26.94   0.941046
   Step 6: Fail to reject H_O,
   Step 7: Conclude that there is not enough evidence to conclude that the variance has changed.

11.9.   No statistical method exists for developing a confidence interval estimate for a population standard deviation directly. Instead we must first convert to variances. This, have a sample variance equal to $s^2 = 6.2^2 = 38.44$.
   Now we compute the interval estimate using:

$$\frac{(n-1)s^2}{\chi_U^2} \leq \sigma^2 \leq \frac{(n-1)s^2}{\chi_L^2}$$

where

   s^2 = sample variance
   n = sample size
   χ_L^2 = Lower Critical Value
   χ_U^2 = Upper Critical Value

   The denominators come from the chi-square distribution with n -1 degrees of freedom. For example, in an application in which the sample size is n = 15 and the desired confidence level is 90%, $\alpha = 0.10$. Then from the chi-square table in Appendix G we get the critical value

$$\chi_U^2 = 23.6848$$

Likewise, we get:

$$\chi_L^2 = 6.5706$$

Now given that the sample variance computed from the sample of n = 15 values is $s^2 = 6.2^2 = 38.44$. Then, we construct the 90% confidence interval as follows:

$$\frac{(15-1)38.44}{23.6848} \leq \sigma^2 \leq \frac{(15-1)38.44}{6.5706}$$

$$22.72 \leq \sigma^2 \leq 81.90$$

Thus, at the 90% confidence level, we conclude that the population variance will fall in the range 22.72 to 81.90. By taking the square root, you can convert to an interval estimate of the population standard deviation as the interval 4.77 minutes to 9.05 minutes.

11.11 The confidence interval estimate for the population variance, σ^2 is computed using Equation 11-2 shown below:

$$\frac{(n-1)s^2}{\chi_U^2} \leq \sigma^2 \leq \frac{(n-1)s^2}{\chi_L^2}$$

Where s^2 = the sample variance, n = the sample size, and α = 1-confidence interval. For a 95% confidence interval we find the following values for χ_L^2 and χ_U^2 with n-1 = 14-1 = 13 degrees of freedom:

$\chi_{0.975}^2 = 5.0087$ and $\chi_{0.025}^2 = 24.7356$.

The sample variance is found to be: $s^2 = 672.39$

The confidence interval is calculated using Equation 11-2:

$$\frac{(14-1)672.39}{24.7356} \leq \sigma^2 \leq \frac{(14-1)672.39}{5.0087} = 353.38 \leq \sigma^2 \leq 1745.18$$

11.13

a. H_o: $\mu \leq 10$
    H_a: $\mu > 10$

b. Using Excel's AVERAGE and STDEV functions

$\bar{x} = 11$ s = 2.5820

$t = (11- 10)/(2.5820/\sqrt{10}) = 1.2247$

$t_{.10} = 1.383$

Since 1.2247 < 1.383 do not reject H_o and conclude that the mean time may be 10 minutes or less. Needed to assume a random sample and the underlying population was normally distributed.

c. H_o: $\sigma^2 \leq 16$
    H_a: $\sigma^2 > 16$

$\chi^2 = [(10-1)(2.5820)^2]/16 = 3.75$

Decision Rule:

If $\chi^2 > 14.6837$, reject H_o, otherwise do not reject H_o

Since 3.75 < 14.6837 do not reject Ho and conclude that the population variance is less than or equal to 16

11.15

a. Hartford's wage average is 19.5 + 0.38(19.5) = \$26.91 and Brownsville's is 19.5 – 0.30(19.5) = \$13.65. Therefore, the range of values is 26.91 – 13.65 = 13.26. The relationship between a normal distribution's range and standard deviation is $\sigma \approx \dfrac{R}{6} = \dfrac{13.26}{6} = 2.21$. Therefore, $\sigma^2 = 4.884$.

b. There are two hypothesis tests called for here. First we perform the test to determine if the standard deviation is smaller in San Antonio. Using the seven steps outlined in the chapter:

Step 1: The parameter of interest is the population variance, σ^2,

Step 2: H_O: $\sigma^2 \geq 4.884$ H_A: $\sigma^2 < 4.884$,

Step 3: $\alpha = 0.05$,

Step 4: The critical value is obtained from a χ^2 distribution with n – 1 = 24 degrees of freedom, i.e., 13.8484.

Step 5: $\chi^2 = \dfrac{(n-1)s^2}{\sigma^2} = \dfrac{(25-1)(1.46)^2}{4.884} = 10.47$,

Step 6: Since the test statistic = 10.47 < the χ^2 critical value = 13.8484, do not reject the null hypothesis.

Step 7: Conclude that the variance of the construction workers in San Antonio is not less than the variance of the nation construction workers as a whole.

Since the variance for wages of the construction workers in San Antonio is (smaller than the nation as a whole but) unknown, a test of hypothesis utilizing the t-distribution is appropriate.

The second part of the problem involves testing a hypothesis about the population mean, μ,

H_O: $\mu \geq 19.5$

H_A: $\mu < 19.5$

$\alpha = 0.05$,

Since σ is unknown, we use a t test statistic $t = \dfrac{\overline{x} - \mu}{\dfrac{s}{\sqrt{n}}} = \dfrac{13.87 - 19.5}{\dfrac{1.46}{\sqrt{25}}} = -19.28$, with $25 - 1 = 24$

degrees of freedom. We reject H_O if $t < -1.7109$.

Since $t = -17.57 < -1.7109$, reject H_O. There is sufficient evidence to conclude that the construction workers average wage is smaller than that of the national construction workers as whole.

11.17

a. For the weight to round off to 2.2, the range of values must be between 2.15 to 2.25. This is a range of 0.10.

The relationship between a normal distribution's range and standard deviation is $\sigma \approx \dfrac{R}{6} = \dfrac{0.10}{6} = 0.0167$.

Therefore, $\sigma^2 = 0.000278$.

b. H_o: $\sigma^2 \leq 0.000278$

H_a: $\sigma^2 > 0.000278$

Using Minitab to test, based on the Catfood data set:

Test and CI for One Variance: C1

```
Test of sigma squared = 0.000278 vs > 0.000278


Chi-Square Method (Normal Distribution)

                            95%
                          Lower
    Variable   N  Variance  Bound  Chi-Square     P
    C1        65  0.000428  0.000327     98.51  0.004
```

Since p-value = 0.004 < 0.01, we conclude that the standard deviation of the weight of crude protein in the 6.6 pound sack of Felidae cat food is too large to meet Canidae's wishes.

Section 11-2 Exercises

11.19

a. Using Appendix H: If the calculated F > 2.278, reject H_0, otherwise do not reject H_0

b. F = 1450/1320 = 1.0985

Since 1.0985 < 2.278 do not reject H_0

11.21

a. Using the F distribution in Appendix H, F = 3.619

b. Using the F distribution in Appendix H, F = 3.106

c. Using the F distribution in Appendix H, F = 3.051

11.23 Using the seven step procedure from the chapter:

Step 1: σ^2,

Step 2: H_O: $\sigma_1^2 \leq \sigma_2^2$, H_A: $\sigma_1^2 > \sigma_2^2$,

Step 3: $\alpha = 0.05$,

Step 4: The critical value is obtained from the F-distribution. F = 6.388. Reject H_O if F > 6.388.

Step 5: $s_1^2 = \dfrac{7.028}{4} = 1.757$ $s_2^2 = \dfrac{\sum(x - \bar{x})^2}{n-1} = \dfrac{8.108}{4} = 2.027$.

The test statistic is $F = \dfrac{s_2^2}{s_1^2} = \dfrac{2.027}{1.757} = 1.154$

Step 6: Since F = 1.154 < 6.388 = $F_{0.05}$, fail to reject H_O.

Step 7: Based on these sample data, there is not sufficient evidence to conclude that population one's variance is larger than population two's variance.

11.25 H_0: $\sigma_m^2 \leq \sigma_f^2$
H_A: $\sigma_m^2 > \sigma_f^2$
Using Appendix H with $D_1 = 24$ & $D_2 = 24$: If the calculated F > 1.984, reject H_0, otherwise do not reject H_0
$F = 2.5^2/1.34^2 = 3.4807$
Since 3.4807 > 1.984 reject H_0 and conclude that there is more variability in male donations than in female donations.

11.27
a. H_0: $\sigma_A^2 \leq \sigma_T^2$
H_A: $\sigma_A^2 > \sigma_T^2$
If the calculated F > 2.534, reject H_0, otherwise do not reject H_0
$F = 0.202^2/0.14^2 = 2.0818$
Since 2.0818 < 2.534 do not reject H_0 and conclude that the Trenton plant is not less variable than the Atlanta plant.
b.   You would have rejected a true null hypothesis, which is a Type I, error. You could decrease the alpha level to decrease the probability of a Type I error or you could increase the sample sizes.

11.29   Using the seven steps outlined in the chapter:

Step 1: σ^2,

Step 2: H_O: $\sigma_1^2 \leq \sigma_2^2$ H_A: $\sigma_1^2 > \sigma_2^2$,

Step 3: $\alpha = 0.05$,

Step 4: The critical value is obtained from the F-distribution. F = 2.526. Reject H_O if F > 2.526.

Step 5: The test statistic is $F = \dfrac{s_1^2}{s_2^2} = \dfrac{(2636)^2}{(1513)^2} = 3.035$,

Step 6: Since F = 3.035 > 2.526 = $F_{0.05}$, reject H_O.

Step 7: Based on these sample data, there is sufficient evidence to conclude that the debt for 4-year degree students is greater than students taking more than 4 years.

11.31 $s_A = 7.1375$ $s_B = 8.6929$

$H_0: \sigma_A^2 = \sigma_B^2$

$H_A: \sigma_A^2 \neq \sigma_B^2$

Using Appendix H with D_1 and D_2 both equal to 19: If the calculated F > 3.027, reject H_0, otherwise do not reject H_0

$$F = 8.6929^2/7.1375^2 = 1.4833$$

Since 1.4833 < 3.027 do not reject H_0 and conclude that there is no difference in the standard deviation of dollars returned between the two brochures.

Excel or Minitab could be used to find the exact p-value = .199. Using the Appendix, the F value is less than the F for α = .05 of 2.168. So the p-value must be greater than .05.

11.33

a.   Since the populations are assumed to be normally distributed, the F-test approach is the appropriate test to determine equality of variances.

Minitab output

Test for Equal Variances: 04Salary, 94Salary

```
95% Bonferroni confidence intervals for standard deviations

            N    Lower    StDev    Upper
04Salary  100  7.36764  8.54544  10.1500
94Salary  100  1.26546  1.46776   1.7434


F-Test (normal distribution)
Test statistic = 33.90, p-value = 0.000


Levene's Test (any continuous distribution)
Test statistic = 83.55, p-value = 0.000
```

Since the p-value = 0, reject the null of equal variances.

b.   Minitab output:

Descriptive Statistics: 94Salary, 04Salary

```
Variable   Mean    StDev
94Salary   1.398   1.468
04Salary   9.603   8.545
```

$$P(x > 1.398) = P\left(z = \frac{1.398 - 9.603}{8.545} \right) = P(z > -0.96) = 0.5000 + 0.3315 = 0.8315.$$

More than 80% or the 2004 CEO salaries are greater than the 1994 average salaries.

Chapter Exercises

11.35   Student answers will vary with the article.

11.37.   Answers will vary, but any examples involving manufacturing, service or scheduling would be appropriate.

11.39   The interval estimate is completed using:

$$\frac{(n-1)s^2}{\chi_U^2} \leq \sigma^2 \leq \frac{(n-1)s^2}{\chi_L^2}$$

where

s^2 = sample variance
n = sample size
χ_L^2 = Lower Critical Value
χ_U^2 = Upper Critical Value

For the 98% interval, with 26 degrees of freedom, we get the critical value

$$\chi_U^2 = \chi_{0.01}^2 = 45.6416$$

Likewise, we get:

$$\chi_L^2 = \chi_{0.99}^2 = 12.1982$$

The 98% confidence interval becomes:

$$\frac{(27-1)1.15^2}{45.6416} \leq \sigma^2 \leq \frac{(27-1)1.15^2}{12.1982}$$
$$0.753 \leq \sigma^2 \leq 2.819$$

By taking the square root, you can convert to an interval estimate of the population standard deviation as the interval 0.868 to 1.679 degrees.

11.41 H_o: $\sigma^2_A = \sigma^2_Z$
H_a: $\sigma^2_A \neq \sigma^2_Z$
$\alpha = 0.05$ $n_A = 24$ $n_Z = 32$

$$F = = \frac{41.3^2}{37.5^2} = 1.2129$$

If F > 2.231, reject the null hypothesis
Since 1.2129 < 2.231, do not reject the null hypothesis and conclude there is no evidence of differences in the variability of the effect time for the 2 drugs.

11.43.

a. H_O: $\sigma^2 = (0.05)^2$
H_A: $\sigma^2 \neq 0.0025$
$\alpha = 0.10$

Reject H_O if $\chi^2 < \chi_L^2 = 10.1170$ or $\chi^2 > \chi_U^2 = 30.1435$ $\chi^2 = \frac{(n-1)s^2}{\sigma^2} = \frac{(20-1)(0.07)^2}{0.0025} =$

37.24

Since $\chi^2 = 37.24 > \chi_U^2 = 30.1435 \rightarrow$ reject H_O. There is enough evidence to conclude that the standard deviation of the amount of Coke in the cans differs from the standard deviation specified by the quality control division.

b. From part a, random sampling would indicate the process is not meeting specifications 10% of the time when it is meeting specifications ($\alpha = 0.10$). The trial has two outcomes: meet specifications or not. There were seven trials. If we assume the trials were random and independent we have a binomial distribution where we are looking for the probability of three or more with n = 7. From the binomial table with p = α = 0.10:

$P(x \geq 3) = 0.0230 + 0.0026 + 0.0002 = 0.0256$.

11.45

a. H_O: $\sigma_1^2 = \sigma_2^2$

H_A: $\sigma_1^2 \neq \sigma_2^2$

The test statistic is F = $\dfrac{s_1^2}{s_2^2} = \dfrac{87025}{22801} = 3.817$

Since F = 3.817 > 1.752 = $F_{0.025}$, reject H_O.

Based on these sample data, there is sufficient evidence to conclude that the two population variances are not equal to each other. The two-sample t could not be used.

b. Regardless of the test to be used in this situation, it would be necessary to determine if the populations' distributions had normal distributions.

11.47 H_o: $\sigma^2 \leq 3,900^2$
H_a: $\sigma^2 > 3,900^2$
$\alpha = 0.10$ s = 3,934.5589   n = 200   df = 200 – 1 = 199

$$\chi^2 = \frac{(n-1)s^2}{\sigma^2} = \frac{(200-1)3,934.5589^2}{3,900^2} = 202.5424$$

Since the table in the book does not contain df = 199, use Excel's CHIINV function to find the critical value. If χ^2 > 224.9568, reject the null hypothesis
Since 202.5424 < 224.9568, do not reject the null hypothesis and conclude that the manager is correct in the consistency of the current routes so he does not need to reroute trucks.

11.49 H_o: $\sigma^2_M \leq \sigma^2_F$
H_a: $\sigma^2_M > \sigma^2_F$
$\alpha = 0.05$
$n_F = 70$ $s_F = 3,694.5429$ $n_M = 67$ $s_M = 5,303.8555$

$$F = = \frac{5,303.8555^2}{3,694.5429^2} = 2.0609$$

If F > 1.4953, reject the null hypothesis
Since 2.0609 > 1.4953, reject the null hypothesis and conclude that the negotiator's concern is valid and that the variability of total charges for male patients is greater than the variability of total charges for female patients.

11.51
    a.   Minitab output:
        Test for Equal Variances: INCOME04, INCOME07
        95% Bonferroni confidence intervals for standard deviations

	N	Lower	StDev	Upper
INCOME04	100	12654.8	14677.9	17433.9
INCOME07	100	11814.9	13703.7	16276.8

        F-Test (normal distribution)
        Test statistic = 1.15, p-value = 0.496
        Since the p-value = $0.496 > 0.05 = \alpha = 0.05$, fail to reject the null hypothesis.

    b.   It would be appropriate to use the two-sample t since the two population variances were determined to be equal to each other. One other requirement must be met: the populations must have normal distributions.

Chapter 12
Analysis of Variance

Section 12-1 Exercises

12.1

a. The calculations for the completed ANOVA table below are:
Between groups df = k-1 where k is the number of magazines = 3-1 = 2
Within groups df = n_t –k, where n_t = 25 subscribers * 3 magazines = 75;
$75 - 3 = 72$
SSW = SST-SSB = 9,271,678,090 – 2,949,085,157 = 6,322,592,933
MSB = 2,949,085,157/2 = 1,474,542,579
MSW = 6,322,592,933/72 = 87,813,791
F = 1,474,542,579/87,813,791 = 16.79

ANOVA

Source of Variation	SS	df	MS	F
Between Groups	2,949,085,157	2	1,474,542,579	16.79
Within Groups	6,322,592,933	72	87,813,791	
Total	9,271,678,090	74		

b. H_o: $\mu_1 = \mu_2 = \mu_3$
H_A: Not all populations have the same mean
F = MSB/MSW = 1,474,542,579/87,813,791 = 16.79
Because the F test statistic = 16.79 > F_α = 2.3778, we do reject the null hypothesis based on these sample data.

12.3

a. The appropriate null and alternative hypotheses are:
$$H_0 : \mu_1 = \mu_2 = \mu_3$$
$$H_A : \text{not all } \mu_j \text{ are equal}$$

b. The one-way ANOVA test is appropriate for testing the null and alternative hypotheses. All the information needed is supplied in the table.

Using the F test approach, because F = 9.84 > critical F = 3.35, we reject the null hypothesis and conclude that the population means are not all equal.

Using the p-value approach, because p-value = 0.0006 < α = 0.05, we reject the null hypothesis and conclude that the population means are not all equal.

c. Because the null hypothesis has been rejected and we conclude that not all population means are equal, we can now apply the Tukey-Kramer method to determine which means are different. We start by calculating the Tukey-Kramer critical range value using:

$$CriticalRange = q_{1-\alpha} \sqrt{\frac{MSW}{2} \left\{ \frac{1}{n_i} + \frac{1}{n_j} \right\}}$$

The value for $q_{0.95}$ with $k = 3$ and $n_T - k$ = 30-3=27 degrees of freedom is found in Appendix J as approximately 3.50. Because the sample sizes are equal in this situation, we need only compute one critical range value shown as follows:

$$CriticalRange = 3.5 \sqrt{\frac{29.42}{2} \left\{ \frac{1}{10} + \frac{1}{10} \right\}} = 6.0$$

We now compare all the possible contrasts of differences between sample means to the Tukey-Kramer critical range value.

Contrast	Significant ?
$\left|\overline{x}_1 - \overline{x}_2\right| = \left|50.72 - 40.58\right| = 10.14 > 6.0$	Yes
$\left|\overline{x}_1 - \overline{x}_3\right| = \left|50.72 - 48.76\right| = 1.96 < 6.0$	No
$\left|\overline{x}_2 - \overline{x}_3\right| = \left|40.58 - 48.76\right| = 8.18 > 6.0$	Yes

Thus, we conclude $\mu_1 > \mu_2$ and $\mu_3 > \mu_2$. Thus, the mean for population 2 is less than the means for the other two populations. However, the sample data do not provide sufficient evidence to conclude that the means for populations one and three are different.

12.5

a. $df_B = 3 = k - 1 \rightarrow k = 4 =$ number of populations.

b.

Source	SS	df	MS	F
Between Samples	483	3	161	11.1309
Within Samples	405	28	14.464	
Total	888	31		

c. H_0: $\mu_1 = \mu_2 = \mu_3 = \mu_4$
H_A: At least two population means are different

d. F critical = 2.9467 (Minitab); from text table use $F_{3, 24} = 3.009$
Since $11.1309 > 2.9467$ reject H_o and conclude that at least two populations means are different.

12.7

a. H_0: $\mu_1 = \mu_2 = \mu_3$

H_A: At least two population means are different.
Because $k - 1 = 2$ and $n_T - k = 12$, $F_{0.05} = 3.885$. The decision rule is if the calculated $F > F_{0.05} = 3.885$, reject H_O, or if the p-value $< \alpha = 0.05$, reject H_O; otherwise, do not reject H_O.
If we assume that the populations are normally distributed, Harley's F_{max} test can be used to test whether the three populations have equal variances. The sample variances are $s_1^2 = \dfrac{\sum(x - \overline{x})^2}{n - 1} = \dfrac{10}{5 - 1} = 2.50$,

$s_2^2 = 0.916$, and $s_3^2 = 1.467$ test statistic is $F_{max} = \dfrac{s_{max}^2}{s_{min}^2} = \dfrac{2.50}{0.916} = 2.729$. From Appendix I, the critical value for alpha $= 0.05$, $k = 3$, and $\overline{n} - 1 = 4$ is 15.5. Because $2.729 < 15.5$, we conclude that the population variances could be equal.

One-way ANOVA: Group1, Group2, Group3

```
Source  DF    SS    MS    F     P
Factor   2  16.85  8.43  5.03  0.026
Error   12  20.08  1.67
Total   14  36.93

S = 1.294   R-Sq = 45.62%   R-Sq(adj) = 36.56%


                          Individual 95% CIs For Mean Based on
                          Pooled StDev
Level   N   Mean   StDev   ----+---------+---------+---------+----
Group1  5  14.000  1.581   (-------*--------)
Group2  4  16.750  0.957                    (---------*--------)
Group3  6  15.333  1.211           (------*-------)
                            ----+---------+---------+---------+----
                            13.5      15.0      16.5      18.0

Pooled StDev = 1.294
```

Since $F = 5.03 > 3.885$, we reject H_O.
We conclude there is sufficient evidence to indicate that at least two of the population means differ.

b. Use the Tukey-Kramer test to determine which populations have different means.
Using Equation 12-7 to construct the critical ranges:

$$q_{1-\alpha}\sqrt{\frac{MSW}{2}\left(\frac{1}{n_i}+\frac{1}{n_j}\right)}$$

For $n_1 = 5$ and $n_2 = 4$, critical range $= 3.77\sqrt{\frac{1.67}{2}\left(\frac{1}{5}+\frac{1}{4}\right)} = 2.311$;

for $n_1 = 5$ and $n_3 = 6$, critical range $= 3.77\sqrt{\frac{1.67}{2}\left(\frac{1}{5}+\frac{1}{6}\right)} = 2.086$;

and for $n_2 = 4$ and $n_3 = 6$, critical range $= 3.77\sqrt{\frac{1.67}{2}\left(\frac{1}{4}+\frac{1}{6}\right)} = 2.224$

The contrast are $|\bar{x}_1 - \bar{x}_2| = |14 - 16.75| = 2.75 > 2.311$,

$|\bar{x}_1 - \bar{x}_3| = |14 - 15.33| = 1.33 < 2.086$, and

$|\bar{x}_2 - \bar{x}_3| = |16.75 - 15.33| = 1.42 < 2.224$

Therefore, we can infer that population 1 and population 2 have different means. However, no other differences are supported by these sample data.

12.9 Using Excel's ANOVA Single Factor Data Analysis tool with an $\alpha = 0.01$, the following ANOVA table was generated. Use this information to answer parts (a and b).
Anova: Single Factor

SUMMARY

Groups	Count	Sum	Average	Variance
Venetti	10	137,277	13,727.7	737,295.12
Madison	10	130,197	13,019.7	888,396.90
Edison	10	122,718	12,271.8	604,286.84

ANOVA

Source of Variation	SS	df	MS	F	P-value	F crit
Between Groups	10,600,877	2	5,300,439	7.131	0.003	5.488
Within Groups	20,069,810	27	743,326			
Total	30,670,687	29				

a. Test to determine if there is a difference in the average time before failure for the three different supplier motors. The null and alternative hypotheses are:

H_o: $\mu_V = \mu_M = \mu_E$
H_A: Not all populations have the same mean
As shown in the ANOVA table above, the F test statistic for this null hypothesis is 7.131.
$F_{\alpha=0.01} = 5.488$ is obtained from the ANOVA table above. Since $F = 7.131 > F_{\alpha=0.01} = 5.488$, reject the null hypothesis. Based on these sample data we can conclude that the average time before failure is different for the three different suppliers.

b. Use the Tukey-Kramer test to determine which populations have different means. Calculate the critical range using Equation 12-7.

q_α has 3 and 27 degrees of freedom. The table (Appendix J) has (3, 24) and (3, 30) degrees of freedom. Since you need (3, 27), take the average of these q-values (4.55 and 4.45) = 4.5. Since the sample sizes are the same for each motor supplier, you only need to calculate one critical range.

$$CR = q_{1-\alpha}\sqrt{\frac{MSW}{2}\left(\frac{1}{n_i}+\frac{1}{n_j}\right)} = 4.5\sqrt{\frac{743,326}{2}\left(\frac{1}{10}+\frac{1}{10}\right)} = 1,226.88$$

Contrast	Conclusions
$\lvert \overline{x}_1 - \overline{x}_2 \rvert = \lvert 13727.7 - 13019.7 \rvert = 708 < 1,226.88$	No significant difference
$\lvert \overline{x}_1 - \overline{x}_3 \rvert = \lvert 13727.7 - 12271.8 \rvert = 1,455.9 > 1,226.88$	Significant difference: $\mu_1 \neq \mu_3$
$\lvert \overline{x}_2 - \overline{x}_3 \rvert = \lvert 13019.7 - 12271.8 \rvert = 747.9 < 1,226.88$	No significant difference

Based on the sample data, EverRun can conclude that Venetti would be preferred to Edison. Based on the sample, there is no difference between Venetti and Madison or between Madison and Edison. EverRun can eliminate Edison motors from further consideration because Venetti motors have a longer mean performance time before repair than Edison and EverRun can also eliminate Madison because there is no difference between Madison's mean time before repair and Edison's.

12.11

a. **Step 1:** The parameters of interest are the mean fire points of the three types of dielectric fluid.

Step 2: H_O: $\mu_1 = \mu_2 = \mu_3$,

H_A: At least two population means are different.

Step 3: The significance level is $\alpha = 0.05$.

Step 4: The selected samples are specified in the heading of this exercise.

Step 5: Because $k - 1 = 2$ and $n_T - k = 12$, $F_{0.05} = 3.885$. The decision rule is if the calculated $F > F_{0.05} = 3.885$, reject H_O, or if the p-value $< \alpha = 0.05$, reject H_O; otherwise, do not reject H_O.

Step 6: Because of the small sample sizes, the box and whisker diagram is used.

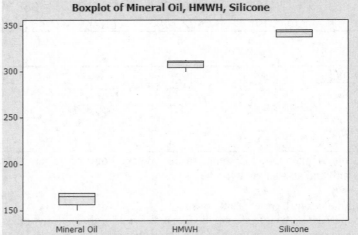

The box plots indicate some skewness but not sufficient to deny normality. If we assume that the populations are normally distributed, Harley's F_{max} test can be used to test whether the three populations have equal variances. The sample variances are $s_1^2 = \dfrac{\sum(x-\overline{x})^2}{n-1} = \dfrac{210}{5-1} = 52.5$, $s_2^2 = 23.2$, and $s_3^2 = 16.8$ test statistic is $F_{max} = \dfrac{s_{max}^2}{s_{min}^2} = \dfrac{52.5}{16.8} = 3.125$. From Appendix I, the critical value for alpha = 0.05, k = 3, and $\overline{n} - 1 = 4$ is 15.5. Because $3.125 < 15.5$, we conclude that the population variances could be equal.

Step 7:

One-way ANOVA: Mineral Oil, HMWH, Silicone

```
Source  DF      SS       MS        F       P
Factor   2   90019.7  45009.9  1459.78  0.000
Error   12    370.0     30.8
Total   14  90389.7

S = 5.553   R-Sq = 99.59%   R-Sq(adj) = 99.52%
```

```
                              Individual 95% CIs For Mean Based on
                              Pooled StDev
Level          N   Mean  StDev  --------+---------+---------+---------+-
Mineral Oil    5  163.00  7.25  (*)
HMWH           5  308.20  4.82                           (*)
Silicone       5  341.40  4.10                                  (*)
                              --------+---------+---------+---------+-
                                    200       250       300       350
```

Step 8: Since F = 1459.78 > 3.885, we reject H_O.

Step 9: We conclude there is sufficient evidence to indicate that at least two of the population means differ.

b. Using Equation 12-7 to construct the critical ranges:

$$q_{1-\alpha}\sqrt{\frac{MSW}{2}\left(\frac{1}{n_i}+\frac{1}{n_j}\right)}$$

For $n_1 = n_2 = n_3 = 5$, critical range $= 3.77\sqrt{\frac{30.8}{2}\left(\frac{1}{5}+\frac{1}{5}\right)} = 9.36$;

The contrast are $|\bar{x}_1 - \bar{x}_2| = |163 - 308.2| = 145.2 > 9.36$,

$$|\bar{x}_1 - \bar{x}_3| = |163 - 341.4| = 178.4 > 9.36, \text{ and}$$

$$|\bar{x}_2 - \bar{x}_3| = |308.2 - 341.4| = 33.2 > 9.36$$

Therefore, we can infer that the mean fire points differ among the three types of dielectic fluids.

12.13

a. H_0: $\mu_1 = \mu_2 = \mu_3 = \mu_4$

H_A: At least two population means are different

Since 10.48326 > 5.9525 reject H_0 and conclude that at least two populations means are different.

Anova: OneWay

SUMMARY

Groups	Count	Sum	Average	Variance
Type A	4	4417	1104.25	11576.25
Type B	4	5343	1335.75	4257.583
Type C	4	4634	1158.5	1845.667
Type D	4	4114	1028.5	8393

ANOVA

rce of Varia	SS	df	MS	F	P-value	F crit
Between G	204993.5	3	68331.17	10.48326	0.001137	5.952529
Within Gro	78217.5	12	6518.125			
Total	283211	15				

b. Using an α value of 0.01, giving a q with 4 and 12 degrees of freedom of 5.50 we find a critical range value of 22.02 and can construct the following table:

	Absolute Difference	Critical Range	Significant?
Type A - Type B	231.5	222.02	Yes
Type A - Type C	54.25	222.02	No
Type A - Type D	75.75	222.02	No
Type B - Type C	177.25	222.02	No
Type B - Type D	307.25	222.02	Yes
Type C - Type D	130.00	222.02	No

Based on the Tukey-Kramer test you can eliminate Type D and A since the mean life is less than B.

12.15

a. H_0: $\mu_1 = \mu_2 = \mu_3$
H_A: At least two population means are different
Anova: Single Factor

SUMMARY

Groups	Count	Sum	Average	Variance
Mini1	5	68	13.6	0.345
Mini 2	3	38.9	12.96667	0.263333
Mini 3	4	59.1	14.775	0.515833

ANOVA

Source of Variation	SS	df	MS	F	P-value	F crit
Between Groups	6.0725	2	3.03625	7.911098	0.010407	4.256492
Within Groups	3.454167	9	0.383796			
Total	9.526667	11				

Since 0.01 < 0.05 reject H_0 and conclude that at least two populations means are different.

b. Using a value of 0.05 we can construct the following table:

	Absolute Differences	Critical Range	Significant?
Mini 1 -Mini 2	0.633	1.264	no
Mini 1 - Mini 3	1.175	1.161	yes
Mini 2 -Mini 3	1.808	1.322	yes

Student reports will vary but they should recommend either 1 or 2 since there is no statistically significance difference between them..

c. The confidence interval is constructed around the difference between the largest sample value and the smallest sample value. The pooled estimator of the population standard deviation is found by taking the square root of the mean square within.

$(14.775 - 12.967) \pm 1.7959(0.6197)\sqrt{(1/3)+(1/4)}$; 0.978 ----- 2.678 range for cents per mile so the maximum and minimum difference in average savings per year would be ($0.00978)(30,000) ----- ($0.02678)(30,000); $293.40 ----- $803.40

12.17

a. Minitab output:

One-way ANOVA: Life versus Manufacturer

```
Source         DF     SS      MS     F      P
Manufacturer    2  2218.2  1109.1  22.05  0.000
Error         132  6640.8    50.3
Total         134  8859.0

S = 7.093   R-Sq = 25.04%   R-Sq(adj) = 23.90%
```

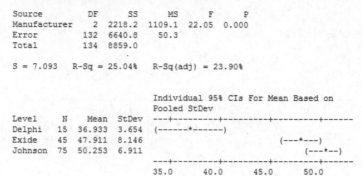

The p-value = 0.000 < α = 0.05. Therefore, there appears to be sufficient evidence to indicate that there is a difference in the average length of life among the batteries from the different manufacturers.

b. Minitab output:

```
Tukey 95% Simultaneous Confidence Intervals
All Pairwise Comparisons among Levels of Manufacturer

Individual confidence level = 98.07%

Manufacturer = Delphi subtracted from:

Manufacturer  Lower   Center  Upper
Exide         5.968   10.978  15.987
Johnson       8.568   13.320  18.072
```

```
Manufacturer = Exide subtracted from:

Manufacturer  Lower   Center  Upper
Johnson       -0.826  2.342   5.510
```

The confidence intervals by Minitab indicate that there is no significant difference in the means if the confidence interval contains 0. The confidence intervals indicate that there is sufficient evidence to conclude that the average length of life differs between Delphi and Exide and also between Delphi and Johnson. There is, however, not enough evidence to indicate that the average lifetime for batteries made by Exide and Johnson differ.

Section 12-2 Exercises

12.19

a. H_0: $\mu_1 = \mu_2 = \mu_3 = \mu_4$

H_A: At least two population means are different

H_0: $\mu_{b1} = \mu_{b2} = \mu_{b3} = \mu_{b4} = \mu_{b5} = \mu_{b6} = \mu_{b7} = \mu_{b8}$

H_A: Not all block means are equal

b.

ANOVA

Source of Variation	SS	df	MS	F	P-value	F crit
Blocks	9123.375	7	1303.339	46.87669	2.08E-11	2.487582
Groups	1158.625	3	386.2083	13.8906	3.26E-05	3.072472
Error	583.875	21	27.80357			
Total	10865.88	31				

c. Since $46.87669 > 2.487582$ reject H_0 and conclude that there is an indication that blocking was necessary.

d. Since p-value $0.0000326 < 0.05$ reject H_0 and conclude that at least two means are different.

e.

Least Significant
Difference (LSD)   5.48280844

	Mean Difference	Absolute Mean Difference	Significant
G1 v. G2	6.625	6.625	YES
G1 v. G3	-0.625	0.625	NO
G1 v. G4	-10.25	10.25	YES
G2 v. G3	-7.25	7.25	YES
G2 v. G4	-16.875	16.875	YES
G3 v. G4	-9.625	9.625	YES

12.21 $H_0 : \mu_1 = \mu_2 = \mu_3$

$H_A : not\ all\ \mu_j\ are\ equal$

The sample data are:

Block	Sample 1	Sample 2	Sample 3
1	30	40	40
2	50	70	50
3	60	40	70
4	40	40	30
5	80	70	90
6	20	10	10

The following sums of squares values are computed:

$SST = 9,000$ $SSB = 33.33$ $SSBL = 7,866.67$ $SSW = 1,100$

The completed ANOVA table is:

ANOVA Source of Variation	SS	df	MS	F	P-value	F crit
Rows (Blocks)	7866.667	5	1573.333	14.30303	0.000277	3.325837
Columns (Populations)	33.33333	2	16.66667	0.151515	0.861341	4.102816
Error (Within)	1100	10	110			
Total	9000	17				

The hypothesis to be tested is:

$H_0 : \mu_1 = \mu_2 = \mu_3 = \mu_4 = \mu_5 = \mu_6$ (blocking is not effective)

$H_A : not\ all\ \mu_j\ are\ equal$ (blocking is effective)

The hypothesis is tested by computing the test statistic F ratio as follows:

$$F = \frac{MSBL}{MSW} = \frac{1,573.33}{110} = 14.3$$

The critical F value from the F-distribution for alpha = 0.05 and degrees of freedom $D_1 = 5 \; and \; D_2 = 10$ is 3.326. Therefore the decision rule is:

> If test statistic F > critical F = 3.326, reject the null hypothesis
> Otherwise, do not reject the null hypothesis

Because F = 14.3 > critical F = 3.326, we reject the null hypothesis and conclude that blocking is effective. Recall that the main hypothesis is:

$$H_0 : \mu_1 = \mu_2 = \mu_3$$

$$H_A : not \; all \; \mu_j \; are \; equal$$

This hypothesis is tested using an F test with the test statistic computed as follows:

$$F = \frac{MSB}{MSW} = \frac{16.67}{110} = 0.1515$$

The critical F value from the F-distribution for alpha = 0.05 and degrees of freedom $D_1 = 2 \; and \; D_2 = 10$ is 4.103. Therefore the decision rule is:

> If test statistic F > critical F = 4.103, reject the null hypothesis
> Otherwise, do not reject the null hypothesis

Because F = 0.1515 < critical F = 4.103, we do not reject the null hypothesis and conclude that the three populations may have the same mean value.

12.23 Using Excel's ANOVA Two-Factor without Replication Data Analysis tool with an α = 0.01, the following ANOVA table was generated. Use this information to answer parts (a and b).

Anova: Two-Factor
Without Replication

SUMMARY	Count	Sum	Average	Variance
Product 1	3	24831	8277	221673
Product 2	3	25595	8531.667	708756.3
Product 3	3	27885	9295	14491
Product 4	3	17519	5839.667	30190.33
Rail	4	31810	7952.5	2035434
Plane	4	30834	7708.5	1965691
Truck	4	33186	8296.5	3118892

ANOVA						
Source of Variation	SS	df	MS	F	P-value	F crit
Rows (blocks)	20107982	3	6702661	32.11967	0.000431	9.779538
Columns (carrier)	698154.7	2	349077.3	1.672805	0.264625	10.92477
Error	1252067	6	208677.8			
Total	22058204	11				

a. Test to determine whether blocking is effective. Four products were examined. These constitute the blocks. The null and alternative hypotheses are:

H_o: $\mu_1 = \mu_2 = \mu_3 = \mu_4$
H_A: Not all populations have the same mean

As shown in the ANOVA table above, the rows represent blocking (products). The F test statistic for this null hypothesis is 32.12.

$F_{\alpha=0.01} = 9.78$ is obtained from the ANOVA table above. Because $F = 32.12 > F_{\alpha=0.01} = 9.78$, reject the null hypothesis. Thus, based on these sample data we conclude that blocking is effective.

b. Conduct the main hypothesis test to determine whether there is a difference due to carrier type. The appropriate null and alternative hypotheses are:

H_o: $\mu_R = \mu_P = \mu_T$
H_A: Not all populations have the same mean

As shown in the ANOVA table above, the columns represent the main test (carrier type). The F test statistic for this null hypothesis is 1.673.

$F_{\alpha=0.01} = 10.925$ is obtained from the ANOVA table above. Because $F = 1.673 < F_{\alpha=0.01} = 10.925$, do not reject the null hypothesis. This means that based on these sample data we cannot conclude average dollar breakage per shipment is different among the three carrier types.

12.25 Using Excel's ANOVA Two-Factor without Replication Data Analysis tool with $\alpha = 0.05$, the following ANOVA table was generated. Use this information to answer parts (a-c).

Anova: Two-Factor Without Replication

SUMMARY	Count	Sum	Average	Variance
Hourly	3	162	54	36
Non-Supervisory	3	122	40.66667	160.3333
Supervisors/Managers	3	98	32.66667	56.33333
Shift 1	3	104	34.66667	142.3333
Shift 2	3	123	41	129
Shift 3	3	155	51.66667	108.3333

ANOVA

Source of Variation	SS	df	MS	F	P-value	F crit
Rows (blocks)	696.8889	2	348.4444	22.32028	0.006763	6.944272
Columns (Shifts)	442.8889	2	221.4444	14.18505	0.01527	6.944272
Error	62.44444	4	15.61111			
Total	1202.222	8				

a. Test to determine whether blocking is effective. Three employee groups were selected. These constitute the blocks. The null and alternative hypotheses are:

H_o: $\mu_H = \mu_N = \mu_S$
H_A: Not all blocks have the same mean

As shown in the ANOVA table above, the rows represent blocking (employee groups). The F test statistic for this null hypothesis is 22.32.

$F_{\alpha=0.05} = 6.944$ is obtained from the ANOVA table above. Because $F = 22.32 > F_{\alpha=0.05} = 6.944$, reject the null hypothesis. Thus, based on these sample data we conclude that blocking is effective.

b. Conduct the main hypothesis test to determine whether there are differences in the average number of hours missed due to illness across the three shifts. The appropriate null and alternative hypotheses are:

H_o: $\mu_1 = \mu_2 = \mu_3$

H_A: Not all populations have the same mean

As shown in the ANOVA table above, columns represent the main test (shifts). The F test statistic for this null hypothesis is 14.185.

$F_{\alpha=0.05} = 6.944$ is obtained from the ANOVA table above. Because $F = 14.185 > F_{\alpha=0.05} = 6.944$, reject the null hypothesis. This means that based on these sample data we can conclude that there are differences in the average number of hours missed due to illness across the three shifts.

c. $LSD = t_{\alpha/2} \sqrt{MSW} \sqrt{\dfrac{2}{b}} = 2.7765\sqrt{15.61}\sqrt{\dfrac{2}{3}} = 8.957$

Where t $\alpha/2$ df = (k-1)(b-1) = (3-1)(3-1) = 4

MSW is taken from the ANOVA table given above

Absolute Difference	Comparison	Conclusion
$\lvert \overline{x}_1 - \overline{x}_2 \rvert = \lvert 34.67 - 41 \rvert = 6.33$	$6.33 < 8.957$	No Significant Difference
$\lvert \overline{x}_1 - \overline{x}_3 \rvert = \lvert 34.67 - 51.67 \rvert = 33.0$	$33.0 > 8.957$	$\mu_1 \neq \mu_3$
$\lvert \overline{x}_2 - \overline{x}_3 \rvert = \lvert 41 - 51.67 \rvert = 10.67$	$10.67 > 8.957$	$\mu_2 \neq \mu_3$

We infer, based on the sample data, that the mean number of hours missed due to illness for Shift 3 exceeds those for Shift 1 and also exceed those for Shift 2. Management may want to study Shift 3 to determine why the mean hours missed due to illness on Shift 3 is greater than that for Shifts 1 and 2.

12.27

a. Minitab output:

Two-way ANOVA: Revenue versus Restaurant, Week

```
Source      DF      SS       MS       F      P
Restaurant   2   26.234  13.1168  11.61  0.004
Week         4  110.123  27.5307  24.36  0.000
Error        8    9.040   1.1300
Total       14  145.396

S = 1.063   R-Sq = 93.78%   R-Sq(adj) = 89.12%
```

The p-value = 0.000 < α = 0.05. This indicates that inserting the week on which the testing was done was necessary.

b. The p-value = 0.004 < α = 0.05. This indicates that we should reject the null hypothesis and conclude that there exists a difference in the average revenue among the three restaurants.

c. If you did conclude that there was a difference in the average revenue, use Fisher's LSD approach to determine which restaurant should be closed.

Source	$\overline{x}_1$	$\overline{x}_2$	$\overline{x}_3$
Between	9.06	8.24	11.37

We calculate $LSD = t_{\alpha/2}\sqrt{MSW}\sqrt{\dfrac{2}{b}} = 2.3060\sqrt{1.13}\sqrt{\dfrac{2}{5}} = 1.550.$

Since $\lvert \overline{x}_1 - \overline{x}_2 \rvert = \lvert 9.06 - 8.24 \rvert = 0.82 < 1.550,$

$\lvert \overline{x}_1 - \overline{x}_3 \rvert = \lvert 9.06 - 11.37 \rvert = 2.31 > 1.550,$

$\lvert \overline{x}_2 - \overline{x}_3 \rvert = \lvert 8.24 - 11.37 \rvert = 3.13 > 1.550,$

$\mu_1 < \mu_3$ and $\mu_2 < \mu_3$.

This indicates that Restaurant 3 has the highest average revenue while there is no evidence of a difference between Restaurant 1's and 2's average revenues.

12.29

a. Minitab output:

General Linear Model: Strength versus Material, Day

```
Factor     Type   Levels  Values
Material   fixed      3   Nylon, Polyester, Polypropylene
Day        fixed     10   1, 2, 3, 4, 5, 6, 7, 8, 9, 10


Analysis of Variance for Strength, using Adjusted SS for Tests

Source     DF    Seq SS    Adj SS    Adj MS      F      P
Material    2  25550400  25550400  12775200  81.36  0.000
Day         9   1119133   1119133    124348   0.79  0.628
Error      18   2826365   2826365    157020
Total      29  29495898


S = 396.258   R-Sq = 90.42%   R-Sq(adj) = 84.56%
```

The p-value = 0.628 < α = 0.05. This indicates that inserting the day on which the testing was done was not necessary.

b. The p-value = 0.000 < α = 0.05. This indicates that we should reject the null hypothesis and conclude that there exists a difference in the average breaking strength of the three materials.

c. We calculate $LSD = t_{\alpha/2}\sqrt{MSW}\sqrt{\dfrac{2}{b}} = 2.1009\sqrt{157020}\sqrt{\dfrac{2}{10}} = 372.304$.

Since $|\bar{x}_1 - \bar{x}_2| = |5328.4 - 4455.5| = 872.9 > 372.304$,

$|\bar{x}_1 - \bar{x}_3| = |5328.4 - 3086.1| = 2242.3 > 372.304$,

$|\bar{x}_2 - \bar{x}_3| = |4455.5 - 3086.1| = 1369.4 > 372.304$,

this indicates that $\mu_1 > \mu_2 > \mu_3$.

Section 12-3 Exercises

12.31 Minitab output:

General Linear Model: Response versus Factor A, Factor B

```
Factor     Type   Levels  Values
Factor A   fixed      3   1, 2, 3
Factor B   fixed      2   1, 2


Analysis of Variance for Response, using Adjusted SS for Tests

Source            DF   Seq SS   Adj SS  Adj MS      F      P
Factor A           2  1020.50  1020.50  510.25  47.10  0.000
Factor B           1    75.00    75.00   75.00   6.92  0.039
Factor A*Factor B  2     3.50     3.50    1.75   0.16  0.854
Error              6    65.00    65.00   10.83
Total             11  1164.00


S = 3.29140   R-Sq = 94.42%   R-Sq(adj) = 89.76%
```

a. H_O: $\mu_{AB1} = \mu_{AB2}$,
H_A: the interaction terms have different response averages.
P-value = 0.854 > α = 0.05. Therefore, fail to reject H_O. Conclude that there is not sufficient evidence to determine that there is interaction between Factor A and Factor B.

b. H_O: $\mu_{A1} = \mu_{A2} = \mu_{A3}$,
H_A: at least two levels have different mean response
F = MSA/MSW = 47.10 $F_{0.05}$ = 5.143. Since F = 47.10 > $F_{0.05}$ = 5.143, reject H_O. Conclude that there is sufficient evidence to indicate that at least two of the Factor A response variable averages differ.

c. H_O: $\mu_{B1} = \mu_{B2}$,
H_A: the two levels of Factor B have different response averages.
P-value = 0.039 < α = 0.05. Therefore, reject H_O. Conclude that there is sufficient evidence to determine that the two mean responses of Factor B differ

12.33

    a. H_0: Factors A and B do not interact

          H_A: Factors A and B do interact

ANOVA

Source of Variation	SS	df	MS	F	P-value	F crit
Factor B	150.2222	1	150.2222	5.753191	0.033605	4.747221
Factor A	124.1111	2	62.05556	2.376596	0.135052	3.88529
Interaction	24.11111	2	12.05556	0.461702	0.640953	3.88529
Within	313.3333	12	26.11111			
Total	611.7778	17				

          Since $0.4617 < 3.8853$ do not reject H_0 and conclude that Factors A and B do not interact.

    b. H_0: $\mu_{\alpha 1} = \mu_{\alpha 2} = \mu_{\alpha 3}$

          H_A: Not all means are equal

          Since $2.3766 < 3.8853$ do not reject H_0 and conclude that all means are equal

    c. H_0: $\mu_{\beta 1} = \mu_{\beta 2}$

          H_A: Not all means are equal

          Since $5.7532 > 4.7472$ reject H_0 and conclude that not all means are equal.

12.35

    a.   Minitab output:

Two-way ANOVA: Response versus Factor A, Factor B

```
Source       DF      SS      MS      F       P
Factor A      2  11133.4  5566.72  53.61  0.000
Factor B      2  10836.8  5418.39  52.18  0.000
Interaction   4  16459.6  4114.89  39.63  0.000
Error         9    934.5   103.83
Total        17  39364.3

S = 10.19   R-Sq = 97.63%   R-Sq(adj) = 95.52%
```

          H_O: AB interaction does not exist,

          H_A: AB interaction does exist

          $F = MSAB/MSW = 39.63$ $F_{0.05} = 3.633$.

          Since $F = 39.63 > F_{0.05} = 3.633$, reject H_O. Conclude that there is sufficient evidence to indicate that interaction exists between Factors A and B.

    b.   Since interaction exists, it is futile to conduct inference on the response means associated with the levels of Factor A and Factor B. Therefore, a one-way analysis of variance using only those values for Factor A associated with level one of Factor B.

          Minitab output:

One-way ANOVA: ResponseB1 versus Factor A B1

```
Source        DF    SS     MS     F      P
Factor A B1    2  276.3  138.2  2.90  0.199
Error          3  143.0   47.7
Total          5  419.3

S = 6.904   R-Sq = 65.90%   R-Sq(adj) = 43.16%
```

          H_O: $\mu_{A1} = \mu_{A2} = \mu_{A3}$ @ Level 1 of Factor B,

          H_A: at least two levels of Factor A have different mean responses @ Level 1 of Factor B

          $F = MSA_{B1}/MSW = 2.90$ $F_{0.05} = 9.552$.

          Since $F = 2.90 < F_{0.05} = 9.552$, fail to reject H_O. Conclude that there is not sufficient evidence to indicate that at least two levels of Factor A have different mean responses @ Level 1 of Factor B.

c.   Minitab output with Factor B at level 2:

One-way ANOVA: ResponseB2 versus Factor A B2

```
Source       DF    SS     MS     F     P
Factor A B2   2  202.3  101.2  3.49  0.165
Error         3   87.0   29.0
Total         5  289.3

S = 5.385   R-Sq = 69.93%   R-Sq(adj) = 49.88%
```

H_0: $\mu_{A1} = \mu_{A2} = \mu_{A3}$ @ Level 2 of Factor B,

H_A: at least two levels of Factor A have different mean responses @ Level 2 of Factor B

$F = MSA_{B2}/MSW = 3.49$ $F_{0.05} = 9.552$.

Since $F = 3.49 < F_{0.05} = 9.552$, fail to reject H_0. Conclude that there is not sufficient evidence to indicate that at least two levels of Factor A have different mean responses @ Level 2 of Factor B.

Minitab output with Factor B at level 3:

One-way ANOVA: Respose B3 versus Factor A B3

```
Source       DF    SS     MS      F     P
Factor A B3   2  27114  13557  57.73  0.004
Error         3    705    235
Total         5  27819

S = 15.32   R-Sq = 97.47%   R-Sq(adj) = 95.78%
```

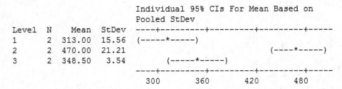

```
                            Individual 95% CIs For Mean Based on
                            Pooled StDev
Level  N   Mean   StDev  ----+---------+---------+---------+-----
1      2  313.00  15.56  (-----*-----)
2      2  470.00  21.21                          (----*-----)
3      2  348.50   3.54        (-----*-----)
                            ----+---------+---------+---------+-----
                            300       360       420       480

Pooled StDev = 15.32
```

H_0: $\mu_{A1} = \mu_{A2} = \mu_{A3}$ @ Level 3 of Factor B,

H_A: at least two levels of Factor A have different mean responses @ Level 3 of Factor B

$F = MSA_{B3}/MSW = 57.73$ $F_{0.05} = 9.552$.

Since $F = 57.73 > F_{0.05} = 9.552$, reject H_0. Conclude that there is sufficient evidence to indicate that at least two levels of Factor A have different mean responses @ Level 2 of Factor B.

12.37   Using Excel's ANOVA Two-Factor with Replication Data Analysis tool with $\alpha = 0.05$, the following ANOVA table was generated. Use this information to answer parts (a-c).

ANOVA

Source of Variation	SS	df	MS	F	P-value	F crit
Sample (Layout Type)	240.3889	2	120.1944	102.2126	0.00000	3.354131
Columns (Lines)	2.722222	2	1.361111	1.15748	0.329386	3.354131
Interaction	4.777778	4	1.194444	1.015748	0.416816	2.727765
Within	31.75	27	1.175926			
Total	279.6389	35				

a.   Test to determine whether there is an interaction effect between the type of layout and the production line. The null and alternative hypotheses are:

   H_0: Type of layout and production line do not interact to affect mean   output

   H_A: Type of layout and production line do interact

   The F test statistic for this null hypothesis is 1.016.

$F_{\alpha=0.05} = 2.728$ is obtained from the ANOVA table above. Because $F = 1.016 < F_{\alpha=0.05} = 2.728$, do not reject the null hypothesis. Based on these sample data we conclude that there is no interaction between type of layout and production line.

b. To test whether there is a difference in mean output due to production line, the appropriate null and alternative hypotheses are:

H_0: $\mu_1 = \mu_2 = \mu_3$
H_A: Not all populations have the same mean
The F test statistic for this null hypothesis is 1.157.

$F_{\alpha=0.05} = 3.354$ is obtained from the ANOVA table above. Because $F = 1.157 < F_{\alpha=0.05} = 3.354$, do not reject the null hypothesis. Based on these sample data we conclude that there is no difference in the average output across the three production lines.

c. To test whether there is a difference in mean output due to type of layout used, the appropriate null and alternative hypotheses are:

H_0: $\mu_1 = \mu_2 = \mu_3$
H_A: Not all populations have the same mean
The F test statistic for this null hypothesis is 102.213.

$F_{\alpha=0.05} = 3.354$ is obtained from the ANOVA table above. Because $F = 102.213 > F_{\alpha=0.05} = 3.354$, reject the null hypothesis. Based on these sample data we conclude that there are differences in the average output across the three layout types.

12.39

a. H_0: Factors A and B do not interact
H_A: Factors A and B do interact

ANOVA

Source of Variation	SS	df	MS	F	P-value	F crit
Hours	0.308888889	2	0.154444444	0.758181818	0.482906	6.012897
Temperature	1.22	2	0.61	2.994545455	0.075393	6.012897
Interaction	2.284444444	4	0.571111111	2.803636364	0.057002	4.579022
Within	3.666666667	18	0.203703704			
Total	7.48	26				

Since p-value = 0.0570 > 0.01 do not reject H_0 and conclude there is no interaction between water temperature and vat hours. Interaction would mean some combination of water temperature and vat time would cause either an unexpected high or low numbers of spin outs.

b. H_0: $\mu_{\alpha1} = \mu_{\alpha2} = \mu_{\alpha3}$
H_A: Not all means are equal
Since 2.9945 < 6.0129 do not reject H_0 and conclude that there is no difference in mean core diameter at the 3 water temperatures.

c. H_0: $\mu_{\beta1} = \mu_{\beta2} = \mu_{\beta3}$
H_A: Not all means are equal
Since p-value = 0.4829 > 0.1 do not reject H_0 and conclude that there is no difference in mean core diameter across the 3 vat times

12.41

a. Minitab output:

Two-way ANOVA: Fat versus Formula, Plant

```
Source        DF    SS      MS       F      P
Formula        4  324.68  81.1700  15.61  0.000
Plant          4   66.08  16.5200   3.18  0.031
Interaction   16   50.52   3.1575   0.61  0.849
Error         25  130.00   5.2000
Total         49  571.28

S = 2.280   R-Sq = 77.24%   R-Sq(adj) = 55.40%
```

H_O: Interaction between Factor A and Factor B does not exist,
H_A: Interaction between Factor A and Factor B does exist,
$\alpha = 0.025 < $ p-value = 0.849. Therefore, fail to reject H_O.
Conclude that there is not sufficient evidence to indicate interaction between the Eukanuba formulas and plant site where they are produced.

b. H_O: $\mu_{A1} = \mu_{A2} = \mu_{A3} = \mu_{A4} = \mu_{A5}$,

H_A: at least two formulas have different averages of percent of crude fat,

$\alpha = 0.025$, F = MSA/MSW = 15.61 $F_{0.025}$ = 3.353. Since F = 15.61 > $F_{0.025}$ = 3.353, reject H_O.

Conclude that there is sufficient evidence to indicate that at least two formulas have different averages of percent of crude fat.

c. H_O: $\mu_{B1} = \mu_{B2} = \mu_{B3} = \mu_{B4} = \mu_{B5}$,

H_A: at least two plant sites have different averages of percent of crude fat,

$\alpha = 0.025$, F = MSB/MSW = 15.61 $F_{0.025}$ = 3.353. Since F = 3.18 < $F_{0.025}$ = 3.353, do not reject H_O.

Conclude that there is not sufficient evidence to indicate that at least two plant sites have different averages of percent of crude fat.

d. In order to provide the answer for this question, you must conduct the test of hypothesis

H_O: $\mu_{A4} = 9$,

H_A: $\mu_{A4} \neq 9$, $\alpha = 0.05$.

This is conducted using a one-sample t-test with a standard error of $\sqrt{MSE/n} = \sqrt{5.200/10} = 0.7211$. Minitab output:

One-Sample T

```
Test of mu = 9 vs not = 9


 N     Mean     StDev   SE Mean      T
10   8.50000   2.28035  0.72111   -0.69
```

The critical value for this test is obtained from a t-distribution with degrees of freedom equal to the degrees of freedom for error in the ANOVA table = 25. This says the critical values are ± 2.0595. Since -2.0595 < t = -0.69 < 2.0595. Fail to reject H_O and conclude that the average percent of crude fat for the "Reduced Fat" formula is equal to the advertised nine percent.

Chapter Exercises

12.43 If the null hypothesis is not rejected we conclude that there is no difference in population means. In this case we would expect that the Tukey-Kramer procedure for multiple comparisons would show no significant difference in any pairwise comparison.

12.45 The randomized complete block design is used whenever we are testing situations where an additional factor affects the observed responses in a one-way design. In this respect, the randomized complete block design is analogous to the paired samples hypothesis testing procedure. Whenever an additional factor could potentially introduce a source of variation on the observed responses the results could be affected. In cases such as this we can control for the additional source of variability by blocking. By blocking we have an additional source of variation to account for called the block variation. The effect of blocking is to reduce the sum of squares within. If the variation in the blocks is significant, the variation within the factor levels will be reduced. This makes it easier to detect a difference in the population means if such a difference actually exists. If we do not block when it is needed we may not be able to detect a difference when in fact it exists.

12.47 In the two-sample t-test for a difference between any two means, the estimate of the population variances only includes data from the two specific samples under consideration. For ANOVA situations where there are three or more groups, we would be disregarding some of the information available to estimate the common population variance. To overcome this problem we base our confidence intervals using as our estimate of the pooled standard deviation the square root of the mean square within (MSW) value. The MSW is the weighted average of all sample variances in the problem under consideration. This is preferred to the two-sample t-test procedure because we are assuming that each of the sample variances is an estimate of the common population variance. Using the MSW enables us to incorporate all the information related to the estimate of the common population variance not just some of it as would be the case with the two-sample t-test approach.

12.49

a. Minitab output:

Two-way ANOVA: KERNELS versus Fertilizer, Seed

```
Source        DF       SS       MS       F      P
Fertilizer     3    19718     6573    0.82  0.506
Seed           2   408209   204105   25.55  0.000
Interaction    6    23993     3999    0.50  0.797
Error         12    95870     7989
Total         23   547790

S = 89.38   R-Sq = 82.50%   R-Sq(adj) = 66.46%
```

H_O: Interaction between Fertilizers and Seeds does not exist,

H_A: Interaction between Fertilizers and Seeds does exist,

$\alpha = 0.05 <$ p-value $= 0.797$. Therefore, fail to reject H_O.

Conclude that there is not sufficient evidence to indicate interaction between the Fertilizers and Seeds exists.

b. H_O: $\mu_{B1} = \mu_{B2} = \mu_{B3}$,

H_A: the average number of kernels of at least two seed types are not equal,

$\alpha = 0.05$, F = MSB/MSW = 25.55, $F_{0.05} = 3.855$. Since F = 25.55 > $F_{0.05} = 3.855$, reject H_O. Conclude that there is sufficient evidence to indicate that the average number of kernels of at least two of the types of seeds are not equal.

c. H_O: $\mu_{A1} = \mu_{A2} = \mu_{A3} = \mu_{A4}$,

H_A: the average number of kernels of at least two fertilizer types are not equal,

$\alpha = 0.05$, F = MSA/MSW = 0.82 $F_{0.05} = 3.940$. Since F = 0.82 < $F_{0.05} = 3.940$, do not reject H_O. Conclude that there is not sufficient evidence to indicate that the average number of kernels of at least two of the types of fertilizers are not equal.

12.51

a. Using the steps outlined in the chapter:

Step 1: The parameters of interest are the average percentage gains accrued by the analyst's customers among the mutual fund types.

Step 2: H_O: $\mu_1 = \mu_2 = ... = \mu_8$,

H_A: At least two population means are different.

Step 3: The significance level is $\alpha = 0.05$.

Step 4: The selected samples are specified in the heading of this exercise.

Step 5: Because of the small sample sizes, the box and whisker diagram is used.

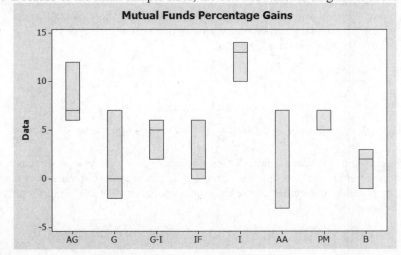

The box plots indicate some skewness but not sufficient to deny normality. If we assume that the populations are normally distributed, Harley's F_{max} test can be used to test whether the three populations have equal variances. The sample variances are $s_1^2 = \dfrac{\sum (x - \bar{x})^2}{n-1} = \dfrac{20.66}{2} = 10.33$, $s_2^2 = 22.33$, and s_3^2

$= 4.33$, $s_4^2 = 10.33$, $s_5^2 = 4.33$, $s_6^2 = 33.33$, $s_7^2 = 1.333$, $s_8^2 = 4.33$, test statistic is $F_{max} = \dfrac{s_{max}^2}{s_{min}^2} = \dfrac{33.33}{1.333} =$

25.004. From Appendix I, the critical value for alpha = 0.05, k = 8, and n - 1 = 2 is 403. Because 25.004 < 403, we conclude that the population variances could be equal.

Step 6:

Anova: Single Factor

SUMMARY

Groups	Count	Sum	Average	Variance
AG	3	25	8.333	10.333
G	3	5	1.667	22.333
G-I	3	13	4.333	4.333
IF	3	7	2.333	10.333
I	3	37	12.333	4.333
AA	3	11	3.667	33.333
PM	3	17	5.667	1.333
B	3	4	1.333	4.333

ANOVA

Source of Variation	SS	df	MS	F	P-value	F crit
Between Groups	297.625	7	42.518	3.752	0.014	2.657
Within Groups	181.333	16	11.333			
Total	478.958	23				

Step 7: Because k − 1 = 7 and $n_T - k = 16$, $F_{0.05} = 2.657$. The decision rule is if the calculated $F > F_{0.05} = 2.657$, reject H_O, or if the p-value $< \alpha = 0.05$, reject H_O; otherwise, do not reject H_O.

Step 8: Since F = 3.752 > 2.657, we reject H_O.

Step 9: We conclude there is sufficient evidence to indicate that there is a difference in the average percentage gains accrued by his customers among the mutual fund types

b. Using Equation 12-7 to construct the critical ranges:

$$q_{1-\alpha}\sqrt{\frac{MSW}{2}\left(\frac{1}{n_i}+\frac{1}{n_j}\right)}$$

For $n_1 = n_2 = ... = n_8 = 3$, critical range $= 4.90\sqrt{\dfrac{11.3}{2}\left(\dfrac{1}{3}+\dfrac{1}{3}\right)} = 9.5099$;

Minitab has a procedure to construct Tukey-Kramer comparisons. They look different from the tables produced in the chapter but present the same information. If you want to compare your answers with those that follow, compare the absolute values of the differences found in the following output with the critical range calculated above.

```
Tukey 95% Simultaneous Confidence Intervals
All Pairwise Comparisons

Individual confidence level = 99.68%

AG subtracted from:

        Lower   Center   Upper   -------+---------+---------+---------+--
G      -16.191  -6.667   2.857      (------*-------)
G-I    -13.524  -4.000   5.524        (-------*-------)
IF     -15.524  -6.000   3.524      (-------*-------)
I       -5.524   4.000  13.524              (-------*-------)
AA     -14.191  -4.667   4.857       (-------*-------)
PM     -12.191  -2.667   6.857        (-------*-------)
B      -16.524  -7.000   2.524      (-------*-------)
                                  -------+---------+---------+---------+--
                                       -12        0        12       24

G subtracted from:

        Lower   Center   Upper   -------+---------+---------+---------+--
G-I     -6.857   2.667  12.191           (-------*-------)
IF      -8.857   0.667  10.191         (-------*------)
I        1.143  10.667  20.191                 (-------*-------)
AA      -7.524   2.000  11.524          (-------*-------)
PM      -5.524   4.000  13.524            (-------*-------)
B       -9.857  -0.333   9.191         (-------*-------)
                                  -------+---------+---------+---------+--
                                       -12        0        12       24

G-I subtracted from:

        Lower   Center   Upper   -------+---------+---------+---------+--
IF     -11.524  -2.000   7.524        (-------*-------)
I       -1.524   8.000  17.524              (-------*-------)
AA     -10.191  -0.667   8.857        (------*-------)
PM      -8.191   1.333  10.857         (-------*-------)
B      -12.524  -3.000   6.524       (-------*------)
                                  -------+---------+---------+---------+--
                                       -12        0        12       24

IF subtracted from:

        Lower   Center   Upper   -------+---------+---------+---------+--
I        0.476  10.000  19.524               (-------*-------)
AA      -8.191   1.333  10.857          (-------*-------)
PM      -6.191   3.333  12.857           (-------*-------)
B      -10.524  -1.000   8.524         (-------*-------)
                                  -------+---------+---------+---------+--
                                       -12        0        12       24

I subtracted from:

        Lower   Center   Upper   -------+---------+---------+---------+--
AA     -18.191  -8.667   0.857     (-------*-------)
PM     -16.191  -6.667   2.857      (------*-------)
B      -20.524 -11.000  -1.476   (-------*-------)
                                  -------+---------+---------+---------+--
                                       -12        0        12       24

AA subtracted from:

        Lower   Center   Upper   -------+---------+---------+---------+--
PM      -7.524   2.000  11.524           (-------*-------)
B      -11.857  -2.333   7.191         (-------*-------)
                                  -------+---------+---------+---------+--
                                       -12        0        12       24

PM subtracted from:

        Lower   Center   Upper   -------+---------+---------+---------+--
B      -13.857  -4.333   5.191       (-------*-------)
                                  -------+---------+---------+---------+--
                                       -12        0        12       24
```

Tukey-Kramer, therefore, indicates that $\mu_I > \mu_B$, $\mu_I > \mu_{IF}$, and $\mu_I > \mu_G$. Other pairwise comparison were deemed to be equal.

12.53

   a.   Minitab output

One-way ANOVA: Salary versus Year

```
Source   DF      SS       MS      F       P
Year      1   3365.3   3365.3   89.53   0.000
Error   198   7442.7     37.6
Total   199  10808.0

S = 6.131    R-Sq = 31.14%    R-Sq(adj) = 30.79%


                              Individual 95% CIs For Mean Based on
                              Pooled StDev
Level     N    Mean   StDev   ---------+---------+---------+---------+
04Salary  100  9.602  8.545                            (---*---)
94Salary  100  1.398  1.468   (---*---)
                              ---------+---------+---------+---------+
                                  3.0       6.0       9.0      12.0

Pooled StDev = 6.131
```

H_O: $\mu_1 = \mu_2$,

H_A: $\mu_1 \neq \mu_2$,

$\alpha = 0.05$,

$F = MSA/MSW = 89.53$, $F_{1,200,0.05} = 3.888 < F_{1,998,0.05} < F_{1,100,0.05} = 3.936$.

Since ($F_{1,200,0.05} = 3.888 < F_{1,998,0.05} < F_{1,100,0.05} = 3.936$) $< F = 89.53$ reject H_O. Conclude that there is a difference in the CEOs average salaries between 1994 and 2004, adjusted for inflation.

   b.   Minitab output:

Two-Sample T-Test and CI: 94Salary, 04Salary

```
Two-sample T for 94Salary vs 04Salary

            N    Mean   StDev   SE Mean
94Salary   100   1.40    1.47      0.15
04Salary   100   9.60    8.55      0.85


Difference = mu (94Salary) - mu (04Salary)
Estimate for difference:  -8.20400
95% CI for difference:  (-9.91385, -6.49415)
T-Test of difference = 0 (vs not =): T-Value = -9.46   P-Value = 0.000   DF = 198
Both use Pooled StDev = 6.1310
```

H_O: $\mu_1 = \mu_2$,

H_A: $\mu_1 \neq \mu_2$,

$\alpha = 0.05$,

$t = -9.46$, $t_{250,0.05} = 1.9695 < t_{998,0.05} < t_{100,0.05} = 1.9840$.

Since $t = -9.46 < (t_{250,0.05} = -1.9695 < t_{998,0.05} < t_{100,0.05} = -1.9840)$ reject H_O. Conclude that there is a difference in the CEOs average salaries between 1994 and 2004, adjusted for inflation. The same result obtained in part a.

   c.   Note that (t-value)^2 = (-9.46)^2 = 89.49 $\approx$ 89.53. Except for rounding, the t^2 and the F test statistic would be equal.

12.55

a. It is set up as a randomized block design. The main hypothesis is the type of scanner with blocking on the basket so that the items in each basket would not influence the results.

b. H_0: $\mu_1 = \mu_2 = \mu_3 = \mu_4$
   H_A: At least two population means are different

c.

ANOVA						
Source of Variation	SS	df	MS	F	P-value	F crit
Carts (Blocks)	89.91042	29	3.100359	20.39312	1.14E-27	1.935817
Scanner	1.540917	3	0.513639	3.378543	0.02187	4.015021
Error	13.22658	87	0.15203			
Total	104.6779	119				

Since 3.3785 < 4.0150 do not reject H_0 and conclude that there is no difference in the average number of errors among the four different scanning systems.

d. H_0: $\mu_{b1} = \mu_{b2} = \mu_{b3} = \mu_{b4} = \mu_{b5} = \mu_{b6} = \mu_{b7} = \mu_{b8} = \ldots = \mu_{b30}$
   H_A: Not all block means are equal
   Since 20.39312 > 1.9358 reject H_0 and conclude that there is an indication that blocking on shopping cart was effective. Maynards was correct in blocking by shopping cart.

e. There is no difference between the scanners.

f. Based strictly on the test you would not upgrade scanners. Student answers will vary but some other factors that might be considered are the age of the current scanners, cost of the scanners, or any additional features that might be on the other scanners that is not available on the current scanners.

12.57

a. Minitab output:

Two-way ANOVA: Nitrogen versus Corn Yield, Plant

```
Source        DF      SS       MS       F       P
Corn Yield     4   35843.2  8960.80  541.98  0.000
Plant          2    7337.6  3668.80  221.90  0.000
Interaction    8     710.4    88.80    5.37  0.003
Error         15     248.0    16.53
Total         29   44139.2

S = 4.066    R-Sq = 99.44%    R-Sq(adj) = 98.91%
```

H_O: interaction does not exist,
H_A: interaction does exist
F = MSAB/MSW = 5.37 $F_{0.05}$ = 2.641.
Since F = 5.37 > $F_{0.05}$ = 2.641, reject H_O. Conclude that there is sufficient evidence to indicate that interaction exists between the yield levels of corn and the crop that had been previously planted in the field.

b. Since interaction exists, it is futile to conduct inference on the major effects. Therefore, a one-way analysis of variance using only those levels associated with the specific crop that had been previously planted will be presented.

Minitab output:

One-way ANOVA: NitroCorn versus Yield Corn

```
Source       DF      SS      MS      F      P
Yield Corn    4  14640.0  3660.0  142.97  0.000
Error         5    128.0    25.6
Total         9  14768.0

S = 5.060   R-Sq = 99.13%   R-Sq(adj) = 98.44%


                            Individual 95% CIs For Mean Based on
                            Pooled StDev
Level  N    Mean   StDev  +---------+---------+---------+---------
  80   2   80.00    2.83  (--*-)
 100   2  110.00    7.07          (-*--)
 120   2  140.00    4.24                   (--*--)
 140   2  160.00    1.41                         (--*-)
 160   2  190.00    7.07                                 (-*--)
                           +---------+---------+---------+---------
                          70        105       140       175

Pooled StDev = 5.06
```

H_O: $\mu_{A1} = \mu_{A2} = \mu_{A3} = \mu_{A4}$ with corn as previous crop,

H_A: at least two levels of corn yields require different amounts of nitrogen with corn as previous crop
$F = MSA_{B1}/MSW = 142.97$ $F_{0.05} = 5.192$.
Since $F = 142.97 > F_{0.05} = 5.192$, reject H_O. Conclude that there is sufficient evidence to indicate that at least two levels of corn yields require different amounts of nitrogen with corn as previous crop.

c. Minitab output with soybeans as the previous crop:

One-way ANOVA: NitroSoy versus Yield Soy

```
Source       DF      SS      MS      F      P
Yield Soy     4   9353.6  2338.4  129.91  0.000
Error         5     90.0    18.0
Total         9   9443.6

S = 4.243   R-Sq = 99.05%   R-Sq(adj) = 98.28%


                            Individual 95% CIs For Mean Based on
                            Pooled StDev
Level  N    Mean   StDev  -+---------+---------+---------+--------
  80   2   80.00    1.41  (--*--)
 100   2   80.00    7.07  (--*--)
 120   2  114.00    1.41              (--*--)
 140   2  130.00    4.24                    (--*--)
 160   2  160.00    4.24                                (--*--)
                          -+---------+---------+---------+--------
                          75        100       125       150
```

H_O: $\mu_{A1} = \mu_{A2} = \mu_{A3} = \mu_{A4}$ with soybeans as previous crop,

H_A: at least two levels of corn yields require different amounts of nitrogen with soy beans as previous crop
$F = MSA_{B2}/MSW = 129.91$ $F_{0.05} = 5.192$.
Since $F = 129.91 > F_{0.05} = 5.192$, reject H_O. Conclude that there is sufficient evidence to indicate that at least two levels of corn yields require different amounts of nitrogen with soy beans as previous crop.

Minitab output with sod grass as previous crop:

One-way ANOVA: Nitro Gras versus Yield Gras

```
Source      DF        SS        MS       F      P
Yield Gras   4  12560.00   3140.00  523.33  0.000
Error        5     30.00      6.00
Total        9  12590.00

S = 2.449   R-Sq = 99.76%   R-Sq(adj) = 99.57%


                            Individual 95% CIs For Mean Based on
                            Pooled StDev
Level  N    Mean  StDev  -----+---------+---------+---------+----
  80   2   50.00   4.24  (-*)
 100   2   70.00   1.41        (*-)
 120   2  100.00   1.41                 (*-)
 140   2  120.00   2.83                        (*)
 160   2  150.00   0.00                                (*)
                         -----+---------+---------+---------+----
                             60        90       120       150
```

H$_0$: $\mu_{A1} = \mu_{A2} = \mu_{A3} = \mu_{A4}$ with sod grass as previous crop,

H$_A$: at least two levels of corn yields require different amounts of nitrogen with sod grass as previous crop
F = MSA$_{B3}$/MSW = 523.33 F$_{0.05}$ = 5.192.
Since F = 523.33 > F$_{0.05}$ = 5.192, reject H$_0$. Conclude that there is sufficient evidence to indicate that at least two levels of corn yields require different amounts of nitrogen with soy beans as previous crop.

CHAPTERS 8—12
SPECIAL REVIEW SECTION

SR.1. Conditions: (1) Parameter of concern: average, (2) sample size = 50 > 30 ==> Use a large sample hypothesis test for the mean of a population. Research hypothesis: average of new starter units is greater than 1000 ==>

H_0: $\mu \leq 1000$

H_A: $\mu > 1000$

$\alpha = 0.05$

$$z = \frac{\overline{x} - \mu}{\dfrac{s}{\sqrt{n}}} = \frac{1010 - 1000}{\dfrac{48}{\sqrt{50}}} = 1.4731$$

Rejection region: z > 1.645

Decision: z = 1.4731 < 1645 = z_α ==> do not reject H_0

Conclusion: The average cycles for the new starter unit is not greater than that of the old starter unit. Do not recommend changing suppliers.

SR.3. Conditions: (1) Parameter of concern: difference between two proportions, (2)

$n_1 \overline{p}_1 = 800(.05) = 40 > 5$; $n_1(1 - \overline{p}_1) = 800(.95) = 760 > 5$;

$n_2 \overline{p}_2 = 900(.09) = 81 > 5$; $n_2(1 - \overline{p}_2) = 900(.91) = 819 > 5$ ==> use a normal approximation ==> Use a large sample hypothesis test for the difference between two proportions. Research hypothesis: There is a difference in the turnover rates for the two trial policies.
==>

H_0: $p_1 - p_2 = 0$

H_A: $p_1 - p_2 \neq 0$

$\alpha = 0.05$ $\qquad \overline{p} = \dfrac{\overline{p}_1 n_1 + \overline{p}_2 n_2}{n_1 + n_2} = \dfrac{40 + 81}{800 + 900} = .0712$

$$z = \frac{\overline{p}_1 - \overline{p}_2 - (p_1 - p_2)}{\sqrt{\overline{p}(1 - \overline{p})\left(\dfrac{1}{n_1} + \dfrac{1}{n_2}\right)}} = \frac{.05 - (.09) - 0}{\sqrt{.0712(.9288)\left(\dfrac{1}{800} + \dfrac{1}{900}\right)}} = -3.2011$$

Rejection region: z < -1.96 or z > 1.96

Decision: z = -3.2011 < -1.96 = $-z_{\alpha/2}$ ==> reject H_0

Conclusion: There is a difference in the turnover rates for the two trial policies.

SR.5. Conditions: (1) Parameter of concern: population variances, (2) assume population is normally distributed ==> Use a hypothesis test for the equality of two variances. Research hypothesis: There is no difference in variability of attendance between downtown and suburban theaters.

$H_0: \sigma_1^2 = \sigma_2^2$

$H_A: \sigma_1^2 \neq \sigma_2^2$

$\alpha = 0.05$

$$F = \frac{s_1^2}{s_2^2} = \frac{1684}{1439} = 1.1703$$

Rejection region: $F > 3.137$

Decision: $F_\alpha = 3.137 > 1.1703 = F$ ==> do not reject H_0

Conclusion: There is no difference in variability of attendance between downtown and suburban theaters.

Conditions: (1) Parameter of concern: population means, (2) sample sizes < 30, (3) population variances unknown, (4) population variances equal, and (5) assume population is normally distributed ==> Use a hypothesis test for the equality of two means. Research hypothesis: There is no difference in mean attendance between downtown and suburban theaters.

$H_0: \mu_1 = \mu_2$

$H_A: \mu_1 \neq \mu_2$

$\alpha = 0.05 \qquad s_p = \sqrt{\dfrac{(11-1)1684 + (10-1)(1439)}{11+10-2}} = 39.5973$

$$t = \frac{\bar{x}_1 - \bar{x}_2 - (\mu_1 - \mu_2)}{s_p \sqrt{\dfrac{1}{n_1} + \dfrac{1}{n_2}}} = \frac{855 - 750}{39.5973\sqrt{\dfrac{1}{11} + \dfrac{1}{10}}} = 6.0689$$

Rejection region: $t < -2.0930$ or $t > 2.0930$

Decision: $t_{\alpha/2} = 2.0930 < 6.0689 = t$ ==> reject H_0

Conclusion: There is a difference in the average attendance between downtown and suburban theaters.

SR.7. Conditions: (1) Parameter of concern: differences among three population means, (2) population variances unknown, (3) samples are independent, and (4) assume population is normally distributed ==> Use an analysis of variance for the difference between population means. Research hypothesis: There is no difference in mean strength of the three types of shocks after 20,000 miles.

The equality of the populations' variances must be verified first.

Conditions: (1) Parameter of concern: population variances, (2) assume population is normally distributed ==> Use a hypothesis test for the equality of population variances. Research hypothesis: There is no difference in variability among the strength of the three types of shocks after 20,000 miles.

$H_0: \sigma_1^2 = \sigma_2^2 = \sigma_3^2$

$H_A:$ at least two σ_i^2 differ

$\alpha = 0.05$

$$F = \frac{s_{max}^2}{s_{min}^2} = \frac{4.0280}{3.0695} = 1.3123$$

Rejection region: $F_H > 10.8$

Decision: $F_H = 10.8 > 1.3123 = F$ ==> do not reject H_0

Conclusion: There is no difference in variability of the strength of the three types of shocks after 20,000 miles.

Anova: Single Factor						
SUMMARY						
Groups	*Count*	*Sum*	*Average*	*Variance*		
Manufacturer	6	64.3	10.71667	3.069667		
Competitor 1	6	61.8	10.3	3.304		
Competitor 2	6	64.3	10.71667	4.029667		
ANOVA						
Source of Variation	*SS*	*df*	*MS*	*F*	*P-value*	*F crit*
Between Groups	0.694444	2	0.347222	0.100128	0.905321	3.682317
Within Groups	52.01667	15	3.467778			
Total	52.71111	17				

H_0: $\mu_1 = \mu_2 = \mu_3$
H_A: at least two μ_i differ
$\alpha = 0.05$

Rejection region: $F > 3.682$
Decision: $F_\alpha = 3.682 > 0.10 = F ==>$ do not reject H_0
Conclusion: There is no difference in average strength of the three types of shocks after 20,000 miles.

SR.9.   Conditions: (1) Parameter of concern: differences among three population means, (2) treatment effects for Phosphor type are different for different levels of the glass type ➔ interaction, (3) samples are independent, and (4) assume population is normally distributed ==> Use a two factor analysis of variance for the difference between population means. Research hypothesis: There is no difference in brightness of the monitors for the three Phosphor types. There is no difference in brightness of the monitors for glass types. There is no interaction between the glass type and relationship between the Phosphor type and the brightness of the monitor types.

Two-way ANOVA: Brightness versus GlassType, PhosType

```
Analysis of Variance for Brightne
Source         DF      SS       MS      F       P
GlassTyp        1    7896     7896    33.11    0.000
PhosType        2     181       90     0.38    0.692
Interaction     2    1650      825     3.46    0.065
Error          12    2861      238
Total          17   12588
```

Test for Interaction: p-value = 0.692 > 0.05 = α. Therefore, do not reject the null hypothesis that interaction does not exist.
Test for Factor 1: Glass type
p-value = 0.065 > 0.05 = α. Therefore, do not reject the null hypothesis that the average brightness of the monitors is not different between the glass types.
Test for Factor 2: Phosphor type
p-value = 0.000 < 0.05 = α. Therefore, reject the null hypothesis that the average brightness of the monitors is not different among the Phosphor types

SR.11. Conditions: (1) Parameter of concern: difference between two proportions, (2)

$$n_1 p_1 = 250\left(\frac{9}{250}\right) = 9 > 5; \; n_1(1-p_1) = 250\left(\frac{241}{250}\right) = 241 > 5 \; ;$$

$$n_2 p_2 = 250\left(\frac{16}{250}\right) = 16 > 5; \; n_2(1-p_2) = 250\left(\frac{234}{250}\right) = 234 > 5 ==> \text{use a normal approximation.}$$

Requires range of possible values ==> Use a large sample confidence interval for the difference between two proportions.
==>

$$p_1 - p_2 \pm z_{\alpha/2}\sqrt{\frac{p_1(1-p_1)}{n_1} + \frac{p_2(1-p_2)}{n_2}} = (\frac{16}{250} - \frac{9}{250}) \pm 1.96\sqrt{\frac{0.064(0.936)}{250} + \frac{0.036(0.964)}{250}} = 0.028 \pm 0.0381 =$$

(0.0019, 0.0781)

Using a 95% confidence level, it is estimated that the percentage of the blenders returned with the old switch is somewhere between 0% and 7% greater than the percentage of blenders returned with the new switch. Therefore the claim that the difference is somewhere between 3% and 6% seems quite plausible.

Chapter 13
Goodness-of-Fit Tests and Contingency Analysis

Section 13-1 Exercises

13.1

# of Defective Batteries Per Package	Observed (o)	Binomial Probability n=50, p = 0.02	Expected Frequency (e)	$(o_i-e_i)^2/e_i$
0	165	0.36417	145.668	2.5656
1	133	0.37160	148.641	1.6458
2	65	0.18580	74.320	1.1688
3	28	0.06067	24.268	0.5740
4 or more	9	0.01776	7.103	0.5065
Total	400			6.4607

The calculated chi-square test statistic is $\chi^2 = 6.4607$.
The decision rule is:
If $\chi^2 > 13.2767$, reject Ho;
Otherwise, do not reject Ho.
Because $\chi^2 = 6.4607 < 13.2767$, do not reject the null hypothesis.
We conclude, based on the sample information and the results of the goodness-of-fit test that the binomial distribution with n = 50 and $\pi = 0.02$ is an appropriate distribution for describing the company's sampling plan.

13.3.

x	o Frequency	Poisson Probability	e Expected Frequency
2 or less	7	0.0620	30.98
3	29	0.0892	44.62
4	26	0.1339	66.93
5	52	0.1606	80.31
6	77	0.1606	80.31
7	77	0.1377	68.84
8	72	0.1033	51.63
9	53	0.0688	34.42
10	35	0.0413	20.65
11	28	0.0225	11.26
12	18	0.0113	5.63
13	13	0.0052	2.60
14 or more	13	0.0036	1.81
Total	500	1.0000	500

Now you need to check to see if any of the expected cell frequencies are less than 5. In this case we see that there are two instances where this is the case. To deal with this, you should collapse categories so that all expected frequencies are at least 5. Doing this gives the following:

x	o Frequency	Poisson Probability	e Expected Frequency
2 or less	7	0.062	29.39
3	29	0.0892	42.28
4	26	0.1339	63.47
5	52	0.1606	76.12
6	77	0.1606	76.12
7	77	0.1377	65.27
8	72	0.1033	48.96
9	53	0.0688	32.61
10	35	0.0413	19.58
11	18	0.0225	10.67
12 or more	44	0.0201	9.53
Total	474	1	474

Now we can compute the chi-square test statistic using equation 13-1 as follows"

$$\chi^2 = \sum \frac{(o-e)^2}{e} = \frac{(7-29.39)^2}{29.39} + \frac{(29-42.28)^2}{42.28} + \ldots + \frac{(9.53-44)^2}{9.53} = 218.62$$

Because $\chi^2 = 218.62 > 18.0370$, we reject the null hypothesis.

The population distribution is not Poisson distributed with a mean of 6.

13.5

Successes	o Observed Successes	Binomial Probability n = 18, p = 0.15	e Expected Frequency	$\frac{(o_i - e_i)^2}{e_i}$
0	80	0.050328	10.0657	485.894
1	75	0.205889	41.1778	27.780
2	39	0.336909	67.3819	11.955
3	6	0.275653	55.1306	43.784
4 - 5	0	0.131220	26.2440	26.244
Total	200	1	200	595.657

The calculated chi-square test statistic is $\chi^2 = 595.657$.

Because the calculated value of $595.657 > 13.2767$, we reject H_O.

There is sufficient evidence to reject that the binomial distribution with n = 18 and $\pi = 0.15$ is the appropriate distribution to describe the distribution of the number of successes.

13.7

Successes	o Observed Successes	Binomial Probability n = 200, p = 0.15	e Expected Frequency	$\dfrac{(o_i - e_i)^2}{e_i}$
≤1	3	0.135888	6.9622	2.25487
2	9	0.184959	9.6179	0.03969
3	11	0.215785	11.2208	0.00435
4	14	0.188812	9.8182	1.78109
5	6	0.132169	6.8728	0.11083
≥6	9	0.144387	7.5081	0.29644
Total	52	1	52	4.48727

The calculated chi-square test statistic is $\chi^2 = 4.48727$.
Because the calculated value of 4.48727 is less than the critical value of 12.8345, we do not reject H_O.
There is not sufficient evidence to conclude that the distribution of loan applicant arrivals is not Poisson, with $\lambda = 3.5$.

13.9

a. H_0: The pipe diameter is normally distributed with a mean of 2.00 and a standard deviation of 0.10.
    H_A: The pipe diameter is not normally distributed with a mean of 2.00 and a standard deviation of 0.10.
    One way to group the data into classes to test this hypothesis is to form six classes of one standard deviation in width. The observed frequency distribution is:

Classes	Frequency	Normal Probability	Expected Frequencies
< 1.70	0	0.0013	0.039
1.70 < 1.80	0	0.0215	0.645
1.80 < 1.90	3	0.1359	4.077
1.90 < 2.00	14	0.3413	10.239
2.00 < 2.10	7	0.3413	10.239
2.10 < 2.20	6	0.1359	4.077
2.20 < 2.30	0	0.0215	0.645
2.30 >	0	0.0013	0.039

Collapse cells so that the expected frequencies are 5 or more. Note, we would need to collapse the data into only two classes to achieve this. If we use four classes, two of the expected frequencies are very close to five.
The chi-square goodness of fit test is:

Class	Observed Frequency	Normal Distribution Probability	Expected Frequency	(O-E)^2/E
Under 1.9	3	0.15865526	4.75965779	0.65055
1.9 to under 2.0	14	0.34134474	10.2403422	1.3803276
2.0 to under 2.1	7	0.34134474	10.2403422	1.0253386
2.1 and over	6	0.15865526	4.75965779	0.3232268

The calculated chi-square statistic is 0.65055 + 1.3803276 + 1.0253386 + 0.3232268 = 3.379443. Since the calculated chi-square test statistic is less than the critical chi-square test statistic for an alpha value of 0.01 and 3 degrees of freedom, 11.3449, we do not reject the null hypothesis and we conclude that the pipe diameter may be normally distributed with a mean of 2.00 inches and a standard deviation of 0.10. Notice, we have two expected values less than 5, but since we do not reject the null hypothesis we don't have to adjust the cell sizes.

b. Based on the test, we have no reason to conclude that the company is not meeting its product specification.

13.11 H_0: Distribution of service time is normally distributed.
H_A: Distribution of service time is not normally distributed.
Students may choose a variety of ways to define the data classes. One suggestion that provides expected cell frequencies of 5 or greater is:

	Observed Frequency	Normal Distribution Probability	Expected Frequency	$(O-E)^2/E$
0.1 to less than 6.5	6	0.1441	7.205	0.1999
6.5 to less than 13	36	0.6818	34.090	0.1070
13 or greater	8	0.1742	8.710	0.0578
				0.3647

The chi-square value of .3647 is less than any Chi-square critical value so you should not reject H_0 and therefore conclude that the distribution of service time may be normally distributed.

13.13 H_0: The arrival distribution is Poisson distributed
H_A: The arrival distribution is not Poisson distributed
The sample mean is 2.30. This will be used to determine the Poisson probabilities since no mean is specified in the null hypothesis.

x	Observed	Poisson	Expected
0	4	0.100259	3.007765
1	6	0.230595	6.91786
2	6	0.265185	7.955539
3	10	0.203308	6.099247
4	3	0.116902	3.507067
5	0	0.053775	1.613251
6	0	0.020614	0.618413
7	0	0.006773	0.203193
8	0	0.001947	0.058418
9	1	0.000498	0.014929
	30		30.00

We combine cells to make the expected cell frequencies 5 or greater.

x	observed	Poisson	expected	$(o-e)^2/e$
less than 2	10	0.3309	9.927	0.0005
2	6	0.2652	7.956	0.4809
3	10	0.2033	6.099	2.4951
greater than 3	4	0.2007	6.021	0.6784
				3.6549

The critical Chi-Square value with an $\alpha = .025$ and k-1 - 1 = 2 degrees of freedom is 7.3778,   The calculated Chi-Square is 3.6549 which is less than 7.3778 so do not reject H_0 and thus conclude that the arrival distribution may be Poisson distributed. Note, one extra degree of freedom is lost since we had to estimate the mean from the sample data.

13.15
a.   Using the steps outlined in the chapter:
Step 1: In this case, the null and alternative hypotheses are
H_0: Distribution of successes is binomial, with n = 15 and $\pi = 0.50$
H_A: Distribution is not binomial, with n = 15 and $\pi = 0.50$
Step 2: $\alpha = 0.05$
Step 3: The degrees of freedom equals k – 1 = 8 – 1 = 7. The critical chi-square value found in Appendix G is 14.0671.

Step 4: Note that expected values of less than 5 required that the values less than 5 and those greater than 10, respectively, required that categories be combined.

Chi-Square Goodness-of-Fit Test for Observed Counts in Variable: FasTrak

```
Using category names in FasTrak11

                   Historical      Test                  Contribution
Category  Observed     Counts  Proportion  Expected         to Chi-Sq
   <5            5   0.059235    0.059235    5.3311           0.02057
    5            7   0.091644    0.091644    8.2480           0.18883
    6           13   0.152740    0.152740   13.7466           0.04055
    7           21   0.196381    0.196381   17.6742           0.62580
    8           18   0.196381    0.196381   17.6742           0.00600
    9           14   0.152740    0.152740   13.7466           0.00467
   10            9   0.091644    0.091644    8.2480           0.06857
  >10            3   0.059235    0.059235    5.3311           1.01934

  N  DF   Chi-Sq  P-Value
 90   7  1.97433    0.961
```

The calculated chi-square test statistic is $\chi^2 = 1.97433$.

Step 5: Because the calculated value of 1.97433 is less than the critical value of 14.0671, we do not reject H_O.

Step 6: There is not sufficient evidence to conclude the distribution of the number of FasTrak users could not be described as a binomial distribution with n = 15 and a population proportion equal to 0.50

b. **Step 1:** $H_O: \pi \le 0.70$, $H_A: \pi > 0.70$

Step 2: $\alpha = 0.05$.

Step 3: Since $\alpha = 0.05$, the critical value is 1.645. Reject H_O if $z > 1.645$,

Step 4: From the data set in 90 days 1350 cars were observed. A total of 673 used the electronic payment system.

$$p = 673/1350 = .499$$

$$z = \frac{p - \pi}{\sqrt{\frac{\pi(1-\pi)}{n}}} = \frac{.499 - .7}{\sqrt{\frac{.7(.3)}{1350}}} = \frac{-0.201}{0.0125} = -16.12$$

Step 5: Since $z = -16.12 < 1.645$, do not reject H_O

Step 6: There is not sufficient evidence to conclude that the percent of tolls paid electronically has increased to more than 70% since Yee's efforts

Section 13-2 Exercises

13.17
a. H_0: Type of car owned is independent of union membership.
H_A: Type of car owned is not independent of union membership.
$\alpha = 0.05$

Observed Frequencies			
	Union Membership		
Car	Yes	No	Total
Domestic	155	470	625
Foreign	40	325	365
Total	195	795	990

Expected Frequencies			
	Union Membership		
Car	Yes	No	Total
Domestic	123.1061	501.8939	625
Foreign	71.8939	293.1061	365
Total	195	795	990

The calculated chi-square test statistic is 8.2630 + 2.0268 + 14.1489 + 3.4705
= 27.9092. The critical value of the chi-square test statistic for $\alpha = 0.05$ and 1 d.f. is 3.8415. Since the calculated value of 27.9092 > 3.8415, we reject the null hypothesis and conclude that type of car owned is not independent of union membership.

b. The p-value can be found using Excel's CHITEST function or Excel's CHIDIST function. The form of the CHITEST function is =CHITEST(Actual_range, Expected_range). The function returns the p-value. The p-value for this test is 0.000001271442. Small p-values provide strong evidence to reject the null hypothesis. The form of the CHIDIST function is =CHIDIST(Chi-Square, Degrees of freedom) or CHIDIST(27.9092, 1) which gives .0000000127, the same value as the CHITEST function

13.19.
a. H_0: Gender is independent of drink preference
H_A: There is a relationship between gender and drink preference
b. The expected cell frequencies are:

	Flavored	Unflavored
Men	83.655	114.345
Women	85.345	116.655

The calculated value of the test statistic is
Chi-square = $(101-83.655)^2/83.655 + (97-114.345)^2/114.345 + (68-85.345)^2/85.345 + (134-116.655)^2/116.655 = 12.331$.
The critical value of the test statistic has 1 degree of freedom and is 3.8415.
Because the calculated value of the test statistic = 12.331 is greater than the critical value of 3.8415, reject the null hypothesis and conclude there is a relationship between gender and drink preference.

13.21

a. H_O: The approval of a loan is independent of the marital status of the customer

H_A: Approval of a loan and marital status are not independent.

	Approved	Rejected	Total
Single	213	189	402
Married	374	231	605
Divorced	358	252	610
Total	945	672	1617

The expected cell frequencies are determined by

$$e_{ij} = \frac{(\text{row total})(\text{column total})}{\text{grand total}}$$

As an example $e_{11} = \dfrac{402(945)}{1617} = 234.94$. The expected cell values for all cells are

	Approved	Rejected	Total
Single	234.94	167.06	402
Married	353.57	251.43	605
Divorced	356.49	253.51	610
Total	945	672	1617

The test statistic is computed using Equation 13.2

$$\chi^2 = \sum\sum \frac{(o_{ij} - e_{ij})^2}{e_{ij}} = \frac{(213 - 234.94)^2}{234.94} + \ldots + \frac{(252 - 253.51)^2}{253.51} = 7.783$$

Because $\chi^2 = 7.783 < 9.2104$, do not reject the null hypothesis.

Approval of a loan and marital status are independent.

b. Since $\chi^2 = 7.783 < 9.2104 = \chi^2_{0.01}$, then $0.01 < $ p-value. The exact p-value can be found using Excel's CHIDIST command or Minitab's CALC>PROBABILITY DISTRIBUTIONS command to find the exact value of 0.0204.

13.23.

a. H_0: Investing preference is independent of employment sector

H_A: Investing preference is not independent of employment sector

$\alpha = 0.01$

The expected cell frequencies are shown below:

	Aggressive	Balanced
Public	182.857	137.143
Private	217.143	162.857

The calculated value of the chi-square text statistic is

$(164-182.857)^2/182.857 + (156-137.143)^2/137.143 + (236-217.143)^2/217.143 + (144-162.857)^2/162.857 = 8.3584$.

Chi-square critical has 1 degree of freedom and for $\alpha = 0.01 = 6.6349$. Because the calculated value of the test statistic $= 8.3584$ is greater than the critical value $= 6.6349$, reject the null hypothesis and conclude that investing preference is not independent of employment sector.

b. The p-value for the test can be found using Excel. P-value $= 0.00384$

13.25 H_0: Account balance and model of washer purchased are independent.

H_A: Account balance and model of washer purchased are not independent.

$\alpha = 0.025$.

		Observed Frequencies				
		Washer Model Purchased				
		Standard	Deluxe	Superior	XLT	Total
Credit Balance	Under $200	10	16	40	5	71
	$200-800	8	12	24	15	59
	Over $800	16	12	16	30	74
	Total	34	40	80	50	204

		Expected Frequencies				
		Washer Model Purchased				
		Standard	Deluxe	Superior	XLT	Total
Credit Balance	Under $200	11.8333	13.9216	27.8431	17.4020	71
	$200-800	9.8333	11.5686	23.1373	14.4608	59
	Over $800	12.3333	14.5098	29.0196	18.1373	74
	Total	34	40	80	50	204

$$\chi^2 = \sum\sum \frac{(o-e)^2}{e} = \frac{(10-11.83)^2}{11.83} + \frac{(16-13.92)^2}{13.92} + \cdots + \frac{(30-18.13)^2}{18.13} = 30.2753$$

The p-value for a chi-square value of 30.2753 and 6 d.f. is 0.00003484. Since the p-value is less than $\alpha = 0.02$, we reject the null hypothesis and conclude that account balance and model of washer purchased are not independent.

13.27

a. H_O: The number of lettuce heads harvested for the two lettuce types is independent of the levels of sodium absorption ratios (SAR).

H_A: The number of lettuce heads harvested for the two lettuce types is not independent of the levels of sodium absorption ratios (SAR).

The following contingency table shows the results of the sampling

SAR	Salinas	Sniper	Total
3	104	109	213
5	160	163	323
7	142	146	288
10	133	156	289
Total	539	574	1113

The expected cell frequencies are determined by

$$e_{ij} = \frac{(\text{row total})(\text{column total})}{\text{grand total}}$$

As an example $e_{11} = \dfrac{213(539)}{1113} = 103.151$. The expected cell values for all cells are

SAR	Salinas	Sniper	Total
3	103.15	109.85	213
5	156.42	166.58	323
7	139.47	148.53	288
10	139.96	149.04	289
Total	539	574	1113

The test statistic is computed using Equation 13.2

$$\chi^2 = \sum\sum \frac{(o_{ij}-e_{ij})^2}{e_{ij}} = \frac{(104-103.15)^2}{103.151} + \ldots + \frac{(156-149.04)^2}{149.04} = 0.932$$

Since $\chi^2_{0.025} = 9.3484 > \chi^2 = 0.932$, then p-value > 0.025. Because p-value > 0.025 = α, do not reject H_O. The number of lettuce heads harvested for the two lettuce types is independent of the levels of sodium absorption ratios (SAR).

b. Examine the average number of heads per SAR level for Salinas and Sniper: $\bar{x}_1 = \frac{\sum x_i}{n} = \frac{539}{4} = 134.75$

and $\bar{x}_2 = \frac{\sum x_i}{n} = \frac{574}{4} = 143.50$. Since H_O was not rejected in part a. even though a difference exists, it could be due to sampling error. A decision could be made for other reasons, like cost.

13.29

a. Minitab output:

Tabulated statistics: Severity, Emotions

Rows: Severity   Columns: Emotions

	Anger	Hostility	Irritability	All
A little	166	151	367	684
Extreme	110	55	113	278
Moderate	101	70	189	360
Quite a bit	81	55	131	267
All	458	331	800	1589

Cell Contents: Count

b. **Step 1:** H_O: The type of emotion felt by patients just before they were injured is independent of the severity of that emotion, H_A: The type of emotion felt by patients just before they were injured is not independent of the severity of that emotion.
Step 2: α = 0.05
Step 3: The critical value for this test will be the chi-square value with (r-1)(c-1) = (4-1)(3-1) = 6 degrees of freedom with α = 0.05. From Appendix G, the critical value is 12.5916.
Step 4: The expected cell frequencies are determined by

$$e_{ij} = \frac{(\text{row total})(\text{column total})}{\text{grand total}}$$. The results are obtained in the following Minitab output:

Tabulated statistics: Severity, Emotions

Rows: Severity   Columns: Emotions

	Anger	Hostility	Irritability	All
A little	166	151	367	684
	197.2	142.5	344.4	684.0
Extreme	110	55	113	278
	80.1	57.9	140.0	278.0
Moderate	101	70	189	360
	103.8	75.0	181.2	360.0
Quite a bit	81	55	131	267
	77.0	55.6	134.4	267.0
All	458	331	800	1589
	458.0	331.0	800.0	1589.0

Cell Contents: Count
                   Expected count

Pearson Chi-Square = 24.439, DF = 6, P-Value = 0.000

Step 5: Because $\chi^2 = 24.439 > 12.5916$, reject the null hypothesis.
Step 6: Conclude that there is sufficient evidence to conclude that the type of emotion felt by patients just before they were injured is not independent of the severity of that emotion.

13.31 H_0 : The plan to stay at the hotel again is independent of whether or not this is the first time the customer has stayed at the hotel.

H_A :   The plan to stay again is not independent of whether the customer has stayed at the hotel before

The contingency table with expected frequencies included is:

		First Stay?		
		Yes	No	Total
	Definitely Will	9	12	21
		14.90	6.10	
	Probably Will	18	2	20
Stay Again?		14.19	5.81	
	Maybe	15	3	18
		12.77	5.23	
	Probably Not	2	1	3
		2.13	0.87	
	Total	44	18	62

We have some expected cell frequencies that are smaller than 5. Before collapsing categories, we will see if the null hypothesis is rejected. If not, then we need not worry about the small expected frequencies. Then the test statistic is:

$$\chi^2 = \sum\sum \frac{(o-e)^2}{e} = 12.9$$

Because $\chi^2 = \sum\sum \frac{(o-e)^2}{e} = 12.9 > 7.8147$ we would reject the null hypothesis. Thus, we need to take care of the small expected frequencies. We will do this by combining the "Maybe" and the "Probably not" categories on the stay again variable with the revised contingency table as follows:

		First Stay?		
		Yes	No	Total
	Definitely Will	9	12	21
		14.90	6.10	
	Probably Will	18	2	20
Stay Again?		14.19	5.81	
	Maybe or	17	4	21
	Probably Not	14.90	6.10	
	Total	44	18	62

The revised test statistic is:

$$\chi^2 = \sum\sum \frac{(o-e)^2}{e} = 11.6$$

and the revised critical value now has (3-1)(2-1) = 2 degrees of freedom and is 5.9915. Therefore,

Because $\chi^2 = \sum\sum \frac{(o-e)^2}{e} = 11.6 > 5.9915$, we reject the null hypothesis.

The company can conclude that whether someone is staying for the first time or not is not independent of plans to stay again. In general, people who have stayed before are more likely to say that they will stay again.

13.33. H_0: Type of warranty problem and shift are independent.
          H_A: The of warranty problem and shift are not independent

Expected Frequencies

Type of Complaint	Plant			Total
	Day	Swing	Graveyard	
Corrosion	23.8636364	9.545454545	1.59090909	35
Cracked Lens	30.6818182	12.27272727	2.04545455	45
Wiring	15.6818182	6.272727273	1.04545455	23
Sound	4.77272727	1.909090909	0.31818182	7
Total	75	30	5	110

Since several of the expected frequencies are less than 5 we need to combine swing and graveyard and combine wiring and sound.

Observed Frequencies:

Type of Complaint	Shift		Total
	Day	Swing and Graveyard	
Corrosion	23	12	35
Cracked Lens	32	13	45
Wiring & Sound	20	10	30
Total	75	35	110

Expected Frequencies:

Type of Complaint	Shift		Total
	Day	Swing and Graveyard	
Corrosion	23.864	11.136	35
Cracked Lens	30.682	14.318	45
Wiring & Sound	20.455	9.545	30
Total	75	35	110

Chi-Square Calculation

Type of Complaint	Shift	
	Day	Swing and Graveyard
Corrosion	0.031	0.067
Cracked Lens	0.057	0.121
Wiring & Sound	0.010	0.022

Chi-Square Critical	5.991
Chi-Square Calculated	0.308
p-value	0.857

Since $0.308 < 5.991$ do not reject H_0 and conclude there is not sufficient evidence to conclude the type of warranty problem and shift are not independent.

Chapter Exercises

13.35 Student answers will vary depending upon the marketing research book selected and what is included in the book.

13.37 The hypothesis test procedure allows the researcher to conduct a one-tail test to determine if one proportion is larger than the other while the contingency analysis establishes independence/dependence (equal proportions/unequal proportions). The second advantage is that the test of proportions allows the test the difference between the two proportions to be something other than zero while the contingency analysis only tests the equality of the proportions.

13.39
a. Students will need to collapse rows to make the expected cell frequencies reach 5 or more.

Readmissions Last Year	Observed Frequency	Poisson Probability Distribution	Expected Frequency
0	139	0.3012	90.3583
1	87	0.3614	108.4299
2	48	0.2169	65.0579
3	14	0.0867	26.0232
4 or more	12	0.0338	10.1400

b. H_0: The distribution of patient readmissions is Poisson distributed with mean of 1.2
H_A: The distribution of patient readmission is not Poisson distributed with mean of 1.2
$\alpha = .05$

Readmissions Last Year	Observed Frequency	Poisson Probability Distribution	Expected Frequency	$(O-E)^2/E$
0	139	0.3012	90.3583	26.18486
1	87	0.3614	108.4299	4.235375
2	48	0.2169	65.0579	4.47253
3	14	0.0867	26.0232	5.554927
4 or more	12	0.0338	10.1400	0.341183
				40.78888

Chi-Square Critical   9.4877
Chi-Square Calculated   40.7889

Since $40.7889 > 9.4877$ reject H_0 and conclude that the distribution of patient readmission is not Poisson distributed with mean of 1.2

13.41

a.

Number of Defectives	Observed Frequency	Binomial Probability Distribution	Expected Frequency	(O-E)2/E
0	209	0.773780938	232.134281	2.30554
1	33	0.203626563	61.0879688	12.91472
2	43	0.021434375	6.4303125	207.9747
3	10	0.001128125	0.3384375	275.814
4	5	2.96875E-05	0.00890625	2797.026
5	0	3.125E-07	9.375E-05	9.38E-05
				3296.035

Need to combine defectives 2-5 to form a category of 2-5.

b. H_0: The number of defectives is binomial distributed with n = 5 and π = 0.05
   H_A: The number of defectives is not binomial distributed with n = 5 and p = 0.05

Number of Defectives	Observed Frequency	Binomial Probability Distribution	Expected Frequency	(O-E)2/E
0	209	0.773780938	232.134281	2.30554
1	33	0.203626563	61.0879688	12.91472
2-5	58	0.0225925	6.77775	387.1077
				402.3279

Chi-Square Critical	4.6052
Chi-Square Calculated	402.327913
p-value	4.3212E-88

Since 402.3279 > 4.6052 reject H_0 and conclude that the number of defectives is not binomial distributed with n = 5 and π = 0.05.

13.43

Step 1: H_O: the type of preferred outdoor activity is not dependent on the year,
  H_A: the type of preferred outdoor activity is dependent on the year.
Step 2: α = 0.05
Step 3: The critical value for this test will be the chi-square value with (r-1)(c-1) = (2 -1)(5-1) = 4 degrees of freedom with α = 0.05.
Step 4: The observed data were
  The expected cell frequencies are determined by

	Bicycling	Swimming	Baseball	Fishing	Touch football	Total
1995	68	60	29	25	16	198
2004	47	42	22	18	10	139
Total	115	102	51	43	26	337

$$e_{ij} = \frac{(row\ total)(column\ total)}{grand\ total}$$

As an example $e_{11} = \dfrac{198(115)}{337} = 67.5668$. The expected cell values for all cells are

The test statistic is computed using Equation 13.2

$$\chi^2 = \sum\sum \frac{(o_{ij} - e_{ij})^2}{e_{ij}} = \frac{(68 - 67.5668)^2}{67.5668} + \ldots + \frac{(10 - 10.7240)^2}{10.7240} = 0.172$$

	Bicycling	Swimming	Baseball	Fishing	Touch football	Total
1995	67.5668	59.9288	29.9644	25.2641	15.2760	198
2004	47.4332	42.0712	21.0356	17.7359	10.7240	139
Total	115	102	51	43	26	337

Step 5: From Appendix G, we see that $P(\chi^2 > 0.2070) = 0.995$. Therefore, p-value $= P(\chi^2 = 0.172) > 0.995$ $> \alpha = 0.05$. Because p-value $> 0.995 > \alpha = 0.05$, do not reject the null hypothesis.

Step 6: There is not sufficient evidence to conclude that the type of preferred outdoor activity is dependent on the year of this survey.

13.45
a. H_0: Airline usage pattern has not changed from a previous study
H_A: Airline usage pattern has changed from a previous study

b.

Airline	Observed	Previous Proportion	Expected	$(O-E)^2/E$
Delta	7	0.2	20	8.45
Horizon	29	0.1	10	36.1
Northwest	18	0.1	10	6.4
Skywest	8	0.03	3	8.333333333
SouthWest	20	0.25	25	1
United	18	0.32	32	6.125
Total	100	1	100	66.40833333

The calculated chi-square test statistic is 66.4083. This calculated value is compared to the critical value of the test statistic for alpha = 0.01 and 5 d.f. of 15.08632. Because the calculated value is greater than the critical value we reject the null hypothesis and conclude that the usage pattern has changed from the pattern reported in the earlier study. Note the p-value for this test (5.71786E-13) is very small indicating that there is strong sample evidence to reject the null hypothesis.

13.47

a.   Minitab output:

Tabulated statistics: Invest, Race

```
Rows: Invest    Columns: Race

               AfricanAmerican  White     All

Don't Invest              175     90     265
                        132.5  132.5   265.0

Invest                    325    410     735
                        367.5  367.5   735.0

All                       500    500    1000
                        500.0  500.0  1000.0


Cell Contents:       Count
                     Expected count
```

b.   **Step 1:** H_O: The proportion of African-Americans does not differ from the proportion of white Americans who invest in stocks in 2005.

   H_A: The proportion of African-Americans differs from the proportion of white Americans who invest in stocks.

Step 2: $\alpha = 0.05$

Step 3: The critical value for this test will be the chi-square value with $(r-1)(c-1) = (2-1)(2-1) = 1$ degrees of freedom with $\alpha = 0.05$. From Appendix G, the critical value is 3.8415.

Step 4: The expected cell frequencies are determined by

$$e_{ij} = \frac{(\text{row total})(\text{column total})}{\text{grand total}}.$$

The results are obtained in the following Minitab output:

Tabulated statistics: Invest, Race

```
Rows: Invest    Columns: Race

               AfricanAmerican  White     All

Don't Invest              175     90     265
                        132.5  132.5   265.0

Invest                    325    410     735
                        367.5  367.5   735.0

All                       500    500    1000
                        500.0  500.0  1000.0


Cell Contents:       Count
                     Expected count


Pearson Chi-Square = 37.094, DF = 1, P-Value = 0.000
Likelihood Ratio Chi-Square = 37.604, DF = 1, P-Value = 0.000
```

Step 5: Because $\chi^2 = 37.094 > 3.8415$, reject the null hypothesis.

Step 6: Conclude there is sufficient evidence to conclude that the proportion of African-Americans differs from the proportion of white Americans who invest in stocks.

Chapter 14
Introduction to Linear Regression and Correlation Analysis

Section 14-1 Exercises

14.1. $H_0 : \rho \le 0.0$

$H_A : \rho > 0.0$

The correlation coefficient is r = 0.57. The test statistic is computed as follows:

$$t = \frac{r}{\sqrt{\dfrac{1-r^2}{n-2}}} = \frac{0.57}{\sqrt{\dfrac{1-0.57^2}{15-2}}} = 2.50$$

Because t = 2.50 > 1.7709, reject the null hypothesis

There is sufficient evidence to conclude there is a positive linear relationship between sales units and marketing expense for companies in this industry.

14.3

a. Minitab output produces the following correlation coefficient:

Correlations: Xi, Yi

```
Pearson correlation of Xi and Yi = 0.206
P-Value = 0.569
```

b. $H_O: \rho = 0$
$H_A: \rho \ne 0$

$$r = \frac{\sum(x - \bar{x})(y - \bar{y})}{\sqrt{[\sum(x - \bar{x})^2][\sum(y - \bar{y})^2]}} = 0.206$$

Compute the *t* test statistic using Equation 14-3.

$$t = \frac{r}{\sqrt{\dfrac{1 - r^2}{n - 2}}} = \frac{0.206}{\sqrt{\dfrac{1 - 0.206^2}{10 - 2}}} = 0.59$$

For an alpha level equal to 0.10, the two-tailed, upper-tail, critical value for n − 2 = 10 − 2 = 8 degrees of freedom is *t* = 1.8595. The decision rule is

If *t* < -1.8595 or *t* > 1.8595 reject H_O;

Otherwise, do not reject the null hypothesis

Because -1.8595 < *t* = 0.59 < 1.8595, we do not reject H_O.

There is not sufficient evidence to conclude that there is a correlation between the two population variables.

14.5

a.

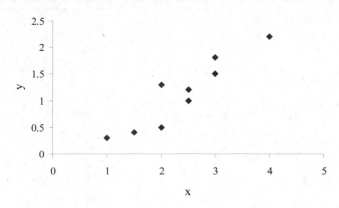

x,y Scatterplot

There appears to be a positive linear relationship.

b. Using Excel's CORREL function, the sample correlation coefficient is 0.9239. The correlation coefficient indicates the strength of the linear relationship between two variables. In this case the relationship is a positive one.

c. H_0: $\rho \le 0$
H_A: $\rho > 0$
d.f. = 10 - 2 = 8
Decision Rule:

  If t > 2.8965, Reject H_0, otherwise do not reject H_0

$$t = 0.9239/\sqrt{(1 - 0.9239^2)/(10 - 2)} = 6.8295$$

Since 6.8295 > 2.8965 reject H_0 and conclude that the correlation coefficient is greater than 0.

14.7

a. There appears to be a fairly strong positive correlation between the standardized mathematics examination and the standardized English examination for these students.

b. Ho: $\rho \le 0$
H_A: $\rho > 0$

$$t = \frac{r}{\sqrt{\dfrac{1-r^2}{n-2}}} = \frac{0.75}{\sqrt{\dfrac{1-(0.75)^2}{50-2}}} = 7.856$$

Because t = 7.856 > 2.4066, reject the null hypothesis
Because the null hypothesis is rejected, the sample data does support the hypothesis that there is a positive linear relationship between the standardized mathematics examination and the standardized English examination.

14.9.

a. The dependent variable will be the variable for which the analysis are interested in explaining or predicting. That would be the average credit card balance. The independent variable is the variable that the analysts will use in an attempt to explain the variation in the dependent variable or to predict the value of the dependent variable. That would be the income variable.

b.   The scatter plot for these two variables is:

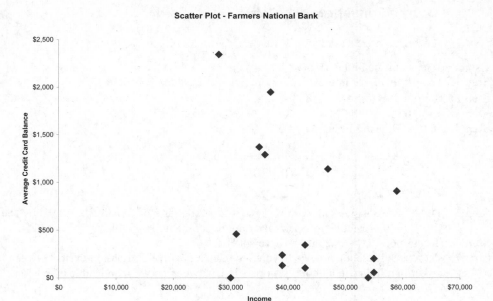

Based on this scatter plot there does not appear to be a strong relationship of any kind between income and credit card balance. If anything, the relationship is negative – as income rises, there is a tendency for credit card balances to be lower.

c.   The correlation coefficient can be computed using the following equation:

$$r = \frac{\sum(x-\overline{x})(y-\overline{y})}{\sqrt{[\sum(x-\overline{x})^2][\sum(y-\overline{y})^2]}}$$

or we can use the algebraic equivalent equation:

$$r = \frac{n\sum xy - \sum x \sum y}{\sqrt{[n\sum(x^2)-(\sum x)^2][n\sum(y^2)-(\sum y)^2]}}$$

Using either of these two, we get r = -0.397

$$H_0 : \rho = 0.0$$

$$H_A : \rho \neq 0.0$$

$$t = \frac{r}{\sqrt{\dfrac{1-r^2}{n-2}}} = \frac{-0.397}{\sqrt{\dfrac{1--0.397^2}{15-2}}} = -1.56$$

Because t = -1.56 > -2.1604, do not reject the null hypothesis

Based on these sample data we have no basis for concluding that the population correlation is different from zero. This means that we can not state that there is a linear relationship between income and credit card balance.

14.11.
  a. Minitab output:

Correlations: Network, Cable

Pearson correlation of Network and Cable = 0.979

  b. Using the steps outline in the chapter:
  Step 1: The parameter of interest is the population correlation coefficient.
  Step 2: $H_O: \rho \le 0$, $H_A: \rho > 0$
  Step 3: $\alpha = 0.05$
  Step 4: $r = 0.979$, using Equation 14-3.

  $$t = \frac{r}{\sqrt{\dfrac{1 - r^2}{n - 2}}} = \frac{0.979}{\sqrt{\dfrac{1 - (0.979)^2}{4 - 2}}} = 6.791$$

  Step 5: The degrees of freedom with n -2 = 4 – 2 = 2 degrees of freedom, t = 2.9200. The decision rule is if t > 2.9200 reject H_O, otherwise, do not reject the null hypothesis.
  Step 6: Because 6.791 > t = 2.9200, we reject H_O.
  Step 7: There is sufficient evidence to conclude that a positive correlation exists between the average non-program minutes in an hour of prime-time between network and cable television.

14.13
  a.

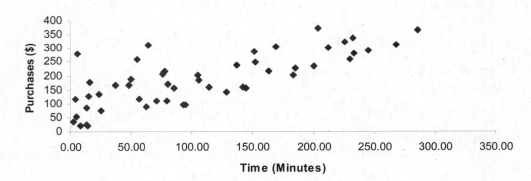

Scatterplot of Time vs. Purchases

There appears to be a positive linear relationship between the time the customer spent shopping the company's on-line catalog that quarter and the dollar value of each customer's quarterly purchases.
  b. Using Excel, the correlation coefficient between the time the customer spent shopping the company's on-line catalog that quarter and the dollar value of each customer's quarterly purchases is found to be 0.75644. The correlation coefficient measures the degree of correlation between the two variables. This correlation coefficient indicates that there is a fairly strong degree of positive correlation between the time the customer spent shopping the company's on-line catalog that quarter and the dollar value of each customer's quarterly purchases.

c. The appropriate null and alternative hypotheses are:

$H_0: \rho \leq 0$

$H_A: \rho > 0$

Using Excel with a significance level of 0.025 and 49 (51-2) degrees of freedom, the critical t value is 2.0096. The decision rule is

If t > 2.0096, reject the null hypothesis;

Otherwise, do not reject the null hypothesis.

Compute the test statistic using Equation 14-3

$$t = \frac{r}{\sqrt{\dfrac{1-r^2}{n-2}}} = \frac{0.75644}{\sqrt{\dfrac{1-(0.75644)^2}{51-2}}} = 8.0957$$

Because t = 8.0957 > 2.0096, reject the null hypothesis and conclude that there is a positive linear relationship between the time the customer spent shopping the company's on-line catalog that quarter and the dollar value of each customer's quarterly purchases.

14.15.

a. Minitab scatter plot:

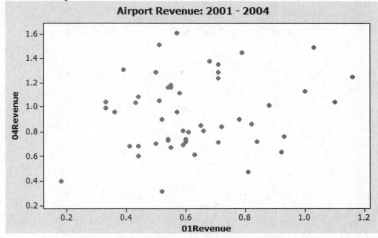

It appears that as 2001 revenue increases there is an increase in the 2004 revenue which can be seen as the upward "tilt" of the scatter plot.

b. Minitab output:

Scatterplot of 04Revenue vs 01Revenue

Correlations: 04Revenue, 01Revenue

Pearson correlation of 04Revenue and 01Revenue = 0.186

This correlation coefficient indicates there is a very weak positive linear relationship between per-person airport spending in 2004 versus 2001. Given this weak relationship, one could not project that the 2004 revenue would increase in response to an increase in 2001 revenue.

c. **Step 1:** The parameter of interest is the population correlation coefficient
    Step 2: H_O: $\rho \leq 0$, H_A: $\rho > 0$
    Step 3: $\alpha = 0.05$
    Step 4: r = 0.186, using Equation 14-3.

$$t = \frac{r}{\sqrt{\dfrac{1-r^2}{n-2}}} = \frac{0.186}{\sqrt{\dfrac{1-(0.186)^2}{51-2}}} = 1.325$$

    Step 5: The degrees of freedom with n -2 = 51 – 2 = 49 degrees of freedom, t = 1.67655 (from Minitab). The decision rule is if t > 1.67655 reject H_O, otherwise, do not reject the null hypothesis.
    Step 6: Because 1.325 $< t$ = 1.67655, we reject do not reject H_O.
    Step 7: There is insufficient evidence to conclude that a positive correlation exists between the per-person spending in 2001 and that in 2004.

Section 14-2 Exercises

14.17.
a. The scatter plot is shown below:

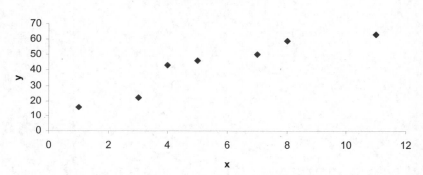

Scatterplot of x vs. y

        There appears to be a positive linear relationship between x and y.
b. Using equation 14-7,

$$b_1 = \frac{\sum xy - \dfrac{\sum x \sum y}{n}}{\sum x^2 - \dfrac{(\sum x)^2}{n}} = \frac{1{,}999 - \dfrac{(39)(299)}{7}}{285 - \dfrac{39^2}{7}} = 4.92$$

$$\bar{y} = \frac{\sum y}{n} = \frac{299}{7} = 42.71 \qquad\qquad \bar{x} = \frac{\sum x}{n} = \frac{39}{7} = 5.57$$

$$b_0 = \bar{y} - b_1 \bar{x} = 42.71 - (4.92)(5.57) = 15.31$$

$$\hat{y} = 15.31 + 4.92(x)$$

b_0 of 15.31 would be the value of y if x were 0; b_1 of 4.92 means that for every one unit increase in x, y will increase by 4.92.

c. Using Excel, the results of the regression analysis are shown below:

SUMMARY OUTPUT

Regression Statistics	
Multiple R	0.9329
R Square	0.8702
Adjusted R Square	0.8443
Standard Error	6.9917
Observations	7

The percentage of the total variation in the dependent variable that can be explained by the independent variable is equal to R^2, which is 0.8702. Therefore, approximately 87% of the total variation is explained by the independent variable. This is the result we would get by dividing SSR, the regression sum of squares, by SST, the total sum of squares.

d. Conduct a test to determine whether the regression model is statistically significant (or whether the population correlation is equal to 0). The null and alternative hypotheses to test the correlation coefficient are:

H_o: $\rho = 0$
H_A: $\rho \neq 0$

Using Excel, the correlation coefficient is:

	x (independent)	y (dependent)
x (independent)	1	
y (dependent)	0.9329	1

The test statistic is

$$t = \frac{r}{\sqrt{\frac{1-r^2}{n-2}}} = \frac{0.9329}{\sqrt{\frac{1-(0.9329)^2}{7-2}}} = 5.7923$$

The critical t for a significant level of 0.01 and 5 degrees of freedom = 4.0321. Because t = 5.7923 > 4.0321, reject H_o and conclude that the overall model is significant. We could also conduct an F-test to determine if ρ^2 is significantly different from zero, or a t-test to determine whether the true regression slope is different from zero. The three tests are equivalent in the simple linear regression model.

e. The null and alternative hypotheses to test whether the regression slope coefficient is equal to zero is:

H_o: $\beta_1 = 0$
H_A: $\beta_1 \neq 0$

Using Excel, the regression results are:

	Coefficients	Standard Error
Intercept	15.3038	5.4215
x (independent)	4.9198	0.8497

The test statistic is $t = \frac{b_1 - \beta_1}{S_{b1}} = \frac{4.9198 - 0}{0.8497} = 5.79$

The critical t for a significant level of 0.01 and 5 degrees of freedom = 4.0321.
Because t = 5.79 > 4.0321, reject H_o and conclude that the regression slope coefficient does not equal zero, meaning that x does provide meaningful information in determining y.

14.19.

a. The slope of the regression equation is given by $b_1 = \dfrac{\sum(x-\bar{x})(y-\bar{y})}{\sum(x-\bar{x})^2} = \dfrac{-269.613}{547.66} = -0.4923$.

The y-intercept $= b_0 = \bar{y} - b_1\bar{x} = 19.175 - (-0.4923)(15.55) = 26.830$. So the regression equation is $\hat{y} = 26.830 - 0.4923x$

b. When x = 10, $\hat{y} = 26.830 - 0.4923(10) = 21.907$.

c. The slope of the equation indicates the change in the average value of y when the x variable increases by 1 unit. Therefore, what is being sought here is ten times the slope = 10(-0.4923) = - 4.923 (a decrease of 4.923 units).

d. A scatter plot of y and x

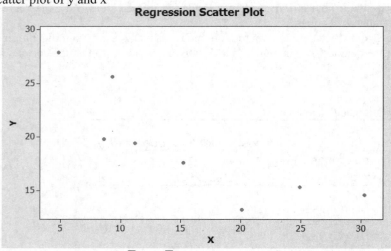

$$r = \frac{\sum(x-\bar{x})(y-\bar{y})}{\sqrt{[\sum(x-\bar{x})^2][\sum(y-\bar{y})^2]}} = \frac{-269.613}{\sqrt{547.66(191.975)}} = -0.8315$$

The slope of the regression equation is given by $b_1 = \dfrac{\sum(x-\bar{x})(y-\bar{y})}{\sum(x-\bar{x})^2} = \dfrac{-269.613}{547.66} = -0.4923$.

The y-intercept $= b_0 = \bar{y} - b_1\bar{x} = 19.175 - (-0.4923)(15.55) = 26.830$.

So the regression equation is $\hat{y} = 26.830 - 0.4923x$

The coefficient of determination is
$$R^2 = r^2 = (-0.8315)^2 = 0.691$$

$H_O: \beta_1 \geq 0$, $H_A: \beta_1 < 0$; $\alpha = 0.025$, the test statistic is $t = \dfrac{b_1 - \beta_1}{S_{b_1}} = \dfrac{-0.4923-0}{0.1343} = -3.67$,

the degrees of freedom = n – 2 = 8 – 2 = 6 and the critical value is $t_{0.025}$ = - 2.4469
The *t* test statistic of -3.67 is less than the *t*-critical value of -2.4469. Reject the null hypothesis. There is sufficient evidence to conclude the regression slope coefficient is less than zero.

14.21

a. The slope coefficient, -10.12, is the average decrease in total dollar volume in business this year for each 1 mile increase in the distance the customer is from corporate headquarters.

b. H_0: $\beta_1 \geq 0$

H_A: $\beta_1 < 0$

Decision Rule

       If $t < -2.407$ reject H_0, otherwise do not reject H_0

        $t = (-10.12-0)/3.12 = -3.2436$,

Since $-3.2436 < -2.407$ reject H_0 and conclude the further a business is from the corporate headquarters the smaller its sales are.

14.23.

a. A scatter plot of y and x

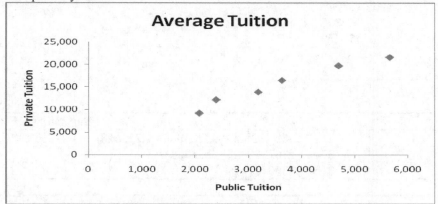

The correlation coefficient for the sample data from Excel:

	Public
Public	1
Private	0.983465

Excel output:

Regression Analysis: Private versus Public

```
The regression equation is
Private = 3372 + 3.36 Public


Predictor     Coef   SE Coef       T        P
Constant      3372      1181    2.86    0.046
Public      3.3606    0.3094   10.86    0.000


  S = 946.565    R-Sq = 96.7%    R-Sq(adj)  = 95.9%
```

The resulting regression equation is $\hat{y} = 3372 + 3.36x$. The coefficient of determination is 96.7%.

Conduct a test to determine whether the regression model is statistically significant (or whether the population slope is equal to zero).

    H_O: $\beta_1 = 0$,

    H_A: $\beta_1 \neq 0$;

    $\alpha = 0.10$,

The test statistic as given by Minitab in Step 4 is $t = 10.86$, the degrees of freedom $= n - 2 = 6 - 2 = 4$ and the critical value is ± 2.1318

The t test statistic of 10.86 is greater than the upper t-critical value of 2.1318.

There is sufficient evidence to conclude that the regression slope coefficient is not zero.

234 Chapter 14 | Introduction to Linear Regression and Correlation Analysis

b. An increase of the average public college tuition of $1 would accompany and increase in the average private college tuition of $3.36 (which is the slope of the regression equation). Therefore, an increase in the average public college tuition of $100 would accompany and increase in the average private college tuition of $3.36(100) = $336.

c. This is just asking what the predicted y value will be when x equals 7500 = $\hat{y}$ = 3372 + 3.36(7500) = $28,572.

14.25.

The completed regression output is shown as follows:

SUMMARY OUTPUT						
Regression Statistics						
Multiple R	0.198732547					
R Square	0.0395					
Adjusted R Square	0.007477779					
Standard Error	8693.34					
Observations	32					
ANOVA						
	df	*SS*	*MS*	*F*	*Significance F*	
Regression	1	93224985.89	93224986	1.233558	0.275539149	
Residual	30	2267222428	75574081			
Total	31	2360447414				
	Coefficients	*Standard Error*	*t Stat*	*P-value*	*Lower 95%*	*Upper 95%*
Intercept	63260.5323	3993.499925	15.84087	4.08E-16	55104.7258	71416.33881
Wins	511.7303371	460.7458564	1.110656	0.275539	-429.2372656	1452.69794

a. The R-square value for the regression model is 0.0395 which can be computed as follows:

$$R^2 = \frac{SSR}{SST} = \frac{93,223,985.89}{2,360,447,414} = 0.0395$$

So approximately 4% of the variation in average home attendance can be explained by knowing the number of games won.

b. The standard error or the estimate is computed as follows:

$$s_e = \sqrt{\frac{SSE}{n-2}} = \sqrt{\frac{2,267,222,428}{30}} = 8,693.34$$

The standard error is the measure of variation between the fitted regression values and the actual y values.

c. The hypothesis test is conducted as follows:

$$H_0 : \beta_1 = 0.0$$

$$H_0 : \beta_1 \neq 0.0$$

$$\alpha = 0.05$$

The test statistic is:

$$t = \frac{b_1 - \beta_1}{s_{b_1}} = \frac{511.73 - 0}{460.75} = 1.11$$

The critical value from the t-distribution for $\alpha = 0.05$ and 30 degrees of freedom is 2.0423. Because t = 1.11 < 2.0423, do not reject the null hypothesis. This means that the number of wins in the season does not explain a significant proportion of the variation in average home attendance.

d. After analyzing the regression model it is clear that using the number of wins in the season to predict average home attendance is not effective. The low R-square (0.0395) indicates just under 4 percent of the attendance variation is explained by the number of wins. The slope coefficient is insignificant. The staff at the NFL office should look for other variables to predict average attendance.

14.27.
a. Minitab scatter plot

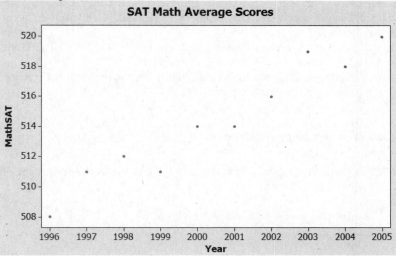

b. Minitab output:

Regression Analysis: MathSAT versus Years

```
The regression equation is
MathSAT = - 1995 + 1.25 Years


Predictor     Coef   SE Coef      T      P
Constant   -1995.4     223.7   -8.92  0.000
Years       1.2545    0.1118   11.22  0.000


S = 1.01578   R-Sq = 94.0%   R-Sq(adj) = 93.3%


Analysis of Variance

Source        DF      SS      MS       F      P
Regression     1  129.85  129.85  125.84  0.000
Residual Error 8    8.25    1.03
Total          9  138.10
```

Minitab produced the equation $\hat{y} = -1995 + 1.25x$

c. The research hypothesis to determine if the the College Board's assertion concerning the improvement in SAT average math test scores over the last 10 years is overly optimistic would be that the slope of the population regression equation is less than average SAT scores divided by 10 years (14/10 = 1.4). The test follows, using the steps outlined in the chapter:

  1: The independent variable is the year the SAT test was taken; the dependent variable is the average SAT math score of all students taking the exam.
  2: The scatter plot is in the solution to part a.
  3: From Minitab:

Correlations: MathSAT, Years

```
Pearson correlation of MathSAT and Years = 0.970
```

4: The regression equation is $\hat{y} = -1995 + 1.2545x$ and the coefficient of determination was given in part b. as $R^2 = 94.0\%$

5: H_O: $\beta_1 \geq 1.4$, H_A: $\beta_1 < 1.4$; $\alpha = 0.05$, the test statistic is

$$t = \frac{b_1 - \beta_1}{S_{b_1}} = \frac{1.2545 - 1.4}{0.1118} = -1.301$$

the degrees of freedom = $n - 2 = 10 - 2 = 8$ and the critical value is $t_{0.05} = -1.8595$. (Note, the significance level was not specified in the problem, students may choose a different value, giving a different critical value.)

6: The *t* test statistic of -1.301 is greater than the *t*-critical value of -1.8595. Therefore, do not reject the null hypothesis.

7: There does not exist enough evidence to indicate that the Average Math SAT score increases less than 1.4 points per year over the last ten years.

14.29.

a. Minitab provides the following regression equation:

$$\hat{y} = 145,000,000 + 1.3220x$$

b. **Step 1:** The independent variable is the gambling revenue of the Las Vegas Strip; the dependent variable is the gambling revenue for all of Clark County.

Step 2: The scatter plot is

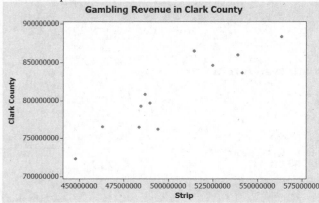

Step 3: From Minitab:

Correlations: Clark County, Strip

```
Pearson correlation of Clark County and Strip = 0.912
```

Step 4: Minitab output:

Regression Analysis: Clark County versus Strip

```
The regression equation is
Clark County = 1.45E+08 + 1.32 Strip


Predictor      Coef   SE Coef     T      P
Constant   144671002  94901882  1.52  0.158
Strip         1.3220    0.1884  7.02  0.000


S = 21438796   R-Sq = 83.1%   R-Sq(adj) = 81.4%


Analysis of Variance

Source           DF         SS          MS      F      P
Regression        1  2.26267E+16  2.26267E+16  49.23  0.000
Residual Error   10  4.59622E+15  4.59622E+14
Total            11  2.72230E+16
```

The regression equation is $\hat{y} = 145,000,000 + 1.3220x$ and the coefficient of determination is $R^2 = 83.1\%$

Step 5: $H_O: \beta_1 = 0$, $H_A: \beta_1 \neq 0$; $\alpha = 0.05$, the test statistic is

$$t = \frac{b_1 - \beta_1}{S_{b_1}} = 7.02$$

the degrees of freedom = $n - 2 = 12 - 2 = 10$ and the upper critical value is $t_{0.025} = 2.2281$. (Note, the significance level was not specified in the problem, students may choose a different value, giving a different critical value.)

Step 6: The *t* test statistic of 7.02 is greater than the *t*-critical value of 2.2281. Therefore, reject the null hypothesis.

Step 7: There does exist enough evidence to indicate that the Las Vegas Strip gambling revenue can be used to predict the gambling revenue for all of Clark County

c. Determining the increase gambling revenue that would accrue to all of Clark County if the gambling revenue on the Las Vegas Strip were to increase by a million dollars would require that we estimate $1,000,000 \, \hat{y} = 1000000(1.322) = \$1,322,000$.

Section 14-3 Exercises

14.31.

a.

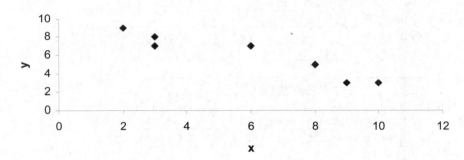

Scatterplot of x vs. y

b. Using equation 14-7,

$$b_1 = \frac{\sum xy - \frac{\sum x \sum y}{n}}{\sum x^2 - \frac{\left(\sum x\right)^2}{n}} = \frac{202 - \frac{(41)(42)}{7}}{303 - \frac{41^2}{7}} = -0.7$$

$$\bar{y} = \frac{\sum y}{n} = \frac{42}{7} = 6 \qquad\qquad \bar{x} = \frac{\sum x}{n} = \frac{41}{7} = 5.857$$

$b_0 = \bar{y} - b_1 \bar{x} = 6 - (-0.7)(5.857) = 10.1$

$\hat{y} = 10.1 + (-0.7)(x)$

c. The confidence interval estimate is

$$b_1 \pm t \, s_{b1}$$

where the degrees of freedom for the critical t is $7 - 2 = 5$. The critical t for a 95% confidence interval estimate are 2.5706, and the interval estimate is

-0.7 ± 2.5706 (0.1009)

-0.7 ± 0.2594

-0.9594 -------------- -0.4406

So, for a one-unit increase in x, y will decrease by an average of between -0.9469 and -0.4531.

d.   Using the equation determined in part (b) the point estimate of the predicted y for a given $x_p = 7$,
$$\hat{y} = 10.1 + (-0.7)(7) = 5.2$$

To determine the 95% prediction interval estimate for a particular y, given x_p, use Equation 14-24

$$\hat{y} \pm t s_e \sqrt{1 + \frac{1}{n} + \frac{(x_p - \bar{x})^2}{\sum (x - \bar{x})^2}}$$

Because this equation can be tedious to use, the results of the calculation using PhStat are shown below:

Confidence Interval Estimate

Data	
X Value	7
Confidence Level	95%

Intermediate Calculations	
Sample Size	7
Degrees of Freedom	5
t Value	2.570582
Sample Mean	5.857143
Sum of Squared Difference	62.85714
Standard Error of the Estimate	0.8
h Statistic	0.163636
Predicted Y (YHat)	5.2

For Average Y	
Interval Half Width	0.831881
Confidence Interval Lower Limit	4.368119
Confidence Interval Upper Limit	6.031881

For Individual Response Y	
Interval Half Width	2.21835
Prediction Interval Lower Limit	2.98165
Prediction Interval Upper Limit	7.41835

The prediction interval for an individual response is
2.98165 ------ 7.41835

14.33.   The interval estimate for the slope coefficient is developed using:
$$b_1 \pm t s_{b_1}$$

For 90% confidence and n-1 = 73 degrees of freedom, the critical t is approximately equal to 1.67. Then:
$$0.0943 \pm 1.67(0.107)$$

$$0.0943 \pm 0.179$$

-0.0847   ---------------------------------   +0.2733

Thus, based on the sample data, with 90% confidence, a one unit increase in x will be associated with an average change in y of anywhere between -0.0847 and 0a +0.2733. The fact the interval contains zero means the true population regression slope may be zero. Thus, it is possible that there is no relationship between the two variables in this study.

14.35.

a. The least square regression model can be developed manually or through the use of software such as Excel or Minitab. The resulting output based on these sample data is:

SUMMARY OUTPUT						
Regression Statistics						
Multiple R	0.706					
R Square	0.498					
Adjusted R Square	0.465					
Standard Error	15991.444					
Observations	17					
ANOVA						
	df	*SS*	*MS*	*F*	*Significance F*	
Regression	1	3810861239	3.81E+09	14.90	0.00154	
Residual	15	3835894055	2.56E+08			
Total	16	7646755294				
	Coefficients	*Standard Error*	*t Stat*	*P-value*	*Lower 95%*	*Upper 95%*
Intercept	58766.11	8193.92	7.17	3.22E-06	41301.2	76231.0
Weeks on the Market	943.58	244.43	3.86	0.001541	422.6	1464.6

The regression equation is:
$$\hat{y} = \$58,766.11 + \$943.58\,(x)$$

b. The hypothesis test is conducted as follows:
$$H_0 : \beta_1 = 0.0$$
$$H_0 : \beta_1 \neq 0.0$$
$$\alpha = 0.05$$

The test statistic is:
$$t = \frac{b_1 - \beta_1}{s_{b_1}} = \frac{943.58 - 0}{244.43} = 3.86$$

The critical value from the t-distribution for alpha = 0.05 and 15 degrees of freedom is 2.1315. Because t = 3.86 > 2.1315, reject the null hypothesis. This means that the number of days a condo is on the market is a significant variable in explaining the variation in the selling prices for condos in the Tempe, Arizona area.

c. $$b_1 \pm ts_{b_1}$$

For 95% confidence and n-1 = 15 degrees of freedom, the critical t = 2.1315. Then:
$$\$943.58 \pm 2.1315(\$244.43)$$
$$\$943.58 \pm \$521$$
$$\$422.58 \text{ --------------------------------- } \$1,464.58$$

Thus, based on the sample data, with 95% confidence, for a one week increase in time that a condo is on the market the mean change in selling price is increased by somewhere between $422.58 and $1,464.58. Note, this interpretation is valid only for the relevant range of data in the study.

14.37.

a. $b_1 = \dfrac{\sum(x - \bar{x})(y - \bar{y})}{\sum(x - \bar{x})^2} = \dfrac{156.4}{173.5} = 0.9014$. The y-intercept = $b_0 = \bar{y} - b_1\bar{x} = 56.4 - (0.9014)(13.4) = 44.3207$

So the regression equation is $\hat{y} = 44.3207 + 0.9014x$

b. To determine if there is a linear relationship we must test the hypotheses:
$H_O: \beta_1 = 0$, $H_A: \beta_1 \neq 0$, $\alpha = 0.05$,

$$s_\varepsilon = \sqrt{\dfrac{SSE}{n-k-1}} = \sqrt{\dfrac{40.621}{15-1-1}} = 1.7677, s_{b_1} = \dfrac{s_\varepsilon}{\sqrt{\sum(x_i - \bar{x})^2}} = \dfrac{1.7677}{\sqrt{173.5}} = 0.1342$$

$$t = \dfrac{b_1 - \beta_1}{s_{b_1}} = \dfrac{0.9014 - 0}{0.1342} = 6.717,$$ the degrees of freedom = $n - 2 = 15 - 2 = 13$. Therefore, the p-value

< 0.05 (since $t = 6.717$ is greater than any value for 13 degrees of freedom shown in the table) and the null hypothesis is rejected. There is sufficient evidence to indicate that there is a linear relationship between the dependent and independent variable.

c. $b_1 \pm ts_{b_1} = 0.9014 \pm 1.7709(0.1342) = (0.6637, 1.1391)$. At the 90% confidence level, the dependent variable will increase somewhere between 0.6637 and 1.1391 units for every unit the independent variable increases.

14.39.

a. The dependent variable (y) is service times (minutes) and the independent variable (x) is number of machines. Using equation 14-7,

$$b_1 = \dfrac{\sum xy - \dfrac{\sum x \sum y}{n}}{\sum x^2 - \dfrac{(\sum x)^2}{n}} = \dfrac{7,552 - \dfrac{(95)(863)}{12}}{825 - \dfrac{95^2}{12}} = 9.8731$$

$$\bar{y} = \dfrac{\sum y}{n} = \dfrac{863}{12} = 71.9167 \qquad\qquad \bar{x} = \dfrac{\sum x}{n} = \dfrac{95}{12} = 7.9167$$

$b_0 = \bar{y} - b_1\bar{x} = 71.9167 - (9.8731)(7.9167) = -6.2457$

$\hat{y} = -6.2457 + (9.8731)(x)$

b. With 6 machines, the expected number of minutes for a routine service call would be:
$\hat{y} = -6.2457 + (9.8731)(6) = 52.9929$ minutes

c. Using the equation determined in part (a) the point estimate of the average y for a given $x_p = 9$,
$\hat{y} = -6.2457 + (9.8731)(9) = 82.61$ minutes

To determine the 90% confidence interval estimate for an average y, given x_p, use Equation 14-23

$$\hat{y} \pm t s_e \sqrt{\dfrac{1}{n} + \dfrac{(x_p - \bar{x})^2}{\sum(x - \bar{x})^2}}$$

Since this equation can be tedious to use, the results of the calculation using PhStat are shown below:

Confidence Interval Estimate

Data	
X Value	9
Confidence Level	90%

Intermediate Calculations	
Sample Size	12
Degrees of Freedom	10
t Value	1.812461
Sample Mean	7.916667
Sum of Squared Difference	72.91667
Standard Error of the Estimate	7.855422
h Statistic	0.099429
Predicted Y (YHat)	82.61257

For Average Y	
Interval Half Width	4.489457
Confidence Interval Lower Limit	78.12311
Confidence Interval Upper Limit	87.10203

For Individual Response Y	
Interval Half Width	14.92869
Prediction Interval Lower Limit	67.68388
Prediction Interval Upper Limit	97.54126

The confidence interval for an average y is

78.123 ------ 87.102

d. Using the equation determined in part (a) the point estimate of the predicted y for a given $x_p = 7$,

$\hat{y} = -6.2457 + (9.8731)(7) = 62.866$ minutes

To determine the 90% prediction interval estimate for a particular y, given x_p, use Equation 14-24

$$\hat{y} \pm t\, s_e \sqrt{1 + \frac{1}{n} + \frac{\left(x_p - \bar{x}\right)^2}{\sum(x - \bar{x})^2}}$$

Since this equation can be tedious to use, the results of the calculation using PhStat are shown below:

Confidence Interval Estimate

Data	
X Value	7
Confidence Level	90%

Intermediate Calculations	
Sample Size	12
Degrees of Freedom	10
t Value	1.812461
Sample Mean	7.916667
Sum of Squared Difference	72.91667
Standard Error of the Estimate	7.855422
h Statistic	0.094857
Predicted Y (YHat)	62.86629

For Average Y	
Interval Half Width	4.385037
Confidence Interval Lower Limit	58.48125
Confidence Interval Upper Limit	67.25132

For Individual Response Y	
Interval Half Width	14.89762
Prediction Interval Lower Limit	47.96866
Prediction Interval Upper Limit	77.76391

The prediction interval for an individual response is
47.96866 ------ 77.76391

14.41.
a. Minitab scatter plot:

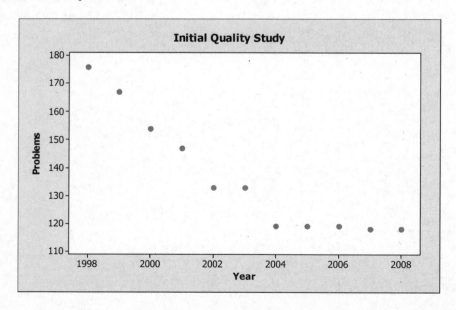

b. Minitab output:

    Step 1: The independent variable is the year for the period 1998-2008; the dependent variable is the average number of reported problems per 100 vehicles over that same period.

    Step 2: The scatter plot is in the solution to part a.

    Step 3: From Minitab:

    Correlations: Year, Problems

```
Pearson correlation of Year and Problems = -0.948
```

    Step 4: Minitab output:

    Regression Analysis: Problems versus Year

```
The regression equation is
Problems = 11991 - 5.92 Year

Predictor       Coef   SE Coef        T       P
Constant       11991      1326     9.04   0.000
Year         -5.9182    0.6620    -8.94   0.000

S = 6.94269    R-Sq = 89.9%    R-Sq(adj) = 88.8%

Analysis of Variance

Source           DF        SS       MS       F       P
Regression        1    3852.7   3852.7   79.93   0.000
Residual Error    9     433.8     48.2
Total            10    4286.5
```

    The regression equation is $\hat{y} = 11991 - 5.92x$ and the coefficient of determination is $R^2 = 89.9\%$

    Step 5: H_O: $\beta_1 \geq 0$, H_A: $\beta_1 < 0$; $\alpha = 0.01$, p-value is 0.000.

    Step 6: The p-value = $0.000 < \alpha = 0.01$. Therefore, reject the null hypothesis.

    Step 7: There does exist enough evidence to indicate that the average number of reported problems per 100 vehicles declines from year to year

c. Minitab output:

```
Predicted Values for New Observations

New
Obs     Fit   SE Fit         95% CI              95% PI
1     95.94    5.08   (84.43, 107.44)   (76.47, 115.40)


Values of Predictors for New Observations
New
Obs   Year
1     2010
```

The 95% prediction interval for the initial quality industry average of the number of reported problems per 100 vehicles for 2010 is (76.47, 115.40).

14.43.

   a. Minitab scatter plot:

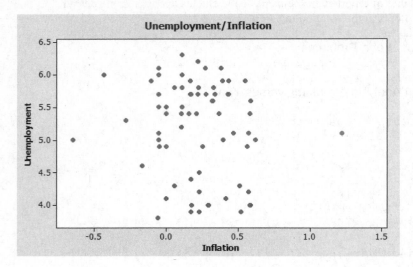

If anything, the relationship may be linear with a slightly negative slope.

   b. The maximum inflation rate is 1/223.

Confidence Interval Estimate

Data	
X Value	1.223
Confidence Level	95%

Intermediate Calculations	
Sample Size	72
Degrees of Freedom	70
t Value	1.994435
Sample Mean	0.220139
Sum of Squared Difference	5.401291
Standard Error of the Estimate	0.729999
h Statistic	0.200091
Predicted Y (YHat)	4.837578

For Average Y	
Interval Half Width	0.651262
Confidence Interval Lower Limit	4.186316
Confidence Interval Upper Limit	5.488839

For Individual Response Y	
Interval Half Width	1.594958
Prediction Interval Lower Limit	3.24262
Prediction Interval Upper Limit	6.432535

The prediction interval is (3.2426, 6.4325).

c.

Confidence Interval Estimate

Data	
X Value	0
Confidence Level	95%

Intermediate Calculations	
Sample Size	72
Degrees of Freedom	70
t Value	1.994435
Sample Mean	0.220139
Sum of Squared Difference	5.401291
Standard Error of the Estimate	0.729999
h Statistic	0.022861
Predicted Y (YHat)	5.252455

For Average Y	
Interval Half Width	0.220135
Confidence Interval Lower Limit	5.03232
Confidence Interval Upper Limit	5.472591

For Individual Response Y	
Interval Half Width	1.472484
Prediction Interval Lower Limit	3.779972
Prediction Interval Upper Limit	6.724939

The prediction interval is (3.78 to 6.5).

d. The equation for the prediction interval is $\hat{y} \pm t_{\alpha/2} s_e \sqrt{1 + \dfrac{1}{n} + \dfrac{(x_p - \overline{x})^2}{\sum (x-x)^2}}$.

Of this $t_{\alpha/2} s_e \sqrt{1 + \dfrac{1}{n} + \dfrac{(x_p - \overline{x})^2}{\sum (x-x)^2}}$ is the margin of error for the prediction interval.

The width of the prediction interval is calculated as

$$\hat{y} + t_{\alpha/2} s_e \sqrt{1 + \dfrac{1}{n} + \dfrac{(x_p - \overline{x})^2}{\sum (x-x)^2}} - \hat{y} - t_{\alpha/2} s_e \sqrt{1 + \dfrac{1}{n} + \dfrac{(x_p - \overline{x})^2}{\sum (x-x)^2}} =$$

$t_{\alpha/2} s_e \sqrt{1 + \dfrac{1}{n} + \dfrac{(x_p - \overline{x})^2}{\sum (x-x)^2}}$ which is 2 times the margin of error. For this example the margin of error =

$(6.7249 - 3.7800)/2 = 1.4724$ when $x_p = 0$. It equals $(6.4325 - 3.2426)/2 = 1.5950$ when $x_p = 1.223$. Thus, the former case has the larger margin of error. The difference between the margin of error for part b. and c. is the specific value of the term $\left(x_p - \overline{x}\right)^2$. The former prediction interval has the largest margin of error since its x_p (= 1.223) is further away from $\overline{x}$ (= 0.2201)than is the other x_p (= 0).

Chapter Exercises

14.45. The correlation is a quantitative measure of the strength of the linear relationship between two variables. The correlation coefficient may range in value between −1.00 and + 1.00. If the correlation coefficient equals −1.00, then the two variables are said to be perfectly negatively correlated, with increases in one variable associated with uniform decreases in the other. If the correlation coefficient equals +1.00, then the two variables are said to be perfectly positively correlated, meaning that the two variables move in the same direction. The value of 0.45 would indicate a relatively weak positive correlation.

14.47. No. The correlation coefficient measures the strength of the linear relationship between two variables. If we conclude that the population correlation coefficient may be zero, then we can say there is no linear relationship between the two variables. However, there may be a very clearly defined nonlinear relationship between the two variables that we have not quantified.

14.49.
   a. No you cannot assume this because correlation does not assume cause and effect. Two unconnected variables could be highly correlated.
   b. On the basis of the correlation coefficient case you can still not assume cause and effect, although an increase in the common dividends may well cause an increase in the stock price. Stock prices are based on expected future value. Individuals will assume that if a company is raising their dividends they must expect future growth. Companies do not raise dividends in one year if they expect to have to decrease dividends in the next year.

14.53.
   a. Minitab output:

   Regression Analysis: Private versus Public

   ```
   The regression equation is
   Private = 3372 + 3.36 Public


   Predictor    Coef   SE Coef      T      P
   Constant     3372      1181   2.86  0.046
   Public     3.3606    0.3094  10.86  0.000


   S = 946.565   R-Sq = 96.7%   R-Sq(adj) = 95.9%


   Analysis of Variance

   Source          DF         SS         MS       F      P
   Regression       1  105696811  105696811  117.97  0.000
   Residual Error   4    3583944     895986
   Total            5  109280755
   ```

   The regression equation is $\hat{y} = 3372 + 3.36x$.
   b. To determine if there is a linear tendency for the average college tuition for private colleges to increase when the average college tuition for public colleges increases we must test the hypotheses:
   $H_O: \beta_1 \leq 0$, $H_A: \beta_1 > 0$, $\alpha = 0.05$,
   From the regression output, $t = 10.86$ and the p-value = 0.000.
   Since the p-value = $0.000 < 0.05 = \alpha$ the null hypothesis is rejected. There is sufficient evidence to indicate that there is a linear tendency for the average college tuition for private colleges to increase when the average college tuition for public colleges increases.

c.   Minitab output:

```
Predicted Values for New Observations

New
Obs    Fit   SE Fit       95% CI           95% PI
  1   26896    1119   (23789, 30003)   (22827, 30966)X
```

X denotes a point that is an outlier in the predictors
The 95% confidence interval is ($23,789, $30,002).

d.   Since the 95% confidence interval is ($23,789, $30,002), this suggests that the largest the average college tuition for private colleges would expect to be is $30,002. Since $35,000 is larger than $30,002, it does not seem to be a plausible value.

14.55.
a.

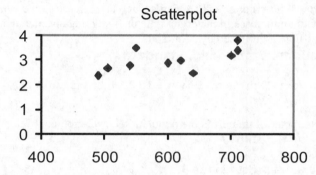

There appears to be a weak positive linear relationship.

b.   (1) $r = 0.6239$

(2) H_0: $\rho = 0$

$\qquad$ H_A: $\rho \neq 0$

$\qquad$ d.f. = 10-2 = 8

Decision Rule:

$\qquad$ If t > 3.3554 or t < -3.3554, Reject H_0, otherwise do not reject H_0

$$t = 0.6239 / \sqrt{(1 - 0.6239)^2)/(10 - 2)} = 2.2581$$

Since 2.2580 < 3.3554 do not reject H_0 and conclude that there is not a correlation between SAT scores and final GPA.

c.   (1). $\hat{y} = 0.9772 + 0.0034(x)$

(2). The y-intercept would indicate the average university GPA of all students who received an SAT score of 0. Such a situation seems highly unlikely. Therefore, the y-intercept has no interpretation in this case. The slope indicates that the average university GPA increases by 0.0034 for each increase of 1 unit in the SAT score.

14.57.

a. Minitab scatter plot:

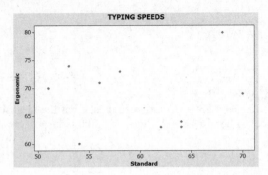

Examining the scatter plot there seems to be a random pattern in the relationship between the typing speed using the standard and ergonomic keyboards since an increase in the standard user's typing speed at times is associated with an increase in the ergonomic user's typing speed and at other times a decrease.

b. Correlation coefficient produced by Minitab is

Correlations: Ergonomic, Standard

```
Pearson correlation of Ergonomic and Standard = 0.071
```

c. **Step 1:** The parameter of interest is the population correlation coefficient.

Step 2: $H_O: \rho \leq 0$, $H_A: \rho > 0$

Step 3: $\alpha = 0.05$

Step 4: r = 0.071, using Equation 14-3.

$$t = \frac{r}{\sqrt{\dfrac{1 - r^2}{n - 2}}} = \frac{0.071}{\sqrt{\dfrac{1 - (0.071)^2}{10\text{-}2}}} = 0.2013$$

Step 5: For $\alpha = 0.05$ with n -2 = 10 − 2 = 8 degrees of freedom, $t = 1.8595$. The decision rule is if $t >$ 1.8595 reject H_O, otherwise, do not reject the null hypothesis.

Step 6: Because $0.2013 < t = 1.8595$, we fail to reject H_O.

Step 7: There is insufficient evidence to conclude that a positive correlation exists between administrative assistants using ergonomic and standard keyboards

14.59.

a.

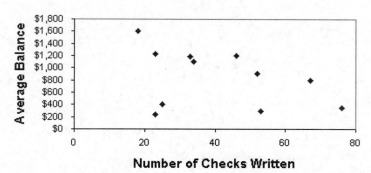

b.

SUMMARY OUTPUT						
Regression Statistics						
Multiple R	0.378864769					
R Square	0.143538513					
Adjusted R Square	0.048376126					
Standard Error	453.9233193					
Observations	11					
ANOVA						
	df	*SS*	*MS*	*F*	*Significance F*	
Regression	1	310790.7635	310791	1.5083534	0.250539111	
Residual	9	1854417.418	206046			
Total	10	2165208.182				
	Coefficients	*Standard Error*	*t Stat*	*P-value*	*Lower 90.0%*	*Upper 90.0%*
Intercept	1219.803532	333.178933	3.66111	0.0052265	609.0486136	1830.558451
Checks Written	-9.119641901	7.425508984	-1.2282	0.2505391	-22.73144531	4.492161507

The regression model is $\hat{y} = 1219.8035 + (-9.1196)(x)$

c. To find the confidence interval for the change in the number of checks, we need to find the confidence interval for the slope coefficient and then multiply it by 25. The interval is found in the output.
Lower 90%: 25 x –22.7314 = -568.285; Upper 90%: 25 x 4.4922 = 112.305

d. H_0: $\beta_1 = 0$
H_A: $\beta_1 \neq 0$
Decision Rule:
If p-value < 0.05 reject H_0, otherwise do not reject H_0.
Since p-value = 0.25 do not reject H_0 and conclude that the overall model is not significant so that an increase in the number of checks written by an individual cannot be used to predict the checking account balance of that individual.

14.61.

a.

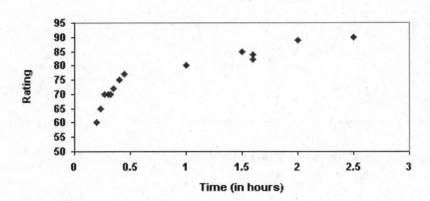

There appears to be a possible positive linear relationship between time (in hours) and rating.

b.

SUMMARY OUTPUT

Regression Statistics	
Multiple R	0.915504887
R Square	0.838149199
Adjusted R Square	0.824661632
Standard Error	3.786842178
Observations	14

ANOVA

	df	SS	MS	F
Regression	1	891.1322016	891.1322	62.14236
Residual	12	172.0820842	14.34017	
Total	13	1063.214286		

	Coefficients	Standard Error	t Stat	P-value
Intercept	66.71114789	1.587951365	42.01083	2.15E-14
Time (x)	10.61666113	1.346772042	7.883042	4.37E-06

$\hat{y} = 66.7111 + 10.6167(x)$

Student reports will vary but they should include a test to determine if the model is significant. Since *p*-value $= 4.37 \times 10^{-6}$ students should conclude that the overall model is significant at the .10 level. They should also comment on what the R^2 is and what this means to the model.

14.63.

    a.   Minitab output:

        Regression Analysis: Nov07Average versus Nov07Median

```
The regression equation is
Nov07Average = 3786 + 1.35 Nov07Median


Predictor        Coef   SE Coef       T       P
Constant         3786      5967    0.63   0.543
Nov07Median   1.35049   0.02845   47.47   0.000


S = 2327.92    R-Sq = 99.6%    R-Sq(adj) = 99.6%


Analysis of Variance

Source          DF            SS            MS        F       P
Regression       1   12210351200   12210351200  2253.15   0.000
Residual Error   8      43353800       5419225
Total            9   12253705000
```

        The regression equation is $\hat{y}$ = 3786 +1.35x

    b. H_O: β_1 = 0, H_A: $\beta_1 \neq$ 0; α = 0.05, the p-value = 0.000. Since the p-value is less than α = 0.05, we reject the null hypothesis.

    c.   Using Minitab

```
Predicted Values for New Observations

New
Obs      Fit  SE Fit        90% CI             90% PI
  1   267132     825  (265597, 268666)  (262539, 271724)


Values of Predictors for New Observations

New
Obs   Nov07Median
  1        195000
```

The confidence interval is ($265597, $26866671724). This indicates that, using a 90% confidence interval, the estimated average selling price during a year in which the median selling price for homes was $195,000 is somewhere between $265597 and $268666.

14.65.

a.

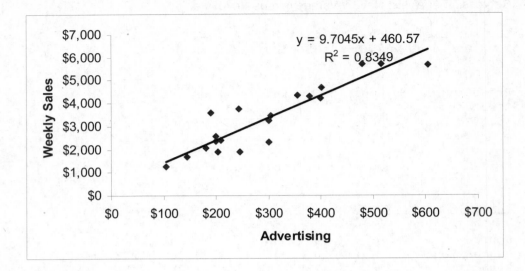

b. The 95% confidence interval for the increase in sales if found by finding the 95% confidence interval for the slope coefficient in the regression model and multiplying it by 50. The interval can be found in the shown output.

	Coefficients	Standard Error	t Stat	P-value	Lower 95%	Upper 95%
Intercept	460.567578	330.389599	1.394014	0.180285	-233.55575	1154.69091
Advertising	9.70447122	1.017240888	9.539993	1.83E-08	7.5673258	11.8416167

Lower 95%: 50 x 7.5673 = 378.365   Upper 95%: 50 x 11.8416 = 592.08
A $50 increase in advertising will result in an increase in sales of $378.365 to $592.08.

c. No it is not appropriate in this case. It is appropriate if the value 0 is in the range of x values in the sample.

d.

For Average Predicted Y (YHat)	
Interval Half Width	286.0036653
Confidence Interval Lower Limit	2115.458156
Confidence Interval Upper Limit	2687.465486

e. The conclusions and inferences made from a regression line are statistically valid only over the range of the data contained in the sample used to develop the regression line. The $100 is outside of the range of the sample.

Chapter 15
Multiple Regression Analysis and Model Building

Section 15-1 Exercises

15.1

a. $\hat{y} = 87.7897 - 0.9705x_1 + 0.0023x_2 - 8.7233x_3$

b. $F = 5.3276 > F_{0.05} = 3.0725$ (Using Excel's FINV) Also, p-value = .00689 < any reasonable alpha.. Therefore, reject H_0: $\beta_1 = \beta_2 = \beta_3 = 0$. At least some part of the model is statistically significant.

c. $R^2 = \dfrac{SSR}{SST} = \dfrac{16646.091}{38517.76} = 0.432$

d. x_1 (p-value = 0.1126 > α = 0.05 ➜ fail to reject H_0: $\beta_1 = 0$) and x_3 (p-value = 0.2576 > α = 0.05 ➜ fail to reject H_0: $\beta_3 = 0$) are not significant.

e. $b_2 = 0.0023$ ➜ $\hat{y}$ increases 0.0023 for each one unit increase of x_2.

$b_3 = -8.7233$ ➜ $\hat{y}$ decreases 8.7233 for each one unit increase of x_3.

f. The confidence intervals for β_1 and β_3 contain 0. This indicates that x_1 and x_3 are not statistically significantly different than 0 in this model.

15.3

a. $b_1 = -412$. This implies that, holding the other independent variables constant and increasing the local unemployment rate by one percent, the average weekly sales is estimated to decrease by 412 dollars.

$b_2 = 818$. This implies that, holding the other independent variables constant and increasing the weekly average high temperature by one degree, the average weekly sales is estimated to increase by 818 dollars.

$b_3 = -93$. This implies that, holding the other independent variables constant and increasing the number of local activities by one, the average weekly sales is estimated to decrease by 93 dollars.

$b_4 = -71$. This implies that, holding the other independent variables constant and increasing the average gasoline price by one dollar, the average weekly sales is estimated to decrease by 71dollars.

b. $\hat{y} = 22{,}167 - 412(5.7) + 818(61) - 93(14) - 71(1.39) = 68{,}315.91$

15.5

a. Minitab output:
Regression Analysis: yi versus x1, x2
The regression equation is
yi = 5.05 - 0.051 x1 + 0.888 x2

Predictor	Coef	SE Coef	T	P	VIF
Constant	5.045	8.698	0.58	0.580	
x1	-0.0513	0.2413	-0.21	0.838	1.1
x2	0.8880	0.1475	6.02	0.001	1.1

S = 6.82197   R-Sq = 84.5%   R-Sq(adj) = 80.1%

Analysis of Variance

Source	DF	SS	MS	F	P
Regression	2	1775.12	887.56	19.07	0.001
Residual Error	7	325.78	46.54		
Total	9	2100.90			

The estimated regression equation is $\hat{y} = 5.05 - 0.0513x_1 + 0.888x_2$

b. Minitab output:
Correlations: yi, x1, x2

	yi	x1
x1	0.206	
x2	0.919	0.257

Cell Contents: Pearson correlation

$$t = \frac{r}{\sqrt{\frac{1-r^2}{n-2}}} = \frac{0.206}{\sqrt{\frac{1-0.206^2}{10-2}}} = 0.5954$$

Since $-2.306 < t = 0.5954 < 2.306$; we fail to reject H_O.
The correlation with the dependent variable is not significant.

c. **Step 1:** The parameters of interest are the population coefficients of x_1 and x_2,
Step 2: H_O: $\beta_1 = \beta_2 = 0$, H_A: at least one $\beta_i \neq 0$
Step 3: $\alpha = 0.05$

Step 4: $F = \dfrac{\dfrac{SSR}{k}}{\dfrac{SSE}{n-k-1}} = \dfrac{\dfrac{1775.12}{2}}{\dfrac{325.78}{10-2-1}} = 19.07$

Step 5: The numerator degrees of freedom are $k = 2$ and the denominator degrees of freedom are
$n - k - 1 = 10 - 2 - 1 = 7$; the critical value = 4.737.
Step 6: Since $F = 19.07 > 4.737$, reject H_O;
Step 7: The overall model is significant.

d. Minitab output:

Predictor	Coef	SE Coef	T	P	VIF
Constant	5.045	8.698	0.58	0.580	
x1	-0.0513	0.2413	-0.21	0.838	1.1
x2	0.8880	0.1475	6.02	0.001	1.1

$S = 6.82197$ R-Sq = 84.5% R-Sq(adj) = 80.1%
A VIF < 5 for a given independent variable indicates that this independent variable is not correlated with the remaining independent variables in the model. Both x_1 and x_2 have VIFs equal to 1.1. Therefore, neither of the independent variable is correlated with the other independent variable. Multicollinearity does not exist between the two independent variables.

15.7

a. Minitab output:
Regression Analysis: Market Value versus 52WK HI, P- E
```
The regression equation is
Market Value = - 977 + 11.2 52WK HI + 118 P- E

Predictor    Coef   SE Coef      T      P  VIF
Constant   -977.1    664.0  -1.47  0.159
52WK HI     11.20    12.57   0.89  0.385  1.0
P- E       117.72    13.27   8.87  0.000  1.0
S = 933.549   R-Sq = 82.4%   R-Sq(adj) = 80.3%

Analysis of Variance
Source           DF         SS         MS      F      P
Regression        2   69367140   34683570  39.80  0.000
Residual Error   17   14815723     871513
Total            19   84182863
```
The estimated regression equation is $\hat{y} = -977.1 + 11.252\text{WK HI} + 117.72\text{P-E}$

b. **Step 1:** The parameters of interest are the population coefficients of x_1 and x_2,
   Step 2: H_O: $\beta_1 = \beta_2 = 0$, H_A: at least one $\beta_i \neq 0$
   Step 3: $\alpha = 0.05$
   Step 4: The test statistic provided by Minitab is F = 39.80
   Step 5: The numerator degrees of freedom are k = 2 and the denominator degrees of freedom are n – k – 1
   = 20 – 2 – 1 = 17; the critical value is 3.592.,
   Step 6: Since F = 39.80 > 3.592, we reject H_O
   Step 7: The overall model is significant.
c. Minitab output:

```
Predicted Values for New Observations

New
Obs   Fit  SE Fit     95% CI        95% PI
  1   1607    268  (1041, 2173)  (-443, 3656)


Values of Predictors for New Observations

New
Obs   52WK HI  P- E
  1      31.0  19.0
```

d. The estimated market value is $\hat{y} = 1607$

15.9
   a. Minitab output:

   Regression Analysis: Sales versus Sales Increase, Return on Capital, ...

```
The regression equation is
Sales = 503 - 10.5 Sales Increase + 2.4 Return on Capital + 0.165 Market Value
        + 1.90 Stock Price


Predictor           Coef  SE Coef      T      P
Constant           502.6    780.7   0.64  0.529
Sales Increase    -10.50    17.26  -0.61  0.552
Return on Capital   2.36    57.60   0.04  0.968
Market Value     0.16455  0.07776   2.12  0.051
Stock Price        1.903    5.975   0.32  0.754


S = 308.537   R-Sq = 39.4%   R-Sq(adj) = 23.2%


Analysis of Variance

Source          DF       SS      MS     F      P
Regression       4   928619  232155  2.44  0.092
Residual Error  15  1427922   95195
Total           19  2356540
```

   The estimated regression equation is $\hat{y}$ = 503 - 10.5x_1 + 2.4x_2 + 0.165x_3 + 1.90x_4
   b. **Step 1:** The parameters of interest are the population coefficients of x_1, x_2, x_3, and x_4
   Step 2: H_O: $\beta_1 = \beta_2 = \beta_3 = \beta_4 = 0$, H_A: at least one $\beta_i \neq 0$,
   Step 3: $\alpha = 0.05$
   Step 4: The test statistic provided by Minitab is F = 2.44.
   Step 5: The numerator degrees of freedom are k = 4 and the denominator degrees of freedom are n – k – 1
      = 20 – 4 – 1 = 15; the critical value is 3.056.
   Step 6: Since F = 2.44 < 3.056, fail to reject H_O
   Step 7: The overall model is not significant.

c. **Step 1:** The parameter of interest is the population coefficient of x_3, market value
Step 2: $H_O: \beta_3 = 0$, $H_A: \beta_3 \neq 0$
Step 3: $\alpha = 0.05$
Step 4: The p-value is 0.051
Step 5: If the p-value is less than α, reject the null hypothesis; otherwise fail to reject the null hypothesis.
Step 6: Since the p-value = 0.051 > 0.05, fail to reject H_O.
Step 7: There is not sufficient evidence to conclude that market value is a significant predictor sales in this model.

d. Minitab output:

Regression Analysis: Sales versus Market Value

```
The regression equation is
Sales = 344 + 0.186 Market Value


Predictor        Coef   SE Coef     T      P
Constant        343.9     100.8   3.41  0.003
Market Value  0.18640   0.05702   3.27  0.004


S = 286.608   R-Sq = 37.3%   R-Sq(adj) = 33.8%


Analysis of Variance

Source         DF       SS       MS      F      P
Regression      1   877948   877948  10.69  0.004
Residual Error 18  1478593    82144
Total          19  2356540
```

The estimated regression equation is $\hat{y} = 344 - 0.186x_1$.

(In this model the p-value associated with market value is 0.004. Since the p-value = 0.004 < 0.05, there is sufficient evidence to conclude that the market value is a significant predictor of sales.

15.11

a.

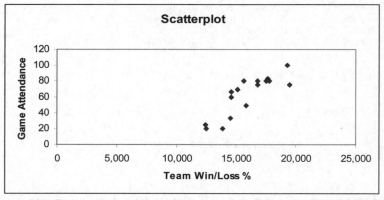

There appears to be a positive linear relationship between team win/loss percentage and game attendance.

Scatterplot

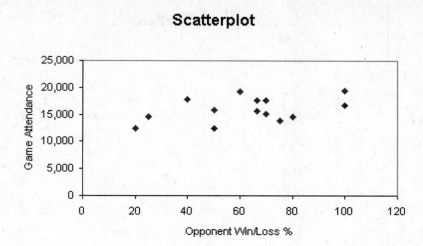

There appears to be a positive linear relationship between opponent win/loss percentage and game attendance.

Scatterplot

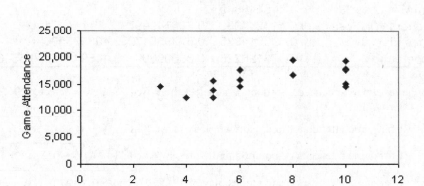

There appears to be a positive linear relationship between games played and game attendance.

Scatterplot

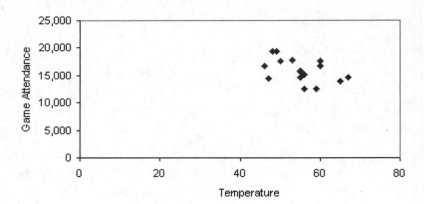

There does not appear to be any relationship between temperature and game attendance.

b.

	Game Attendance	Team Win/Loss %	Opponent Win/Loss %	Games Played	Temperature
Game Attendance	1				
Team Win/Loss %	0.848748849	1			
Opponent Win/Loss %	0.414250332	0.286749997	1		
Games Played	0.599214835	0.577958172	0.403593506	1	
Temperature	-0.476186226	-0.330096097	-0.446949168	-0.550083219	1

No alpha level was specified. Students will select their own. We have selected .05.

Critical t = ± 2.1448

t for game attendance and team win/loss % = $0.8487/\sqrt{(1-0.8487^2)/(16-2)}$ = 6.0043

t for game attendance and opponent win/loss % = $0.4143/\sqrt{(1-0.4143^2)/(16-2)}$ = 1.7032

t for game attendance and games played = $0.5992/\sqrt{(1-0.5992^2)/(16-2)}$ = 2.8004

t for game attendance and temperature = $-0.4762/\sqrt{(1-(-0.4762)^2)/(16-2)}$ = -2.0263

There is a significant relationship between game attendance and team win/loss % and games played. Therefore a multiple regression model could be effective.

c. Multiple regression equation using x_1, x_2, x_3, x_4 as independent variables to predict y

Regression Analysis

Regression Statistics	
Multiple R	0.880534596
R Square	0.775341175
Adjusted R Square	0.693647057
Standard Error	1184.124723
Observations	16

ANOVA

	df	SS	MS	F	Significance F
Regression	4	53230058.97	13307514.74	9.490783318	0.001427993
Residual	11	15423664.97	1402151.361		
Total	15	68653723.94			

	Coefficients	Standard Error	t Stat	P-value	Lower 95%
Intercept	14122.24086	4335.791765	3.25713079	0.007637823	4579.222699
Team Win/Loss %	63.15325348	14.93880137	4.227464568	0.001418453	30.27315672
Opponent Win/Loss %	10.09582009	14.31396102	0.705312811	0.49528028	-21.40901163
Games Played	31.50621796	177.129782	0.177870811	0.862057676	-358.3540008
Temperature	-55.4609057	62.09372861	-0.89318047	0.390882768	-192.12835

d. $R^2 = 0.7753$ so 77.53% is explained.

e. H_0: $\beta_1 = \beta_2 = \beta_3 = \beta_4 = 0$
   H_A: at least one β_i does not equal 0
   Decision Rule:
   If p-value $< \alpha = 0.05$, , reject H_o, otherwise do not reject H_o
   Since p-value (Significance F) = .00143 reject H_o and conclude that the overall model is significant.

f. For team win/loss % the p-value = 0.0014 < 0.08 so this variable is significant
   For opponent win/loss % the p-value = 0.4953 > 0.08 so this variable is not significant
   For games played the p-value = 0.8621 > 0.08 so this variable is not significant
   For temperature the p-value = 0.3909 > 0.08 so this variable is not significant

g. The standard error of the estimate is 1184.1274. Practical significance is a decision made based on whether an interval of $\pm 2(1184.1274)$ is small enough to add value to the value being estimated. .

h. Multicollinearity is present when the independent variables are correlated with one another. This is indicated if the VIF for pairs of variables is greater than 5. The VIF for the variables in this problem are:

	VIF
Team Win/Loss Percentage and all other X	1.569962033
Temperature and all other X	1.963520336
Games Played and all other X	1.31428258
Opponent Win/Loss Percentage and all other X	1.50934547

The low VIF values indicate multicollinearity is not a problem since no VIF is greater than 5.

i.

	Coefficients	Standard Error	t Stat	P-value	Lower 95%	Upper 95%
Intercept	14122.24086	4335.791765	3.25713079	0.007637823	4579.222699	23665.25902
Team Win/Loss %	63.15325348	14.93880137	4.227464568	0.001418453	30.27315672	96.03335024
Opponent Win/Loss %	10.09582009	14.31396102	0.705312811	0.49528028	-21.40901163	41.6006518
Games Played	31.50621796	177.129782	0.177870811	0.862057676	-358.3540008	421.3664367
Temperature	-55.4609057	62.09372861	-0.89318047	0.390882768	-192.12835	81.20653863

Because the confidence intervals for Opponent win/loss %, games played, and temperature all include the value 0 it is indicating the same thing as the t-tests in that these variables are not significantly different from 0. The interpretation of the interecept would not be relevant since none of the predictor variables is likely to be zero.

Section 15-2 Exercises

15.13

a. $y = \beta_0 + \beta_1 x_1 + \beta_2 x_2 + \varepsilon$; x_1 = {0 for level 1, 1 for level 2}

b. β_0 = the average value of y when x_1 = level one and $x_2 = 0$.

 β_1 = the difference in the average value of y when x_1 is changed from level one to level two while holding x_2 constant.

 β_2 = the amount of change in the average value of y when x_2 is increased by one unit while holding x_1 constant.

15.15

a. Since the apartment is in the town center, $x_2 = 1$ which implies $\hat{y} = 145 + 1.2(1500) + 300(1) = 2245$.

b. Since the apartment is not in the town center, $x_2 = 0$ which implies $\hat{y} = 145 + 1.2(1500) + 300(0) = 1945$.

c. The difference between the answers in part a. and b. (2245 -1945 = 300) equals the value of b_2. Therefore, b_2 indicates the average premium paid for living in the city's town center.

15.17

a. As the vehicle weight increases by 1 pound, the average highway mileage rating would decrease by 0.003 for a specified type of transmission.

b. If the car has standard transmission the highway mileage rating will increase by 4.56 holding the weight constant.

c. $\hat{y} = 34.2 - 0.003x_1 + 4.56(1) = 38.76 - 0.003x_1$

d. $\hat{y} = 34.2 - 0.003(4394) + 4.56(0) = 21.02$

e. Incorporating the dummy variable essentially gives two regression equations with the same slope but different intercepts depending upon whether the automobile as an automatic or standard transmission. The regression model for an automatic transmission is $E(y) = \beta_0 + \beta_1 x_1$; if the automobile has a standard transmission the equation becomes $E(y) = (\beta_0 + \beta_2) + \beta_1 x_1$

15.19

a.   Minitab output:

Regression Analysis: PP100 versus X1, X2

```
The regression equation is
PP100 = 197 - 43.6 X1 - 51.0 X2


Predictor    Coef  SE Coef      T      P
Constant   196.57    12.95  15.18  0.000
X1         -43.57    18.31  -2.38  0.029
X2         -51.00    18.31  -2.79  0.012


S = 34.2535   R-Sq = 33.5%   R-Sq(adj) = 26.1%


Analysis of Variance

Source          DF     SS    MS     F      P
Regression       2  10628  5314  4.53  0.026
Residual Error  18  21119  1173
Total           20  31747
```

$$\hat{y} = 197 - 43.6x_1 - 51x_2$$

b.   When $x_1 = 0$ and $x_2 = 0$, the model becomes $y_i = \beta_O + \varepsilon$. Therefore, β_O = the average PP100 of the Korean-branded vehicles. When $x_1 = 1$ and $x_2 = 0$, the model becomes $y_i = \beta_O + \beta_1 + \varepsilon$ which represents the average PP100 for Domestic vehicles. Therefore, β_1 = the difference in the average PP100 between Domestic and Korean vehicles. When $x_1 = 0$ and $x_2 = 1$, the model becomes $y_i = \beta_O + \beta_2 + \varepsilon$ which represents the average PP100 for European vehicles. Therefore, β_2 = the difference in the average PP100 between European and Korean vehicles.

c.   **Step 1:** The parameters of interest is the population coefficients of x_1 and x_2. In order for the averages to be equal, it must be true that $\beta_1 = \beta_2 = 0$

Step 2: H_O: $\beta_1 = \beta_2 = 0$, H_A: at least one $\beta_i \neq 0$

Step 3: $\alpha = 0.05$

Step 4: The test statistic provided by Minitab is F = 4.53

Step 5: The numerator degrees of freedom are k = 2 and the denominator degrees of freedom are n – k – 1 = 21 – 2 – 1 = 18; the critical value is 3.555

Step 6: Since F = 4.53 > 3.555, we reject H_O

Step 7: There is sufficient evidence to conclude that the average PP100 is the not same for the three international automobile production regions

15.21
   a.

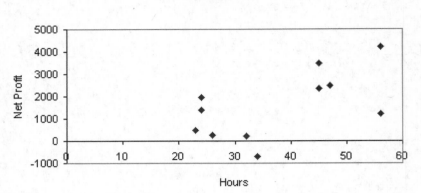

There appears to be a weak positive linear relationship between hours and net profit.

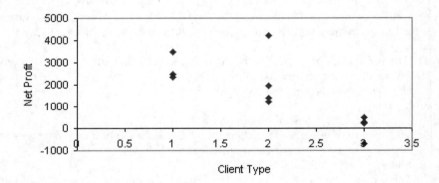

There appears to be a weak negative linear relationship between client type and net profit. However, students should recognize that it is not appropriate to construct a scatter plot when one or both variables are nominal as in the case of client type. The result would be sensitive to how the nominal variable has been coded.

   b. $\hat{y} = -1{,}012.0542 + 69.1471(x_1)$

This model indicates that if the hours increase by 1 the net profit will increase by \$69.1471

c.

Regression Analysis

Regression Statistics	
Multiple R	0.595748747
R Square	0.35491657
Adjusted R Square	0.283240633
Standard Error	1257.145502
Observations	11

ANOVA

	df	SS	MS	F
Regression	1	7825714.315	7825714.315	4.951683728
Residual	9	14223733.32	1580414.813	
Total	10	22049447.64		

	Coefficients	Standard Error	t Stat	P-value
Intercept	-1012.05421	1224.030842	-0.826820841	0.429713772
Hours (x1)	69.14707843	31.07401609	2.225237904	0.053108059

The p-value for hours is 0.0531 so at a 5% or 1% significance level this variable would not be useful in predicting the net profit earned by a client. The R^2 is also only 0.3549

15.23

a. Minitab output:

Regression Analysis: MathSAT versus Gender, VerbalSAT

```
The regression equation is
MathSAT = 390 - 37.0 Gender + 0.263 VerbalSAT


Predictor    Coef  SE Coef      T      P
Constant   390.00    35.97  10.84  0.000
Gender    -36.966    1.807 -20.45  0.000
VerbalSAT 0.26338  0.06998   3.76  0.000


S = 7.77253   R-Sq = 86.8%   R-Sq(adj) = 86.4%


Analysis of Variance

Source          DF     SS     MS      F      P
Regression       2  29779  14889 246.46  0.000
Residual Error  75   4531     60
Total           77  34310
```

The regression equation is $\hat{y} = 390 - 37.0x_1 + 0.263x_2$

b. While implausible, β_O = the average math SAT score for females who score 0 on the verbal portion of the SAT examination. β_1 = the difference in the average math SAT scores between males and females for those who score a specific average value on the verbal portion of the SAT examination. β_2 = the amount the average math SAT score changes as the average verbal SAT score increases by one point given the specific gender of the student taking the examination.

c. **Step 1:** The parameter of interest is the population coefficient of x_1
    Step 2: H_O: $\beta_1 = 0$, H_A: $\beta_1 \neq 0$
    Step 3: $\alpha = 0.05$
    Step 4: The test statistic provided by Minitab in part a. is t = -20.45
    Step 5: The numerator degrees of freedom are n-k-1 = 78 – 2 – 1 = 75 the lower critical value provided by Minitab is -1.9921
    Step 6: Since t = -20.45< -1.9921, we reject H_O
    Step 7: There is sufficient evidence to conclude that the gender of the student taking the SAT examination is a significant predictor of the students' average math SAT score for a given verbal SAT score.

d. $\hat{y}$ = 390 - 37.0x_1 + 0.263x_2 = 390 - 37.0(1) + 0.263(500) = 484.5 $\approx$ 485.

Section 15-3 Exercises

15.25

a.

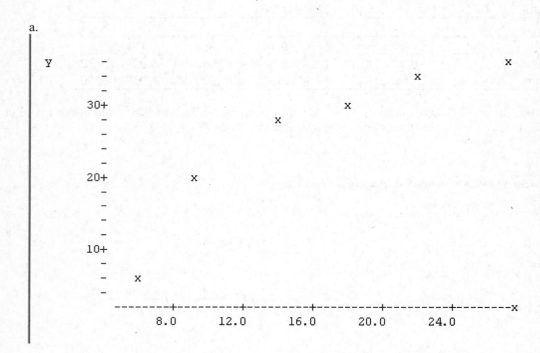

b. $\hat{y} = 4.937 + 1.2643x$

Predictor	Coef	SE Coef	T	P
Constant	4.937	5.448	0.91	0.416
x	1.2643	0.3102	4.08	0.015

$S = 5.498$ R-Sq = 80.6%   R-Sq(adj) = 75.7%

Analysis of Variance

Source	DF	SS	MS	F	P
Regression	1	501.94	501.94	16.61	0.015
Residual Error	4	120.89	30.22		
Total	5	622.83			

The p-value = 0.015 < α = 0.05. Therefore, reject H_0 and conclude that there is a linear relationship between the dependent and independent variables.

c. $\hat{y} = -25.155 + 18.983 \ln x$

Predictor	Coef	SE Coef	T	P
Constant	-25.155	6.917	-3.64	0.022
lnx	18.983	2.561	7.41	0.002

$S = 3.251$ R-Sq = 93.2%   R-Sq(adj) = 91.5%

Analysis of Variance

Source	DF	SS	MS	F	P
Regression	1	580.57	580.57	54.95	0.002
Residual Error	4	42.27	10.57		
Total	5	622.83			

The adjusted R^2 (91.5%)for the curvilinear model exceeds the R^2 of the simple linear model. The model's variance estimate is smaller for the curvilinear model and the F-test has a smaller p-value. It appears that the logarithmic model provides a better fit of the data.

15.27

a.   Minitab scatterplot:

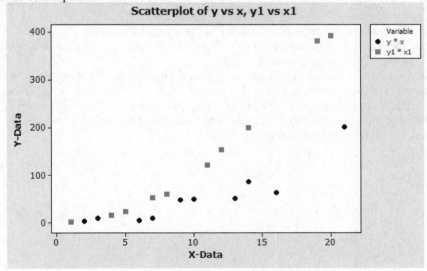

b. The scatter plot indicates that there are two quadratic models. Since the two models are not equal distance from each other, this indicates that there is interaction between x_2 and the quadratic relationship between y and x_2.

```
The regression equation is
y = 4.9 - 3.58 x1 - 0.014 x1sq + 1.42 x1x2 + 0.528 x1sqx2


Predictor      Coef   SE Coef       T       P
Constant       4.90     10.84    0.45   0.658
x1           -3.580     3.671   -0.98   0.345
x1sq        -0.0140    0.2067   -0.07   0.947
x1x2          1.424     2.002    0.71   0.488
x1sqx2       0.5276    0.1231    4.29   0.001


S = 15.0083   R-Sq = 98.7%   R-Sq(adj) = 98.3%


Analysis of Variance

Source           DF       SS      MS       F       P
Regression        4   255018   63755  283.04   0.000
Residual Error   15     3379     225
Total            19   258397
```

The equation is $\hat{y}_i = 4.9 - 3.58x_1 - 0.014x_1^2 + 1.42x_1x_2 + 0.528x_1^2x_2$.

c. The two interaction terms are $\beta_3 x_1 x_2$ *and* $\beta_4 x_1^2 x_2$. So you must conduct two hypothesis tests:

(i) To determine if there is interaction between x_2 and the linear relationship between x_1 and y, we must test to determine if $\beta_3 = 0$.
Step 1: The parameter of interest is the population coefficient of x_1x_2
Step 2: H_O: $\beta_3 = 0$, H_A: $\beta_3 \neq 0$
Step 3: $\alpha = 0.05$
Step 4: The p-value is 0.488
Step 5: If the p-value is less than α, reject the null hypothesis; otherwise fail to reject the null hypothesis
Step 6: Since the p-value = 0.488 > 0.05, we fail to reject H_O
Step 7: There is not sufficient evidence to conclude that there is interaction between x_2 and the linear relationship between x_1 and y.

(ii) To determine if there is interaction between x_2 and the quadratic relationship between x_1 and y, we must test to determine if $\beta_4 = 0$. The p-value for $\beta_4 = 0.001$, there is sufficient evidence to conclude that there is interaction between x_2 and the quadratic relationship between x_1 and y.

d. The second hypothesis indicated that there was sufficient evidence to conclude that there is interaction between x_2 and the quadratic relationship between x_1 and y.

15.29

a. The complete model is $y_i = \beta_0 + \beta_1 x_1 + \beta_2 x_2 + \beta_3 x_3 + \beta_4 x_4 + \varepsilon_i$. The reduced model is $y_i = \beta_0 + \beta_1 x_1 + \beta_2 x_2 + \varepsilon_i$. Therefore, to conduct a test of hypothesis to to determine if the independent variables x_3 and x_4 belong in the complete regression model, the following hypothesis must be tested: H_O: $\beta_3 = \beta_4 = 0$, H_A: at least one $\beta_i \neq 0$

SSE$_C$ = 201.72. So MSE$_C$ = SSE$_C$/(n-c-1) = 201.72/(10 – 4-1) = 40.344 and SSE$_R$ =1343. The hypothesis test follows:

Step 1: The parameters of interest are the population coefficients of x_3 and x_4. In order for the averages to be equal, it must be true that $\beta_3 = \beta_4 = 0$

Step 2: H_O: $\beta_3 = \beta_4 = 0$, H_A: at least one $\beta_i \neq 0$

Step 3: $\alpha = 0.05$

Step 4: The test statistic is

$$F = \frac{(SSE_R - SSE_C)/(c-r)}{MSE_C} = \frac{(1343 - 201.72)/(4-2)}{40.344} = 14.144$$

Step 5: The numerator degrees of freedom are $c - r = 4 - 2 = 2$ and the denominator degrees of freedom are $n - c - 1 = 10 - 4 - 1 = 5$. The critical value is 5.786

Step 6: Since F = 14.144 > 5.786, we reject H_O

Step 7: There is sufficient evidence to conclude that at least one of the independent variables x_3 and x_4 belongs in the complete regression model

b. The complete model is $y_i = \beta_0 + \beta_1 x_1 + \beta_2 x_2 + \beta_3 x_3 + \beta_4 x_4 + \varepsilon_i$. The reduced model is $y_i = \beta_0 + \beta_1 x_3 + \beta_2 x_4 + \varepsilon_i$. Therefore, to conduct a test of hypothesis to determine if the independent variables x_1 and x_2 belong in the complete regression model, the following hypothesis must be tested: H_O: $\beta_1 = \beta_2 = 0$, H_A: at least one $\beta_i \neq 0$

SSE$_C$ = 201.72. So MSE$_C$ = SSE$_C$/(n-c-1) = 201.72/(10 – 4-1) = 40.344 and SSE$_R$ = 494.6. The hypothesis test follows:

Step 1: The parameters of interest are the population coefficients of x_1 and x_2. In order for the averages to be equal, it must be true that $\beta_1 = \beta_2 = 0$

Step 2: H_O: $\beta_1 = \beta_2 = 0$, H_A: at least one $\beta_i \neq 0$

Step 3: $\alpha = 0.05$

Step 4: The test statistic is

$$F = \frac{(SSE_R - SSE_C)/(c-r)}{MSE_C} = \frac{(494.6 - 201.72)/(4-2)}{40.344} = 3.630$$

The numerator degrees of freedom are $c - r = 4 - 2 = 2$ and the denominator degrees of freedom are $n - c - 1 = 10 - 4 - 1 = 5$. The p-value = $P(F \geq 3.630) = 0.1062$

Step 5: If the p-value is less than α, reject the null hypothesis; otherwise fail to reject the null hypothesis

Step 6: Since the p-value = 0.1062 > 0.05, we fail to reject H_O

Step 7: There is sufficient evidence to conclude that at least one of the independent variables x_1 and x_2 belong in the complete regression model.

15.31
a. You will need two dummy variables for the type of client
$x_2 = 1$ if manufacturing, 0 otherwise
$x_3 = 1$ if service, 0 otherwise
SUMMARY OUTPUT

Regression Statistics	
Multiple R	0.835474124
R Square	0.698017012
Adjusted R Square	0.568595732
Standard Error	975.3064045
Observations	11

ANOVA

	df	SS	MS	F
Regression	3	15390889.56	5130296.519	5.393371239
Residual	7	6658558.078	951222.5826	
Total	10	22049447.64		

	Coefficients	Standard Error	t Stat	P-value
Intercept	-586.2555597	974.2029083	-0.601779727	0.566292865
Hours (x1)	22.86106295	29.33445824	0.779324532	0.461318736
Manufacturing (x2)	2302.267018	895.0615733	2.572188425	0.036889988
Service (x3)	1869.813042	764.538844	2.445674352	0.044387958

b.

Regression Statistics						
Multiple R	0.857349507					
R Square	0.735048178					
Adjusted R	0.55841363					
Standard E	986.7489828					
Observatio	11					

ANOVA

	df	SS	MS	F	Significance F	
Regression	4	16207406.31	4051851.576	4.161407	0.059614012	
Residual	6	5842041.33	973673.5551			
Total	10	22049447.64				

	Coefficients	Standard Error	t Stat	P-value	Lower 95%	Upper 95%
Intercept	5828.692045	7074.147002	0.823942737	0.441486	-11481.13475	23138.52
x1	-334.4059583	391.2641671	-0.854680766	0.425533	-1291.795586	622.9837
x1 sq	4.557139444	4.976413466	0.915747752	0.395113	-7.619714546	16.73399
x2	2694.801455	1001.890131	2.689717536	0.036066	243.2628268	5146.34
x3	1287.495477	1001.336851	1.285776585	0.245912	-1162.689323	3737.68

Looking only at the r-square, the second order model is a slight improvement. However, because of the added variable, the adjusted R-square is actually lower for the second order model. In neither model was the hours variable significant. In the second order model, only x2 , the manufacturing dummy variable was significant. Neither model is very effective at explaining variation in the dependent variable.

15.33

a. Minitab scatter plot:

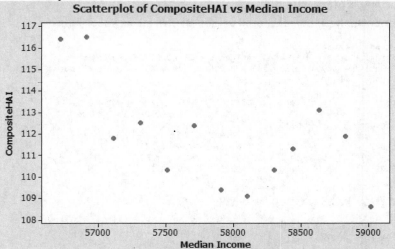

b. There appears to be one curve in the sample data. Therefore, a second-order polynomial seems to be the correct model.

Minitab output:

Regression Analysis: CompositeHAI versus Median Income, Median IncomeSq

```
The regression equation is
CompositeHAI = 8083 - 0.273 Median Income + 0.000002 Median IncomeSq


Predictor              Coef      SE Coef      T      P
Constant               8083         3540   2.28  0.046
Median Income        -0.2734       0.1224  -2.23  0.049
Median IncomeSq  0.00000234   0.00000106   2.22  0.051


S = 1.72721   R-Sq = 59.6%   R-Sq(adj) = 51.5%


Analysis of Variance

Source          DF      SS      MS      F      P
Regression       2  44.004  22.002   7.38  0.011
Residual Error  10  29.833   2.983
Total           12  73.837
```

The estimated regression equation is $\hat{y} = 8083 - 0.273x + 0.000002x^2$.

c. The model that would contain the specified interaction terms is
$$y = \beta_o + \beta_1 x_1 + \beta_2 x_1^2 + \beta_3 x_2 + \beta_4 x_1 x_2 + \beta_5 x_1^2 x_2 + \varepsilon$$
Minitab provides an analysis of this model:

Regression Analysis: CompositeHAI versus Median Incom, Median Incom, ...

```
The regression equation is
CompositeHAI = 4038 - 0.127 Median Income + 0.000001 Median IncomeSq
               - 4.38 Monthly P&I + 0.000141 IncomePI - 0.000000 IncomeSqPI


Predictor                Coef      SE Coef       T      P
Constant                 4038         3623    1.11  0.302
Median Income         -0.1269       0.1257   -1.01  0.346
Median IncomeSq    0.00000105   0.00000109    0.97  0.366
Monthly P&I           -4.383        3.265    -1.34  0.221
IncomePI            0.0001415    0.0001132    1.25  0.252
IncomeSqPI        -0.00000000   0.00000000   -1.19  0.273


S = 0.0452312   R-Sq = 100.0%   R-Sq(adj) = 100.0%


Analysis of Variance

Source          DF      SS       MS        F      P
Regression       5  73.823   14.765  7216.78  0.000
Residual Error   7   0.014    0.002
Total           12  73.837
```

The two interaction turns are $\beta_4 x_1 x_2$ *and* $\beta_5 x_1^2 x_2$. So you must conduct two hypothesis tests:

(i) To determine if there is interaction between x_2 and the linear relationship between x_1 and y, we must test to determine if $\beta_4 = 0$, so we hypothesize $\beta_4 = 0$. Since the p-value for $\beta_4 = 0.252 > 0.05$, we fail to reject H_O, there is not sufficient evidence to conclude that there is interaction between x_2 and the linear relationship between x_1 and y.

(ii) To determine if there is interaction between x_2 and the quadratic relationship between x_1 and y, we must test to determine if $\beta_5 = 0$. We hypothesize $\beta_5 = 0$. Since the p-value for $\beta_5 = 0.273 > 0.05$, we fail to reject H_O; there is not sufficient evidence to conclude that there is interaction between x_2 and the quadratic relationship between x_1 and y.

15.35

a. Minitab scatter plot:

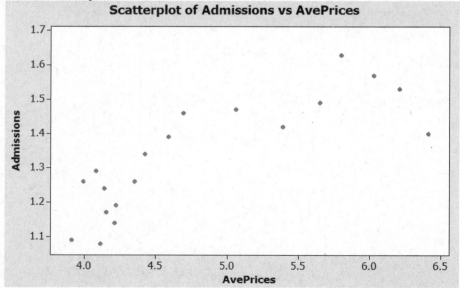

b. There appears to be three "curves." This would suggest a fourth order polynomial.
c. Minitab output:

Regression Analysis: Admissions versus AvePrices, AP2, AP3, AP4

```
The regression equation is
Admissions = - 30.0 + 24.5 AvePrices - 7.3 AP2 + 0.98 AP3 - 0.0499 AP4


Predictor     Coef  SE Coef      T      P
Constant    -30.00    56.96  -0.53  0.607
AvePrices    24.49    45.55   0.54  0.599
AP2          -7.31    13.54  -0.54  0.598
AP3          0.984    1.772   0.56  0.588
AP4       -0.04990  0.08621  -0.58  0.572


S = 0.0772561   R-Sq = 82.8%   R-Sq(adj) = 77.9%


Analysis of Variance

Source           DF       SS       MS      F      P
Regression        4  0.40256  0.10064  16.86  0.000
Residual Error   14  0.08356  0.00597
Total            18  0.48612
```

Note that the F-test has a p-value of 0.000. However, the individual t-tests all have very large p-values. There is also a substantial difference in the adjusted and unadjusted coefficient of determination. This suggests that there may be some components that are redundant and should be removed from the model.

d. To determine if the fourth order components should be removed we must determine if $\beta_4 = 0$. We test the hypothesis $\beta_4 = 0$. Since the p-value $= .572 > 0.05$, we fail to reject H_O; there is sufficient evidence to remove the fourth order component.

(ii) Minitab output:

Regression Analysis: Admissions versus AvePrices, AP2, AP3

```
The regression equation is
Admissions = 2.71 - 1.76 AvePrices + 0.510 AP2 - 0.0414 AP3


Predictor      Coef  SE Coef      T      P
Constant      2.709    6.990   0.39  0.704
AvePrices    -1.764    4.173  -0.42  0.679
AP2          0.5098   0.8205   0.62  0.544
AP3        -0.04141  0.05317  -0.78  0.448
```

To determine if the third order components should be removed we must determine if $\beta_3 = 0$. Since its p-value $= 0.488 > 0.05$, there is sufficient evidence to remove the third order component.

(iii) Minitab output:

```
The regression equation is
Admissions = - 2.68 + 1.47 AvePrices - 0.129 AP2


Predictor      Coef  SE Coef      T      P
Constant    -2.6842   0.9447  -2.84  0.012
AvePrices    1.4722   0.3800   3.87  0.001
AP2        -0.12856  0.03723  -3.45  0.003


S = 0.0745897   R-Sq = 81.7%   R-Sq(adj) = 79.4%


Analysis of Variance

Source           DF       SS       MS      F      P
Regression        2  0.39710  0.19855  35.69  0.000
Residual Error   16  0.08902  0.00556
Total            18  0.48612
```

To determine if the second order components should be removed we must determine if $\beta_2 = 0$. Since its p-value $= 0.003 < 0.05$, there is sufficient evidence to retain the second order component.

The resulting equation is $\hat{y}_i = -2.68 + 1.47x_1 - 0.129x_1^2$

15.37
a.   The second order polynomial is

```
The regression equation is
HAI = 8083 - 0.273 Median Income + 0.000002 MedIncome2


Predictor              Coef     SE Coef       T       P
Constant               8083        3540    2.28   0.046
Median Income       -0.2734      0.1224   -2.23   0.049
MedIncome2       0.00000234  0.00000106    2.22   0.051


S = 1.72721   R-Sq = 59.6%   R-Sq(adj) = 51.5%


Analysis of Variance

Source         DF       SS      MS       F       P
Regression      2   44.004  22.002    7.38   0.011
Residual Error 10   29.833   2.983
Total          12   73.837
```

b.   To determine if the polynomial is useful we must test if at least one of β_1 and β_2 is different from 0. This is accomplished using a "global-F" test.

Step 1: The parameters of interest is the population coefficient of x_1x_2

Step 2: H_O: $\beta_1 = \beta_2 = 0$, H_A: at least one $\beta_i \neq 0$

Step 3: $\alpha = 0.01$

Step 4: The p-value obtained from Minitab above is 0.011

Step 5: If the p-value is less than α, reject the null hypothesis; otherwise fail to reject the null hypothesis

Step 6: Since the p-value = 0.011 > 0.01, we do not reject H_O

Step 7: There is not sufficient evidence to conclude that the polynomial is useful.

c. and d. The regression equation containing the interaction terms is

Regression Analysis: HAI versus Median Income, MedIncome2, ...

```
The regression equation is
HAI = - 815 + 0.0414 Median Income - 0.000000 MedIncome2 - 0.000011 MediP&I
      + 0.000000 Medi2P&I


Predictor              Coef     SE Coef       T      P
Constant             -814.6       256.7   -3.17  0.013
Median Income       0.04140     0.01013    4.09  0.003
MedIncome2       -0.00000041  0.00000010   -4.11  0.003
MediP&I          -0.00001054  0.00000131   -8.06  0.000
Medi2P&I          0.00000000  0.00000000    6.70  0.000


S = 0.0474453   R-Sq = 100.0%   R-Sq(adj) = 100.0%


Analysis of Variance

Source           DF       SS       MS       F      P
Regression        4   73.819   18.455  8198.26  0.000
Residual Error    8    0.018    0.002
Total            12   73.837
```

The complete model is $y_i = \beta_0 + \beta_1 x_1 + \beta_2 x_1^2 + \beta_3 x_1 x_2 + \beta_4 x_1^2 x_2 + \varepsilon_i$. The reduced model is $y_i = \beta_0 + \beta_1 x_1 + \beta_2 x_1^2 + \varepsilon_i$. Therefore, to conduct a test of hypothesis to determine if monthly principle and interest interacts with the relationship between the HAI and the median family income, the following hypothesis must be tested: H_0: $\beta_3 = \beta_4 = 0$, H_A: at least one $\beta_i \neq 0$. $SSE_C = 0.018$. So $MSE_C = SSE_C/(n-c-1)$ = 0.018/(13 − 4-1) = 0.002 and SSE_R =29.833. The hypothesis test follows:

Step 1: The parameters of interest are the population coefficients of x_3 and x_4. In order for the averages to be equal, it must be true that $\beta_3 = \beta_4 = 0$

Step 2: H_0: $\beta_3 = \beta_4 = 0$, H_A: at least one $\beta_i \neq 0$

Step 3: $\alpha = 0.025$

Step 4: The test statistic is

$$F = \frac{(SSE_R - SSE_C)/(c-r)}{MSE_C} = \frac{(29.833 - 0.018)/(4-2)}{0.002} = 7453.75$$

Step 5: The numerator degrees of freedom are c − r = 4 - 2 = 2 and the denominator degrees of freedom are n − c - 1 = 13 − 4 − 1 = 8. The critical value is 11.04

Step 6: Since F = 14.144 > 11.04, we reject H_0

Step 7: There is sufficient evidence to conclude that the monthly principle and interest interacts with the relationship between the HAI and the median family income

Section 15-4 Exercises

15.39
    a. x_2 and x_4 were the only variables to enter the model because x1 and x3 did not have high enough coefficients of partial determination to add significantly to the model.
    b.   The stepwise model and the "full" model with the same variables would be identical. Stepwise regression is just a variable selection procedure. After the variables have been selected, the method of least squares is used to obtain estimates of the parameters for both the full model and stepwise regression. This results in the same estimates for both procedures.
    c.   Stepwise regression cannot have a larger R^2 than the full model since R^2 is increased every time a new variable is added. So the full model will have an R^2 at least as large as the Stepwise model. This of course assumes the same pool of independent variables is used for both procedures.

15.41
    a.

```
                 y         x1         x2
    x1      -0.088
             0.765

    x2       0.062     -0.366
             0.834      0.198

    x3       0.383     -0.128      0.129
             0.176      0.664      0.660

    Cell Contents: Pearson correlation
                   P-Value
```

None of the independent variables are significantly (at the 0.05 significance level) correlated with the dependent variable. It would appear that no independent variables will enter the first step of the stepwise regression model. However, using a more liberal significance level (such as Minitab's 0.25), x_3 would be the most likely variable to enter the model.

    b.

```
Alpha-to-Enter: 0.25  Alpha-to-Remove: 0.25
Response is yi on 3 predictors, with N = 14

Step                 1
Constant         26.19

xi3               0.42
T-Value           1.44
P-Value          0.176

S                 4.46
R-Sq             14.68
R-Sq(adj)         7.57
Mallows C-p       0.0
```

c.

```
The regression equation is
y = 27.9 - 0.035 x1 - 0.002 x2 + 0.412 x3


Predictor         Coef      SE Coef         T         P
Constant         27.92        22.47      1.24     0.243
x1             -0.0346       0.2699     -0.13     0.901
x2             -0.0017       0.2608     -0.01     0.995
x3              0.4120       0.3217      1.28     0.229


S = 4.886       R-Sq = 14.8%      R-Sq(adj) = 0.0%

Analysis of Variance

Source              DF           SS          MS         F         P
Regression           3        41.60       13.87      0.58     0.641
Residual Error      10       238.76       23.88
Total               13       280.36
```

Of course, the difference between the two models is that the full model has more independent variables. However, each of the variables and the entire model are not significant. The adjusted R^2 is 0% for the full model and 7.57% for the standard selection model. Neither model offers a good approach to fitting this data.

15.43

a. Minitab output:

Stepwise Regression: y versus x1, x2, x3, x4

```
   Alpha-to-Enter: 0.15  Alpha-to-Remove: 0.15


Response is y on 4 predictors, with N = 10


Step             1       2       3
Constant     80.19   47.99   32.08


x3            -8.7    -7.1    -5.0
T-Value      -4.72   -4.90   -2.98
P-Value      0.001   0.002   0.025


x1                    0.91    0.76
T-Value               2.91    2.68
P-Value              0.023   0.037


x4                            0.95
T-Value                       1.83
P-Value                      0.117


S             9.85    7.09    6.13
R-Sq         73.60   88.05   92.34
R-Sq(adj)    70.30   84.64   88.51
Mallows C-p   13.3     4.7     3.6
```

The resulting equation is $\hat{y} = 32.08 + 0.76x_1 - 5x_3 + 0.95x_4$

b.   Minitab output:

Stepwise Regression: y versus x1, x2, x3, x4

```
Forward selection.  Alpha-to-Enter: 0.25


Response is y on 4 predictors, with N = 10


Step               1      2      3
Constant        80.19  47.99  32.08


x3              -8.7   -7.1   -5.0
T-Value         -4.72  -4.90  -2.98
P-Value         0.001  0.002  0.025


x1                     0.91   0.76
T-Value                2.91   2.68
P-Value                0.023  0.037


x4                            0.95
T-Value                       1.83
P-Value                       0.117


S               9.85   7.09   6.13
R-Sq            73.60  88.05  92.34
R-Sq(adj)       70.30  84.64  88.51
Mallows C-p     13.3    4.7    3.6
```

The resulting equation is $\hat{y} = 32.08 + 0.76x_1 - 5x_3 + 0.95x_4$

c.   Minitab output:

Stepwise Regression: y versus x1, x2, x3, x4

```
Backward elimination.  Alpha-to-Remove: 0.1

Response is y on 4 predictors, with N = 10

Step               1      2      3
Constant        32.80  32.08  47.99

x1              0.47   0.76   0.91
T-Value         0.98   2.68   2.91
P-Value         0.373  0.037  0.023

x2              0.55
T-Value         0.77
P-Value         0.478

x3              -4.8   -5.0   -7.1
T-Value         -2.69  -2.98  -4.90
P-Value         0.043  0.025  0.002

x4              0.93   0.95
T-Value         1.74   1.83
P-Value         0.143  0.117

S               6.35   6.13   7.09
R-Sq            93.14  92.34  88.05
R-Sq(adj)       87.66  88.51  84.64
Mallows C-p      5.0    3.6    4.7
```

The resulting equation is $\hat{y} = 32.08 + 0.76x_1 - 5x_3 + 0.95x_4$

Note: This is the model from step 2, it is chosen because of the higher adjusted R square value.

d. Minitab output:

Best Subsets Regression: y versus x1, x2, x3, x4

```
Response is y

                        Mallows          x x x x
Vars  R-Sq  R-Sq(adj)    C-p      S      1 2 3 4
  1   73.6    70.3      13.3    9.8544       X
  1   70.1    66.3      15.8   10.492            X
  2   88.1    84.6       4.7    7.0872   X   X
  2   86.9    83.1       5.6    7.4255   X X
  3   92.3    88.5       3.6    6.1293   X   X X
  3   91.8    87.7       4.0    6.3288       X X X
  4   93.1    87.7       5.0    6.3517   X X X X
```

Using adjusted R^2 as the criterion, the resulting equation is $\hat{y} = 32.08 + 0.76x_1 - 5x_3 + 0.95x_4$.

15.45

a.

```
Backward elimination.  Alpha-to-Remove: 0.05

Response is Calls Re on  3 predictors, with N =   12


     Step        1        2        3
 Constant   -269.84  -248.04   -18.33

 Ads Plac         5
 T-Value       0.24
 P-Value      0.817

 Calls Re      0.83     0.92     1.07
 T-Value       1.59     2.57     2.74
 P-Value      0.150    0.030    0.021

 Airline      0.089    0.093
 T-Value       1.62     1.87
 P-Value      0.145    0.094

 S             86.2     81.5     91.1
 R-Sq         59.11    58.82    42.83
 R-Sq(adj)    43.78    49.67    37.12
 C-p            4.0      2.1      3.2
```

$\hat{y} = -18.33 + 1.07x_2$

b. There is one independent variable (x_2) and one dependent variable (y)..

c. x_1 was the first variable removed. It was removed because the p-value associated with it (0.817) was larger than the specified significance level (0. 05). x_3 was the last variable removed. It was removed because the p-value associated with it (0.094) was larger than the specified significance level (0. 05).

15.47

a.   Minitab scatter plot:

(1)

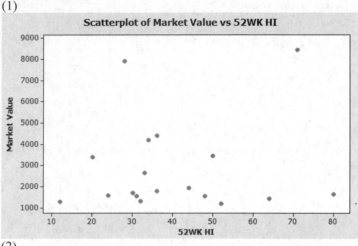

(2)

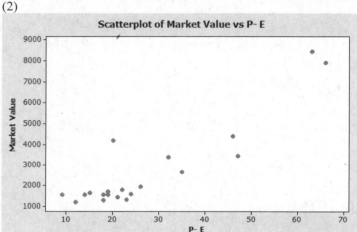

Examining the first scatter plot, it would appear that there are two outliers. However, the slope on the regression equation seems to almost equal 0 with no curves. The second scatter plot seems to have a slight concave curvature, supporting the analyst's decision to produce a second-order polynomial.

b.   Minitab output:

Stepwise Regression: Market Value versus 52WK HI, P- E, HISq, PESq, HIPE

```
Forward selection.  Alpha-to-Enter: 0.25


Response is Market Value on 5 predictors, with N = 20



Step            1
Constant     1110

PESq         1.60
T-Value     11.48
P-Value     0.000

S             750
R-Sq        87.99
R-Sq(adj)   87.32
Mallows C-p  -0.3
```

The equation is $\hat{y} = 1110 + 1.60x_2^2$

c.   The forward selection stepwise regression agrees with the analyst's decision to produce a second-order polynomial since the square of the P-E ratio is in the resulting regression equation. The fact that the p-value = 0.000 provides inferential support to this statement.

15.49

a. Minitab output:

Stepwise Regression: CPI versus Gas Price, Heat Oil, Diesel, Crude Oil

```
Backward elimination.  Alpha-to-Remove: 0.1


Response is CPI on 4 predictors, with N = 15

* ERROR * X-matrix is (nearly) singular.
```

The message indicates that there is multicollinearity among the predictor variables.

b. Minitab output:

Correlations: CPI, Gas Price, Heat Oil, Diesel, Crude Oil

```
              CPI  Gas Price  Heat Oil    Diesel
Gas Price   0.507
            0.054

Heat Oil    0.858    0.703
            0.000    0.003

Diesel      0.582    0.867     0.834
            0.023    0.000     0.000

Crude Oil   0.582    0.867     0.834     1.000
            0.023    0.000     0.000        *


Cell Contents: Pearson correlation
               P-Value
```

Either crude oil or diesel prices should be removed since they have the same correlation coefficient with the dependent variable and a correlation coefficient with each other of 1.

c. Crude oil prices were removed for the following stepwise procedure.

Minitab output:

Stepwise Regression: CPI versus Gas Price, Heat Oil, Diesel

```
Backward elimination.  Alpha-to-Remove: 0.1


Response is CPI on 3 predictors, with N = 15


Step               1        2
Constant      0.8739   0.8741

Gas Price    0.00005
T-Value         0.41
P-Value        0.689

Heat Oil     0.00089  0.00089
T-Value         4.97     5.14
P-Value        0.000    0.000

Diesel      -0.00029 -0.00023
T-Value        -1.53    -1.84
P-Value        0.154    0.091

S            0.00639  0.00616
R-Sq           79.65    79.33
R-Sq(adj)      74.09    75.89
Mallows C-p      4.0      2.2
```

The resulting equation is $\hat{y} = 0.8741 + 0.00089x_2 - 0.00023x_3$

Section 15-5 Exercises

15.51.

a. The regression equation is
$$\hat{y} = -16.02 + 2.1277x$$

b. $H_0 : B_1 = 0.0$

$H_A : B_1 \neq 0.0$

Predictor	Coef	SE Coef	T	P
Constant	-16.02	10.22	-1.57	0.156
x	2.1277	0.2658	8.00	0.000

S = 18.54   R-Sq = 88.9%   R-Sq(adj) = 87.5%

Analysis of Variance

Source	DF	SS	MS	F	P
Regression	1	22013	22013	64.07	0.000
Residual Error	8	2749	344		
Total	9	24762			

The p-value equals 0.000 which is smaller than the significance level = 0.05. Thus, the regression equation is found to be significant.

c. Note, the solution was done using Minitab. The Minitab standardized residuals will be slightly different than those computed in Excel (Minitab uses Studentized Standardized Residuals) . The plots will still provide the same general conclusions.

RESI1	SRES1
8.2567	0.50886
16.8735	1.02038
14.2350	0.83940
-7.2759	-0.42265
-3.7867	-0.21760
-10.4253	-0.59423
-22.1916	-1.26229
-30.3627	-1.79839
18.2325	1.15838
16.4445	1.24124

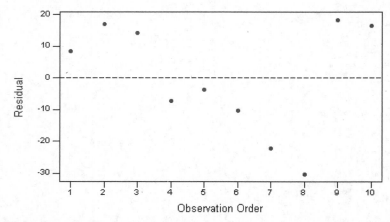

Residuals Versus the Order of the Data
(response is y)

This graph indicates that the error terms are not independent of each other. Some "time" related factor is influencing the randomness of the residuals.

No evidence is available to refute the assumption that the residuals have equal variances at each value of the independent variable.

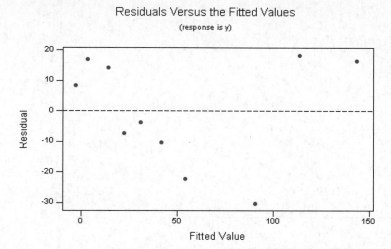

The residuals are positive for small values, negative for the intermediate values, and positive again for the large values of the fitted values. This indicates that, perhaps, a 2nd order term be placed into the model.

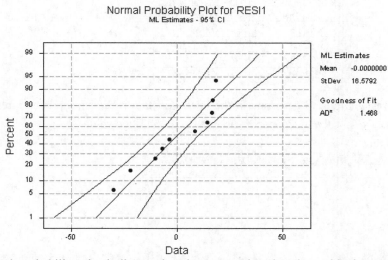

The normal probability plot indicates that the assumption that the residuals possess a normal distribution cannot be rejected.

15.53

a.   Minitab output:

Regression Analysis: y versus x1, x2

```
The regression equation is
y = 17.0 + 1.54 x1 - 0.119 x2


Predictor      Coef  SE Coef      T      P
Constant     17.010    6.199   2.74  0.029
x1           1.5416   0.2811   5.48  0.001
x2          -0.1193   0.2811  -0.42  0.684


S = 8.50528   R-Sq = 85.8%   R-Sq(adj) = 81.8%
```

The equation is $\hat{y} = 17.0 + 1.54x_1 - 0.119x_2$

b.

e_i	r_i
3.2646	0.53825
10.8786	1.59564
-10.1214	-1.48457
-5.7773	-0.87248
-2.9528	-0.48684
-11.5668	-1.43995
5.3218	0.68149
3.3218	0.42538
7.7253	0.98443
-0.0939	-0.01356

c.   The appropriate residual plot to determine if the linear function is the appropriate regression function is a plot of the residuals versus the independent variable (x) or the fitted value ($\hat{y}_i$).

Minitab plot:

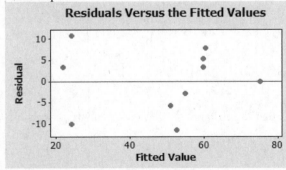

This residual plot shows the residuals scattered about 0. The residual plot supports the choice of the linear model.

d. The appropriate residual plot to determine if the residuals have a constant variance is a plot of the residuals versus the independent variable (x) or the fitted value ($\hat{y}_i$).

Minitab plot:

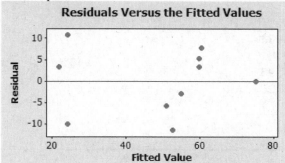

The residual plot does not display any non-random pattern. This indicates that the residuals do have a constant variance.

e. The appropriate residual plot to determine if the residuals are independent is a plot of the residuals versus a "time" variable.

Minitab plot:

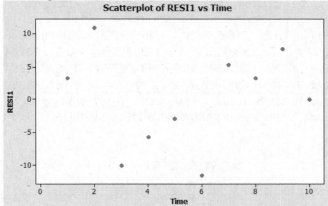

This residual plot shows positive residuals early in the experiment. In the middle of the experiment, the residuals are negative, and at the end they are positive again.

f. Minitab probability plot:

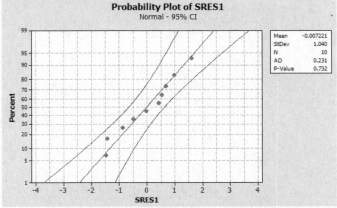

The probability plot shows all of the standardized residuals within the confidence bounds. This indicates that the error terms are normally distributed.

15.55

  a.

Regression Analysis

Regression Statistics	
Multiple R	0.768833636
R Square	0.591105161
Adjusted R Square	0.437769596
Standard Error	86.185825
Observations	12

ANOVA

	df	SS	MS	F	Significance F
Regression	3	85904.27855	28634.75952	3.854977555	0.056364409
Residual	8	59423.97145	7427.996431		
Total	11	145328.25			

	Coefficients	Standard Error	t Stat	P-value
Intercept	269.8384166	216.5685514	-1.245972302	0.248024888
Ads Place Previous Week	4.952788772	20.69902397	0.23927644	0.81690744
Calls Received the Previous Week	0.834047965	0.523880632	1.592057261	0.150036794
Airline Bookings	0.088664991	0.054832052	1.617028492	0.144533989

The overall model is not significant as can be seen by a p-value of 0.0564 and none of the independent variables are significant as can be seen by the p-values of 0.8169, 0.1500 and 0.1445.

  b.

Scatterplot

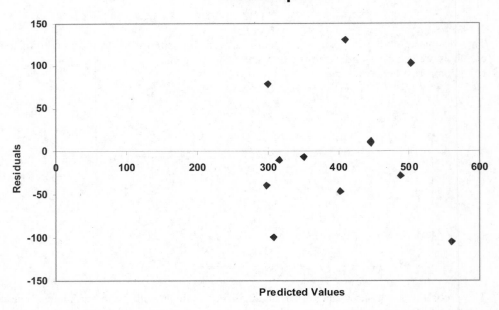

The plot appears to have a uniform shape, which means the assumption of constant variance has not been violated.

c.   Students should state that it would be inappropriate to test for randomness using a plot of the residuals over time since the weeks were randomly selected and are not in sequential, time-series order.

d.

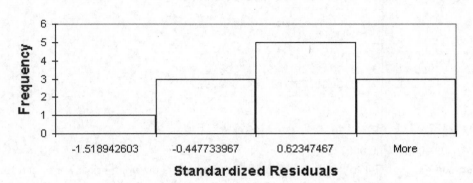

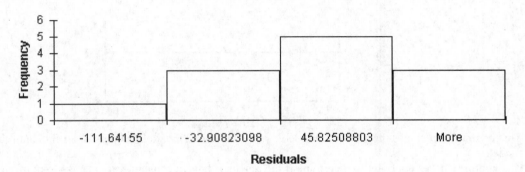

The residuals appear to be fairly normally distributed so the model meets the assumption of normally distributed error terms.

15.57
   a.   Minitab output:

Regression Analysis: CPI versus Heat Oil, Diesel

```
The regression equation is
CPI = 0.874 + 0.000887 Heat Oil - 0.000235 Diesel


Predictor        Coef      SE Coef        T       P
Constant      0.87406      0.02134    40.95   0.000
Heat Oil    0.0008873    0.0001728     5.14   0.000
Diesel     -0.0002347    0.0001279    -1.84   0.091


S = 0.00616296   R-Sq = 79.3%   R-Sq(adj) = 75.9%
```

$\hat{y} = 0.874 + 0.000887x_1 - 0.000235x_2$

   b.   The appropriate residual plot to determine if the linear function is the appropriate regression function is a plot of the residuals versus the independent variable (x) or the fitted value ($\hat{y}_i$).

       Minitab plot:

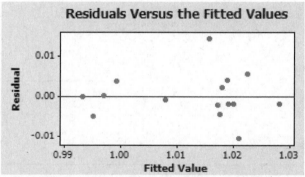

This residual plot shows the residuals scattered about 0. The residual plot supports the choice of the linear model.

   c.   The appropriate residual plot to determine if the residuals have a constant variance is a plot of the residuals versus the independent variable (x) or the fitted value ($\hat{y}_i$).

       Minitab plot:

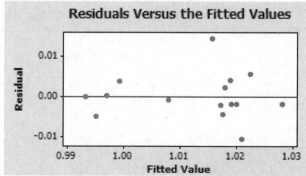

The residual plot seems to indicate that the dispersion gets larger for larger fitted values. This indicates that the residuals do not have constant variances.

d. The appropriate residual plot to determine if the residuals are independent is a plot of the residuals versus a "time" variable.
Minitab plot:

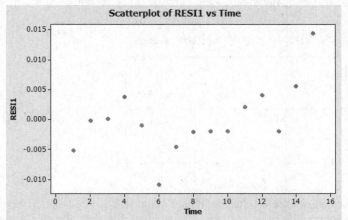

This residual plot shows the residuals scattered about 0. The residuals, however, follow a pattern of being negative, positive, negative, and positive. The linear model appears to be insufficient.

e. Minitab probability plot:

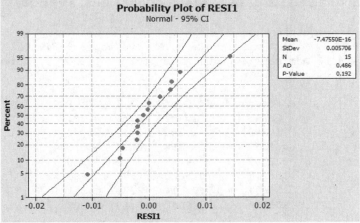

The probability plot shows all of the standardized residuals within the confidence bounds. This indicates that the error terms are normally distributed.

15.59

a. Minitab output:

Regression Analysis: Grosses versus Admissions, AvePrices, Total Screens

```
The regression equation is
Grosses = - 6.81 + 5.29 Admissions + 1.51 AvePrices - 0.000033 Total Screens


Predictor            Coef      SE Coef        T       P
Constant          -6.8099       0.1834   -37.13   0.000
Admissions         5.2878       0.2731    19.36   0.000
AvePrices          1.51364      0.05053   29.95   0.000
Total Screens  -0.00003251  0.00001011    -3.22   0.006


S = 0.0788179    R-Sq = 99.9%    R-Sq(adj) = 99.8%
```

The equation is $\hat{y} = -6.81 + 5.29x_1 + 1.51x_2 - 0.000033x_3$

b. The appropriate residual plot to determine if the linear function is the appropriate regression function is a plot of the residuals versus the independent variable (x) or the fitted value ($\hat{y}_i$).

Minitab plot:

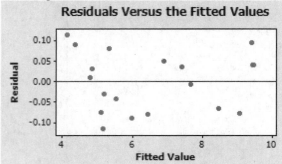

This residual plot shows the residuals scattered about 0. The residuals, however, follow a pattern of being positive, negative, positive, and positive. The residual plot indicates that a higher order model may be in order.

c. Minitab output:

Regression Analysis: Grosses versus Admissions, AvePrices, ...

```
The regression equation is
Grosses = 0.97 - 3.20 Admissions + 0.285 AvePrices + 0.000029 Total Screens
        + 3.12 AdmissSq + 0.103 AvePriceSq - 0.000000 TScrenSq
```

Predictor	Coef	SE Coef	T	P
Constant	0.966	1.404	0.69	0.505
Admissions	-3.205	1.394	-2.30	0.040
AvePrices	0.2852	0.4254	0.67	0.515
Total Screens	0.00002897	0.00004661	0.62	0.546
AdmissSq	3.1217	0.5025	6.21	0.000
AvePriceSq	0.10307	0.03814	2.70	0.019
TScrenSq	-0.00000000	0.00000000	-0.69	0.503

```
S = 0.0413482   R-Sq = 100.0%   R-Sq(adj) = 100.0%
```
The equation is $\hat{y} = 0.97 - 3.20x_1 + 0.285x_2 + 0.000029x_3 + 3.12x_1^2 + 0.103x_2^2 - 0.000000x_3^2$

d. Minitab plot:

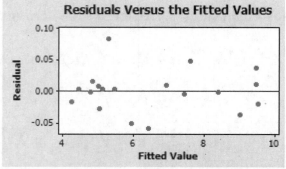

The residual plot does not display any non-random pattern. This indicates that the addition of the quadratic terms have alleviated the non-randomness with the residuals.

e. Minitab probability plot:

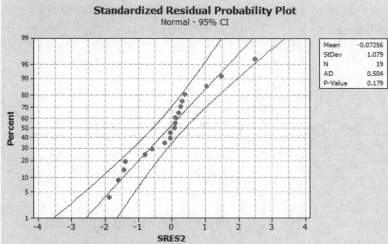

The probability plot shows all of the standardized residuals within the confidence bands. This indicates that the error terms are normally distributed.

Chapter Exercises

15.61 Simple linear and multiple linear regression are similar in almost all aspects except that (1) more than one independent variable is used in multiple regression; (2) the plot of a multiple regression equation is a hyperplane instead of a straight line, and (3) matrix algebra is used to compute the regression coefficients.

15.63. The regression assumptions are:
   a. The relationship between the dependent and each independent variable is linear.
   b. The residuals are independent.
   c. The variances of the residuals are constant over the range of the independent variables.
   d. The residuals are normally distributed.

15.65
   a. The coefficient of x_1 indicates that the average y increases by three units *holding x_2 constant*.
   b. The interpretation provided in part a. true regardless of the value of x_2 since x_2 only affects the y-intercept of this model.
   c. When $x_2 = 1$, $E(y) = 5 + 3x_1 + 5(1) + 4x_1(1) = 10 + 7x_1$. Note that the coefficient of x_1 actually equals 7 when $x_2 = 1$. Therefore, the interpretation is that the coefficient of x_1 indicates that the average y increases by 7 units *when $x_2 = 1$*.
   d. When $x_2 = 2$, $E(y) = 5 + 3x_1 + 5(2) + 4x_1(2) = 15 + 11x_1$. Note that now the coefficient of x_1 actually equals 11 when $x_2 = 2$. Therefore, the interpretation is that the coefficient of x_1 indicates that the average y increases by 11 units when $x_2 = 1$. For this model, the interpretation in part a is no longer true.
   e. When interaction terms exist in the model, those coefficients affected by the interaction terms have conditional interpretations.

15.67

	Volumes Sold Y	Pages X1	Competing Books X2	Advertising Budget X3	Age of Author X4
Volumes Sold Y	1				
Pages X1	0.62156877	1			
Competing Books X2	0.3554432	0.50109	1		
Advertising Budget X3	0.62034992	0.09128	0.383834666	1	
Age of Author X4	0.48517364	-0.01886	-0.11345564	0.26509575	1

The critical t for all pairs would be 2.1604

Volumes Sold (y) – Pages

$t = 0.6216/\sqrt{(1-0.6216^2)/(15-2)} = 2.8611 > 2.1604$ so highly correlated

Volumes Sold (y) – Competing Books

$t = 0.3554/\sqrt{(1-0.3554^2)/(15-2)} = 1.3709 < 2.1604$ so not highly correlated

Volumes Sold (y) – Advertising Budget.

$t = 0.6203/\sqrt{(1-0.6203^2)/(15-2)} = 2.8514 > 2.1604$ so highly correlated

Volumes Sold (y) – Age of Authors

$t = 0.4852/\sqrt{(1-0.4852^2)/(15-2)} = 2.0001 < 2.1604$ so not highly correlated

15.69

	Volumes Sold Y	Pages X1	Competing Books X2	Advertising Budget X3	Age of Author X4	Production Expenditures (x5)	Number of Reviewers (x6)
Volumes Sold Y	1						
Pages X_1	0.621568766	1					
Competing Books X_2	0.355443199	0.50108903	1				
Advertising Budget X_3	0.620349915	0.09127632	0.383834666	1			
Age of Author X_4	0.48517364	-0.01885537	-0.11345564	0.265095752	1		
Production Expenditures X_5	0.895786702	0.66950558	0.269519652	0.539371855	0.43762765	1	
Number of Reviewers X_6	0.660445191	0.37703987	0.291358466	0.354945062	0.52844266	0.737261383	1

a. Students should recognize that the number of independent variables is quite large given the sample size. The critical t for all pairs would be 2.1604

Volumes Sold (y) – Production Expenditures

$t = 0.8958/\sqrt{(1-0.8958^2)/(15-2)} = 7.270 > 2.1604$ so highly correlated

Volumes Sold (y) – Number of Reviewers

$t = 0.6604/\sqrt{(1-0.6604^2)/(15-2)} = 3.1709 > 2.1604$ so highly correlated

Volumes Sold (y) – Pages

$t = 0.6216/\sqrt{(1-0.6216^2)/(15-2)} = 2.86 > 2.1604$ so significantly correlated

Volumes Sold (y) – Competing Books

$t = 0.3554/\sqrt{(1-0.3554^2)/(15-2)} = 1.37 < 2.1604$ so no correlation

Volumes Sold (y) – Advertising Budget

$t = 0.6203/\sqrt{(1-0.6203^2)/(15-2)} = 32.85 > 2.1604$ so significantly correlated

Volumes Sold (y) – Age of Author

$t = 0.4852/\sqrt{(1-0.4852^2)/(15-2)} = 2.00 < 2.1604$ so not correlated

b.
SUMMARY OUTPUT

Regression Statistics	
Multiple R	0.934087733
R Square	0.872519893
Adjusted R Square	0.776909812
Standard Error	24165.94185
Observations	15

ANOVA

	df	SS	MS	F	Significance F
Regression	6	31976458035	5329409672	9.125815	0.003196409
Residual	8	4671941965	583992745.7		
Total	14	36648400000			

	Coefficients	Standard Error	t Stat	P-value
Intercept	-100834.5029	37274.89669	-2.705158481	0.026859
Pages X1	94.76853711	86.04152462	1.101427916	0.302742
Competing Books X2	-346.6236856	2660.369448	-0.13029156	0.899552
Advertising Budget X3	1.004264711	0.733503779	1.369133657	0.20816
Age of Author X4	1042.959943	782.0739662	1.333582228	0.21906
Production Expenditures (x5)	0.836522569	0.927136395	0.902264838	0.39327
Number of Reviewers (x6)	596.0263426	5749.306694	0.103669255	0.919984

Based upon the p-values determined in the regression model I would not retain any of the variables in the problem since all p-values > 0.05. One option would be to start removing the least significant variables and see if any of the other variables become significant.

c. Critical F = 3.581; Since F = 9.1258 > 3.581 conclude that the overall model is significant.

d. The things to look for when checking for multicolinearity include changes between the correlation sign and the sign on the regression coefficient (no sign changes) and variables that were individually significant but are not significant in the presence of the other variables (Four instances of this). Thus, there may be multicolinerarity affects here. However, the change in significance may also be due to the small sample size (n =15) relative to the number of independent variables (k = 6).

e. $\pm 2(24,165.9419) = \pm 48,331.8$; most people would probably not be willing to accept this kind of variation in volumes sold. The model needs improvement. Increased sample size would be the first step following by adding useful independent variables.

f.

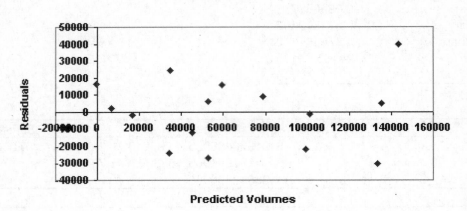

It appears that the constant variance assumption is satisfied.

g.

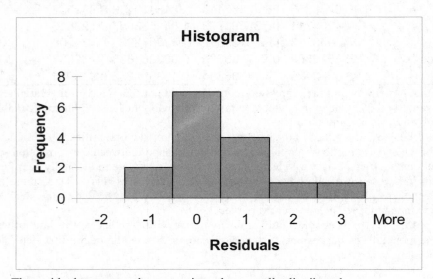

The residuals appear to be approximately normally distributed.

h.

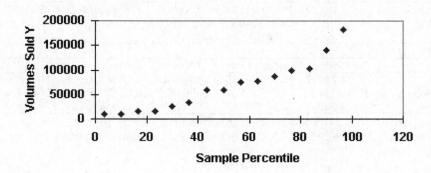

It appears that the model satisfies the normal distribution assumption.

Also, in part f. the plot of the residuals against the predicted values does not show a problem with non constant variance.

The model could be improved by adding sample size (More text books) and then looking for other useful independent variables.

15.71.   The t-critical for all pairs would be ± 2.0687

For family size – family income

$t = 0.2718/\sqrt{(1-0.2718^2)/(25-2)} = 1.354 < 2.0687$ so not highly correlated

For family income and age

$t = 0.0513/\sqrt{(1-0.0513^2)/(25-2)} = 0.246 < 2.0687$ so not highly correlated

For family size and age

$t = 0.5037/\sqrt{(1-0.5037^2)/(25-2)} = 2.7963 > 2.0687$ so highly correlated

For purchase volume and age

$t = -0.4057/\sqrt{(1-(-0.4057^2))/(25-2)} = -2.1287 < 2.0687$ so highly correlated

For purchase volume and family income

$t = 0.4591/\sqrt{(1-0.4591^2)/(25-2)} = 2.4784 > 2.0687$ so highly correlated

For purchase volume and family size

$t = -0.2445/\sqrt{(1-(-0.2445^2))/(25-2)} = 1.2093 < 2.0687$ so not highly correlated

15.73.   The significance F = 0.0210 is the p-value for the F-distribution and since this is smaller than any significance level except 0.01 conclude that the overall model at this step is significant.

15.75.

Age X1 entered.

	df	SS	MS	F	Significance F
Regression	2	15235.41902	7617.709511	7.19814255	0.003935699
Residual	22	23282.34098	1058.288226		
Total	24	38517.76			

	Coefficients	Standard Error	t Stat	P-value	Lower 95%	Upper 95%
Intercept	82.8874522	25.31844215	3.273797485	0.00347108	30.38016058	135.394744
Family Income X2	0.00208703	0.000719902	2.899044278	0.00832364	0.00059404	0.00358001
Age X1	-1.31806521	0.50826742	-2.59325141	0.01659161	-2.37214845	-0.26398196

The R^2 at step 1 was 0.2108 and the standard error at step 1 was 36.3553. The R^2 at step 2 is 0.3955 and the standard error at step 2 is 32.5313. The overall model is significant at step 2 based upon the significance F = 0.00395.

15.77. This occurs because the other variables that enter into the model partially overlap with the other included variables in its ability to explain the variation in the dependent variable. To be truly independent, the x variables need to be uncorrelated. We see from the correlation matrix that there is some correlation in the sample data between the x variables. This intercorrelation could result in the value of a variable changing at each step. In this situation the change is relatively small.

15.79. The plot of the residuals against the predicted values indicates that the residuals appear to have a constant variance.

a.

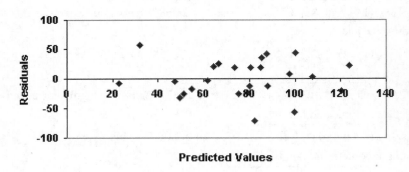

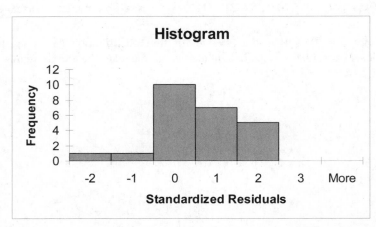

This does appear to meet the assumption of normal distribution of the residuals.

b. The model appears to fit the assumptions, but is not a good predictor of the independent variable. Going back to exercise 15-69, note the selected independent variables are not highly correlated with the dependent variable. A search should be conducted for different independent variables.

15.81

a. Minitab output:

Regression Analysis: Market Value versus 52WK HI, P- E, HISq, PESq, HIPE

```
The regression equation is
Market Value = 2857 - 26.4 52WK HI - 80.6 P- E + 0.115 HISq + 2.31 PESq
             + 0.542 HIPE


Predictor     Coef  SE Coef      T      P
Constant      2857     1674   1.71  0.110
52WK HI     -26.36    51.02  -0.52  0.613
P- E        -80.63    69.80  -1.16  0.267
HISq        0.1151   0.5240   0.22  0.829
PESq        2.3133   0.8019   2.88  0.012
HIPE        0.5421   0.6228   0.87  0.399


S = 803.423   R-Sq = 89.3%   R-Sq(adj) = 85.4%


Analysis of Variance

Source          DF        SS        MS      F      P
Regression       5  75146023  15029205  23.28  0.000
Residual Error  14   9036840    645489
Total           19  84182863
```

The estimated regression equation is $\hat{y} = 2857 - 26.4x_1 - 80.6x_2 + 0.115x_1^2 + 2.31x_2^2 + 0.542x_1x_2$

b. The appropriate residual plot to determine if the linear function is the appropriate regression function is a plot of the residuals versus the independent variable (x) or the fitted value ($\hat{y}_i$).

Minitab plot:

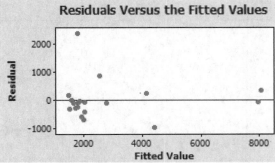

This residual plot shows the residuals scattered about 0 in a band. The residual plot supports the choice of the linear model.

c. The appropriate residual plot to determine if the residuals have a constant variance is a plot of the residuals versus the independent variable (x) or the fitted value ($\hat{y}_i$).

Minitab plot:

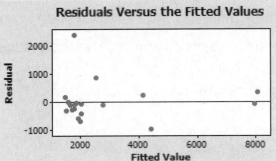

With the exception of what might be an outlier, the residual plot indicates that the dispersion is constant for any given fitted value taking in to account that the residuals are samples. This indicates that the residuals do have constant variances.

d. The appropriate residual plot to determine if the residuals are independent is a plot of the residuals versus a "time" variable.

Minitab plot:

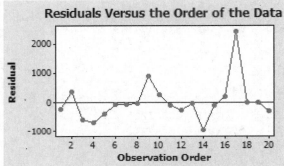

This residual plot shows the residuals exhibit a "wave form." The linear model appears to be insufficient. The addition of an independent variable representing time is indicated.

e. Minitab probability plot:

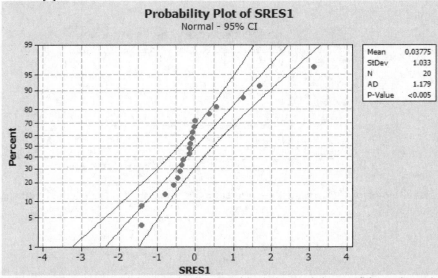

The probability plot shows two of the standardized residuals beyond the confidence bounds. This indicates that the error terms are not normally distributed. A transformation of the independent or dependent variables is required.

15.83

a. The scatterplot is

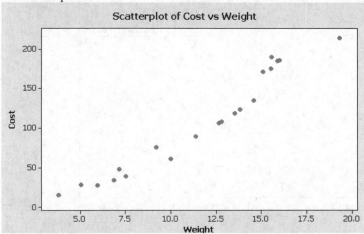

The scatterplot indicates that a quadratic relationship exists between cost and weight.

b. The correlation coefficient obtained using Minitab is

Correlations: Cost, Weight

```
Pearson correlation of Cost and Weight = 0.963
P-Value = 0.000
```

To determine if the population correlation coefficient is significantly different from zero, we conduct the following hypothesis test.

Step 1: The parameters of interest is the correlation coefficient, ρ.

Step 2: H_O: $\rho = 0$, H_A: $\rho \neq 0$

Step 3: $\alpha = 0.05$

Step 4: The p-value obtained from Minitab above is 0.000

Step 5: If the p-value is less than α, reject the null hypothesis; otherwise fail to reject the null hypothesis

Step 6: Since the p-value = 0.000 > 0.05, we reject H_O

Step 7: There is sufficient evidence to conclude that the population correlation coefficient is significantly different from zero.

c. The estimate of the simple linear regression model is

Regression Analysis: Cost versus Weight

```
The regression equation is
Cost = - 64.06 + 14.92 Weight


S = 17.7185    R-Sq = 92.8%    R-Sq(adj) = 92.4%


Analysis of Variance

Source        DF        SS        MS        F        P
Regression     1   72744.3   72744.3   231.71   0.000
Error         18    5651.0     313.9
Total         19   78395.3
```

The plot of the estimate of the simple linear model is

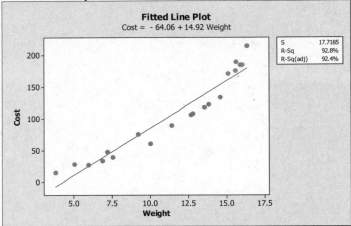

The residuals form a "+, -, +" pattern which indicates that a quadratic model would be superior to that of the simple linear model.

d. The estimate of the quadratic model is

Regression Analysis: Cost versus Weight, WeightSq

```
The regression equation is
Cost = 43.8 - 9.22 Weight + 1.14 WeightSq

Predictor      Coef    SE Coef       T      P
Constant      43.76      18.44    2.37  0.030
Weight       -9.218      3.885   -2.37  0.030
WeightSq     1.1432     0.1821    6.28  0.000

S = 10.0094    R-Sq = 97.8%    R-Sq(adj) = 97.6%

Analysis of Variance

Source          DF      SS      MS       F      P
Regression       2   76692   38346  382.74  0.000
Residual Error  17    1703     100
Total           19   78395
```

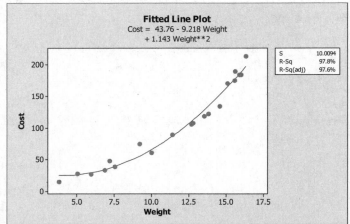

Comparing the R^2_{adj} for the quadratic equation (97.6%) and the R^2 for the simple linear equation (92.8%), the quadratic equation appears to fit better. Also the p-value (0.000) obtained for testing the second order component of the quadratic equation indicates that the quadratic term is useful in predicting the average cost. Therefore, it would appear that a nonlinear model would better fit the sample data.

15.85 To deal with the categorical variables, we will recode the data, using dummy variables, as follows:

Driver Sex: Male = 1   Female = 0

Seat belt status:	D1	D2	D3	
Not observed		0	0	0
Wearing	1	0	0	
Not wearing		0	1	0
Not required		0	0	1
Knowledge of seat belt law	D4	D5	D6	
No response		0	0	0
Aware		1	0	0
Not aware		0	1	0
Uncertain		0	0	1
Employment Status	D7	D8	D9	
No response		0	0	0
Employed		1	0	0
Unemployed		0	1	0
Retired	0	0	1	

Insurance Certificate	D10	D11	D12
Not observed	0	0	0
In vehicle	1	0	0
Not in vehicle	0	1	0
Other	0	0	1

Because D9 and D12 have no entries, they must be eliminated before the correlation matrix is determined. The correlation matrix becomes: (See next page)

Because of the large number of independent variables neither Excel or the PHStat programs will handle this problem. Using the stepwise option in Minitab we find:

Stepwise Regression: Vehicle Year versus Driving Cita, Driver Sex, ...

```
Alpha-to-Enter: 0.15  Alpha-to-Remove: 0.15

Response is Vehicle Year on 17 predictors, with N = 100

Step                   1      2      3
Constant           90.57  71.45  73.18

Driver Sex         -11.4  -10.1   -9.1
T-Value            -2.65  -2.37  -2.16
P-Value            0.009  0.020  0.034

Years Education            1.53   1.39
T-Value                    2.24   2.06
P-Value                    0.028  0.043

D3                                  -24
T-Value                           -2.04
P-Value                           0.044

S                   20.5   20.1   19.8
R-Sq                6.67  11.25  14.95
R-Sq(adj)           5.72   9.42  12.29
```

So only the drivers' gender (male or female), years education and the dummy variable associated with not being required to wear a seat belt are significant in the model. However, only 14.959% of the variation in the year of the vehicle can be explained by the available data.

	Driv Citat	Vehil Year	Sex	Age	D1	D2	D3	D4	D5	D6	D7	D8	Year In State	Regis Vehic	Years Ed	D10	D11	Ins Status
Driv Citat	1																	
Vehic Year	0.030071	1																
Sex	0.257473	-0.25833	1															
Year	-0.290971	0.116277	-0.04182	1														
D1	0.017898	0.155711	-0.12042	0.064997	1													
D2	-0.012496	-0.06634	0.052132	-0.08079	-0.907	1												
D3	0.016939	-0.24442	0.129048	-0.01959	-0.107	-0.262	1											
D4	0.103341	0.189027	0.045194	-0.06644	0.1669	-0.099	-0.182	1										
D5	-0.08893	0.073879	-0.11676	-0.00231	-0.107	0.118	-0.031	-0.641	1									
D6	-0.00774	-0.22917	0.104828	0.181912	-0.087	-0.059	0.3936	-0.521	-0.0251	1								
D7	0.134696	-0.09875	0.192186	-0.30686	-0.107	0.083	0.0098	0.0392	0.0098	-0.1905	1							
D8	-0.134696	0.098752	-0.19219	0.306856	0.107	-0.083	-0.01	-0.039	-0.0098	0.1905	-1	1						
Year in State	-0.174276	0.12232	0.088115	0.610012	-0.113	0.092	-0.05	0.0234	-0.0856	0.0744	-0.039	0.0391	1					
No. Veh	-0.176535	-0.04777	0.136736	0.330033	0.1512	-0.129	0.0028	0.0265	-0.0433	0.0584	-0.012	0.0118	0.285945	1				
Years Edu	-0.005358	0.247238	-0.13712	0.048782	0.2284	-0.206	-0.116	0.1549	0.0024	-0.287	-0.059	0.0593	0.055306	0.108400	1			
D10	-0.067598	0.070845	-0.02452	0.034299	-0.004	0.035	-0.001	0.2242	-0.0012	-0.2036	0.1382	-0.138	0.103962	0.189502	-0.1026	1		
D11	0.067597	-0.07084	0.024523	-0.0343	0.0043	-0.035	0.0012	-0.224	0.0012	0.2036	-0.138	0.1382	-0.10396	-0.189502	0.1026	-1	1	
Ins Stat	-0.002831	0.060221	0.127365	0.046721	-0.098	0.07	0.0482	0.0783	-0.1815	0.0392	-0.042	0.0425	0.166711	0.149672	-0.0169	0.1409	-0.141	1

Chapter 16
Analyzing and Forecasting Time-Series Data

Section 16-1 Exercises

16.1. Past measurement of the variable of interest measured at successive points in time is a good definition of time series data. Examples of time series data are the quarterly revenues of a publicly traded company, temperatures taken hourly, the daily patient population count of a local hospital, the number of houses sold every month. Any past measurement of the variable of interest taken at successive points in time is time series data.

16.3 Generally, quantitative forecasting techniques can be used whenever historical data related to the variable of interest exist, the historical data can be quantified and the past is prologue to the future. That is to say, we believe that the historical patterns will continue into the future. Whenever these conditions do not exist, for example, when a new product is introduced for which there is no historical data, then a qualitative technique, which relies on expert opinion, market surveys, or managerial judgment, must be used for forecasting the product's demand.

16.5. The trend component is one of four generally recognized components of time series data. These components are the trend, the seasonal, the cyclical, and the random. Not every time series exhibits all of these components, but every time series will exhibit at least one of these components.

   The trend is the long-term increase or decrease in a variable being measured over time. Trends can be classified as either linear or nonlinear, depending on whether their rate of change is relatively constant or not. A good way to identify whether or not a trend component is present in a time series is to use a time series plot.

16.7
- a. The forecasting horizon is the lead time: the number of periods between when the forecast is made and time period to which it applies. Here the forecast is made in March and is applicable in September. There are six time periods (months) between March and September. Therefore, the forecasting horizon is 6 months.
- b. The medium term forecast has a forecasting horizon of three months to two years. Since this forecasting horizon is six months, it would be considered to me a medium term forecast.
- c. The forecasting period is the unit of time for which forecasts are to be made. Here that unit of time is a month.
- d. The forecasting interval is the frequency with which new forecasts are prepared. Here a forecast is made each year (every 12 months). Therefore, the forecasting interval is 12months.

16.9.
- a. This part of the exercise is done using Equation 16-1 following the steps shown in Example 16-1. Radio advertising has a base value of 300 and newspaper advertising has a base value of 400.

Year	Radio advertising	Index	Newspaper Ad	Index
1	300	100.00	400	100
2	310	103.33	420	105
3	330	110.00	460	115
4	346	115.33	520	130
5	362	120.67	580	145
6	380	126.67	640	160
7	496	165.33	660	165

- b. The unweighted aggregate index is found using Equation 16-2 following the steps shown in Example 16-2.

Year	Radio advertising	Newspaper Ad	Sum	Index
1	300	400	700	100.00
2	310	420	730	104.29
3	330	460	790	112.86
4	346	520	866	123.71
5	362	580	942	134.57
6	380	640	1020	145.71
7	496	660	1156	165.14

c. The Laspreyres Index is found using Equation 16-4 following Example 16-4.

Year	Radio	% radio	Newspaper	Laspeyres
1	300	0.3	400	100
2	310	0.42	420	104.59
3	330	0.42	460	113.78
4	346	0.4	520	126.43
5	362	0.38	580	139.08
6	380	0.37	640	151.89
7	496	0.43	660	165.08

d. The Paasche Index is constructed using Equation 16-3 following Example 16-3.

Year	Radio	% radio	Newspaper	Paasche
1	300	0.3	400	100
2	310	0.42	420	104.41
3	330	0.42	460	113.22
4	346	0.4	520	124.77
5	362	0.38	580	136.33
6	380	0.37	640	148.12
7	496	0.43	660	165.12

16.11.

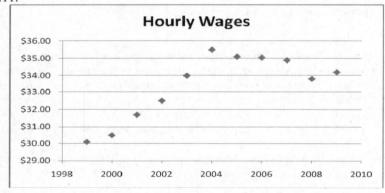

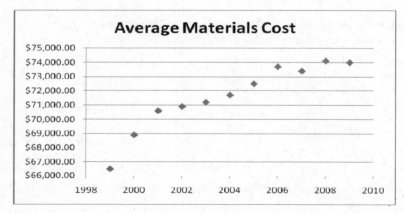

Both graphs show an upward trend with random components. The average material cost time series exhibits a cyclical component with a recurrence period of five years. The hourly wages time series may be indicating a cyclical component with a recurrence period of nine years. However, there is not enough data to determine if this pattern will repeat.

16.13 This exercise should be done using Equation 16-4 following the steps shown in Example 16-4. However, first we must convert hourly wages to reflect their impact on the cost of a town house. So, in 1999:

$$.6(\text{cost of a house}) = \$66500$$
$$\text{Cost of a townhouse} = \$110833$$
$$\text{Labor cost} = \$110833 - 66500 = \$44333$$

Year	Labor Costs	Material Costs	% Matarials	% Labor	Laspeyres Index
1999	44333	66500	60	40	100
2000	49893	68900	58	42	106.36
2001	57764	70600	55	45	113.59
2002	58009	70900	55	45	114.07
2003	55943	71200	56	44	112.95
2004	61078	71700	54	46	117.03
2005	67015	72500	52	48	122.09
2006	73700	73700	50	50	127.88
2007	67754	73400	52	48	123.44
2008	74100	74100	50	50	128.57
2009	83447	74000	47	53	134.95

16.15

a. The sum $\Sigma p_{1993} = 1.07 + 6.16 + 8.32 = 15.55$.

Year	Gas Price	Natural Gas	Electricity	Σp_t	I_t
1993	1.07	6.16	8.32	15.55	100.00
1994	1.08	6.41	8.38	15.87	102.06
1995	1.16	6.06	8.4	15.62	100.45
1996	1.27	6.34	8.36	15.97	102.70
1997	1.24	6.94	8.43	16.61	106.82
1998	1.07	6.82	8.26	16.15	103.86
1999	1.18	6.69	8.16	16.03	103.09
2000	1.52	7.76	8.24	17.52	112.67
2001	1.46	9.63	8.63	19.72	126.82
2002	1.39	7.89	8.46	17.74	114.08
2003	1.60	9.63	8.7	19.93	128.17
2004	1.90	10.75	8.97	21.62	139.04
2005	2.31	12.81	9.1	24.24	155.88
2006	2.63	13.71	8.9	25.24	162.32
2007	2.81	13.03	8.91	24.75	159.16
2008	3.26	13.67	9.64	26.57	170.87

b. The aggregate energy price index for 2008 is 170.87. This means that the actual percentage change in the aggregate energy prices for 2008 is 70.87% above that for 1993.

c. The aggregate energy price index for 1998 is 103.86. Therefore, to determine the actual percentage change in the aggregate energy prices, the calculation is

$$\frac{170.87 - 103.86}{103.86} 100 = 64.52\%.$$

16.17
a.   The Laspeyres Index (for instance) for the 1st Qtr of 2000 is calculated as

$$I_t = \frac{\sum q_o p_t}{\sum q_o p_o} = \frac{736784(0.994) + 5838(0.006)}{720122(0.994) + (4615)(0.006)}(100) = 102.31.$$ The other indexes are

			Total Sales	E-Commerce	% E-C	I$_t$
4th	quarter	2008	980135	37073	3.8	136.13
3rd	quarter	2008	1021320	31613	3.1	141.85
2nd	quarter	2008	1048726	32509	3.1	145.65
1st	quarter	2008	965500	32383	3.4	134.10
4th	quarter	2007	1072153	38992	3.6	148.91
3rd	quarter	2007	1015408	32504	3.2	141.03
2nd	quarter	2007	1009517	31602	3.1	140.21
1st	quarter	2007	996673	29758	3.0	138.42
4th	quarter	2006	977869	28311	2.9	135.81
3rd	quarter	2006	976919	26989	2.8	135.68
2nd	quarter	2006	971912	25824	2.7	134.98
1st	quarter	2006	950892	25218	2.6	132.06
4th	quarter	2005	922500	23569	2.5	128.12
3rd	quarter	2005	920884	22656	2.4	127.89
2nd	quarter	2005	901813	21410	2.3	125.24
1st	quarter	2005	882446	20118	2.2	122.55
4th	quarter	2004	872468	19146	2.1	121.17
3rd	quarter	2004	852892	18024	2.1	118.45
2nd	quarter	2004	838525	17091	2.0	116.45
1st	quarter	2004	831010	16407	1.9	115.41
4th	quarter	2003	814969	15372	1.9	113.18
3rd	quarter	2003	814198	14630	1.8	113.07
2nd	quarter	2003	791446	13679	1.7	109.91
1st	quarter	2003	787291	12772	1.6	109.33
4th	quarter	2002	779680	12317	1.6	108.28
3rd	quarter	2002	778522	11559	1.5	108.12
2nd	quarter	2002	768926	10835	1.4	106.78
1st	quarter	2002	763071	10094	1.3	105.97
4th	quarter	2001	776493	9419	1.2	107.83
3rd	quarter	2001	751150	8314	1.1	104.31
2nd	quarter	2001	757004	8394	1.1	105.12
1st	quarter	2001	748652	8254	1.1	103.96
4th	quarter	2000	745258	7876	1.0	103.49
3rd	quarter	2000	740730	7353	1.0	102.86
2nd	quarter	2000	734915	6495	0.9	102.06
1st	quarter	2000	736784	5838	0.8	102.31
4th	quarter	1999	720122	4615	0.6	100.00

b.   The Laspeyres Index for 1st Qtr of 2004 is 115.41 This means that the actual percentage change in the retail sales for the period of the 4th Qtr 1999 to the 1st Qtr of 2004 is 15.41%.

c.   The Laspeyres Index for 1st Qtr of 2004 is 115.41. Therefore, to determine the actual percentage change in the retail sales for the period of the 1st Qtr 2004 to the 1st Qtr of 2006 is, the calculation is

$$\frac{132.06 - 115.41}{115.41}100 = 14.43\%.$$

Section 16-2 Exercises

16.19 This exercise follows the procedure outlined in Figures 16-19 and 16-20.

Month	Sales	12-Period Moving Average	Centered Moving Average	Ratio to MA
1	23500			
2	21700			
3	18750			
4	22000			
5	23000			
6	26200	28337.500		
7	27300	28337.500	28337.500	0.963
8	29300	28479.167	28408.333	1.031
9	31200	28700.000	28589.583	1.091
10	34200	28883.333	28791.667	1.188
11	39500	29208.333	29045.833	1.360
12	43400	29500.000	29354.167	1.478
13	23500	29816.667	29658.333	0.792
14	23400	30075.000	29945.833	0.781
15	21400	30350.000	30212.500	0.708
16	24200	30475.000	30412.500	0.796
17	26900	30683.333	30579.167	0.880
18	29700	30616.667	30650.000	0.969
19	31100	31241.667	30929.167	1.006
20	32400	31825.000	31533.333	1.027
21	34500	32525.000	32175.000	1.072
22	35700	33216.667	32870.833	1.086
23	42000	33850.000	33533.333	1.252
24	42600	34191.667	34020.833	1.252
25	31000	34450.000	34320.833	0.903
26	30400	34808.333	34629.167	0.878
27	29800	35241.667	35025.000	0.851
28	32500	35800.000	35520.833	0.915
29	34500	35933.333	35866.667	0.962
30	33800	36333.333	36133.333	0.935
31	34200	36450.000	36391.667	0.940
32	36700	36883.333	36666.667	1.001
33	39700	37000.000	36941.667	1.075
34	42400	37175.000	37087.500	1.143
35	43600	37366.667	37270.833	1.170
36	47400	37525.000	37445.833	1.266
37	32400	37800.000	37662.500	0.860
38	35600	38075.000	37937.500	0.938
39	31200	38366.667	38220.833	0.816
40	34600	38725.000	38545.833	0.898
41	36800	39266.667	38995.833	0.944
42	35700	39658.333	39462.500	0.905
43	37500			
44	40000			
45	43200			
46	46700			
47	50100			
48	52100			

16.20. The ratio to moving averages are found using Equation 16-14, as done in Figure 16-21. While the values shown below have some variability for the same month from year to year, the pattern, and relative magnitude of the changes appears to be relatively stable.

Month	Sales	12-Period Moving Average	Centered Moving Average	Ratio to MA
1	23500			
2	21700			
3	18750			
4	22000			
5	23000			
6	26200	28337.500		
7	27300	28337.500	28337.500	0.963
8	29300	28479.167	28408.333	1.031
9	31200	28700.000	28589.583	1.091
10	34200	28883.333	28791.667	1.188
11	39500	29208.333	29045.833	1.360
12	43400	29500.000	29354.167	1.478
13	23500	29816.667	29658.333	0.792
14	23400	30075.000	29945.833	0.781
15	21400	30350.000	30212.500	0.708
16	24200	30475.000	30412.500	0.796
17	26900	30683.333	30579.167	0.880
18	29700	30616.667	30650.000	0.969
19	31100	31241.667	30929.167	1.006
20	32400	31825.000	31533.333	1.027
21	34500	32525.000	32175.000	1.072
22	35700	33216.667	32870.833	1.086
23	42000	33850.000	33533.333	1.252
24	42600	34191.667	34020.833	1.252
25	31000	34450.000	34320.833	0.903
26	30400	34808.333	34629.167	0.878
27	29800	35241.667	35025.000	0.851
28	32500	35800.000	35520.833	0.915
29	34500	35933.333	35866.667	0.962
30	33800	36333.333	36133.333	0.935
31	34200	36450.000	36391.667	0.940
32	36700	36883.333	36666.667	1.001
33	39700	37000.000	36941.667	1.075
34	42400	37175.000	37087.500	1.143
35	43600	37366.667	37270.833	1.170
36	47400	37525.000	37445.833	1.266
37	32400	37800.000	37662.500	0.860
38	35600	38075.000	37937.500	0.938
39	31200	38366.667	38220.833	0.816
40	34600	38725.000	38545.833	0.898
41	36800	39266.667	38995.833	0.944
42	35700	39658.333	39462.500	0.905
43	37500			
44	40000			
45	43200			
46	46700			
47	50100			
48	52100			

16.21 The individual ratio to moving average values are shown below, along with the normalized values.
The normalized index for January, .849, compared to July, .966, indicates that both months have sales below the average trend value for the year, but January's are lower than July's.

	Ratio to MA Values			Total	Seasonal Index	Normalized Index
January	0.792	0.903	0.860	2.556	0.852	0.849
February	0.781	0.878	0.938	2.598	0.866	0.863
March	0.708	0.851	0.816	2.375	0.792	0.789
April	0.796	0.915	0.898	2.608	0.869	0.866
May	0.880	0.962	0.944	2.785	0.928	0.925
June	0.969	0.935	0.905	2.809	0.936	0.933
July	0.963	1.006	0.940	2.909	0.970	0.966
August	1.031	1.027	1.001	3.060	1.020	1.016
September	1.091	1.072	1.075	3.238	1.079	1.075
October	1.188	1.086	1.143	3.417	1.139	1.135
November	1.360	1.252	1.170	3.782	1.261	1.256
December	1.478	1.252	1.266	3.996	1.332	1.327
				Sum =	12.045	

16.23 This exercise is completed using the procedures outlined in Figure 16-18 through 16-24.

a.

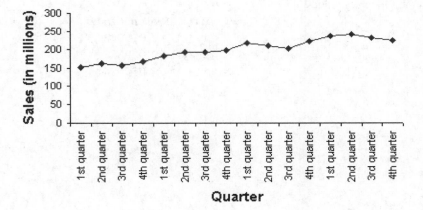

There appears to be an upward linear trend but you also see a seasonal component as a slight drop in the 3rd quarter.

b.

Year	Quarter	Period	Actual Sales	4 Period Moving Average	Centered Moving Average	Ratio to MA	Deseasonalized Sales
2006	1st quarter	1	152				146.858
	2nd quarter	2	162	159.5			158.684
	3rd quarter	3	157	167	163.250	0.962	163.553
	4th quarter	4	167	174.5	170.750	0.978	169.689
2007	1st quarter	5	182	183	178.750	1.018	175.843
	2nd quarter	6	192	190.5	186.750	1.028	188.070
	3rd quarter	7	191	199.25	194.875	0.980	198.972
	4th quarter	8	197	203.5	201.375	0.978	200.172
2008	1st quarter	9	217	206.25	204.875	1.059	209.659
	2nd quarter	10	209	212.25	209.250	0.999	204.722
	3rd quarter	11	202	217	214.625	0.941	210.431
	4th quarter	12	221	225.25	221.125	0.999	224.558
2009	1st quarter	13	236	232.5	228.875	1.031	228.016
	2nd quarter	14	242	233.25	232.875	1.039	237.046
	3rd quarter	15	231				240.642
	4th quarter	16	224				227.607

Because the seasonal index numbers do not add to 4, we normalize them by multiplying each by 4/4.00445 to get the following values:

Quarter	Seasonal Index
1	1.035013
2	1.020898
3	0.959934
4	0.984154

c.

SUMMARY OUTPUT					
Regression Statistics					
Multiple R	0.977				
R Square	0.954				
Adjusted R Square	0.951				
Standard Error	6.499				
Observations	16.000				
ANOVA					
	df	*SS*	*MS*	*F*	*Significance F*
Regression	1	12297.687	12297.687	291.180	9.14188E-11
Residual	14	591.276	42.234		
Total	15	12888.963			
	Coefficients	*Standard Error*	*t Stat*	*P-value*	
Intercept	147.913	3.408	43.402	2.5E-16	
Period	6.014	0.352	17.064	9.14E-11	

RESIDUAL OUTPUT					
Observation	*Predicted Deseasonalized Sales*	*Residuals*	*Squared Residuals*	Absolute Value	
1	153.927	-7.069	49.966	7.069	
2	159.941	-1.257	1.580	1.257	
3	165.955	-2.402	5.770	2.402	
4	171.969	-2.280	5.199	2.280	
5	177.983	-2.140	4.580	2.140	
6	183.997	4.072	16.585	4.072	
7	190.011	8.961	80.292	8.961	
8	196.026	4.146	17.192	4.146	
9	202.040	7.620	58.057	7.620	
10	208.054	-3.332	11.103	3.332	
11	214.068	-3.637	13.226	3.637	
12	220.082	4.476	20.037	4.476	
13	226.096	1.920	3.688	1.920	
14	232.110	4.936	24.363	4.936	
15	238.124	2.517	6.336	2.517	
16	244.139	-16.532	273.303	16.532	
			MSE	MAD	
			36.955	4.831	

Values of the MSE and MAD are best used to compare two or more forecasting models. For this model the MAD, for instance indicates the average forecasting error is less than five (million). For the final period of data this is about 2%, which might be considered acceptable.

d. and e.

Quarter	Period	Seasonally Unadjusted Forecast	Seasonal Index	Seasonally Adjusted Forecast
Quarter 1 2010	17	250.15	1.035	258.91
Quarter 2 2010	18	265.17	1.0209	261.52
Quarter 3 2010	19	262.18	0.9599	251.68
Quarter 4 2010	20	268.2	0.9842	263.95

16.25

a. As an example, the first moving averages is calculated as $\dfrac{2+12+23+20}{4} = 14.25$.

Minitab output:

t	Yt	MA
1	2	*
2	12	14.25
3	23	18.25
4	20	23.25
5	18	29.50
6	32	34.75
7	48	39.00
8	41	44.00
9	35	51.75
10	52	57.25
11	79	*
12	63	*

b. The centered moving average is the average of each adjacent pair of moving averages. As an example, the moving average for time period 2 = $\dfrac{14.25+18.25}{2} = 16.25$

Minitab output:

t	Yt	MA	Centered MA
1	2	*	*
2	12	14.25	*
3	23	18.25	16.250
4	20	23.25	20.750
5	18	29.50	26.375
6	32	34.75	32.125
7	48	39.00	36.875
8	41	44.00	41.500
9	35	51.75	47.875
10	52	57.25	54.500
11	79	*	*
12	63	*	*

c. To calculate the ratio-to-moving-averages, each time series value is divided by the corresponding centered moving average. As an example, the first ratio-to-moving-average is calculated as 23/16.25 = 1.41538. The ratio-to-moving-averages are

t	Yt	MA	Centered MA	Ratio
1	2	*	*	*
2	12	14.25	*	*
3	23	18.25	16.250	1.41538
4	20	23.25	20.750	0.96386
5	18	29.50	26.375	0.68246
6	32	34.75	32.125	0.99611
7	48	39.00	36.875	1.30169
8	41	44.00	41.500	0.98795
9	35	51.75	47.875	0.73107
10	52	57.25	54.500	0.95413
11	79	*	*	*
12	63	*	*	*

d. To calculate the seasonal indexes, the average of the ratio-to-moving-averages are calculated for each quarter. As an example, the seasonal index for the first quarter is calculated as $\frac{0.68246 + 0.73107}{2} =$ 0.70676; the second quarter = 0.97512; the third quarter = 1.35854; and the fourth quarter = 0.97590. The sum of the seasonal indexes = 4.01632. The indexes are adjusted by dividing each by the sum of the seasonal indexes and multiplying the result by 4 (for quarterly data). Thus, the first = [0.70676/4.01632]4 = 0.70389, the second 0.97116, the third 1.35302, and the fourth 0.97194.

e. We deseasonalize the data by dividing the actual data by the appropriate seasonal index. As example, the first observation is deseasonalized by 2/0.70389 = 2.84135.

    Minitab output:

t	Yt	Deseasonalized
1	2	2.8414
2	12	12.3564
3	23	16.9990
4	20	20.5774
5	18	25.5722
6	32	32.9503
7	48	35.4762
8	41	42.1837
9	35	49.7237
10	52	53.5442
11	79	58.3879
12	63	64.8188

f. The trend line is produced using Minitab
    Minitab output:

Regression Analysis: Deseasonalized versus t

```
The regression equation is
Deseasonalized = - 0.607 + 5.42 t

Predictor     Coef   SE Coef      T      P
Constant   -0.6067    0.8505  -0.71  0.492
t           5.4194    0.1156  46.90  0.000

S = 1.38186   R-Sq = 99.5%   R-Sq(adj) = 99.5%

Analysis of Variance

Source            DF      SS      MS        F      P
Regression         1  4199.9  4199.9  2199.40  0.000
Residual Error    10    19.1     1.9
Total             11  4219.0

Predicted Values for New Observations

New
Obs     Fit  SE Fit         95% CI              95% PI
  1  69.845   0.850  (67.950, 71.740)  (66.230, 73.461)
  2  75.265   0.954  (73.139, 77.390)  (71.523, 79.006)
  3  80.684   1.060  (78.322, 83.046)  (76.803, 84.565)X
  4  86.103   1.168  (83.501, 88.706)  (82.072, 90.135)X
```

The equation is $\hat{y}_t = -0.607 + 5.42t$

g. The unadjusted forecasts are produced, as an example, by $\hat{y}_{13} = -0.607 + 5.42(13) = 69.845$, $\hat{y}_{14} = 75.265$, $\hat{y}_{15} = 80.684$, and $\hat{y}_{16} = 86.103$. To provide the seasonalized adjusted forecasts, the unadjusted forecasts are multiplied by the appropriate seasonal index. So $\hat{y}_{13} = 0.70389(69.845) = 49.1632$, $\hat{y}_{14} = 0.97116(75.265) = 73.0944$, $\hat{y}_{15} = 1.35302(80.684) = 109.1671$, and $\hat{y}_{16} = 0.97194(86.103) = 83.6870$.

16.27

a. Minitab time series plot:

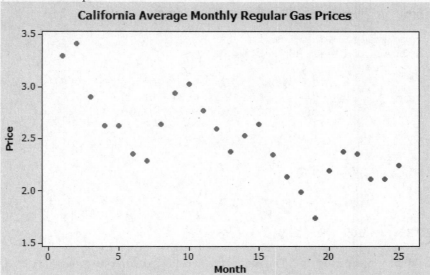

The time series exhibits a linear trend as it moves from left to right. A cyclical component is evidenced by the wave form which re-occurs approximately every 6 months. Finally, random components are evident throughout the time series indicated by the random deviations from a "smooth" wave form.

b. The random components make reading the scatter plot somewhat difficult. However, if the focus is on the valleys instead of the peaks, there appears to be two major valleys with randomness in between. Therefore, it appears that the recurrence period is 12 months.

The seasonal indexes generated by Minitab are

Seasonal Indices

Month	Index
1	1.02349
2	1.07969
3	1.16502
4	1.12147
5	0.98695
6	0.83324
7	0.86807
8	0.91287
9	0.97699
10	1.07311
11	1.01382
12	0.94529

c. The linear trend model fitted to the deseasonalized data is given by Minitab

```
Regression Analysis: Deseasonalized versus Month

The regression equation is
Deseasonalized = 1.98 + 0.0459 Month

Predictor      Coef     SE Coef      T        P
Constant     1.97604    0.07988    24.74    0.000
Month       0.045936   0.005591     8.22    0.000


S = 0.189593    R-Sq = 75.4%    R-Sq(adj) = 74.3%

Analysis of Variance

Source           DF       SS        MS       F        P
Regression        1    2.4266    2.4266   67.51    0.000
Residual Error   22    0.7908    0.0359
Total            23    3.2174
```

d. July 2006 would be time period 25. Therefore, the unadjusted forecast would be $F_{25} =$ 1.97621 + 0.0459(25) = 3.12. The adjusted forecast is F_{25} = (1.02349)(3.12) = 3.19. For July 2010, the time period is 25 + 4(12) = 73. The unadjusted forecast would be F_{73} = 1.97621 + 0.0458589(73) = 5.32. The adjusted forecast is F_{73} = (1.02349)(5.32) = 5.44.

16.29 This exercise is completed using the procedures outlined in Figures 16-18 through 16-24.

a.

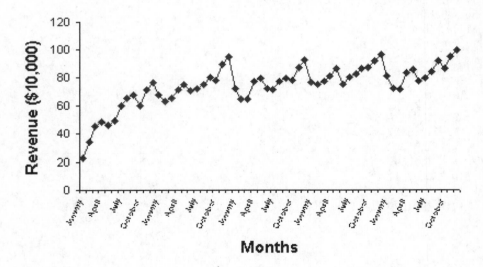

The graph indicates a seasonal component to the data.

b. Regression analysis can be used to find the linear model needed to make forecasts for periods 13 – 16.

SUMMARY OUTPUT

Regression Statistics	
Multiple R	0.59044058
R Square	0.34862008
Adjusted R Square	0.28348208
Standard Error	17.9108678
Observations	12

ANOVA

	df	SS	MS	F	Significance F
Regression	1	1716.924825	1716.925	5.352024	0.043253006
Residual	10	3207.991841	320.7992		
Total	11	4924.916667			

	Coefficients	Standard Error	t Stat	P-value
Intercept	211.893939	11.02337709	19.22223	3.16E-09
Period	3.46503497	1.497782006	2.313444	0.043253

	Period	Forecast	Actual	Forecast Error	Forecast Error Squared	Absolute Error
Qtr. 1	13	256.9393939	229	-27.93939394	780.6097337	27.93939394
Qtr. 2	14	260.4044289	221	-39.4044289	1552.709017	39.4044289
Qtr. 3	15	263.8694639	248	-15.86946387	251.8398835	15.86946387
Qtr. 4	16	267.3344988	231	-36.33449883	1320.195806	36.33449883

MSE	MAD
976.33861	29.88694639

Values of the MSE and MAD are best used to compare two or more forecasting models. For this model the MAD, for instance indicates the average forecasting error is about 30. This is better than 10% of data values. The firm might decide this level of average error is too high.

c.

Quarter		1	2	3	4
		1.0655	0.9124	1.0752	0.9593
		0.9990	0.9349	1.0894	0.9897
Total		2.0645	1.8473	2.1646	1.9490
Seasonal Index		1.0323	0.9236	1.0823	0.9745

Since the index values do not add to 4, we normalize them by multiplying each one by 4/4.0127.

Quarter	Index
1	1.0290
2	0.9207
3	1.0789
4	0.9714

d. Run the regression model based upon the deseasonalized sales

2009	Period	Forecast
Qtr. 1	13	256.5620033
Qtr. 2	14	260.0884382
Qtr. 3	15	263.614873
Qtr. 4	16	267.1413079

e.

Period	Forecast	Seasonal Index	Adjusted Forecast	Actual	Differences	Difference Squared	Absolute Differences
13	256.562	1.0290	264.0107	229	-35.0107	1225.7504	35.0107
14	260.0884	0.9207	239.4574	221	-18.4574	340.6745	18.4574
15	263.6149	1.0789	284.4074	248	-36.4074	1325.4997	36.4074
16	267.1413	0.9714	259.5053	231	-28.5053	812.5503	28.5053
						MSE	*MAD*
						926.1187	*29.5952*

f. The adjusted model has a lower MSE and MAD so I would recommend the deseasonalized data model.

16.31 This exercise combines the linear model components developed in the Taft Ice Cream example with the nonlinear elements in the Harrison Equipment example.

a.

Regression Statistics	
Multiple R	0.9319
R Square	0.8685
Adjusted R Square	0.8583
Standard Error	19.6357
Observations	15

ANOVA

	df	SS	MS	F	Significance F
Regression	1	33092.6286	33092.63	85.82961	4.33333E-07
Residual	13	5012.3048	385.5619		
Total	14	38104.9333			

	Coefficients	Standard Error	t Stat	P-value
Intercept	36.0952	10.6692	3.3831	0.0049
Month	10.8714	1.1735	9.2644	0.0000

Forecast for period 16 without transformation = 36.0952 + 10.8714(16) = 210.0376

Regression Statistics	
Multiple R	0.9856
R Square	0.9715
Adjusted R Square	0.9693
Standard Error	9.1432
Observations	15

ANOVA

	df	SS	MS	F	Significance F
Regression	1	37018.1611	37018.16	442.8123	1.99795E-11
Residual	13	1086.7722	83.59786		
Total	14	38104.9333			

	Coefficients	Standard Error	t Stat	P-value
Intercept	65.2986	3.6207	18.0348	0.0000
Month Sq	0.6988	0.0332	21.0431	0.0000

Forecast for period 16 with transformation $= 65.2986 + 0.6988(16)^2 = 244.1914$

Actual cash balance for Month 16 was 305. The transformed model had a smaller error than the model without the transformation. Based on this analysis and the analysis from problem 16-30 students should prefer the transformed model.

b. Model without transformation:

For Individual Response Y	
Interval Half Width	48.27804189
Prediction Interval Lower Limit	161.7600534
Prediction Interval Upper Limit	258.3161371

Model with transformation:

For Individual Response Y	
Interval Half Width	23.89550188
Prediction Interval Lower Limit	220.29634337
Prediction Interval Upper Limit	268.08734713

The model without the transformation has the wider interval so based on this you should select the model with the transformation.

16.33

a. Minitab scatter plot:

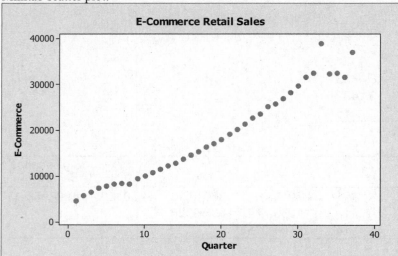

There appears to be a linear trend evidenced by the slope from small to large values. Randomness is exhibited since not all of the data points would lie on a straight line. Unusual points are seen for the 4th quarters of the last two years.

b. Minitab output:

Regression Analysis: E-Commerce versus Quarter

```
The regression equation is
E-Commerce = 1733 + 903 Quarter


Predictor     Coef   SE Coef       T       P
Constant    1733.1     638.9    2.71   0.010
Quarter     903.11     29.31   30.81   0.000


S = 1903.89    R-Sq = 96.4%    R-Sq(adj) = 96.3%


Analysis of Variance

Source          DF           SS          MS        F       P
Regression       1   3440258484  3440258484   949.09   0.000
Residual Error  35    126867819     3624795
Total           36   3567126303
```

To determine if a linear trend exists, we test that the slope is equal to zero: H_O: $\beta_1 = 0$, H_A: $\beta_1 \neq 0$; $\alpha = 0.10$, Minitab lists the p-value as 0.000. Therefore, reject the null hypothesis. There does exist enough evidence to indicate that there exists a linear trend in this data

c.   Minitab output:

```
Predicted Values for New Observations
New
Obs    Fit   SE Fit       95% CI            95% PI
  1  36051      639  (34754, 37348)   (31974, 40128)
  2  36955      665  (35605, 38304)   (32861, 41048)
  3  37858      691  (36456, 39260)   (33746, 41969)
  4  38761      717  (37305, 40216)   (34631, 42891)
```

The fitted values are $F_{38} = 36051$, $F_{39} = 36955$, $F_{40} = 37858$, and $F_{41} = 38761$

d.   The forecast bias is calculated as

$$\frac{\sum (y_t - F_t)}{n} = \frac{(35916 - 36051) + (36432 - 36955) + (35096 - 37858) + (36807 - 38761)}{4} = \frac{-5374}{4} = -1343.5.$$

This says that, on average, the model over forecasts the e-commerce retail sales an average of $1343.5 million.

Section 16-3 Exercises

16.35
  a.

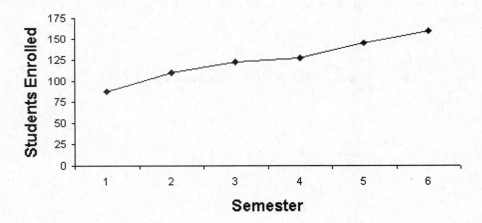

b.   Yes it does appear that trend is present.
c.   Equation 16-16 is used for this part of the exercise following Example 16-6.

Semester	Actual Enrollment	Forecast Enrollment	Forecast Error	Alsolute Forecast Error
1	87	90	-3.00	3.00
2	110	88.95	21.05	21.05
3	123	96.32	26.68	26.68
4	127	105.66	21.34	21.34
5	145	113.13	31.87	31.87
6	160	124.28	35.72	35.72
7		136.78		
			Sum	139.67

Alpha	0.35
MAD	23.278

d.   Equations 16-18, 19 and 20 are used here following Example 16-7.

Semester	Actual Enrollment	Constant	Trend	Forecast Enrollment	Forecast Error	Alsolute Forecast Error
Initial Values		*80*	*10*			
1	87	89.4	9.85	90	-3	3
2	110	101.4	10.39	99.25	10.75	10.75
3	123	114.03	10.95	111.79	11.21	11.21
4	127	125.38	11.05	124.98	2.02	2.02
5	145	138.15	11.48	136.43	8.57	8.57
6	160	151.7	12	149.62	10.38	10.38
7				163.69		
					Sum	45.93

Alpha	0.2
Beta	0.25
MAD	7.655

e.   The MAD for the single exponential smoothing forecast was 23.278
     The MAD for the double exponential smoothing forecast was 7.655
     The double exponential smoothing forecast appears to be doing the better job of forecasting course enrollment.

16.37

a.   Minitab scatter plot:

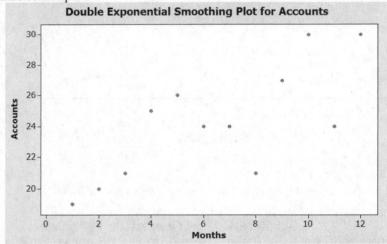

The time series contains a strong upward trend, so a double exponential smoothing model is selected.

b. Minitab output:

Regression Analysis: Accounts versus Months

```
The regression equation is
Accounts = 19.4 + 0.752 Months


Predictor    Coef  SE Coef     T      P
Constant   19.364    1.550  12.49  0.000
Months     0.7517   0.2106   3.57  0.005


S = 2.51867   R-Sq = 56.0%   R-Sq(adj) = 51.6%


Analysis of Variance

Source           DF      SS      MS      F      P
Regression        1  80.813  80.813  12.74  0.005
Residual Error   10  63.437   6.344
Total            11 144.250
```

The equation is $\hat{y}_t = 19.364 + 0.7517t$. Since $C_o = b_o$, $C_o = 19.364$. $T_o = b_1 = 0.7517$.

c. $F_1 = C_o + T_o = 19.3644 + 0.7517 = 20.1154$

$C_1 = \alpha y_1 + (1 - \alpha)(C_o + T_o) = 0.15(19) + (1 - 0.15)(20.1154) = 19.9481$

$T_1 = \beta(C_1 - C_o) + (1 - \beta)T_o = 0.25(19.9481 - 19.3644) + 0.75(0.7517) = 0.709921$

$F_2 = C_1 + T_1 = 19.9483 + 0.7098 = 20.6580$

Calculations proceed in a similar way to produce

Months	Accounts	Ct	Tt	Ft
1	19	19.9481	0.709921	20.1154
2	20	20.5593	0.685246	20.6580
3	21	21.2079	0.676076	21.2445
4	25	22.3513	0.792928	21.8839
5	26	23.5726	0.900018	23.1443
6	24	24.4018	0.882293	24.4727
7	24	25.0914	0.834142	25.2840
8	21	25.1867	0.649432	25.9256
9	27	26.0108	0.693076	25.8362
10	30	27.1983	0.816682	26.7038
11	24	27.4127	0.666122	28.0149
12	30	28.3670	0.738166	28.0788

The forecast is given by Minitab:

```
Forecasts


Period  Forecast    Lower    Upper
13       29.1052  23.9872  34.2231
```

d. MAD as calculated by Minitab:

```
Accuracy Measures


MAPE  8.58150
MAD   2.08901
MSD   6.48044
```

16.39

a.

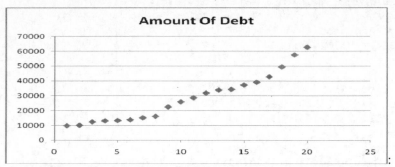

The time series contains a strong upward trend, so a double exponential smoothing model is selected.

The equation is $\hat{y}_t = 990 + 2622.8t$. Since $C_o = b_o$, $C_o = 990$. $T_o = b_1 = 2622.8$.

b. $F_1 = C_o + T_o = 990 + 2622.8 = 3612.8$

$C_1 = \alpha y_1 + (1 - \alpha)(C_o + T_o) = 0.20(9914) + (1 - 0.20)(3612.8) = 4872.7$

$T_1 = \beta(C_1 - C_o) + (1 - \beta)T_o = 0.30(4872.7 - 990) + 0.70(2622.8) = 3000.93$

$F_2 = C_1 + T_1 = 4872.7 + 3000.93 = 7873.6$

Calculations proceed in a similar way to produce

Year	FedLoans	C_t	T_t	F_t
1	9914	4872.7	3000.93	3612.4
2	10182	8335.3	3139.43	7873.6
3	12493	11678.4	3200.53	11474.7
4	13195	14542.1	3099.49	14878.9
5	13414	16796.1	2845.84	17641.6
6	13890	18491.5	2500.72	19641.9
7	15232	19840.2	2155.11	20992.3
8	16221	20840.5	1808.65	21995.3
9	22557	22630.7	1803.12	22649.1
10	26011	24749.2	1897.75	24433.8
11	28737	27065.0	2023.15	26647.0
12	31906	29651.7	2192.22	29088.1
13	33930	32261.2	2317.39	31843.9
14	34376	34538.0	2305.23	34578.5
15	37228	36920.2	2328.32	36843.3
16	39101	39219.0	2319.47	39248.5
17	42761	41783.0	2392.82	41538.5
18	49360	45212.6	2703.87	44175.8
19	57463	49825.8	3276.66	47916.5
20	62614	55004.8	3847.35	53102.5

c. The forecast is given by Minitab:

```
Forecasts

Period  Forecast    Lower    Upper
21       58852.1  50560.4  67143.9
```

d. MAD as calculated by Minitab:

```
Accuracy Measures

MAPE        16
MAD       3384
MSD   19786728
```

16.41

a. Minitab time series plot:

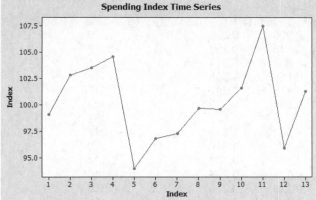

There does not appear to be any trend component in this time series.

b. The forecast is calculated as an example $F_1 = F_2 = 99.1$. Then $F_3 = 0.25y_2 + (1 - 0.25)F_2 = 0.25(102.8) + 0.75(99.1) = 100.025$. The forecasts are given in this Minitab output:

Time	Index	Smooth	Predict	Error
1	99.1	99.100	99.100	0.00000
2	102.8	100.025	99.100	3.70000
3	103.5	100.894	100.025	3.47500
4	104.6	101.820	100.894	3.70625
5	94.0	99.865	101.820	-7.82031
6	96.8	99.099	99.865	-3.06523
7	97.3	98.649	99.099	-1.79893
8	99.7	98.912	98.649	1.05081
9	99.6	99.084	98.912	0.68810
10	101.6	99.713	99.084	2.51608
11	107.5	101.660	99.713	7.78706
12	95.9	100.220	101.660	-5.75971
13	101.3	100.490	100.220	1.08022

c. $\text{MAD} = \dfrac{\sum \left| y_t - F_t \right|}{n} = \dfrac{42.4476}{13} = 3.2652$

d. $F_{14} = 0.25y_{13} + (1 - 0.25)F_{13} = 0.25(101.3) + 0.75(100.22) = 100.49$

16.43

a. Minitab time series plot:

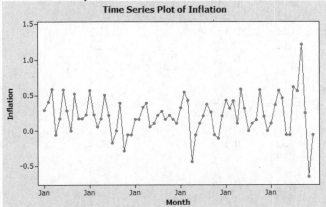

The time series does not exhibit a trend, so a single exponential smoothing model is selected.
There does not appear to be any trend component in this time series.

b. The forecast is calculated as an example $F_1 = F_2 = 0.296$. Then $F_3 = 0.15y_2 + (1 - 0.15)F_2 = 0.15(0.413) + 0.85(0.296) = 0.3136$. The forecasts are given in this Minitab output:

Year	Month	Inflation (%)	Forecast	Absolute Value (Actual - Forecast)
2000	1	0.296	0.296	0.000
2000	2	0.413	0.296	0.117
2000	3	0.588	0.314	0.274
2000	4	-0.058	0.355	0.413
2000	5	0.176	0.293	0.117
2000	6	0.584	0.275	0.309
2000	7	0.290	0.322	0.032
2000	8	0.000	0.317	0.317
2000	9	0.521	0.269	0.252
2000	10	0.173	0.307	0.134
2000	11	0.173	0.287	0.114
2000	12	0.230	0.270	0.040
2001	1	0.573	0.264	0.309
2001	2	0.228	0.310	0.082
2001	3	0.057	0.298	0.241
2001	4	0.170	0.262	0.092
2001	5	0.510	0.248	0.262
2001	6	0.226	0.287	0.061
2001	7	-0.169	0.278	0.447
2001	8	0.000	0.211	0.211
2001	9	0.395	0.179	0.216
2001	10	-0.281	0.212	0.493
2001	11	-0.056	0.138	0.194
2001	12	-0.056	0.109	0.165
2002	1	0.169	0.084	0.085
2002	2	0.169	0.097	0.072
2002	3	0.337	0.108	0.229
2002	4	0.392	0.142	0.250
2002	5	0.056	0.180	0.124
2002	6	0.111	0.161	0.050
2002	7	0.223	0.153	0.070
2002	8	0.278	0.164	0.114
2002	9	0.166	0.181	0.015
2002	10	0.221	0.179	0.042
2002	11	0.166	0.185	0.019
2002	12	0.110	0.182	0.072
2003	1	0.330	0.171	0.159
2003	2	0.549	0.195	0.354
2003	3	0.436	0.248	0.188
2003	4	-0.435	0.276	0.711
2003	5	-0.055	0.170	0.225
2003	6	0.109	0.136	0.027
2003	7	0.218	0.132	0.086
2003	8	0.381	0.145	0.236
2003	9	0.271	0.180	0.091
2003	10	-0.054	0.194	0.248
2003	11	-0.108	0.157	0.265
2003	12	0.217	0.117	0.100
2004	1	0.432	0.132	0.300
2004	2	0.323	0.177	0.146
2004	3	0.429	0.199	0.230
2004	4	0.107	0.233	0.126
2004	5	0.587	0.214	0.373

(table continued on next page)

Year	Month	Inflation (%)	Forecast	Absolute Value (Actual - Forecast)
2004	6	0.318	0.270	0.048
2004	7	0.000	0.277	0.277
2004	8	0.106	0.236	0.130
2004	9	0.158	0.216	0.058
2004	10	0.580	0.208	0.372
2004	11	0.210	0.263	0.053
2004	12	0.000	0.255	0.255
2005	1	0.105	0.217	0.112
2005	2	0.366	0.200	0.166
2005	3	0.573	0.225	0.348
2005	4	0.466	0.277	0.189
2005	5	-0.052	0.306	0.358
2005	6	-0.052	0.252	0.304
2005	7	0.619	0.206	0.413
2005	8	0.564	0.268	0.296
2005	9	1.223	0.313	0.910
2005	10	0.252	0.449	0.197
2005	11	-0.653	0.420	1.073
2005	12	-0.051	0.259	0.310
			0.212	Sum = 15.765

c.   MAD = 15.765/71 = 0.222

d. $F_{73} = 0.15y_{72} + (1 - 0.15)F_{72} = 0.15(-0.051) + 0.85(0.259) = 0.212$

16.45

a.   The time-series plot of the data indicates an upward trend over time. A forecasting model that can explicitly incorporate this trend effect is needed. The double exponential smoothing model will incorporate the trend effect.

b.   Use Equations 16-18, 19 and 20 and follow Example 16-7.

Month	Actual Shirts Sold	Constant	Trend	Forecast Shirts Sold	Absolute Forecast Error	MAD
Initial Values		28848.00	2488.96			
1	37630	32595.57	2866.54	31336.96	6293.04	6293.04
2	34780	35325.69	2825.62	35462.11	682.11	3487.58
3	35150	37551.04	2645.54	38151.30	3001.30	3325.48
4	45990	41355.26	2993.14	40196.58	5793.42	3942.47
5	36130	42704.73	2500.04	44348.41	8218.41	4797.66
6	47090	45581.81	2613.15	45204.76	1885.24	4312.25
7	37220	45999.97	1954.65	48194.96	10974.96	5264.07
8	49180	48199.70	2028.18	47954.63	1225.37	4759.23
9	40010	48184.30	1415.10	50227.88	10217.88	5365.75
10	50720	49823.53	1482.34	49599.41	1120.59	4941.23
11	63560	53756.69	2217.59	51305.87	12254.13	5606.04
12	48470	54473.42	1767.33	55974.28	7504.28	5764.23
13	64350	57862.60	2253.89	56240.76	8109.24	5944.61
14	69590	62011.19	2822.30	60116.49	9473.51	6196.68
15	69000	65666.79	3072.29	64833.49	4166.51	6061.33
16	71196	69230.46	3219.70	68739.08	2456.92	5836.06
17				72450.17		
Alpha	0.2					
Beta	0.3					

SUMMARY OUTPUT

Regression Statistics	
Multiple R	0.88774671
R Square	0.78809422
Adjusted R Square	0.77295809
Standard Error	6360.26152
Observations	16

Initial constant = 28848.
Initial trend = 2488.96

ANOVA

	df	SS	MS	F	Significance F
Regression	1	2.106E+09	2106266471	52.0670974	4.4544E-06
Residual	14	566340973	40452926.6		
Total	15	2.673E+09			

	Coefficients	Standard Error	t Stat	P-value	Lower 95%
Intercept	28848.00	3335.3493	8.64916912	5.4595E-07	21694.3809
X Variable 1	2488.96	344.93361	7.21575342	4.4544E-06	1749.146207

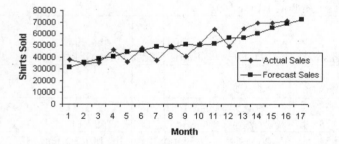

Actual vs. Forecast Sales

The MAD produced by the double exponential smoothing model at the end of month 16 is smaller than the MAD produced by the single exponential smoothing model. This is due to the fact that the double exponential smoothing model explicitly incorporates the trend effect that is present in the time series, thus, producing a more accurate forecast.

c.

Beta Values 5136.51	Alpha Values 0.05	0.1	0.15	0.2	0.25	0.3	0.35	0.4
0.05	5136.51	5259.61	5338.25	5410.42	5538.97	5664.36	5779.94	5893.95
0.1	5161.78	5314.37	5413.38	5490.21	5636.92	5756.44	5863.68	5969.74
0.15	5190.25	5373.74	5489.53	5587.58	5728.26	5835.69	5929.96	6055.09
0.2	5221.54	5435.98	5563.39	5680.04	5807.55	5897.36	5975.45	6140.21
0.25	5258.63	5499.53	5632.25	5763.76	5871.37	5939.32	6053.73	6213.94
0.3	5304.15	5563.03	5693.97	5836.06	5917.96	5961.39	6121.89	6284.81
0.35	5351.00	5631.84	5746.89	5895.15	5946.77	6024.47	6178.71	6394.69
0.4	5398.88	5697.43	5817.68	5940.06	5958.25	6080.76	6226.07	6497.20
0.45	5447.51	5758.44	5883.23	5970.43	5971.96	6126.74	6325.85	6591.03
0.5	5496.65	5814.14	5939.24	5986.43	6023.34	6162.71	6417.80	6675.50
0.55	5546.03	5866.59	5985.16	5988.63	6065.82	6218.98	6501.02	6750.50
0.6	5595.43	5913.91	6020.70	5977.92	6099.54	6305.10	6575.09	6816.40
0.65	5644.63	5954.43	6045.79	5985.32	6124.84	6383.23	6639.99	6873.95
0.7	5693.43	5987.86	6060.56	6024.76	6144.13	6452.95	6696.06	6924.16
0.75	5741.63	6013.98	6065.31	6057.17	6223.13	6514.11	6743.92	6968.24
0.8	5789.07	6032.66	6060.45	6082.70	6295.19	6566.84	6784.40	7007.50
0.85	5835.56	6066.82	6046.53	6101.58	6359.94	6611.48	6818.49	7043.24
0.9	5880.96	6098.20	6024.14	6114.14	6417.20	6648.56	6847.27	7076.77
0.95	5925.12	6127.30	6004.03	6126.16	6466.98	6678.76	6871.87	7109.26

d. and e. Student reports will vary but could include comments such as: The data table shows the MAD values for different combinations of alpha and beta values. Of the combinations considered the minimum MAD at the end of month 16 occurs when alpha = 0.05 and beta = 0.05. The forecast for month 17 with alpha = 0.05 and beta = 0.05 is 71,128.45.

Chapter Exercises

16.47
a. Since the recurrence period is less than one year, a seasonal component exists in the time series.
b. The pattern is linear with a positive slope. This indicates that a linear trend component exists.
c. Since the recurrence period is more than one year, a cyclical component exists in the time series.
d. The time series is exhibiting changes in time with no other components. Therefore, the time series is exhibiting a random component.
e. The steady decrease indicates a linear trend component. The "wave-like" shape with recurrence period of 10 years indicates that a cyclical component also exists.

16.49. A seasonal component is one that is repeated throughout a time series and has a recurrence period of at most one year. A cyclical component is one that is represented by wavelike fluctuations that has a recurrence period of more than one year. Seasonal components are more predictable.

16.51.

a.   This problem should be solved using the steps outlined in the Taft Ice Cream example of section 16-2.

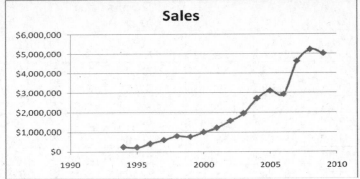

There does appear to be an upward linear trend

b.

SUMMARY OUTPUT						
Regression Statistics						
Multiple R	0.9479					
R Square	0.8985					
Adjusted R Square	0.8913					
Standard Error	567012.9456					
Observations	16					
ANOVA						
	df	*SS*	*MS*	*F*	*Significance F*	
Regression	1	3.98574E+13	3.99E+13	123.9719	2.43055E-08	
Residual	14	4.50105E+12	3.22E+11			
Total	15	4.43585E+13				
	Coefficients	*Standard Error*	*t Stat*	*P-value*	*Lower 95%*	*Upper 95%*
Intercept	-682238010.3021	61455226.5311	-11.1014	2.52E-08	-814046479.3	-5.5E+08
Year	342385.2941	30750.5945	11.1343	2.43E-08	276431.7698	408338.8

It is expected that as time increases by one year the sales are expected to increase by $342,385.2941. There is a fairly strong relationship since the correlation coefficient is 0.9479. Since 123.9719 > 4.6001 you would conclude that there is a significant relationship.

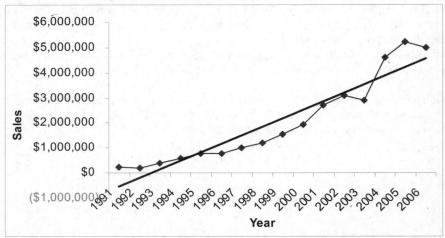

c.

Observation	Predicted Sales	Residuals	Absolute Residual
1	(548,889.7059)	788,889.7059	788,889.7059
2	(206,504.4118)	424,504.4118	424,504.4118
3	135,880.8823	269,119.1177	269,119.1177
4	478,266.1764	108,733.8236	108,733.8236
5	820,651.4706	(25,651.4706)	25,651.4706
6	1,163,036.7647	(401,036.7647)	401,036.7647
7	1,505,422.0588	(507,422.0588)	507,422.0588
8	1,847,807.3529	(630,807.3529)	630,807.3529
9	2,190,192.6471	(620,192.6471)	620,192.6471
10	2,532,577.9412	(585,577.9412)	585,577.9412
11	2,874,963.2353	(163,963.2353)	163,963.2353
12	3,217,348.5294	(113,348.5294)	113,348.5294
13	3,559,733.8236	(641,733.8236)	641,733.8236
14	3,902,119.1177	703,880.8823	703,880.8823
15	4,244,504.4118	971,495.5882	971,495.5882
16	4,586,889.7059	423,110.2941	423,110.2941
		MAD =	461,216.7279

d.

Year	Forecast
2010	4,929,275.00
2011	5,271,660.29
2012	5,614,045.59
2013	5,956,430.88
2014	6,298,816.18

e.

For Individual Response Y

Interval Half Width	1232095.322
Prediction Interval Lower Limit	5066720.854
Prediction Interval Upper Limit	7530911.499

16.53. Use Equations 16-18, 19, 20 and follow the steps outlined in Example 15-7.

    a.   The starting values (-891,270.00) and (342,385.29) for this model are determined using simple linear regression with the time defined as 1, 2, . . . 16.

0.2
0.4
$ (891,275.00)
$ 342,385.29

Period	Year	Sales	Constant	Trend	Forecast	Error	Absolute Error
1	1994	$240,000.00	$(391,111.76)	$405,496.47	$(548,889.71)	$788,889.71	$788,889.71
2	1995	$218,000.00	$55,107.76	$421,785.69	$14,384.71	$203,615.29	$203,615.29
3	1996	$405,000.00	$462,514.77	$416,034.22	$476,893.46	$(71,893.46)	$71,893.46
4	1997	$587,000.00	$820,239.19	$392,710.30	$878,548.98	$(291,548.98)	$291,548.98
5	1998	$795,000.00	$1,129,359.59	$359,274.34	$1,212,949.49	$(417,949.49)	$417,949.49
6	1999	$762,000.00	$1,343,307.14	$301,143.63	$1,488,633.93	$(726,633.93)	$726,633.93
7	2000	$998,000.00	$1,515,160.61	$249,427.56	$1,644,450.77	$(646,450.77)	$646,450.77
8	2001	$1,217,000.00	$1,655,070.54	$205,620.51	$1,764,588.18	$(547,588.18)	$547,588.18
9	2002	$1,570,000.00	$1,802,552.84	$182,365.23	$1,860,691.05	$(290,691.05)	$290,691.05
10	2003	$1,947,000.00	$1,977,334.45	$179,331.78	$1,984,918.07	$(37,918.07)	$37,918.07
11	2004	$2,711,000.00	$2,267,532.99	$223,678.48	$2,156,666.23	$554,333.77	$554,333.77
12	2005	$3,104,000.00	$2,613,769.17	$272,701.56	$2,491,211.47	$612,788.53	$612,788.53
13	2006	$2,918,000.00	$2,892,776.59	$275,223.90	$2,886,470.74	$31,529.26	$31,529.26
14	2007	$4,606,000.00	$3,455,600.40	$390,263.87	$3,168,000.50	$1,437,999.50	$1,437,999.50
15	2008	$5,216,000.00	$4,119,891.41	$499,874.72	$3,845,864.26	$1,370,135.74	$1,370,135.74
16	2009	$5,010,000.00	$4,697,812.91	$531,093.43	$4,619,766.13	$390,233.87	$390,233.87
17	20010				$5,228,906.34		
						MAD	$526,262.47

    b.

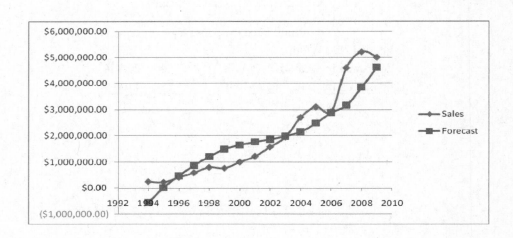

c.

$ 526,262.47		Beta Values		
		0.5	0.4	0.3	0.2

<table>
<tr><td rowspan="5">Alpha Values</td></tr>
<tr><td>0.1</td><td>$568,793.54</td><td>$547,728.21</td><td>$523,915.68</td><td>$498,375.36</td></tr>
<tr><td>0.2</td><td>$538,592.87</td><td>$526,262.47</td><td>$515,577.21</td><td>$497,639.06</td></tr>
<tr><td>0.3</td><td>$481,539.18</td><td>$466,164.76</td><td>$459,595.63</td><td>$452,681.23</td></tr>
<tr><td>0.4</td><td>$454,803.56</td><td>$449,962.38</td><td>$436,850.70</td><td>$421,877.56</td></tr>
</table>

Different combinations of alpha and beta, including the initial values of 0.2 and 0.4, were evaluated using Excel's data table feature. Note that the combination of alpha = 0.4 and Beta = 0.2 produced the smallest MAD of the alpha/beta combinations evaluated.

16.54.

Methods	MAD
Regression	$461,216.73
Single Exponential	$806,724.10
Double Exponential	$421,877.56

Based upon the MAD I would use the Double Exponential method.

16.55

a. Excel scatter plot:

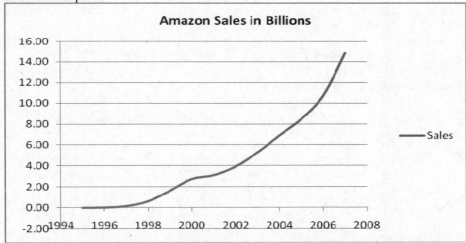

The time series contains a strong upward trend, so a double exponential smoothing model is selected.

b.
SUMMARY OUTPUT

Regression Statistics	
Multiple R	0.9420889
R Square	0.8875315
Adjusted R Square	0.8773071
Standard Error	1.6168892
Observations	13

ANOVA

	df	SS	MS	F	Significance F
Regression	1	226.9373378	226.9373	86.80514	1.49216E-06
Residual	11	28.75763669	2.614331		
Total	12	255.6949745			

	Coefficients	Standard Error	t Stat	P-value	Lower 95%	Upper 95%
Intercept	-2229.921	239.8238705	-9.29816	1.52E-06	-2757.769914	-1702.07
Year	1.1166505	0.1198518	9.316928	1.49E-06	0.852858517	1.380443

Since $C_o = b_o$, $C_o = -2229.9$ $T_o = b_1 = 1.12$.

c. $F_1 = C_o + T_o = -2229.9 + 1.12 = -2228.78$

$C_1 = \alpha y_1 + (1 - \alpha)(C_o + T_o) = 0.10(0.0) + (1 - 0.10)(-2228.78) = -2005.9$

$T_1 = \beta(C_1 - C_o) + (1 - \beta)T_o = 0.20(-2005.9 - (-2229.9)) + 0.80(1.12) = 45.696$

$F_2 = C_1 + T_1 = -2005.9 + 45.696 = -1960.2$

Calculations proceed in a similar way to produce

Year	Sales	C_t	T_t	Forecast	Absolute Deviation
0		-2229.9	1.12		
1	0.00	-2005.9	45.696	-2228.78	222.878
2	0.02	-1764.18	84.900	-1960.21	196.022
3	0.15	-1511.34	118.489	-1679.28	167.943
4	0.61	-1253.51	146.358	-1392.85	139.346
5	1.64	-996.269	168.534	-1107.15	110.879
6	2.76	-744.686	185.144	-827.736	83.050
7	3.12	-503.276	196.397	-559.542	56.267
8	3.93	-275.798	202.613	-306.879	31.081
9	5.26	-65.340	204.182	-73.184	7.845
10	6.92	125.650	201.544	138.843	13.192
11	8.49	295.324	195.170	327.194	31.870
12	10.71	442.515	185.574	490.493	47.978
13	14.84	566.764	173.309	628.089	61.325
14				740.073	MAD = 89.975

d.   MAD shown in part c.

16.57

a.

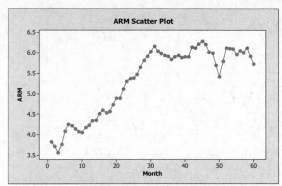

A cyclical component is evidenced by the wave form which recurs approximately every 10 months. There is an increasing linear trend component for the first 30 months. Finally, random components are evident throughout the time series indicated by the random deviations from a "smooth" wave form.

b. If recurrence period, as explained in part a., is 10 months
The seasonal indexes generated by Minitab are

```
Period    Index
     1  0.98230
     2  1.01378
     3  1.00906
     4  1.00979
     5  0.99772
     6  1.01583
     7  0.99739
     8  1.00241
     9  0.98600
    10  0.98572
```

c. The nonlinear trend model (using t and t^2) fitted to the deseasonalized.

```
Regression Analysis: ARM versus Month, MonthSq
The regression equation is
ARM = 3.28 + 0.114 Month - 0.00117 MonthSq
Predictor        Coef     SE Coef        T       P
Constant      3.28256     0.09086    36.13   0.000
Month        0.113789    0.006873    16.56   0.000
MonthSq    -0.0011668   0.0001092   -10.68   0.000
S = 0.226824    R-Sq = 92.9%    R-Sq(adj) = 92.7%


Analysis of Variance
Source          DF       SS       MS        F       P
Regression       2   38.556   19.278   374.70   0.000
Residual Error  57    2.933    0.051
Total           59   41.488
```

d. January 2009 would be time period 61. Therefore, the unadjusted forecast would be $F_{61} = 3.28 + 0.114(61) - .00117(61)^2 = 5.8804$. Since January 2009 has index 1 associated with it, the adjusted forecast is $F_{61} = (0.9823)(5.8804) = 5.7763$.

e. The following values have been computed:
   $R^2 = 92.9\%$, F-statistic = 374.70, and standard error = 0.226824
The model explains a significant amount of variation in the ARM.
Next we test for autocorrelation by calculating the Durbin-Watson d statistic:
Minitab output:

```
Durbin-Watson statistic = 0.378224
```

The null and alternative hypotheses for testing for positive autocorrelation are H: $\rho = 0$ and H_A: $\rho > 0$. The Durbin-Watson table for $\alpha = 0.05$, with k = 1 has value $d_L = 1.35$ and $d_u = 1.49$. Because d = 0.378224 < $d_L = 1.35$, we reject the null hypothesis and conclude that significant positive autocorrelation exists in the regression model. This indicates that the wrong model has been chosen.

16.59

a. Use Equation 16-16 or 16-17 and follow the steps shown in Example 16-6.

Alpha	0.3
Initial Forecast	22,525

	Month Number	Calls Received	Forecast Calls	Error	Absolute Error
Jan	1	23,500	22,525.0	975.0	975.0
	2	21,700	22,817.5	-1,117.5	1,117.5
	3	18,750	22,482.3	-3,732.3	3,732.3
	4	22,000	21,362.6	637.4	637.4
	5	23,000	21,553.8	1,446.2	1,446.2
	6	26,200	21,987.7	4,212.3	4,212.3
	7	27,300	23,251.4	4,048.6	4,048.6
	8	29,300	24,466.0	4,834.0	4,834.0
	9	31,200	25,916.2	5,283.8	5,283.8
	10	34,200	27,501.3	6,698.7	6,698.7
	11	39,500	29,510.9	9,989.1	9,989.1
	12	43,400	32,507.6	10,892.4	10,892.4
Jan	13	23,500	35,775.4	-12,275.4	12,275.4
	14	23,400	32,092.7	-8,692.7	8,692.7
	15	21,400	29,484.9	-8,084.9	8,084.9
	16	24,200	27,059.4	-2,859.4	2,859.4
	17	26,900	26,201.6	698.4	698.4
	18	29,700	26,411.1	3,288.9	3,288.9
	19	31,100	27,397.8	3,702.2	3,702.2
	20	32,400	28,508.5	3,891.5	3,891.5
	21	34,500	29,675.9	4,824.1	4,824.1
	22	35,700	31,123.1	4,576.9	4,576.9
	23	42,000	32,496.2	9,503.8	9,503.8
	24	42,600	35,347.3	7,252.7	7,252.7
Jan	25	31,000	37,523.1	-6,523.1	6,523.1
	26	30,400	35,566.2	-5,166.2	5,166.2
	27	29,800	34,016.3	-4,216.3	4,216.3
	28	32,500	32,751.4	-251.4	251.4
	29	34,500	32,676.0	1,824.0	1,824.0
	30	33,800	33,223.2	576.8	576.8
	31	34,200	33,396.2	803.8	803.8
	32	36,700	33,637.4	3,062.6	3,062.6
	33	39,700	34,556.2	5,143.8	5,143.8
	34	42,400	36,099.3	6,300.7	6,300.7
	35	43,600	37,989.5	5,610.5	5,610.5
	36	47,400	39,672.7	7,727.3	7,727.3
Jan	37	32,400	41,990.9	-9,590.9	9,590.9
	38	35,600	39,113.6	-3,513.6	3,513.6
	39	31,200	38,059.5	-6,859.5	6,859.5
	40	34,600	36,001.7	-1,401.7	1,401.7
	41	36,800	35,581.2	1,218.8	1,218.8
	42	35,700	35,946.8	-246.8	246.8
	43	37,500	35,872.8	1,627.2	1,627.2
	44	40,000	36,360.9	3,639.1	3,639.1
	45	43,200	37,452.7	5,747.3	5,747.3
	46	46,700	39,176.9	7,523.1	7,523.1
	47	50,100	41,433.8	8,666.2	8,666.2
	48	52,100	44,033.7	8,066.3	8,066.3
	49		46,453.6		

MAD	4,767.2

b.

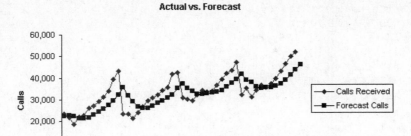

c.

Alpha	MAD
0.1	5270.7
0.2	4960.6
0.3	4767.2
0.4	4503.3
0.5	4212.4

Of the alpha values considered, alpha = 0.5 provides the lowest MAD. This is due to the fact that the time series exhibits an upper trend (also seasonality). The larger alpha value responds more quickly to the increasing value of the series over time. However, the forecasting procedure is incapable of explicitly incorporating the trend and because of this the forecast will always lag the trend. Also, the procedure is incapable of incorporating the seasonal effect.

d. The single exponential smoothing model is designed to be used with a fairly stable time series. Since both the trend and seasonality components are ignored by the single exponential smoothing model, we would expect the MAD to be quite high indicating a poor fit of the forecasted values to the actual values.

16.61

a. Minitab time series plot

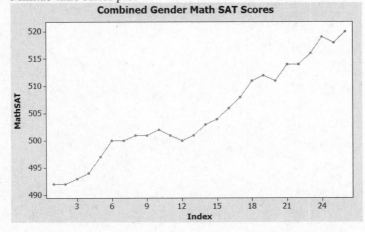

b.   Minitab output:

Regression Analysis: MathSAT versus Years

```
The regression equation is
MathSAT = 490 + 1.09 Years


Predictor      Coef  SE Coef        T       P
Constant    490.249    0.728   673.64   0.000
Years       1.09265  0.04712    23.19   0.000


S = 1.80215   R-Sq = 95.7%   R-Sq(adj) = 95.5%


Analysis of Variance

Source          DF      SS      MS       F       P
Regression       1  1746.1  1746.1  537.62   0.000
Residual Error  24    77.9     3.2
Total           25  1824.0
```

Using 1980 = year 1, the estimated regression equation is $\hat{y}_t = 490.249 + 1.09265t$ and the coefficient

of determination is $R^2 = 95.7\%$. H_O: $\beta_1 \le 0$, H_A: $\beta_1 > 0$; $\alpha = 0.10$, the test statistic is t $= \dfrac{b_1 - \beta_1}{S_{b_1}} = 23.19$

the degrees of freedom $= n - 2 = 26 - 2 = 24$ and the critical value is $t_{0.10} = 1.3178$, (6) The t test statistic of 23.19 is larger than the upper t-critical value of 1.3178. Therefore, reject the null hypothesis. There is sufficient evidence to indicate that the average SAT Math scores of students continue to increase during this period.

c.   The year 2010 is represented by the time value $= 31$. Therefore, the forecast is

$$\hat{y}_t = 490.249 + 1.09265(31) = 524.1212.$$

d.   Time series forecasts are based on the assumption that the structure that has occurred in the past will continue to occur in the future. Since the SAT math examination was changed in March 2005, it is quite dubious that the historical structure will repeat itself in the future. Making a forecast, as in part c., is an example of the regression concept of extrapolation.

Chapter 17
Introduction to Nonparametric Statistics

Section 17-1 Exercises

17.1 The hypotheses are: H_O: $\tilde{\mu} \geq 14$

$\quad\quad\quad\quad\quad\quad\quad\quad\quad$ H_A: $\tilde{\mu} < 14$

W is found as follows:

Values	Difference	Absolute Difference	Rank	R+	R-
10.21	0.21	0.21	1	1	
13.65	3.65	3.65	9	9	
12.30	2.30	2.30	6	6	
9.51	-0.49	0.49	2		2
11.32	1.32	1.32	3	3	
12.77	2.77	2.77	8	8	
6.16	-3.84	3.84	10		10
8.55	-1.45	1.45	4		4
11.78	1.78	1.78	5	5	
12.32	2.32	2.32	7	7	
				W = 39	

Since this is an lower tail test, and n = 11, letting $\alpha = .05$, we reject if W < 13. Therefore, there is

17.3 The hypotheses are: H_O: $\tilde{\mu} = 4$

$\quad\quad\quad\quad\quad\quad\quad\quad\quad$ H_A: $\tilde{\mu} \neq 4$

W is found as follows:

Values	Difference	Absolute Difference	Rank	R+	R-
3.1	-0.9	0.9	3		3
4.8	0.8	0.8	2	2	
2.3	-1.7	1.7	7		7
5.6	1.6	1.6	6	6	
2.8	-1.2	1.2	5		5
2.9	-1.1	1.1	4		4
4.4	0.4	0.4	1	1	
				W = 9	W = 19

From appendix P we see the critical values for n = 7, assuming $\alpha = .1$ are 3 and 25. For this problem we cannot reject the null hypothesis.

17.5

a. The hypotheses are: H_O: $\widetilde{\mu} \le 4$

H_A: $\widetilde{\mu} > 4$

b. Using the Wilcoxon Signed Rank test we find W as follows:

Seconds	Minutes	Differences	Absolute Differences	Rank	R+	R-
194	3.23	-0.77	0.77	8		8
278	4.63	0.63	0.63	7	7	
302	5.03	1.03	1.03	10	10	
140	2.33	-1.67	1.67	11		11
245	4.08	0.08	0.08	1	1	
234	3.90	-0.10	0.10	2		2
268	4.47	0.47	0.47	5	5	
208	3.47	-0.53	0.53	6		6
102	1.70	-2.30	2.30	12		12
190	3.17	-0.83	0.83	9		9
220	3.67	-0.33	0.33	4		4
255	4.25	0.25	0.25	3	3	
					W = 26	

Since this is an upper tail test and n = 12, letting α = .05, sum the positive ranks and reject if W > 61. Therefore, there is not enough evidence to reject the null hypothesis and the manager can conclude the median time does not exceed 4 minutes.

17.7 By agreeing the mean weight is 11 ounces, but also claiming that more than 50% of the candy bars contain less than 11 ounces, the consumer group is stating the distribution is skewed to the right and the median is less than 11 ounces. Putting the claim in the alternative hypothesis we are testing:

H_O: $\widetilde{\mu} \ge 11$

H_A: $\widetilde{\mu} < 11$

Using the Wilcoxon Signed Rank test we find W as follows:

Ounces	Difference	Absolute Differences	Rank	R+	R-
10.9	-0.1	0.1	1.5		1.5
11.7	0.7	0.7	15	15	
10.5	-0.5	0.5	12		12
11.8	0.8	0.8	17	17	
10.2	-0.8	0.8	17		17
11.5	0.5	0.5	12	12	
10.8	-0.2	0.2	4.5		4.5
11.2	0.2	0.2	4.5	4.5	
11.8	0.8	0.8	17	17	
10.7	-0.3	0.3	8		8
10.6	-0.4	0.4	10		10
10.9	-0.1	0.1	1.5		1.5
11.6	0.6	0.6	14	14	
11.2	0.2	0.2	4.5	4.5	
11	0	0			
10.7	-0.3	0.3	8		8
10.8	-0.2	0.2	4.5		4.5
10.5	-0.5	0.5	12		12
11.3	0.3	0.3	8	8	
10.1	-0.9	0.9	19		19
				W = 92	

Since one of the differences equaled 0, we only rank 19 values. This is a lower tail test with n = 19 and α = .05. We reject if W < 53. Therefore, there is not enough evidence to support the consumer group's claim.

17.9 Since we are interested in differences both above and below 30, this should be a two tailed test. The appropriate hypotheses are:

$$H_O: \quad \widetilde{\mu} = 30$$

$$H_A: \quad \widetilde{\mu} \neq 30$$

Using the Wilcoxon Signed Rank test we find W as follows:

Ounces	Difference	Absolute Differences	Rank	R+	R-
25	-5	5	10.5		10.5
24	-6	6	14.5		14.5
21	-9	9	17		17
35	5	5	10.5	10.5	
25	-5	5	10.5		10.5
25	-5	5	10.5		10.5
35	5	5	10.5	10.5	
38	8	8	16	16	
32	2	2	4	4	
36	6	6	14.5	14.5	
35	5	5	10.5	10.5	
29	-1	1	1.5		1.5
30	0	0			
27	-3	3	6.5		6.5
28	-2	2	4		4
27	-3	3	6.5		6.5
31	1	1	1.5	1.5	
32	2	2	4	4	
30	0	0			
30	0	0			
				W = 71.5	W = 81.5

Because some of the differences are 0, n = 17. From Appendix P, the upper and lower values for the Wilcoxon test are 34 and 119 for $\alpha = .05$. We do not reject the hypothesis.

17.11

a. The chi-square table will vary depending on how students construct the data classes, but using data classes one standard deviation wide, with the data mean of 7.6306 and a standard deviation of .2218, we find the following table and chi-square value.

e	o	$(o-e)^2/e$
14.9440	21	2.45417
32.4278	31	0.06287
32.4278	27	0.90851
14.9440	16	0.07462 sum = 3.5002

Testing at the $\alpha = .05$ level, $\chi_\alpha^2 = 5.9915$. Since the calculated $\chi^2 = 3.5002$ we do not reject the hypothesis the data come from a normal distribution.

b. Since we concluded the data come from a normal distribution we test the following:

$$H_O: \quad \mu \geq 7.4$$

$$H_A: \quad \mu < 7.4$$

Decision Rule: If z < -1.645, reject H_0, otherwise do not reject.

$$z = \frac{7.6306 - 7.4}{\frac{.2218}{\sqrt{95}}} = 10.13$$

Therefore, we do not reject the null hypothesis and conclude the average pH level is at least 7.4.

Section 17-2 Exercises

17.13 This exercise can be done following the steps shown in the Blaine County Highway District Example.
   a. Putting the claim in the alternate hypothesis:

$$H_0: \ \widetilde{\mu}_1 - \widetilde{\mu}_2 \geq 0$$

$$H_A: \ \widetilde{\mu}_1 - \widetilde{\mu}_2 < 0$$

   b. Test using the Mann-Whitney U Test
   Using Equations 17-2 and 17-3 to find U_1 and U_2.

Sample 1	Rank (Sample 1)	Sample 2	Rank (Sample 2)
12	7	9	3
21	16	18	13
15	10	16	11
10	4	17	12
11	5	20	15
14	9	7	1
12	7	12	7
8	2	19	14
	Sum of Ranks = 60		Sum of Ranks = 76

$$U_1 = n_1 n_2 + \frac{n_1(n_1 + 1)}{2} - \sum R_1 = 8(8) + \frac{8(8 + 1)}{2} - 60 = 40$$

$$U_2 = n_1 n_2 + \frac{n_2(n_2 + 1)}{2} - \sum R_2 = 8(8) + \frac{8(8 + 1)}{2} - 76 = 24$$

Since the alternate hypothesis indicates population 2 has the higher median, we use U_2 as the test statistic. Using Table L for $n_1 = 8$ and $n_2 = 8$ and $U = 24$, we find a p-value = .221. Since this is greater than α we do not reject the null hypothesis.

17.15 This exercise can be done following the steps shown in the Blaine County Highway District Example.
   a. Putting the claim in the alternate hypothesis:

$$H_0: \ \widetilde{\mu}_1 - \widetilde{\mu}_2 \leq 0$$

$$H_A: \ \widetilde{\mu}_1 - \widetilde{\mu}_2 > 0$$

   b. Constructing the table of ranks we find:

Sample 1	Rank (Sample 1)	Sample 2	Rank (Sample 2)
4.4	15.5	3.7	11
2.7	5	3.5	9.5
1	1	4	12
3.5	9.5	4.9	17
2.8	6.5	3.1	8
2.6	4	4.2	13
2.4	3	5.2	18
2	2	4.4	15.5
2.8	6.5	4.3	14
	Sum of Ranks = 53		Sum of Ranks = 118

Since the alternate hypothesis indicates population 1 should have the larger median we use U_1.

$$U_1 = n_1 n_2 + \frac{n_1(n_1 + 1)}{2} - \sum R_1 = 12(12) + \frac{12(12 + 1)}{2} - 182 = 40$$

Using Appendix M for $n_1 = 12$ and $n_2 = 12$ we find the decision rule:

Reject if $U \leq 31$

Since $U = 40$, we do not reject the null hypothesis.

17.17 The hypotheses to test are:

$$H_0: \ \widetilde{\mu}_1 - \widetilde{\mu}_2 = 0$$

$$H_A: \ \widetilde{\mu}_1 - \widetilde{\mu}_2 \neq 0$$

This problem can be solved using Minitab.
Mann-Whitney Test and CI: C1, C2
C1   N = 40   Median =   481.50
C2   N = 35   Median =   505.00
Point estimate for ETA1-ETA2 is   -25.00
95.1 Percent CI for ETA1-ETA2 is (-62.00,9.00)
W = 1384.0
Test of ETA1 = ETA2 vs ETA1 not = ETA2 is significant at 0.1502
The test is significant at 0.1501 (adjusted for ties)
Cannot reject at alpha = 0.05

17.19 This exercise can be done following the steps shown in Example 17-2.
  a.   The hypotheses to test are:

$$H_0: \ \widetilde{\mu}_1 - \widetilde{\mu}_2 = 0$$

$$H_A: \ \widetilde{\mu}_1 - \widetilde{\mu}_2 \neq 0$$

Using Appendix N, with n = 8, the decision rule is:
Reject if T ≤ 4

Item	Sample 1	Sample 2	d	Rank of d	Rank with smallest sum
1	3.4	2.8	0.6	3	
2	2.5	3	-0.5	-1.5	1.5
3	7	5.5	1.5	7	
4	5.9	6.7	-0.8	-4	4
5	4	3.5	0.5	1.5	
6	5	5	0		
7	6.2	7.5	-1.3	-6	6
8	5.3	4.2	1.1	5	
					T = 11.5

The following table is found:
  Since T = 11.5, we do not reject the null hypothesis.
  b.   Assuming a normal distribution and equal variances, since the mean and median are equal, we can use the paired sample t test.

t-Test: Paired Two Sample for Means		
	Sample 1	Sample 2
Mean	4.9125	4.775
Variance	2.298393	2.959286
Observations	8	8
Pearson Correlation	0.830005	
Hypothesized Mean Difference	0	
df	7	
t Stat	0.403628	
P(T<=t) one-tail	0.349266	
t Critical one-tail	1.894578	
P(T<=t) two-tail	0.698531	
t Critical two-tail	2.364623	

17.21 This exercise can be done following the steps shown in Example 17-2.

The hypotheses to test are:

$$H_0: \ \widetilde{\mu}_1 - \widetilde{\mu}_2 = 0$$

$$H_A: \ \widetilde{\mu}_1 - \widetilde{\mu}_2 \neq 0$$

Using Appendix N, with n = 7, the decision rule is:

Reject if $T \leq 2$

The following table is found:

Sample 1	Sample 2	d	Rank of d	Rank with smallest sum
1004	1045	-41	-2	2
1245	1145	100	4.5	
1360	1400	-40	-1	1
1150	1000	150	6	
1300	1350	-50	-3	3
1450	1350	100	4.5	
900	1140	-240	-7	7
				T = 13

Since T = 13, we do not reject the null hypothesis.

17.23 This exercise can be done following the steps shown in Example 17-2.

$$H_0: \ \widetilde{\mu}_2 = \widetilde{\mu}_1$$

$$H_A: \ \widetilde{\mu}_2 \neq \widetilde{\mu}_1$$

Sample 1	Sample 2	d	Rank	Ranks with smallest sum
234	245	-11	-5	
221	224	-3	-2	
196	194	2	1	1
245	267	-22	-6	
234	230	4	3	3
204	198	6	4	4
				T = 8

If $T \leq 0$ reject H_0, otherwise do not reject H_o

Since 8 > 0 do not reject H_0 and conclude that the medians are the same.

17.25 $H_0: \ \widetilde{\mu}_W - \widetilde{\mu}_{WO} \leq 0$

$H_A: \ \widetilde{\mu}_W - \widetilde{\mu}_{WO} > 0$

U1 = (7)(5) + (7)(7+1)/2 − 42 = 21

U2 = (7)(5) + (5)(5+1)/2 − 36 = 14

Utest = 21

Since 21 is not in the table you cannot determine the exact p-value but you know that the p-value will be greater than 0.562 which means you would not reject the null hypothesis and would conclude that the median score with the course is not larger than the median score without the course.

17.27 This problem can be worked like Example 17-2

   a.   a. H$_0$: $\tilde{\mu}_1 \leq \tilde{\mu}_2$

        H$_A$: $\tilde{\mu}_1 > \tilde{\mu}_2$

   b.

Assessed	Market	Difference	ABS Diff	Ranks	Ranks With Smallest Expected Sum
$302,000.00	$198,000.00	$104,000.00	104000	14	
$176,000.00	$182,400.00	($6,400.00)	6400	12	12
$149,000.00	$154,300.00	($5,300.00)	5300	9	9
					Eliminated Difference =
$198,500.00	$198,500.00	$0.00	0	1	0
$214,000.00	$218,000.00	($4,000.00)	4000	7	7
$235,000.00	$230,000.00	$5,000.00	5000	8	
$305,000.00	$298,900.00	$6,100.00	6100	11	
$187,500.00	$190,000.00	($2,500.00)	2500	6	6
$150,000.00	$149,800.00	$200.00	200	1	
$223,000.00	$222,000.00	$1,000.00	1000	2	
$178,500.00	$180,000.00	($1,500.00)	1500	3	3
$245,000.00	$250,900.00	($5,900.00)	5900	10	10
$167,000.00	$165,200.00	$1,800.00	1800	5	
$219,000.00	$220,700.00	($1,700.00)	1700	4	4
$334,000.00	$320,000.00	$14,000.00	14000	13	

                                                                                            T = 51

Since T = 51 is greater than 16, do not reject Ho and conclude that assessed values are not greater than market values.

   c.   Housing values are typically skewed with a few very expensive houses skewing the distribution to the right.

17.29   H$_0$: $\tilde{\mu}_1 = \tilde{\mu}_2$

       H$_A$: $\tilde{\mu}_1 \neq \tilde{\mu}_2$

       $\mu = 40(40+1)/4 = 410$

       $\sigma = \sqrt{40(40+1)(80+1)/24} = 74.3976$

       $z = (480 - 410)/74.3976 = 0.94$

       p-value $= (0.5 - 0.3264)2 = (0.1736)(2) = 0.3472$. Therefore do not reject H$_o$ and conclude that the median weight gains are not different

17.31 This exercise can be done following the steps shown in Example 17-2.
  a. Want to use a paired-t test
      H_0: $\mu_d \geq 0$
      H_A: $\mu_d < 0$

Old Material	New Material	d
45.5	47.0	-1.5
50.0	51.0	-1.0
43.0	42.0	1.0
45.5	46.0	-0.5
58.5	58.0	0.5
49.0	50.5	-1.5
29.5	39.0	-9.5
52.0	53.0	-1.0
48.0	48.0	0.0
57.5	61.0	-3.5
	Average	-1.7
	Std. Dev.	3.011091

$$t = (-1.7)/(3.011091/\sqrt{10}) = -1.785$$

Since $-1.785 > $ t critical $= -2.2622$ do not reject H_0 and conclude that the soles made from the new material do not have a longer mean lifetime than those made from the old material.

  b. H_0: $\widetilde{\mu}_O \geq \widetilde{\mu}_N$

      H_A: $\widetilde{\mu}_O < \widetilde{\mu}_N$

Old Material	New Material	d	Rank d	Ranks with smallest expected sum
45.5	47.0	-1.5	-6.5	
50.0	51.0	-1.0	-4	
43.0	42.0	1.0	4	4.0
45.5	46.0	-0.5	-1.5	
58.5	58.0	0.5	1.5	1.5
49.0	50.5	-1.5	-6.5	
29.5	39.0	-9.5	-9	
52.0	53.0	-1.0	-4	
57.5	61.0	-3.5	-8	
			T=	5.5

One observation was removed because the difference was 0. Using $\alpha = 0.025$ the decision rule becomes:
        If T $\leq$ 6 reject H_o, otherwise do not reject H_o
Since $5.5 < 6$ reject H_o and conclude that the medians are not the same.
  c. Because you cannot assume the underlying populations are normal you must use the technique from part b.

17.33 This exercise can be done following the steps shown in the Future Vision Example.
  a. H_0: $\tilde{\mu}_N \geq \tilde{\mu}_C$

   H_A: $\tilde{\mu}_N < \tilde{\mu}_C$

$$U1 = (140)(75) + (140)(140+1)/2 - 16073 = 4,297$$
$$U2 = (140)(75) + (75)(75+1)/2 - 7147 = 6,203$$
$$\mu = 140(75)/2 = 5,250$$
$$\sigma = \sqrt{140(75)(140+75+1)/12} = 434.7413$$
$$z = (4297-5250)/434.7413 = -2.19$$
$$\text{p-value} = 0.5 - 0.4857 = 0.0143$$

Since $0.0143 < 0.10$ reject H_0 and conclude that California drivers do have a higher median driving speed than Nevada drivers.
  b. A type I error is rejecting a true null hypothesis. Since we rejected that Nevada drivers drive at least as fast as California drivers we could be concluding that California drivers drive faster when in fact they do not.

17.35 This exercise can be done following the steps shown in Example 17-2.
  a. Since the typists are rating the software systems, the data are ordinal
  b. (1) No, because the data is not at least interval; (2) the median would be the best measure
  c. H_0: $\tilde{\mu}_1 = \tilde{\mu}_2$

   H_A: $\tilde{\mu}_1 \neq \tilde{\mu}_2$

Typist	System 1	System 2	d	Rank of d	Ranks with smallest sum
1	82	75	7	4.5	
2	76	80	-4	-2.5	2.5
3	90	70	20	8	
4	55	58	-3	-1	1
5	49	53	-4	-2.5	2.5
6	82	75	7	4.5	
7	90	80	10	6.5	
9	70	80	-10	-6.5	6.5
				T=	12.5

One observation was removed because the difference was 0. Using $\alpha = .01$, the decision rule is:
   If $T \leq 2$ reject H_0, otherwise do not reject H_0
Since $12.5 > 2$ do not reject H_0 and conclude that the medians are the same for both types of word processing systems
  d. Since there is no significant difference in the measures of central tendency the decision could be made based on some other factor, such a cost..

Section 17-3 Exercises

17.37 This exercise can be done following the steps shown in Example 17-3.

a. H_0: $\widetilde{\mu}_1 = \widetilde{\mu}_2 = \widetilde{\mu}_3$

H_A: Not all population medians are equal

b. The following is the table of ranks:

Group 1		Group 2		Group 3	
10	7	8	2.5	13	16
9	4.5	6	1	12	12.5
11	9.5	8	2.5	12	12.5
12	12.5	9	4.2	11	9.5
13	16	10	7	13	16
12	12.5	10	7	15	17
	Sum = 62		Sum = 24.5		Sum = 83.5

Since many of the ranks are tied, we have to find the H statistic adjusted for ties.

$$H = \frac{\frac{12}{N(N+1)}\sum_{i=1}^{k}\frac{R_i^2}{n_i} - 3(N+1)}{1 - \frac{\sum_{i=1}^{g}(t_i^3 - t_i)}{N^3 - N}} = 10.98$$

Since, with $\alpha = .05$, $\chi_\alpha^2 = 5.9915$, and H $= 10.98$, we reject the null hypothesis of equal medians and conclude at least one of the medians is different.

17.39

a. H_0: $\widetilde{\mu}_1 = \widetilde{\mu}_2 = \widetilde{\mu}_3 = \widetilde{\mu}_4$

H_A: Not all population medians are equal

b. Using Equation 17-10.

$$H = \frac{12}{N(N+1)}\sum_{i=1}^{k}\frac{R_i^2}{n_i} - 3(N+1) =$$

$$\frac{12}{80(80+1)}\left(\frac{409600}{20} + \frac{608400}{20} + \frac{211600}{20} + \frac{1849600}{20}\right) - 3(81) = 42.11$$

Selecting $\alpha = .05$, $\chi_\alpha^2 = 7.8147$, since H $= 42.11$, we reject the null hypothesis of equal medians.

17.41

a. Salaries in general are usually thought to be skewed with more higher end salaries than lower end salaries and this is especially true in sports salaries. Because of this it is better to use the median as a measure of the center rather than the mean.

b. The top salaried players get extremely high salaries compared to the other players.

c. H_0: $\widetilde{\mu}_1 = \widetilde{\mu}_2 = \widetilde{\mu}_3$

H_A: Not all population medians are equal

H = [12/(20+30+40)(20+30+40+1)][(1655^2/20) + (1100^2/30) + (1340^2/40)] − 3(20+30+40+1) = 52.531

If $\alpha = .05$, $\chi_\alpha^2 = 5.9915$

Since 52.531 > 5.9915 reject H_o and conclude that not all population medians are equal

17.43   This exercise can be done following the steps shown in Example 17-3.

H_0: $\widetilde{\mu}_1 = \widetilde{\mu}_2 = \widetilde{\mu}_3 = \widetilde{\mu}_4$

H_A: Not all population medians are equal

Using PHStat:

Level of Significance	0.01
Group 1	
Sum of Ranks	26
Sample Size	4
Group 2	
Sum of Ranks	58
Sample Size	4
Group 3	
Sum of Ranks	37
Sample Size	4
Group 4	
Sum of Ranks	15
Sample Size	4
Sum of Squared Ranks/Sample Size	1408.5
Sum of Sample Sizes	16
Number of groups	4
H Test Statistic	11.13971
Critical Value	11.34488
p-Value	0.010994

Do not reject the null hypothesis

Adjusting for ties, the test statistic is 11.21 which is smaller than the critical value (11.34488). Therefore the null hypothesis is not rejected.

17.45 H_0: $\widetilde{\mu}_1 = \widetilde{\mu}_2 = \widetilde{\mu}_3$

H_A: Not all population medians are equal

Constructing a table like that shown in Table 17-5, find the following values.

Rank Car 1	Rank Car 2	Rank Car 3
85.5	25.5	120

$H = [12/(21)(21+1)][(85.5^2/8) + (25.5^2/6) + (120^2/7)] - 3(21+1) = 13.9818$

Testing at $\alpha = .05$, $\chi_\alpha^2 = 5.9915$

Since $13.9818 > 5.9915$ reject H_0 and conclude that not all population medians are equal

Chapter Exercises

17.47 Student answers will vary depending upon the organization selected.

17.49 Student answers will vary depending upon the journal articles selected.

17.51
a. and b.

Possible Sets	Sum of Ranks	Probability
none	-	1/16
1	1	1/16
2	2	1/16
3	3	1/16
4	4	1/16
1,2	3	1/16
1,3	4	1/16
1,4	5	1/16
2,3	5	1/16
2,4	6	1/16
3,4	7	1/16
1,2,3	6	1/16
1,2,4	7	1/16
1,3,4	8	1/16
2,3,4	9	1/16
1,2,3,4	10	1/16

c.

T	0	1	2	3	4	5	6	7	8	9	10
P(T)	1/16	1/16	1/16	2/16	2/16	2/16	2/16	2/16	1/16	1/16	1/16

17.53 H_0: $\widetilde{\mu}_1 - \widetilde{\mu}_2 = 0$

H_A: $\widetilde{\mu}_1 - \widetilde{\mu}_2 \neq 0$

Plan 1	Rank 1	Plan 2	Rank 2
1711	7	2100	14
1915	11	2210	17
1905	10	1950	13
2153	16	3004	22
1504	3	2725	21
1195	1	2619	20
2103	15	2483	18
1601	6	2520	19
1580	4	1904	9
1475	2	1875	8
1588	5	1943	12
	80		173

U1 = (11)(11) + (11)(11+1)/2 − 80 = 107
U2 = (11)(11) + (11)(11+1)/2 − 173 = 14
Choosing the smallest value: Utest = 14
With α = .05, U_α = 30
Since 14 < 30 reject H_0 and conclude that the medians are different. Plan 2 appears to produce higher sales

17.55
  a. This data is ordinal data and you cannot assume a normal distribution so should use a nonparametric test.

  b. H$_0$: $\widetilde{\mu}_O - \widetilde{\mu}_N \geq 0$

      H$_A$: $\widetilde{\mu}_O - \widetilde{\mu}_N < 0$

Original	Rank 1	New	Rank 2
76	15	55	7
34	4	90	18
70	11	72	12
23	3	17	2
45	5	56	8
80	16	69	10
10	1	91	19
46	6	95	20
67	9	86	17
75	14	74	13
	84		126

U1 = (10)(10) + (10)(10+1)/2 – 84 = 71
U2 = (10)(10) + (10)(10+1)/2 – 126 = 29
Utest = 29
If α = .05, U$_\alpha$ = 27
Since 29 > 27 do not reject H$_0$ and conclude that the medians are not different.

17.57 The hypotheses being tested are:

  H$_0$: $\widetilde{\mu}$ = 1989.32

  H$_A$: $\widetilde{\mu}$ ≠ 1989.32

Using the Wilcoxon Signed Rank test we find W as follows:

This is a two tailed test with n = 18. With α = .05, using Appendix P, we reject if W ≤ 40 or W > 131. Looking at the two values in the table we see there is not enough evidence to conclude the median has changed from $1989.32.

Balance	Difference	Absolute Differences	Rank	R+	R-
1827.85	-161.47	161.47	15		15
1992.75	3.43	3.43	1	1	
2012.35	23.03	23.03	7	7	
1955.64	-33.68	33.68	9		9
2023.19	33.87	33.87	10	10	
1998.52	9.2	9.2	3	3	
2003.75	14.43	14.43	6	6	
1752.55	-236.77	236.77	17		17
1865.32	-124	124	13		13
2013.13	23.81	23.81	8	8	
2225.35	236.03	236.03	16	16	
2100.35	111.03	111.03	12	12	
2002.02	12.7	12.7	5	5	
1850.37	-138.95	138.95	14		14
1995.35	6.03	6.03	2	2	
2001.18	11.86	11.86	4	4	
2252.54	263.22	263.22	18	18	
2035.75	46.43	46.43	11	11	
				W = 103	W = 68

17.59

a. The hypotheses being tested are:

H_0: $\widetilde{\mu} = 8.03$

H_A: $\widetilde{\mu} \neq 8.03$

b. Using the Wilcoxon Signed Rank test we find W as follows:

Fill	Difference	Absolute Differences	Rank	R+	R-
7.95	-0.08	0.08	14.5		14.5
8.02	-0.01	0.01	2.5		2.5
8.07	0.04	0.04	10.5	10.5	
8.06	0.03	0.03	8.5	8.5	
8.05	0.02	0.02	6	6	
8.04	0.01	0.01	2.5	2.5	
7.97	-0.06	0.06	13		13
8.01	-0.02	0.02	6		6
8.04	0.01	0.01	2.5	2.5	
8.05	0.02	0.02	6	6	
8.08	0.05	0.05	12	12	
8.11	0.08	0.08	14.5	14.5	
7.99	-0.04	0.04	10.5		10.5
8	-0.03	0.03	8.5		8.5
8.02	-0.01	0.01	2.5		2.5
				W = 62.5	W = 57.5

This is a two tailed test with n = 15. Since the significance level is not given, students will have to make a choice. If α = .05, using Appendix P, we reject if W $\leq$ 25 or W > 95. Looking at the two values in the table we see there is not enough evidence to conclude the median is different from 8.03 oz.

17.61

a. The hypotheses to be tested are:

H_0: $\tilde{\mu}_1 = \tilde{\mu}_2$

H_A: $\tilde{\mu}_1 \neq \tilde{\mu}_2$

Constructing the paired difference table:

Student	Test 1	Test 2	d	Rank	Ranks with smallest sum
1	42	34	8	12.5	
2	36	34	2	3	
3	44	45	-1	-1	1
4	27	30	-3	-6	6
5	40	45	-5	-9.5	9.5
6	34	32	2	3	0
8	50	44	6	11	0
9	29	32	-3	-6	6
10	43	40	3	6	0
11	42	34	8	12.5	0
12	22	32	-10	-14	14
13	26	30	-4	-8	8
14	45	40	5	9.5	0
15	41	39	2	3	0
				T=	44.5

Using Appendix N, with $\alpha = .05$, Reject if $T \leq 21$ or if $T \geq 84$

Since $44.5 > 21$ do not reject H_0 and conclude that the medians are the same.

b. A Type II error is the probability of accepting a false null hypothesis. In this case a Type II error would mean we accepted the null hypothesis that the medians of the two tests are the same when, in fact, they are not the same.

17.63

a. They should use the Wilcoxon Matched-Pairs Signed Rank test since the problem does not say you can assume a normal distribution and because you are using matched pairs.

b. Putting the claim in the alternate hypothesis:

H_0: $\tilde{\mu}_{w/oA} \geq \tilde{\mu}_A$

H_A: $\tilde{\mu}_{w/oA} < \tilde{\mu}_A$.

Automobile	Without Additive	With Additive	d	rank of d	Ranks with smallest expected sum
1	28	28.5	-0.5	-1	
2	25	26	-1	-3	
4	22	21	1	3	3
5	24	26	-2	-6	
6	19	21	-2	-6	
7	26	25	1	3	3
8	27	29	-2	-6	
				T =	6

Using $\alpha = .025$, $T_\alpha = 4$

c. Since $6 > 4$ do not reject H_0 and conclude the additive does not improve the mileage. The claim is not supported.

Chapter 18
Introduction to Quality and Statistical Process Control

Section 18-1 Exercises

18.1 Both Deming and Juran emphasized that quality was the key component to business competitiveness and that the best way to improve quality came from improving the processes and systems that produce products and deliver services. There are, however, some differences in the philosophies of the two quality pioneers. While Juran focused on quality planning and helping businesses drive down costs by eliminating waste from their processes, Deming advocated a philosophy known as total quality management (TQM), which focused on continuous process improvement directed toward customer satisfaction. In his 14 points, Deming emphasized the importance of leadership if a company is to become a world-class organization. Juran is credited with being one of the first to apply the Pareto Principle to quality improvement activities. This principle is designed to focus management attention on the vital few quality problems that exist in the organization. A primary difference between Deming and Juran is evident in their views regarding goals and targets. While Juran advocated the use of goals and targets in quality improvement activities, Deming argued that goals and targets were detrimental to the constancy of purpose designed to foster a commitment to long-term continuous process improvement activities.

18.3 Student answers will vary. Some students, especially those unfamiliar with the advantage that higher quality can provide a firm, may argue that quality improvement efforts are expensive, since they demand that workers be trained properly and that managers fix quality problems. They may think that these quality improvement costs are never fully recovered by firms in competitive markets. However, others will realize that improving quality can eliminate or reduce rework and scrap. Higher quality may allow a firm to reduce its warranty expense. Also, improved quality translates into greater customer satisfaction and some marketing studies have shown that it is less expensive to keep the customers that you have than it is to try and get new customers. Students who appreciate the strategic importance that high quality can play in an organization will argue that while there are costs to quality, the benefits of having good quality more than make up for any costs incurred in improving the firm's overall product and service quality. Because rework, scrap, and warranty expenses decrease with higher quality, prices for certain high quality goods and services can be competitive.

While student examples will vary, they may cite the experience of electronics manufactures where costs have been declining but quality has increased. Other examples may include automobiles, camping equipment, and personal computers.

18.5 Student answers will vary depending on the process at their school. A simple example would be

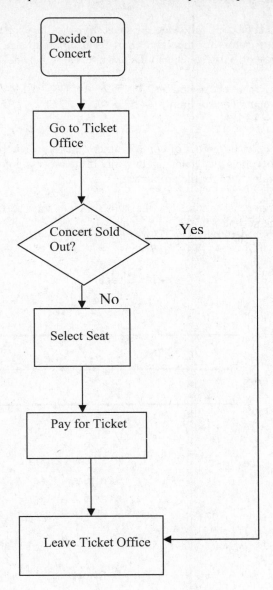

18.7 Student answers will vary depending upon answers to Exercise 18.6.

18.9 Student answers will vary. Some possible causes by category are:
      People: Too Few Drivers, High Driver Turnover
      Methods: Poor Scheduling, Improper Route Assignments
      Equipment: Buses Too Small, Bus Reliability, Too Few Buses
      Environment: Weather, Traffic Congestion, Road Construction

Section 18-2 Exercises

18.11 This exercise can be done following the steps shown in the Cattleman's Bar and Grill Example.
    a.   The Shewhart factors for the x-bar chart for a subgroup size of 5 is $A_2 = 0.577$. For the R-chart with a subgroup size of 5 the Shewhart factors are $D_3 = 0$ and $D_4 = 2.114$ for the lower and upper limits, respectively.
    b.   The R-chart upper control limit is 2.114*5.6 =11.838. The R-chart lower control limit is 0*5.6 = 0.
    c.   X-bar chart upper control limit = 44.52 + (0.577*5.6) = 47.751. X-bar chart lower control limit = 44.52 - (0.577*5.6) = 41.289.

18.13 Because a process can go out of control rather quickly it is imperative that the control charts be updated as soon as information becomes available. In this way if the process is found to be out of control it can be stopped to determine the assignable cause for the problem.

18.15 This exercise can be done following the steps shown in the Cattleman's Bar and Grill Example.
    a.   x-bar chart centerline = 0.753
        UCL = 0.753 + (0.577*0.074) = 0.7957
        LCL = 0.753 - (0.577*0.074) = 0.7103

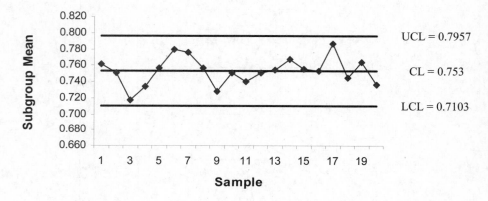

    b.   R-chart centerline = 0.074
        UCL = 2.114*0.074 = 0.1564
        LCL = 0*0.074 = 0.000

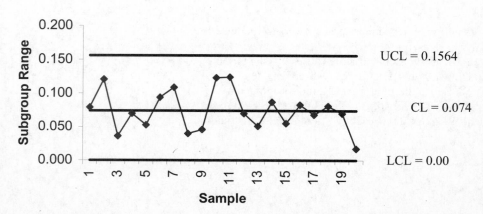

c. There are no subgroup means outside of the upper or lower control limits on the x-bar chart. The pattern appears to be randomly distributed about the centerline. For the R-chart, there are no subgroup ranges outside the control limits. The subgroup ranges appear to be randomly distributed about the centerline. From the control charts there does not appear to be any evidence of special cause variation that requires attention.

18.17

a.

Period	Mean	Range
31	5.3325	1.05
32	4.7875	1.25
33	4.975	0.84
34	5.4425	0.91
35	4.8525	1.47
36	5.3025	1.16
37	5.3375	0.65
38	5.38	0.61
39	6.08	2.09
40	6.2525	1.17

Looking at the mean values of these observations it appears that the process has gone out of control since all but 2 observations and the 1st 8 in sequence are below the LCL.

b. Note: The differences in the control chart limits shown here and in problem 18-14 are due only to rounding differences reflected in the type of software used.

X-bar Chart

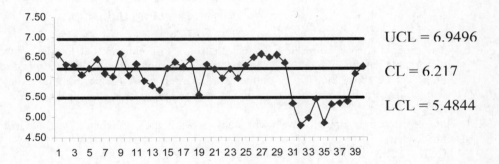

UCL = 6.9496

CL = 6.217

LCL = 5.4844

R-chart

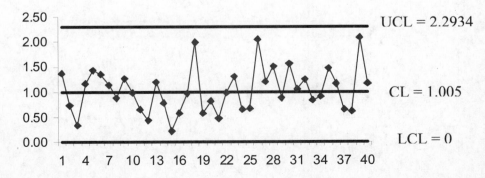

UCL = 2.2934

CL = 1.005

LCL = 0

The report will vary with the student, but should certainly comment on the R-chart being in control but the X-bar chart going out of control in periods 31-38. An assignable cause should be found.

18.19 This exercise can be done following the steps shown in the Chandler Tile Example.

    a.   The type of process control chart needs to be the c-chart.

    b. $\bar{c}$ = 3.2841; since this is not greater than 5 the company needs to form a sampling unit by combining 2 doors to form the sampling unit. The mean of these new sampling units will be 2(3.2841) = 6.5682

$$UCL = 6.5682 + 3(\sqrt{6.5682}) = 14.2568$$

$$LCL = 6.5682 - 3(\sqrt{6.5682}) = -1.1204 \text{ so set to } 0$$

The control chart is:

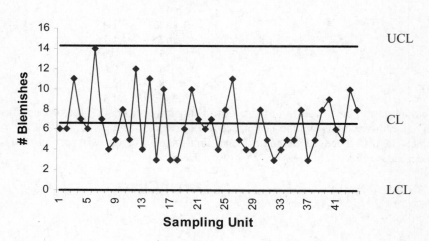

c-Chart

    c.   The process appears to be in statistical control. No points are outside the control limits and there is no discernable pattern in the chart. The sixth sampling unit, with 14 blemishes, is close to the UCL, however, no points are above the UCL or on the LCL. Also, because the pattern within the control limits is random, with no discernable trend or pattern, the process is said to be in statistical control.

18.21 This exercise can be done following the steps shown in the Cattleman's Bar and Grill Example.

    a.   For R-chart
        UCL = 2.282 * 100.375 = 229.056
        CL = 100.375
        LCL = 0 * 100.375 = 0

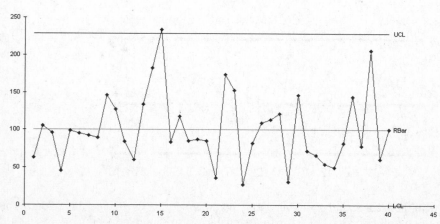

R Chart

b. For x-bar chart
    UCL = 415.3 + 0.729(100.375) = 488.473
    CL = 415.3
    LCL = 415.3 − 0.729(100.375) = 342.127

XBar Chart

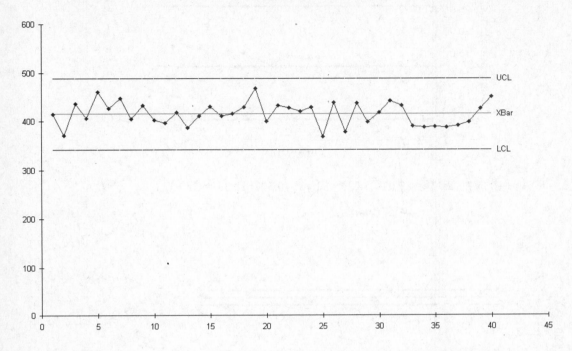

c. The process appears to have lost control with respect to its variability, which is measured by the R-chart. Note that week 15 is above the upper control limit on the R-chart. The range chart measures the dispersion or spread of the process. Ajax should investigate for an assignable cause that could explain the higher variability in week 15. Furthermore, since the range chart shows that the process is out of control, we should question the validity of the x-bar chart. Whenever the range chart reflects an out of control situation, the x-bar chart, which is determined using the average range of the subgroups, is compromised.

18.23 This exercise can be done following the steps shown in the Cattleman's Bar and Grill Example.
a. The x-bar and R-charts are used together to monitor a process where the characteristic of interest is a variable (i.e., a characteristic measured on a continuous scale). Since time is measured, the machine downtime that is being monitored is a variable characteristic and requires that both the x-bar and R-charts be used.
b. The centerline for the x-bar chart is the average of the subgroup means and equals 82.46.
c. The centerline for the R-chart is the average of the subgroup ranges and equals 12.33.

d.   UCL = 2.114*12.33 = 26.07   and LCL = 0*12.33 = 0

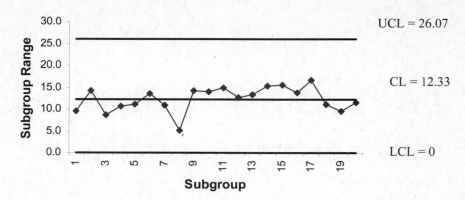

R-Chart

UCL = 26.07

CL = 12.33

LCL = 0

e.   UCL = 82.46 + (0.577*12.33) = 89.57   LCL = 82.46 - (0.577*12.33) = 75.35

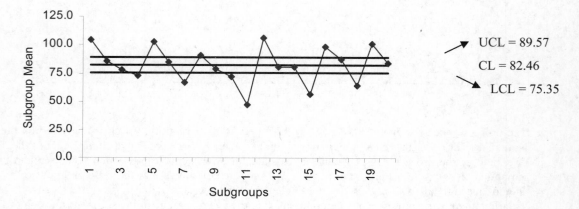

x-Bar Chart

UCL = 89.57

CL = 82.46

LCL = 75.35

f.   While the range chart has no points outside the control chart limits, there is a run of 9 values above the centerline, which indicates a possible loss of statistical control. The x-bar chart exhibits an out of statistical control condition given that there are several subgroup means above the upper control limit and several below the lower control limit. This provides strong evidence that the process was not in statistical control at the time the control chart was developed.

18.25 This exercise can be done following the steps shown in the Hilder's Publishing Example.

    a.   The appropriate control chart for this data is the p-chart.

    b. $\bar{p}$ = 441/(300*50) = 0.0294

$$s_{\bar{p}} = \sqrt{(0.0294)(1-0.0294)/50} = 0.0239$$

UCL = 0.0294 + 3(0.0239) = 0.1011
LCL = 0.0294 − 3(0.0239) = -0.0423 so set to 0

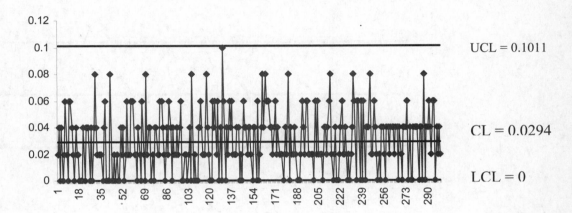

    c.

Sample Number	301	302	303
p-bar	0.12	0.18	0.14

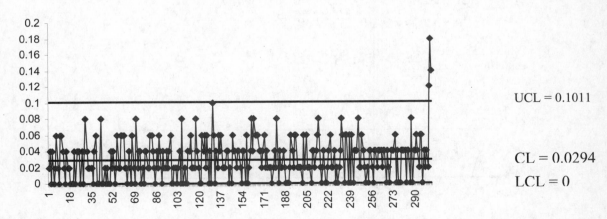

All of these points are above the UCL which indicates that the process has gone out of control.

    d.   The new sample proportion would be 0.28 which is again above the UCL. This suggests that the process is still out of control and getting further out of control.

18.27 This exercise can be done following the steps shown in the Chandler's Tile Example.

    a. $\bar{c}$ = 29.3333

        UCL = 29.3333 + 3($\sqrt{29.3333}$) = 45.5814

        LCL = 29.3333 - 3($\sqrt{29.3333}$) = 13.0852

c-chart

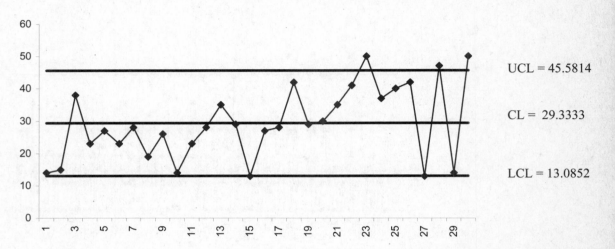

UCL = 45.5814

CL = 29.3333

LCL = 13.0852

    b.   The process seems to be out of control since several observations are above the UCL or right at the LCL and there seems to be a run (observation 4 – 12) below the center line and observations 27 – 30 seem to be alternating one above or near the upper UCL and the next below the LCL, etc.

    c.   Need to convert the data to bags per passenger by dividing bags by 40 and then developing a U-chart based upon the explanation in the optional topics.

        CL = 29.333/40 = 0.7333

        UCL = 0.7333 + 3* $\sqrt{0.7333/40}$ = 1.1395

        LCL = 0.7333 - 3* $\sqrt{0.7333/40}$ = 0.3271

u-chart

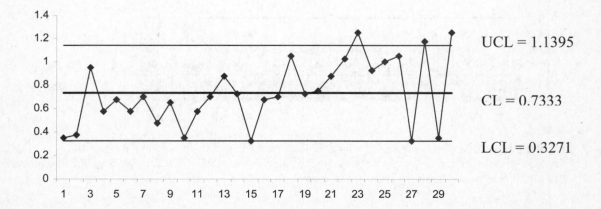

UCL = 1.1395

CL = 0.7333

LCL = 0.3271

Chapter Exercises

18.29

a. The Shewart factor for the x-bar chart with a subgroup size of 3 is A2 = 1.023. The Shewart factors for the range chart are D3 = 0.0 and D4 = 2.575 for the lower and upper control limits, respectively.

b. UCL = 2.575*0.80 = 2.06   LCL = 0*0.80 = 0

c. UCL = 2.33 + (1.023*0.80) = 3.1468   LCL = 2.33 - (1.023*0.80) = 1.512

18.31 The centerline of the control chart is the average proportion of defective = 720/(20*150) = 0.240. For 3-sigma control chart limits we find

$$UCL = 0.240 + 3 * \sqrt{\frac{0.240 * (1 - 0.240)}{150}} = 0.345$$

$$LCL = 0.240 - 3 * \sqrt{\frac{0.240 * (1 - 0.240)}{150}} = 0.135$$

18.33 The appropriate chart is the p-chart. $\bar{p} = 0.0524$

$$s_{\bar{p}} = \sqrt{\frac{0.0524 * (1 - 0.0524)}{100}} = 0.0223$$

The 3-sigma control limits are computed as follows:
Lower Control Limit = 0.0524 - 3*0.0223 = -0.0145 so set to 0
Centerline = 0.0524
Upper Control Limit = 0.0524 + 3*0.0223 = 0.1193
The control chart is shown below.

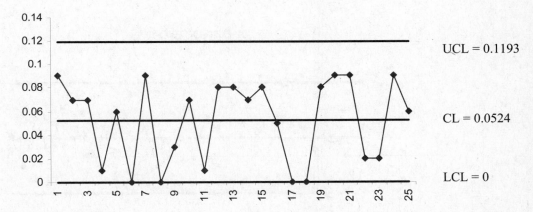

p-chart

The process appears to be in control. Management should investigate points 6,8,17 and 18 where defects were 0 to determine possible improvement in the process.

18.35   The appropriate control chart for monitoring this process is a c-chart.
The centerline for the process is equal to the average number of defects for the sampled output and equals
690/30 = 23.00. The standard error is estimated to be the square root of the centerline and equals 4.7958.
The 3-sigma upper control limit is 23.00 + (3*4.7958) = 37.3875.
The 3-sigma lower control limit is 23.00 - (3*4.7958) = 8.6125.
The chart is shown below.

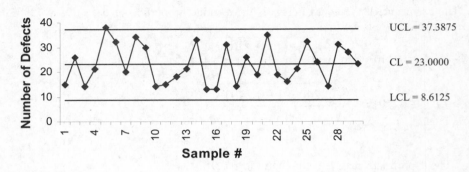

Note that sample number 5 with 38 defects is above the upper control limit. This is an indication of a loss
of statistical process control. The company should investigate for an assignable cause.

18.37
   a.   x-bar chart: CL = 0.7499
         UCL = 0.7499 + (0.577)(0.0115) = 0.7565
         LCL = 0.7499 – (0.577)(0.0115) = 0.7433

         R-chart: CL = 0.0115
         UCL = (0.0115)(2.114) = 0.0243
         LCL = (0.0115)(0) = 0

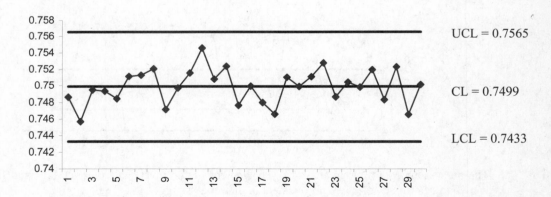

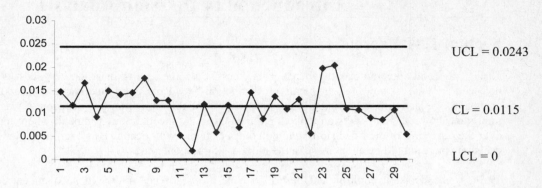

The process appears to be in control.

b.

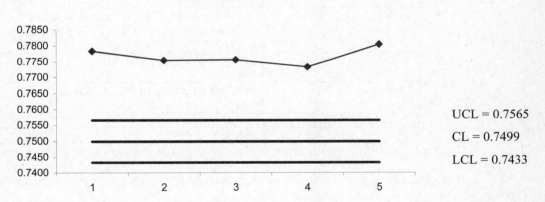

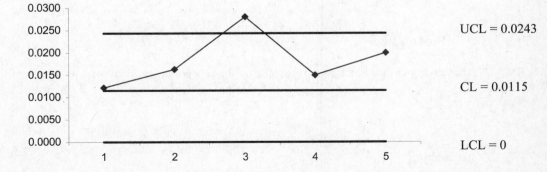

It now appears that the process is out of control. All of the averages are above the UCL and in the range chart one value is above the UCL.

Online Chapter 19
Introduction to Decision Analysis

Section 19-1 Exercises

19.1   A good outcome occurs whenever the "best" outcome results, or at the very least, the worst outcome does not occur. There is, however, an important distinction between a good outcome and a good decision. In decision analysis if we have properly used all the information available in making the decision, it was a good decision. It is important, however, that decision makers realize that in an uncertain environment, where they do not have control over the outcomes of their decisions, bad outcomes can, and will, occur. However, in the long run, by making good decisions there should be an increase in the number of good outcomes.

19.3   The decision environment described here is one of certainty. In such an environment the results of selecting each alternative are known before the decision is made. In this problem, Varsity Contracting knows what outcomes will occur in terms of the time required and the costs involved. The following table provides a breakdown of the revenues and expenses for the decision facing Varsity.

Annual Revenues & Costs	Accept Contract	Reject Contract
Annual Revenues	$0.10 * 100,000 * 12 months = $120,000	$0.00
Costs:		
Labor	2 workers @ $8.00 per hour for 8 hours per night for 5 nights per week for 52 weeks = $33,280	$0.00
Supplies	$200 per week for 52 weeks = $10,400	$0.00
Overhead	20% of Labor Cost (0.2*$33,280) = $6,656	$0.00
Total Annual Costs	$50,336	$0.00
Profit	$69,664	$0.00

Given that Varsity will realize an annual profit of $69,664, Varsity should sign the contract.

19.5   Multiplying each state of nature outcome by the appropriate probabilities, we find the following table: Select the alternative with the largest expected value, A_3.

		States of Nature			Expected Values
		S_1	S_2	S_3	
	A_1	150	80	-20	51
Alternatives	A_2	60	40	45	48.5
	A_3	240	70	-10	81
Probabilities		0.3	0.2	0.5	

19.7   Multiplying each state of nature outcome by the appropriate probabilities, we find the following table:

		States of Nature				Expected Values
		S_1	S_2	S_3	S_4	
	A_1	170	45	-60	100	32.0
Alternatives	A_2	30	190	175	-65	91.5
	A_3	145	-50	120	110	85.5
	A_4	-40	80	10	70	37.0
Probabilities		0.1	0.2	0.4	0.3	

Select the alternative with the largest expected value, A_2.

19.9

a.

	Demand			
Purchase	10,000	15,000	20,000	25,000
10,000	8,500	8,500	8,500	8,500
15,000	5,250	12,750	12,750	12,750
20,000	2,000	9,500	17,000	17,000
25,000	(1,250)	6,250	13,750	21,250

b. 1. The maximum values are 8500, 12750, 17000 and 21250, in order, so purchase 25,000 hotdogs and buns.

2. The minimum values are 8500, 5250, 2000 and –1250, in order, so purchase 10,000 hotdogs and buns.

3.

Opportunity Loss Table				
	Demand			
Purchase	10,000	15,000	20,000	25,000
10,000	-	4,250	8,500	12,750
15,000	3,250	-	4,250	8,500
20,000	6,500	3,250	-	4,250
25,000	9,750	6,500	3,250	-

The maximum regret values are 12750, 8500, 6500, 9750, so purchase 20,000 hotdogs and buns.

19.11

a.

	Demand			
Production	20000	40000	60000	80000
20000	$ 2,800,000.00	$ 2,600,000.00	$ 2,400,000.00	$ 2,200,000.00
40000	$ 1,800,000.00	$ 5,800,000.00	$ 5,600,000.00	$ 5,400,000.00
60000	$ 800,000.00	$ 4,800,000.00	$ 8,800,000.00	$ 8,600,000.00
80000	$ (200,000.00)	$ 3,800,000.00	$ 7,800,000.00	$ 11,800,000.00

Acquisition Cost	$ 200,000.00
Selling Price	$ 250.00
Discount Price	$ 50.00
Coupon (Demand Exceeds Supply)	$ 10.00
Variable Production Cost	$ 100.00

b. Maximin: Max(2200000, 1800000, 800000, -200000) so produce 20,000.

Maximax: Max(2800000, 5800000, 8800000, 11800000) so produce 80,000.

19.13   This problem should be done following the steps shown in Example 19-1.

Purchases	Demand 100,000	150,000	200,000	225,000	250,000
100,000	1000000	1000000	1000000	1000000	1000000
150,000	675000	1575000	1575000	1575000	1575000
200,000	350000	1250000	2150000	2150000	2150000
225,000	187500	1087500	1987500	2437500	2437500
250,000	25000	925000	1825000	2275000	2725000

Fixed Cost	150,000
Variable Cost	5
Shipping	1.5
Sales Price	18

Probabilities	0.1	0.4	0.2	0.2	0.1

Purchases	Expected Value
100,000	1,000,000
150,000	1,485,000
200,000	1,610,000
225,000	1,582,500
250,000	1,465,000

Using the expected value criterion, 200,000 dozen roses should be purchased.   The expected profit of purchasing this amount is $1,610,000.

19.15   This problem should be done following the steps shown in Example 19-1.

Probability of Demand	0.15	0.2	0.2	0.3	0.15
	Demand				
Supply	500	1000	2000	4000	7000
500	$ (7,000.00)	$ (7,000.00)	$ (7,000.00)	$ (7,000.00)	$ (7,000.00)
1000	$ (8,500.00)	$ (4,000.00)	$ (4,000.00)	$ (4,000.00)	$ (4,000.00)
2000	$(11,100.00)	$ (6,600.00)	$ 2,400.00	$ 2,400.00	$ 2,400.00
4000	$(16,700.00)	$(12,200.00)	$ (3,200.00)	$ 14,800.00	$14,800.00
7000	$(23,000.00)	$(18,500.00)	$ (9,500.00)	$ 8,500.00	$35,500.00

Supply	Expected Value
500	-7000
1000	-4675
2000	-1425
4000	1075
7000	-1175

Best Expected Value Decision
Supply 4,000 for EV of 1,075

19.17

a.

Revenue per unit	$	600,000
Variable Cost per unit		$350,000
Salvage Cost per unit		$150,000

States of Nature (possible successful restaurants)

Purchase	0	1	2	3	4	5
0	-	-	-	-	-	-
1	(200,000)	250,000	250,000	250,000	250,000	250,000
2	(400,000)	50,000	500,000	500,000	500,000	500,000
3	(600,000)	(150,000)	300,000	750,000	750,000	750,000
4	(800,000)	(350,000)	100,000	550,000	1,000,000	1,000,000
5	(1,000,000)	(550,000)	(100,000)	350,000	800,000	1,250,000

The maximum values for each alternative are 0; 250,000; 500,000; 750,000; 1,000,000; and 1,250,000, so purchase 5 restaurants for a maximum profit of $1,250,000.

b. The minimum values for each alternative are 0; -200,000; -400,000; -600,000; -800,000; and -1,000,000, so purchase no restaurants for a profit of $0.

c.

Mall Option:

Revenue per unit	$	500,000
Variable Cost per unit		$250,000(includes franchise cost)
Salvage Cost per unit		$100,000

States of Nature (possible successful restaurants)

Purchase	0	1	2	3	4	5
0	-	-	-	-	-	-
1	(150,000)	250,000	250,000	250,000	250,000	250,000
2	(300,000)	100,000	500,000	500,000	500,000	500,000
3	(450,000)	(50,000)	350,000	750,000	750,000	750,000
4	(600,000)	(200,000)	200,000	600,000	1,000,000	1,000,000
5	(750,000)	(350,000)	50,000	450,000	850,000	1,250,000

Larger Buildings:

Revenue per unit	$	1,000,000
Variable Cost per unit		$500,000(includes franchise cost)
Salvage Cost per unit		$200,000

States of Nature (possible successful restaurants)

Purchase	0	1	2	3	4	5
0	-	-	-	-	-	-
1	(300,000)	500,000	500,000	500,000	500,000	500,000
2	(600,000)	200,000	1,000,000	1,000,000	1,000,000	1,000,000
3	(900,000)	(100,000)	700,000	1,500,000	1,500,000	1,500,000
4	(1,200,000)	(400,000)	400,000	1,200,000	2,000,000	2,000,000
5	(1,500,000)	(700,000)	100,000	900,000	1,700,000	2,500,000

d. Mall Option:
    Maximax: The maximum values for each alternative are 0, 250,000; 500,000; 750,000; 1,000,000; 1,250,000, so purchase 5 franchises for a maximum profit of 1,250,000
    Maximin: The minimum values for each alternative are 0; -150,000; -300,000; -450,000; -600,000; -750,000, so purchase 0 franchises for a profit of $0.
    Larger Building Option:
    Maximax: The maximum values for each alternative are 0, 500,000; 1,000,000; 1,500,000; 2,000,000; 2,500,000, so purchase 5 franchises for a maximum profit of 2,500,000
    Maximin: The minimum values for each alternative are 0, -300,000; -600,000; -900,000; -1,200,000; -1,500,000, so purchase 0 franchises for a profit of $0

e.

Purchase	Expected Profit	
0	-	
1	223,000	
2	401,000	
3	489,000	Optimal
4	397,000	
5	251,000	

Mall Option:

Purchase	Expected Profit	
0	-	
1	230,000	
2	420,000	
3	550,000	
4	580,000	Optimal
5	490,000	

Larger Building Option:

Purchase	Expected Profit	
0	-	
1	428,000	
2	736,000	Optimal
3	844,000	
4	632,000	
5	364,000	

Based on the expected value criteria they should purchase 3 franchises with the larger building option for an expected profit of $844,000.

Section 19-2 Exercises

All the problems in this section can be done following the steps shown in Exercise 19-2.

19.19

a.

	Opportunity Loss Table		
	States of Nature		
Probabilities	0.5	0.2	0.3
Alternative	S_1	S_2	S_3
A_1	0	25	40
A_2	15	15	20
A_3	35	0	0

b.

		States of Nature			Expected Values
		S_1	S_2	S_3	
	A_1	145	55	80	107.5
Alternatives	A_2	130	65	100	108.0
	A_3	110	80	120	107.0
Probabilities		0.5	0.2	0.3	

$$EVUC = .5(145) + .2(80) + .3(120) = 124.5$$
$$EVPI = 124.5 - 108.0 = 16.5$$

19.21

	Demand			
Production	20000	40000	60000	80000
20000	$ 2,800,000	$ 2,600,000	$ 2,400,000	$ 2,200,000
40000	$ 1,800,000	$ 5,800,000	$ 5,600,000	$ 5,400,000
60000	$ 800,000	$ 4,800,000	$ 8,800,000	$ 8,600,000
80000	$ (200,000)	$ 3,800,000	$ 7,800,000	$ 11,800,000

					EVUC
Prob.	0.1	0.3	0.4	0.2	
EVUC	$ 280,000	$ 1,740,000	$ 3,520,000	$ 2,360,000	$7,900,000

Production	Expected Value
20000	$ 2,460,000.00
40000	$ 5,240,000.00
60000	$ 6,760,000.00
80000	$ 6,600,000.00

EVPI = $7,900,000 - $6,760,000 = $1,140,000

19.23

Probability of Demand	0.15	0.2	0.2	0.3	0.15	
	Demand					
Supply	500	1000	2000	4000	7000	
500	$ (7,000.00)	$ (7,000.00)	$ (7,000.00)	$ (7,000.00)	$ (7,000.00)	
1000	$ (8,500.00)	$ (4,000.00)	$ (4,000.00)	$ (4,000.00)	$ (4,000.00)	
2000	$(11,100.00)	$ (6,600.00)	$ 2,400.00	$ 2,400.00	$ 2,400.00	
4000	$(16,700.00)	$(12,200.00)	$ (3,200.00)	$ 14,800.00	$14,800.00	
7000	$(23,000.00)	$(18,500.00)	$ (9,500.00)	$ 8,500.00	$35,500.00	EVUC
EVUC	$ (1,050.00)	$ (800.00)	$ 480.00	$ 4,440.00	$ 5,325.00	$8,395.00

Supply	Expected Value
500	-7000
1000	-4675
2000	-1425
4000	1075
7000	-1175

EVPI = $8,395 - $1,075 = $7,320

Section 19-3 Exercises

All the problems in this section can be done following the steps in Example 19-3.

19.25

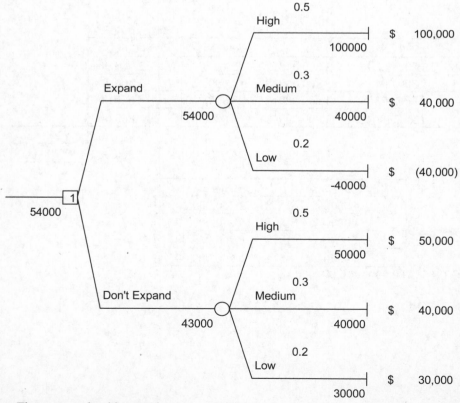

The owners should expand.

19.27

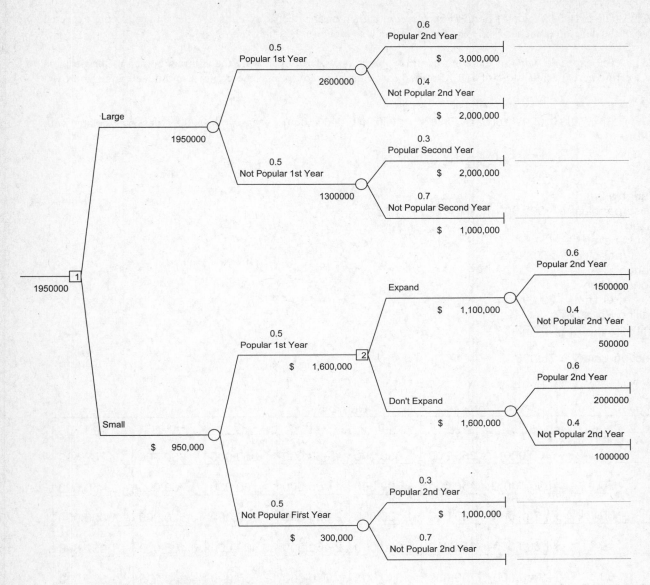

The developer should build the large resort.

End of Chapter Exercises

19.29 The expected value of the *Do Not Develop* branch on the decision tree is $78 per unit while the expected value of the develop branch is $82. The best decision is to work on the improved model.

19.31 The expected value of the don't contract branch is $82. By evaluating the contract branch of the decision tree we find an expected value of $81. So the best decision is not to sign the contract and develop the improved model.

19.33 Max (-400,000; -800,000; -1,200,000; -1,600,000; -2,000,000) so Max = -400,000 which is associated with build 10

19.35

Variable Land
Cost (per block)   200,000
Fixed
Construction
Cost (per block) 250,000
Variable
Construction
Cost (Per Unit)   70,000
Selling Price(per
unit)   200,000

Auction Value   75,000

Build	Demand 0	10	20	30	40	50	EV
10	(400,000)	850,000	850,000	850,000	850,000	850,000	787,500
20	(800,000)	450,000	1,700,000	1,700,000	1,700,000	1,700,000	1,450,000
30	(1,200,000)	50,000	1,300,000	2,550,000	2,550,000	2,550,000	1,800,000
40	(1,600,000)	(350,000)	900,000	2,150,000	3,400,000	3,400,000	1,837,500
50	(2,000,000)	(750,000)	500,000	1,750,000	3,000,000	4,250,000	1,625,000
Probabilities	0.05	0.10	0.25	0.25	0.20	0.15	

Optimal decision based on expected value would be build 40 at an expected profit of $1,837,50

19.37

Decision	Failure	Successful	EV
Don't Market	-	-	-
Market	(20,000,000)	50,000,000	22,000,000
Probabilities	0.4	0.6	

Based on the expected value the company should market the product.

19.39

Decision	Exellent	Good	Fair	Poor	EV
Don't Market	-	-	-	-	0
Market	70,000,000	50,000,000	10,000,000	(20,000,000)	31,000,000
Probabilities	0.3	0.3	0.1	0.3	

Based on the expected value the company should market the product.

19.41

Demand

Prepare	3	4	5	6	7	8	EV
3	10.5	7	3.5	0	-3.5	-7	3.325
4	8.5	14	10.5	7	3.5	0	9.425
5	6.5	12	17.5	14	10.5	7	12.825
6	4.5	10	15.5	21	17.5	14	13.975
7	2.5	8	13.5	19	24.5	21	13.325
8	0.5	6	11.5	17	22.5	28	11.775
Probabilities	0.1	0.3	0.25	0.2	0.1	0.05	

Based on the expected value they should prepare 6 orders for an expected value of $13.975

19.43
Opportunity
Loss Table:

Demand

Build	0	10	20	30	40	50	EOL
10	-	-	850,000	1,700,000	2,550,000	3,400,000	1,657,500
20	400,000	400,000	-	850,000	1,700,000	2,550,000	995,000
30	800,000	800,000	400,000	-	850,000	1,700,000	645,000
40	1,200,000	1,200,000	800,000	400,000	-	850,000	607,500
50	1,600,000	1,600,000	1,200,000	800,000	400,000	-	820,000
Probabilities	0.05	0.10	0.25	0.25	0.20	0.15	

To minimize the EOL you would build 40 units for an expected opportunity loss of $607,500. This is the EVPI. The $607,500 is the most you would pay for perfect information so if someone is willing to sell it to you for $10,000 you would definitely purchase it.

19.45   The following decision tree represents the decision faced by Graciela Grimm and the Grimm Group.

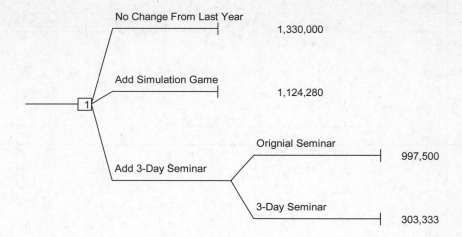

19.47   If the original margins can be maintained, then the revenues and costs become (use new demand values in calculating revenues):

Seminar	Revenues	Costs	Profits
Quality	$1,320,000	$792,000	$528,000
Material	$1,035,000	$621,000	$414,000
JIT	$1,609,800	$1,046,370	$563,430

The total profit is $1,505,430 if margins can be maintained.

The decision tree with the new information becomes:

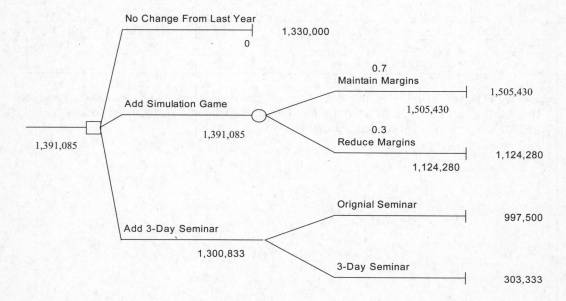

As can be seen from the tree, the best decision now is to add the simulation game.

19.49   NOTE: The solution below is based upon a correction that needs to be made to the textbook problem. On problem 19.48, in the table entitled "League Race" the Yes/No column needs to be reversed. The table should be as follows:

League Race		
Player Strike	*Tight*	*Not Tight*
No	$5.00	$2.50
	p = 0.42	p = 0.28
Yes	$4.00	$2.00
	p = 0.18	p = 0.12

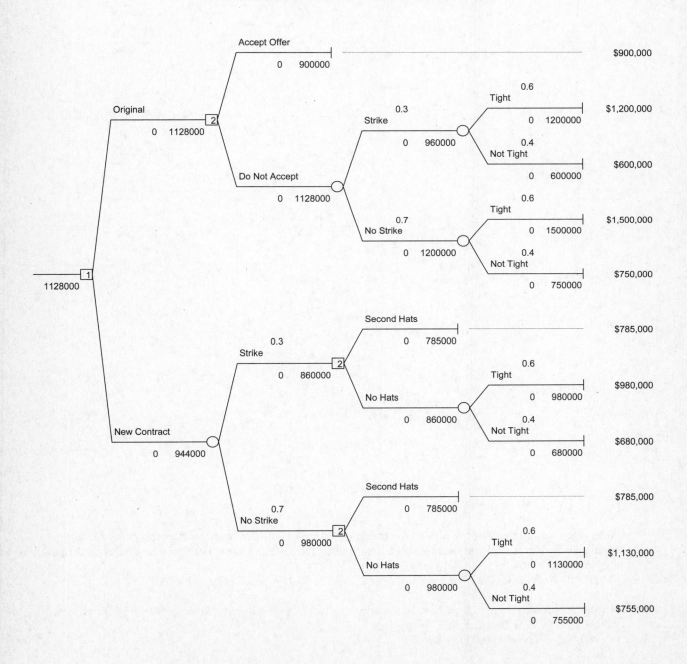

19.51   The expected cost to you for the above proposal is $944,000. The expected cost of buying them on the open market is $1,128,000. In this case since we are discussing cost you would accept the proposal if you were the purchasing manager.

19.53   The decision tree for the Gregston Corporation is shown below. By folding back the decision tree the expected values for the various alternatives are determined. Based on expected profits, Gregston should Not Test and Drill.

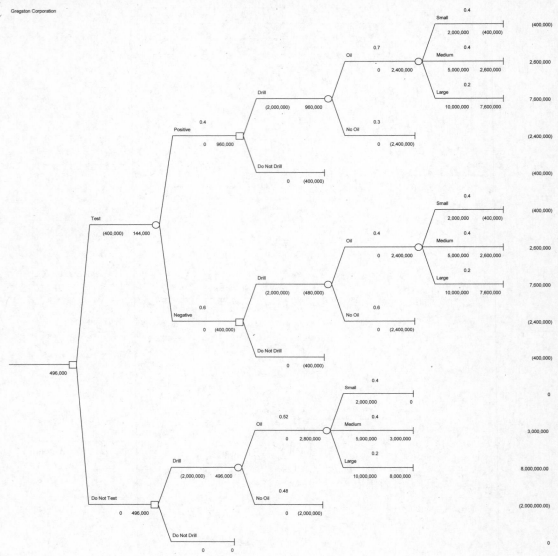

Note: the probabilities associated with the branches No Test –Drill are based on the probability the test has been positive in this area and the probabilities of finding oil when the test is both positive and when the test is negative as follows:
$(0.7*0.4) + (0.6*0.4) = 0.52$ = probability of Oil. $1-0.52 = 0.48$ = probability of No Oil.

19.55   For the decision to change, the expected value of the Test branch will have to be greater than the expected value of the Do Not Test branch.
$(x)(960,000) + (1-x)(-400,000) \geq 496,000; x \geq 0.66$